CONSTRUCTIVISM

Origins and Evolution

WITHDRAWN

CONSTRUCTIVISM
Origins and Evolution

REVISED EDITION

GEORGE RICKEY

GEORGE BRAZILLER   New York

To Gabo

For information, please address the publisher:
George Braziller, Inc.
60 Madison Avenue
New York, New York 10010

Catalogue data on this volume is available at The Library of Congress
ISBN 0-8076-1381-9

Designed by Jennie Bush
Printed in Hong Kong
First printing, 1967
First printing of the Revised Edition, March, 1995

Acknowledgments

The author wishes to thank Dr. Peter Selz for reading the manuscript at a painfully early stage and for his sympathy and encouragement; Mrs. Jean Lipman, Editor of *Art in America*, for voicing her confidence at a critical moment; Mr. Michel Seuphor for his interest, and wide knowledge, and personal recollections of Neo-Plasticism in the Low Countries and in Paris. The author is grateful to Mr. Rudolf Oxenaar, Director of the Kröller-Müller Museum, for access to his documents of De Stijl, the Bauhaus, and Constructivism; to Mr. Henk Peeters for sharing his knowledge and his documents of contemporary movements in Holland and Germany; to Dr. J. Leering, Director of the van Abbemuseum in Eindhoven, for comment on Lissitzky; to Madame Chalette Lejwa for discussions of Constructivist influences in Poland, Paris, and the United States; and to Mr. Joost Baljeu for photographs and comment on Dutch "Structurist" art.

For patient and persevering help with photographs, the author wishes to thank Mr. Richard Tooke of the Museum of Modern Art, Mr. Steven Weil of the Marlborough-Gerson Gallery, Miss Ellen Joosten of the Kröller-Müller Museum, Dr. Marian Minich of the Muzeum Sztuki in Lodz, Frau Lydia Dorner for photostats of Lissitzky's original designs for the *Abstrakt Kabinett*, Mr. Walter Gropius for photographs of his model for the Chicago Tribune building, Mr. Almir Mavignier for photographs of the ruins of Pella, Mr. William Bernoudy for a photograph of his Frank Lloyd Wright window, Mr. Max Bill for photographs of the works of Vantongerloo; also Mrs. Lillian Florsheim, Mrs. Barnett Malbin, Miss Inge Bodesohn, Galerie Denise René, Galerie Chalette, and the numerous collectors, galleries, and museums who provided illustrations.

The author also wishes to thank Mr. Alexei Pevsner for permission to quote from the memoir of his brothers, Gabo and Antoine; Dr. William Arrowsmith, who provided a new translation of a passage from Plato; Mr. Joel Stein and Yvaral for their accounts of "Nouvelle Tendance"; Dr. Carlo Belloli for information about Italian Futurism; Dr. Udo Kulterman and Dr. Werner Schmalenbach for comment on recent trends in Germany; Mr. Jules Langsner for his account of the origin of "Hard Edge"; Professor Bernd Forester, who clarified the meaning of Dutch terms; and Mrs. John S. Cox for compiling the biographical notes and the index.

The author is also grateful to Penny Calfiotis for her meticulous and sympathetic editing of the manuscript, and to Jennie Bush for the design of the book.

Besides furnishing a unique bibliography of Constructivism, Dr. Bernard Karpel of the Museum of Modern Art gave invaluable information about documents, photographs, exhibitions, catalogues, and manifestos. The publication of the bibliography was made possible by grants, for composition and printing costs, from The Joseph H. Hirshhorn Foundation, The Rita and Taft Schreiber Foundation, and The Frederick and Marcia Weisman Foundation. The author gratefully acknowledges this aid.

The author particularly appreciates the patient cooperation of all the artists with whom he corresponded and conversed and who have sent him the information, catalogues, and photographs which provide the documentary basis of this book, including those whose work appears on the cover and who exemplify the wide distribution of the style; Yenceslav Richter (Yugoslavia); Morellet (France); Mack, Piene, von Graevenitz, (Germany); Mari (Italy); Gerstner (Switzerland); Noland, Glarner, L. P. Smith (U.S.); Equipo 57 (Spain); Sedgley (England).

The first draft of the manuscript was written in March 1963, in the solitude of Yaddo, which the author deeply appreciated. All the subsequent work was done in East Chatham, New York, where the author's wife, Edith, patiently typed and retyped successive versions of the manuscript and served as librarian, picture editor, proofreader, archivist, and cook for visiting artists. Her enthusiasm and sensitive awareness of the subject matter lightened the task and assured its completion.

Preface

In the spring of 1961, I visited the great "Movement" exhibition, "Bewogen Beweging," at the Stedelijk Museum in Amsterdam, and then again at its second installation in the Modern Museum in Stockholm. I met many young artists, saw much new work, heard of even more—some of it not particularly involved with *movement*, but all in striking contrast with the prevailing Expressionist styles of that time.

Then, and in subsequent travels, I began to realize the breadth and strength of the forces behind this disciplined non-objective art and how little of it was known. In spite of jet planes, magazines, and an international art market, most of these artists were known outside their cities or regions only to a few alert and inquisitive people in Paris, Milan, Amsterdam and Antwerp, in Switzerland and the German Ruhr. Even their contacts with one another were limited; yet, in spite of isolation, there was an astonishing concurrence in their thinking. It seemed that this concurrence must have been a reaction against international "art informel" and, furthermore, that it had developed from a conscious or unconscious identity with the principles of what has been called "Constructivism."

"Constructivism" is a familiar but elusive word in art circles. Supposedly invented by the Russian artist Vladimir Tatlin, who assembled "corner constructions" in 1914, it is one of those words which become technical terms without ever having been defined. It was carefully skirted by Tatlin's compatriot, Naum Gabo, who always used the more generic term "constructive" for his art instead of "constructivist." Tatlin's word had topical political overtones in 1920 which it was to lose, however, when exported later to the rest of the world.

The word evidently filled a vacuum in the art vocabulary of the period and, still undefined, went into vague but common use in the twenties. It was loosely applied not only to the Russians' work but to any objects *built* rather than cast or carved, to any designs in two or three dimensions reminiscent of Euclid (either because they were flat and rectilinear or because they were made with straight edge and compass as Euclid's constructions were), or to the spare vertical-horizontal painting and sculpture of the new Dutch group, led by Piet Mondrian, called "De Stijl."

To add to the confusion, such art was also sometimes still more loosely called "abstract"—an antonym of "concrete." But "abstract" also means abstracted *from* nature, as was Cubist art, which thus retains a representational component, however much modified. Constructivism on the other hand represented nothing. Nor is "constructivist" identical with "non-objective," a term introduced by another Russian, Alexander Rodchenko, and applied by still another, Kasimir Malevich, to his flat paintings of squares, rectangles, and crosses. "Non-objective" has since been used to describe any subjectless art, whether geometrical or not.

In the pages to follow, "constructivist" will refer to the work of a group of Russians between 1913 and 1922, which include Tatlin, Malevich, Rodchenko, El Lissitzky, Naum Gabo, Antoine Pevsner, and briefly, Wassily Kandinsky. Their work was, in general, geometrical and non-mimetic. It will refer also to the Dutch art which resembled that of the Russians but did not derive from it, to the ensuing painting and sculpture in Europe and America which emanated from the two groups, including "Concrete Art" and "Kalte Kunst," and to much of the work done in such groups as "Cercle et Carré," "Réalités Nouvelles," and "American Abstract Artists." The term will also encompass more recent work characterized by such neologisms as "hard edge," "post-painterly abstraction," and "primary structures," as well as the most all-embracing European term, "new tendency," which was a cry of mutual recognition rather than a definition of style.

Though the characteristics of Constructivism are discussed in detail, no attempt has been made to establish a "constructivist" orthodoxy against which an artist could be tested for inclusion. What is "constructivist" is better revealed by works of art than by words. Failing a comprehensive exhibition, numerous and diverse reproductions can best define the school. Since no comprehensive exhibition was in sight in 1961, and still is not in 1967, I thought a well-documented book could be of interest and fill a need. I had observed illustrated art books on the shelves of artists and their readiness to refer to them. They had Malraux's "museum without walls" in their studios. Unfortunately, however, this "museum" was almost totally lacking a Constructivist wing.

Not only was there apathy outside the studios toward Constructivist art, early or late, there was also profound ignorance as to what it was, who had made it, and on whom and through what channels it had exercised influence. The museums, with three or four exceptions, were still indifferent in 1963 (see Museum Chart, page 245). Among the exceptions was the Guggenheim Museum in New York, which was founded expressly as a museum of non-objective art and therefore unique. Because of the Katherine Dreier bequest, the Yale University Art Gallery was also outstanding for its interest in Constructivist art. The Museum of Modern Art in New York had recorded the existence of the movement, but without affection.

The Musée d'Art Moderne in Paris was in effect the "Musée d'Art Moderne *Français*"—the rest of modern art *n'y éxistait pas*; its holdings of Antoine Pevsner's work were due only to the coincidence of his having worked in Paris and being honored as a French citizen. The Tate Gallery's record was deplorable, although this has changed rapidly in recent years. Boston had nothing and remains slow to recognize Constructivism as compared to other twentieth century movements. Glasgow, which owned important Rembrandts and spent a lot of money on Dali a few years ago, was matched only by St. Louis and the National Gallery of Canada in its neglect. In addition, the extremely limited number of one-man shows of Constructivist artists demonstrated the sharp distinction between being "known" and being "accepted."

The Dutch museums have been exceptional in their continuous appreciation of Constructivism, thanks to their respect for Mondrian and their luck with Malevich, whose paintings are almost all locked up in Russia except for those represented in the 1927 Bauhaus exhibition, which were left by the artist in the care of Alexander Dorner, director of the Landes Museum in Hannover. Of these, fifteen were lent to the Museum of Modern Art, in New York, where they still are; the rest were bought by the Stedelijk Museum in Amsterdam (see note 48).

The situation has changed since the 1963 survey. Interest in the history of Constructivism has increased, and the museums have begun to show and to buy such works. They are also discovering the young. In the last three years, artists of the youthful "New Tendency" have been shown and bought by public museums in London, Paris, Stockholm, Holland, Germany, Italy, Switzerland, Belgium, and the United States. In 1966, the Venice Biennale crowned the movement by awarding the first prize to Julio le Parc of the "Groupe de Recherche d'Art Visuel" in Paris. In 1967, the Museum of Contemporary Art in Montreal assigned to the Galerie Denise René—for twenty years the undaunted exhibitor of Constructivist art in Paris—the choice of a contemporary art exhibition in conjunction with Expo '67. Forty-three artists were picked, of whom all but five are discussed in this book.

No comprehensive history of Constructivism has been published, and its masters, though renowned, are still unfamiliar. The attempt here is to present neither a detailed nor a balanced history, but rather a sufficient outline of events to explain their continuity, to define the points of view of the masters, and then to trace influences on the younger generation, whose work is the true subject of this book. I do not treat all artists equally. Some important ones are hardly more than mentioned, while others receive more attention because of their influence or ability to codify fundamental ideas. The sole survivor of the first generation of Constructivists, Naum Gabo, the clearest, deepest and most revolutionary thinker of the movement, is dwelt on at length. He is also an invaluable source of information about his colleagues and their times.

The history of the past is fixed; one has but to find it. The history of the present alters as one watches (sometimes *because* one watches), and the relation of the actors changes like poles seen from a moving train. Some of the artists I originally chose to study have changed their style and have become, artistically, other people.

The art explosion introduces so many new names and new kinds of work that we are approaching the time when, as Larry Rivers says, "Everybody will be famous." An original limitation to fifty artists soon seemed too rigid. Certain activities I describe—such as the "New Tendency"—were more important when I began than they are now; they are already history. On the other hand, a trend like "depersonalization" is much stronger now than when I first discerned it five years ago; it also may soon pass its zenith. I sometimes describe anachronisms. Artists do not stand still for historians.

Nor is my critical evaluation definitive. My teacher, Richard Offner, once confided, "If I can be considered to have accomplished anything, it is that I have distinguished thirty-six hands in the school of Orcagna alone, where only half a dozen were recognized before." I have not tried to define minute differences between artists nor to establish which of two came first in order to apportion the precise share of credit due. However, to identify the source can sometimes explain the essential character of an influence. Terms and their definitions in art derive partly from history, partly from aesthetic theory, partly from the works themselves. These, too, change with time, usage, and misusage and must be examined.

Constructivists have been accused of being formalistic, conventional, mechanical, and lacking in individuality. Even in the most depersonalized works, however, there is room for individual differences. No two Constructivists had styles as similar as those of early Braque and Picasso. Mondrian, to be sure, has had disciples who come very close to him, but no major painter can be confused with him. Gabo, Pevsner, Ben Nicholson or Josef Albers have had no imitators, yet all have influenced work quite different from their own. The clarity of purpose of the Constructivists permits sharp differences between artists. Also, it carries each artist directly to the frontier, where, as in the sciences, there is room for all to work independently.

With their slow evolution, their steadfastness, their independence coupled with self-effacement, one possibly surprising quality persists—the irrepressible humanity of these supposedly lackluster artists.[1] Even at its most austere and geometrical, art still reveals the man. There is style in non-style.

Criteria separate; artists, as they work, set up their own and become distinct from one another. The first Constructivists, when young, had much in common, yet they differed in what they were devoted to and in what they rejected. With varying degrees of consciousness or loyalty, the next generation has shared the Constructivist inheritance, including their renunciation. Gabo's Manifesto is a list of rejections. The contemporary generation has a list—somewhat longer—of its own, and shows itself to be, in general, anti-aesthetic, anti-mimetic, anti-romantic, anti-symbolic, anti-nostalgic, and sometimes, quite positively, anti-art. There is another list, not of renunciations, but of traditional qualities toward which these artists are now strictly, sometimes belligerently, neutral. They don't care for taste, harmony, unity, composition, pleasure-giving, technical virtuosity, competitiveness, connoisseurship, or its corollary, fame.

It is considered imprudent for an artist to write, for he loses time; rash for him to write about art, for he loses status as an artist. To write about his contemporaries seems especially foolhardy, for he loses not only time and status, but his friends as well. Yet, artists may *talk* at great length about art and their contemporaries and still be granted immunity. I take the risk of offering something more specific, concrete, and discussible: I have commented on the pictures selected and have tried to describe ideas objectively. I have met most of the artists discussed in this book and have seen much of their work. I admit my deep interest in their art, which is not necessarily the same as admiration.

The thesis of this book is that the pioneer work of the early Constructivists established a base from which many of the diverse and inventive non-objective tendencies of the decade 1957–67 have sprung. The book cannot be taken as a manifesto of the author's own aesthetic position; he writes here about what he sees, not about what he does.

George Rickey

East Chatham, N.Y.
July, 1967

Preface to the Revised Edition

It is not easy to pick up what one wrote, a quarter century ago, about fellow artists, with whom one had discussed, intimately and in detail, what to say and how to say it. I wrote in the present tense. We were talking, working, explaining, and we might see one another next week. Was the paint dry? Did you have the tools? Was that an empty, ephemeral idea, or had you taken on more than you could see your way to managing? Had you met so-and-so and seen his work?

Much between these covers wrote itself, in discussion, explanation, argument, that then translated itself into action in some studio in Paris, Milan, Venice, or Bern. The "Zero" group came to New York, showed at Howard Wise, and came to my house in the country for Thanksgiving, 1964. Marisol, Heinz Mack, and Gunther Uecker made little sculptures or drew in our guest book, after eating turkey and mince pie.

The hopeful camaraderie was noted, of course, in the present tense. Twenty-seven years later, some are now famous, some have died, and my present tense may read strangely. Yet the "historic present" is precisely what this was and still is—not recollection, but the daily, hour-to-hour exploration, speculation, unhesitating action—to bring these improbable creations into the world we were living *then,* on *that* stage.

So I have left the text alone, for whatever it meant in that temporal and social context.

The visual verities of time, space, color, light, texture, contrast, passage, impact, echo, void, shape, acute, obtuse, concave, convex, sound, and silence, are still waiting, like the keys of a piano, for a human touch.

Now, as then, another generation takes over, from what had been seen through the glass darkly, but then face-to-face.

December 27, 1994

George Rickey

CONTENTS

Chronology

1895   Art Nouveau.

1905   Einstein publishes *Theory of Relativity.*
        "Fauves," term first used by critic Louis Vauxcelles.

1907   Picasso, *Demoiselles d'Avignon*—Cubism begins.

1908   Kandinsky's first revelation of non-objective art [*Rückblick*, autobiography published by *Der Sturm* (1913); translated by Boris Berg and published by Solomon R. Guggenheim Foundation, N.Y. (1945)].
        Publication of Wilhelm Worringer's *Abstraction and Empathy*. Kandinsky carries on discussion with Worringer in Munich.

1909   Marinetti's "Futurist Manifesto" translated into Russian; he possibly visited Russia that year while on a propaganda tour.

1910   Picasso, portraits of *Fanny Tellier, Kahnweiler*, etc.—analytical Cubism in full flower.
        Kandinsky, first non-objective water color (some doubt Kandinsky's own dating of this work).

1911   Larionov and Goncharova claim to have made first "Rayonnist" painting, developed from Cubist-Futurist influences.
        First abstract painting by Kupka.
        "Expressionism" first used by Worringer in article referring to Cubism for August issue of *Der Sturm*.
        Picasso's first collages.

1912   Morgan Russell comments in his notebook on painting without subject.
        First abstract paintings by Arthur Dove.
        Kandinsky publishes *Concerning the Spiritual in Art* in German, stating his principle of "inner necessity," symbolic color, mathematical abstract construction, etc.
        Picasso's *Guitar*—three-dimensional collage in colored paper and string.

        Boccioni publishes his "Futurist Manifesto" ("Manifesto technica della sculptura futurista").
        Delaunay paints *Simultaneous Discs.*
        Kupka arrives at abstract color "music" from Seurat's theories, not from Cubism (Werner Haftmann, *Painting in the Twentieth Century*, Vol. 1, p. 114). Exhibits *Fugue in Red and Blue* in Salon d'Automne.
        Balla paints totally abstract and geometrical series of *Iridescent Interpenetration* in Düsseldorf.

1913   Picasso constructs reliefs of wood, glass, string, and other materials.
        Parts of Kandinsky's *Concerning the Spiritual in Art* translated into Russian.
        Larionov and Goncharova manifesto on Rayonnism.
        Tatlin visits Picasso in Paris; exhibits abstract constructions (*Hanging Reliefs*) in Moscow.
        Tatlin founds "Constructivism."
        Rodchenko founds "Non-Objectivism."
        Malevich paints *Black Square on a White Square* (according to his recollection) and other Suprematist canvases.
        Morgan Russell and Macdonald-Wright exhibit "Synchromies" in Paris.
        Russolo defines in a Futurist manifesto "The Art of Noise," and gives concerts in Italy, Paris, and London with the first "noise organ."
        Year given by van Doesburg (in fifth anniversary number of *De Stijl*, 1922) for Mondrian's arrival at the principles of "Nieuwe Beeldung"—Neo-Plasticism.
        First German Autumn Salon—"Der Sturm."
        Armory Show in New York.

1914   Rodchenko makes his first abstractions using a compass and ruler.
        Picasso's *Mandoline*—construction in wood.
        Marinetti visits Russia.
        291 published in U.S.A. by Stieglitz.

1

1915 Gabo makes his first construction—a head of wooden planes.
Exhibition of thirty-six Suprematist pictures by Malevich.
"Suprematist Manifesto" by Malevich.
First geometrical abstractions of Magnelli.

1915–22 Kandinsky in Russia except for short trips.

1917 De Stijl movement founded at Leyden by van Doesburg and Mondrian.
Publication of *De Stijl* at Leyden by van Doesburg and Mondrian. Mondrian formulates, in eleven successive installments, "Die Nieuwe Beeldung in de Schilderkunst."
Macdonald-Wright exhibits at Stieglitz Gallery.

1918 Kandinsky, professor of Fine Arts at the Academy in Moscow.

1919 "Dialog Over de Nieuwe Beeldung" by Mondrian in two issues of *De Stijl*.
Bauhaus formed by Gropius in Weimar from the Saxon State School of Arts and Crafts and Academy of Fine Arts.
First Bauhaus proclamation: "A guild of craftsmen without class distinction."

1919–20 Mondrian publishes "Naturlijke en Abstracte Realiteit" (Naturalism in Abstract Reality) in thirteen installments in *De Stijl*. (Cf. "real" in Gabo's Manifesto of same year.)
Kandinsky reorganizes Russian museums and founds Museums of Pictorial Culture. Teaches Moscow Academy and University of Moscow.

1920 Katherine Dreier, Marcel Duchamp, and Man Ray found the "Société Anonyme" in New York.
"Realist Manifesto" of Gabo and Pevsner (applies only to sculpture). Answered by a manifesto of Tatlin.
Lissitzky meets Moholy-Nagy in Düsseldorf.
"Le Néo-Plasticisme"—Mondrian writes in French, published by *L'Effort Moderne*, Paris.
Kandinsky, professor at University of Moscow; one-man show organized by government.

1921 Van Doesburg visits the Bauhaus in Weimar, lectures to the students on "De Stijl."
Hans Richter's abstract film *Rhythm 21*; Eggeling's *Diagonal Symphony*.

1922 Van Doesburg meets Mies van der Rohe and Le Corbusier.
Lissitzky and Gabo leave Russia for Berlin. Gabo stays until 1933, with frequent visits to Paris.
Lissitzky and Ilya Ehrenburg edit Constructivist magazine in Berlin, *Veshch, Objet, Gegenstand*. Bauhaus contact.
Van Doesburg organizes a Weimar section of De Stijl but, according to the Bauhaus (MOMA) book, his influence was in conflict with their principles and soon waned.
By this year, according to Seuphor, "Suprematism," "Non-Objectivism," and "Constructivism" can be used indiscriminately for both painting and sculpture.
Russian Constructivist show at Galerie Van Diemen, first in Berlin with works by Archipenko, Burliuk, Chagall, Gabo, Kandinsky, Lissitzky, Malevich, Mansurov, Rodchenko, Tatlin, then in Amsterdam. Other Russian works were shown.
"Blok," non-objective artists group founded in Lodz by Strzeminski, who developed "Unism."
Kandinsky appointed to Bauhaus faculty.
Lissitzky publishes "The Story of Two Squares" in Russian and also in Dutch in *De Stijl*.

1922–23 Van Doesburg in Berlin; influences Mies van der Rohe.

1923 Moholy-Nagy joins Bauhaus and shares with Albers (a recent Bauhaus student) the second semester Foundation Course.
Van Doesburg in Paris. De Stijl show at Galerie Léonce Rosenberg—influence on Le Corbusier.
Lissitzky comes into close contact with van Doesburg and Moholy-Nagy, increasing the Constructivist influence on the Bauhaus.
Pevsner leaves Russia and goes to Paris, where he remains until his death in 1962.

1924 Vordemberge-Gildewart joins De Stijl.
Mondrian withdraws from De Stijl because van Doesburg begins to use diagonals in his paintings.

1925 "Die Neue Gestaltung" (a translation of Mondrian's 1920 pamphlet "Néo-Plasticisme") published by the Bauhaus.
Lissitzky returns to Russia.

"Foundation of Neo-Plastic Art" by van Doesburg, published by Bauhaus.
Katherine Dreier meets Mondrian.
Gerhard Marcks leaves Bauhaus.

1926 Malevich comes to Germany to publish the "Non-Objective World" (it had been Rodchenko's phrase) at the Bauhaus; returns to Russia.
Bauhaus moves to Dessau and into Gropius' new buildings whose design showed influence of De Stijl and Constructivism.
Van Doesburg publishes manifesto on "Elementarism" in *De Stijl*. Mondrian is exhibited in U.S. through Katherine Dreier, at "Société Anonyme International" in Brooklyn. She buys several of his paintings.

1926–27 Gonzalez first forged iron works.

1926–28 Lissitzky at Kestnergesellschaft in Hannover where he was commissioned by Dorner to design an "Abstract Gallery," (first in Europe) in Provinzial Museum, Hannover.
Collaboration of van Doesburg with Arp and Sophie Taeuber-Arp in designing Restaurant l'Aubette, Strasbourg.

1927 Gallatin Collection of Cubists installed in library of N.Y.U. on Washington Square, N.Y.C., "Gallery of Living Art." Non-objective art added after 1935.

1927–29 Max Bill studies architecture at the Bauhaus.
1928 Picasso "construction" of iron wire—non-objective geometrical design.
Gropius, Moholy-Nagy, Bayer leave Bauhaus; Hannes Meyer takes over.
Len Lye draws the first film directly on celluloid.

1929 Vasarely attends the Budapest Bauhaus lectures of Moholy-Nagy; sees works of Malevich, Mondrian, Gropius, Kandinsky, Le Corbusier.

1930 "Cercle et Carré" founded in Paris by Seuphor and Torrès-Garcia. Calder visits Mondrian's studio.
Hélion meets van Doesburg and comes under Mondrian influence.

1930–31 Gonzalez gives Picasso technical assistance in his welded sculptures; his own work becomes abstract.

1930–33 Mies van der Rohe, director of Bauhaus.
1931 Van Doesburg dies.
Picasso "construction" of wrought iron (82¾" high).

1931–35 Gonzalez discovers ways to "project and design in space."

1932 Gonzalez joins "Cercle et Carré."
"Abstraction-Création" founded in Paris by Vantongerloo and Herbin; yearly exhibitions continue for five years.
Social Realism made the official style of Soviet Union.
Calder mobile exhibit at Galerie Maeght, Paris.

1933 Albers goes to Black Mountain College; stays until 1950.
Bauhaus closed by Hitler. Breuer to London; Kandinsky to Paris; Klee to Bern; Gabo to London.

1934 Diller becomes disciple of Mondrian (they meet nine years later).
Gropius to London.
First abstract works of De Kooning.
Mondrian is visited in Paris by Holtzman (then twenty-two) and Ben Nicholson (then forty). They later arrange his departure.

1935 Vantongerloo admits the curve into his work and studies "the indeterminate."
Max Bill opposes "abstract art" in favor of "concrete art."
"Abstract Art in America"—comprehensive exhibition at Whitney Museum, N.Y.
Death of Malevich in Moscow.

1936 "Cubism and Abstract Art" at MOMA (Europeans only—historical show); book of same name published by Alfred H. Barr.
Fifth and last "Abstraction-Création" exhibition.
"American Abstract Artists" organized under Bolotowsky and Balcomb Green. First exhibition in 1937, yearly ones thereafter.
Abstract Gallery in Hannover destroyed by Nazis.

1937 Museum of Non-Objective Art founded in New York (Solomon R. Guggenheim Museum) with Hilla Rebay as director.
Mortensen comes to Paris, participates in organization of exhibition of avant-garde artists—Miró, Klee, Kandinsky, etc., which

later is shown in Copenhagen.

Nicholson edits *Circle* (London) with Gabo.

"Konstruktivisten" exhibition in Basel.

Gropius goes to Harvard.

Moholy-Nagy establishes new Bauhaus in Chicago (called "Institute of Design" after 1939).

1938   Mies van der Rohe to U.S. to teach at Armour Institute, Chicago.

Mondrian writes to Nicholson and Gabo that he is coming to London. They find him a studio in Hampstead.

1938–40   Mondrian lives next door to Nicholson in Hampstead.

1938   "Abstrakte Kunst" exhibition in Stedelijk Museum, Amsterdam.

1939   Lissitzky designs dining room of Soviet Pavilion, N.Y. World's Fair.

1940   "American Abstract Artists" picket MOMA for refusal to show abstract art.

Mondrian to New York.

Pollock's first abstract painting.

Charmion von Wiegand meets Mondrian in New York.

1941   Death of Lissitzky.

1942   Peggy Guggenheim's Art of This Century gallery opens in New York.

1943   Glarner meets Mondrian (at same time as Diller).

Mondrian exhibition at Valentine Dudensing Gallery, New York.

1944   Exhibition of "Concrete Art," Kunsthalle, Basel.

Mondrian's death.

1945   "Art Concret" exhibit at Galerie Drouin, Paris, of abstract works secretly painted during the occupation.

Mondrian retrospective at MOMA.

Rothko turns to abstraction.

1946   "Réalités Nouvelles" founded in Paris by Frederic Sidès for the flock of new postwar abstract artists.

Gabo to U.S.

"Madi" exhibition organized by Kosice in Buenos Aires has strong Constructivist orientation.

1947   Pasmore turns to abstract painting.

1948   Ellsworth Kelly to Paris.

Guston turns to abstract painting.

Max Bill shows in Stuttgart with Arp and Albers.

1949   Bill shows in Zürich with Vantongerloo and Pevsner.

Galerie Maeght, Paris, exhibition "The First Masters of Abstract Art."

Seuphor publishes *Abstract Art, Its Origin, Its First Masters.*

1950   Robert Coates introduces term "Abstract Expressionism" (*New Yorker*, Nov. 25, 1950).

Albers becomes chairman, Yale University School of Design.

Kelly meets Arp, Vantongerloo, Seuphor.

1951   Bill gets first prize in São Paulo at the first Bienal.

MOMA exhibition "Abstract Painting and Sculpture in America."

Large retrospective of Bill in São Paulo Museum influences young Latin Americans.

Bill appointed rector of Hochschule für Gestaltung, Ulm; remains until 1956.

England: Pasmore's first relief; Mary Martin's first relief; first ICA exhibition of abstract art; Gimpel exhibition of British abstract art; Thomas Hess lectures on abstract art in London; Pasmore reads Biederman.

1952   Harold Rosenberg coins term "Action Painting."

Tapié uses terms "Art Autre" and "Art Informel."

"MAC" (Movimento Arte Concreta), Milan, publishes manifestos calling for synthesis of plastic arts through integration of mobility and transformability.

1953   Bill lectures in Brazil.

Seuphor's date for the beginning of "Tachism."

1954   "Eight Argentine Abstract Painters" at Stedelijk Museum, Amsterdam.

1955   "Five American Abstract Painters" at Stedelijk Museum, Amsterdam.

"Mouvement" exhibition at Galerie Denise René includes Calder, Duchamp, Vasarely, Agam, Tinguely, Bury, Soto, and Jacobsen.

1959   Jules Langsner invents term "Hard Edge" for

4

the works of Benjamin, Hammersley, Feitelson, and McLaughlin.

"Edition MAT" (Multiplication d'Oeuvres d'Art), exhibition, organized by Daniel Spoerri—first mass-produced, multiple art objects; new editions issued 1964, 1965.

"Vision in Motion—Motion in Vision" exhibition, Hessenhuis, Antwerp.

1960 "Konkrete Kunst" exhibition, Helmhaus, Zürich.

"Kinetische Kunst," at Kunstgewerbemuseum, Zürich.

1961 International exhibition, "Bewogen Beweging" (Movement in Art), Stedelijk Museum, Amsterdam; Modern Museum, Stockholm; Louisiana, Copenhagen.

"Nove Tendencije" exhibition, in Zagreb, Yugoslavia.

1962 "Painters of the Bauhaus" exhibition, Marlborough New London Gallery, London.

"Arte Programmata," organized by Munari, sponsored by Olivetti, opened Milan; shown Royal College of Art, London; then at Smithsonian Institute, Washington, D.C. in 1964, and other U.S. cities in 1965.

First international meeting of "Nouvelle Tendance, recherche continuelle" (NTrc), in Paris.

1963 Albers exhibition, Hamburg Kunsthalle.

"Groupe de Recherche d'Art Visuel" given place of honor at entrance of Paris Biennale; receives first prize "d'équipe."

Vasarely retrospective exhibition, Musée des Arts Décoratifs, Louvre, Paris.

"Esquisse d'un Salon" exhibition, Galerie Denise René, gives broad survey of Constructivist, Hard Edge, Concrete, and Research Art.

"Nove Tendencije 2" exhibition, Zagreb, emphasizes optical, kinetic, depersonalized art.

"Europäische Avantgarde," in Frankfurt am Main, includes "Arte Programmata," "Neue Tendenzen," and "Zero."

IV Biennale Internazionale d'Arte, San Marino—substantial representation of "New Tendency."

1964 "On the Move," international exhibition of kinetic art, Howard Wise Gallery, N.Y.

"Nouvelle Tendance," Musée des Arts Décoratifs, Paris.

"13 Konkrete," Kunstverein, Ulm.

"Documenta III" exhibition, includes "Zero," "NTrc," in Kassel, Germany.

"Movement," Gimpel Hanover Galerie, Zürich.

"Mouvement Deux," Galerie Denise René, Paris.

Venice Biennale, includes "Zero," "NTrc."

1965 "The Responsive Eye," at Museum of Modern Art, N.Y.

"Art Today—Kinetic and Optic," Albright-Knox Art Gallery, Buffalo, N.Y.

"Kinetische Kunst uit (from) Krefeld," Gemeentemuseum, The Hague; Stedelijk van Abbemuseum, Eindhoven.

"Espaces de l'Art Abstrait," Musées Royaux des Beaux-Arts de Belgique, Brussels.

"NUL" exhibition, Stedelijk Museum, Amsterdam.

"Nova Tendencija 3," Zagreb.

"Art et Mouvement (Art Optique et Cinétique)," Musée de Tel Aviv; organized by Denise René.

"Licht und Bewegung," Kunsthalle, Bern; travels to Palais des Beaux-Arts, Brussels (as "Lumière, Mouvement et Optique"); Kunsthalle, Baden-Baden; Kunstverein, Düsseldorf; ends April 1966.

Yves Klein retrospective, Stedelijk Museum, Amsterdam.

"White on White," De Cordova Museum, Lincoln, Mass.

"El Lissitzky," Stedelijk van Abbemuseum, Eindhoven.

1966 "The Inner and Outer Space," exhibition featuring Malevich, Gabo, Klein, in Modern Museum, Stockholm.

"Two Kinetic Sculptors: Schöffer and Tinguely," the Jewish Museum, N.Y.

"Directions in Kinetic Sculpture," the University Art Museum, University of California, Berkeley.

"Primary Structures," the Jewish Museum, N.Y.

"Weiss auf Weiss," Kunsthalle, Bern.

"Tendenzen Strukturaler Kunst," Kunstverein, Münster.

Julio le Parc (representing Argentina) wins Grand Prize, and Robert Jacobsen (Denmark) First Prize Sculptor, Venice Biennale.

5

"Kunst Licht Kunst," Stedelijk van Abbemuseum, Eindhoven.

1967 "Nuova Tendenza," Arte Programmata Italiana, Modena.

"Lights in Orbit," Howard Wise Gallery, N.Y.

Yves Klein retrospective, the Jewish Museum, N.Y.

Denise René chooses exhibition for Museum of Contemporary Art, Montreal—in conjunction with Expo '67.

Expo 67 in Montreal prominently displays art by Max Bill, Calder, Groupe de Recherche, Kemeny, Soto, Tinguely, Vasarely and others showing Constructivist tendencies.

Denise René Rive Gauche gallery opens, devoted to "Multiples" mostly by "Nouvelle Tendence."

"Edition MAT" (Multiplication d'Oeuvres d'Art) reissued by Daniel Spoerri.

Corcoran Gallery, Washington, shows single gigantic sculptures by Barnett Newman, Ronald Bladen, Tony Smith.

1968 "Documenta IV," Kassel, emphasizes light, movement, geometric forms, "minimal" art, etc., as important segment of its documentation.

"+ by —" exhibition at Albright-Knox Gallery, Buffalo, including Gabo retrospective and reconstruction of the Tatlin *Monument*.

"de Stijl," Camden Art Centre, London.

Biennale, Venice. First prize to Bridget Riley; international exhibition: "From the Informal to the Constructed."

Bauhaus exhibition opens in Stuttgart with Gropius present.

"Le Silence du Movement," Kröller-Müller Museum, Otterlo, with Mack, Soto, Yvaral, Le Parc, Morellet, Rickey, etc.

1969 Julio Gonzalez exhibitions at MOMA, Saidenberg Gallery, N.Y.; Arts Club, Chicago.

"The Machine as Seen at the End of the Mechanical Age," MOMA, N.Y.; prepared by K. C. Hultén.

David Smith retrospective, Guggenheim Museum, N.Y.

Addenda:

1913 "Target" exhibition in Moscow, with works by Malevich.

1938–39 "Bauhaus" exhibition at MOMA, N.Y.

1942 "Cubism and Abstract Art" exhibition at MOMA, N.Y., including Larionov, Lissitzky, Malevich, Mondrian, Pevsner, Rodchenko, Wilfred.

PART ONE

The Legacy of Constructivism

1/Origins

At the end of the nineteenth century numerous but isolated artists were already considering an art without subject. For example, around 1890, August Endell, the Munich Jugendstil sculptor and architect, envisioned a new art:

> An art which stirs the human soul through forms which resemble nothing known, which represent nothing, and which symbolize nothing; an art which works solely through freely invented forms, like music through freely invented notes.[2]

This description appeared more than twenty years in advance of Constructivism, but it provides a serviceable definition which includes the renunciation of symbolism.

The idea was not new even then. Plato had written in the *Philebus*, concerning geometric forms:

> For I say that these things are beautiful not in relation to something else, but naturally and permanently beautiful, in and of themselves, and give certain characteristic pleasures, not at all like the pleasures produced by physical stimuli. And colors of this sort are beautiful because they have the same character and produce the same pleasures.[3]

Prototypes of the Constructivist image had appeared in many forms: in painted pottery over thousands of years, in geometrical mosaics on the floors of Roman baths and early Christian churches, in Islamic lattices, tile and plaster work, in Celtic interlaces, in heraldic checks and quarterings, in flags, in iron grills, stained glass patterns, woven tartans and rugs, and in the stylized knot drawings of Dürer and Leonardo *(Figs. 1–6)*. This abstract imagery crept into the visual arts by the back door, as applied or useful art—sometimes as space-fillers between naturalistic elements, sometimes just for the love of doing it. In Islam, prohibition of the figure combined with a love of mathematics to enrich surfaces with intricate geometry. Such "applied" art used geometry, proportion, and optical play for their own sake. It had no use for illusionism; it was passed on from generation to generation, was modified slowly from epoch to epoch, and appeared in similar forms in different cultures. But it was neither folk art nor the traditional decoration of the sign-painter. It had a vocabulary of images, such as the circle, square, rhombus, checkerboard, key, stripe, interlace, chevron—the

9

1. Pella, mosaic floor, end of fourth century B.C. Photo Mavignier.

2. Ardebil, mosque of Schech Safi (mausoleum of the Blessed—*detail*). Photo Dr. Franz Stoedner.

3. Konia, mosaic from the Medresse of Kara Tai. Photo Dr. Franz Stoedner.

4. Celtic illuminated page. Photo Dr. Franz Stoedner.

5. Albrecht Dürer, from series *Six Knots*, 1505–07. The Metropolitan Museum of Art, N.Y.

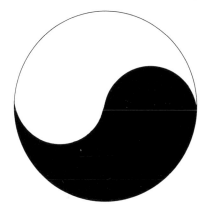

6. Yin and Yang.

basic repertory of heraldry *(Fig. 7)*—which have been extraordinarily viable in diverse cultures and have, in Western art, been considered the province of artisans. This vocabulary had been handed down quite separately from the ebb and flow of schools in "fine" art. For example, the stained glass Frank Lloyd Wright, as architect, designed *(Fig. 8)* for the Coonley children's playhouse in Riverside, Illinois was made in 1912, five years before Mondrian arrived at the same point with paint and canvas. It was not until our epoch that the very neutrality, the self-effacement, of such craftsmanship was to become an aesthetic principle characteristic of a significant group of artists.

11

7. Six Heraldic Devices, thirteenth century (from left to right): Gyronny, Barry dancetty, paly wavy, Mascle, Paly-bendy, Chevronny.

8. Frank Lloyd Wright, *Leaded Glass Window*, 1912. Coonley estate, children's playhouse, Riverside, Ill. Coll. William Bernoudy, St. Louis, Mo.; photo Steve Carver.

9. Pablo Picasso, *Girl with a Mandolin (Fanny Tellier)*, 1910. Private collection, N.Y.; photo Charles Uht.

Conscious use of geometric forms first appeared in twentieth-century art with Cézanne's famous phrase, "treat nature by the cylinder, the sphere, the cone,"[4] which was a personal formula for rendering objects in nature. This provided a rationale for Cubism, a geometric mold into which the shapes of nature were forced, usually with the proportions left unchanged *(Fig. 9)*. Constructivism owes much to the Cubists, who made the leap away from nineteenth century verisimilitude.

The evolution of Cubism was rapid. Five years—1908 to 1913—in Paris, sufficed for its development, including an ideological extension into Futurism (the abortive attempt to add a time-dimension to its geometry), its technical extension by means of collage ("you can paint with anything that will stick"), and its dematerialization in Mikhail Larionov's *(Fig. 10)* 1913 Rayonnism ("spatial forms which are obtained through the crossing of reflected rays from various objects . . . perceived out of time and in space . . . a sensation of what one may call the 'fourth dimension' "[5]). There were immediate converts to Cubism from everywhere—Russians, Americans, Italians, Germans had been infected in Paris within a year or two. But, even in France itself, a widening circle of influence quickly resulted in varied interpretations and programs.

Cubism was robust enough to exert a profound influence on artistic development for fifty years, and it attracted great and long-lived men; Braque, Picasso, Villon, Laurens, Archipenko, for example, were, in 1962, still alive and vigorously productive, still looking at nature after half a century through Cubist-tinted lenses, even though their styles were no longer "pure" Cubism.

But the standard still-lifes had been only an excuse for studying form, and Cubist survivors like Ben Nicholson, Rufino Tamayo, Wifredo Lam, or Marino Marini still remain subject-haunted. Others found Cubism becoming too sensuous, too lyrical, too permissive. They believed that once the object as subject had been dethroned, it should be liquidated.

Three statements made in 1912 by earlier converts to Cubism epitomize such thinking:

Albert Gleizes: "Let the picture imitate nothing and let it present nakedly its raison d'être."[6]

Morgan Russell: "It is purposely that there is no subject (image), it is to glorify other realms of the spirit."[7]

Umberto Boccioni: "The straight line is the only means that can lead to the primitive virginity of a new architectural construction of sculptural masses and zones."[8]

The paintings made at that time illustrated the theory: *The First Step* of Frank Kupka *(Fig. 11)*, and Robert Delaunay's *Simultaneous Discs* (1912)—"[Colors mean] nothing more than what is actually seen—colours in contrasts, arranged

11. Frank Kupka, *The First Step*, 1909. Museum of Modern Art, N.Y.

10. Mikhail Larionov, *Rayonnist Composition Number 8*, 1911?. Museum of Modern Art, N.Y.

in circles, and opposed to each other'';[9] Giacomo Balla's *Iridescent Interpenetration (Fig. 12)*, Malevich's square and cross drawings (geometry, not religion), as well as the "Synchromies" of Macdonald-Wright and Morgan Russell *(Fig. 13)*. After exposure in Paris, the Florentine Alberto Magnelli *(Fig. 14)* adopted geometrical abstraction in 1915, but abandoned it three years later.

In 1918, a reform of Cubism called "Purism" was attempted by Jeanneret—the architect known as Le Corbusier—*(Fig. 15)*, and Ozenfant, who published a manifesto calling for "an art as pure and rigorous as the machine," even though they retained subject matter.

The limitations of Cubism in sculpture were seen most clearly during the decade 1910–20. Ossip Zadkine, Henri Laurens, Jacques Lipchitz *(Fig. 16)*, and Alexander Archipenko were imposing a borrowed Cubist idiom on a surviving Renaissance concept of the figure. Boccioni saw this trap as early as 1912 *(Fig. 17)* and had called for "plastic configurations in space," composed of industrial materials such as glass, iron, cement, mirrors, to make a sculpture he defined as "transposing into material forms the spatial planes that enclose and traverse an object."[10] But he did not do it; his own Futurist sculpture of that year was essentially Cubist and remained preoccupied with the subject.

14

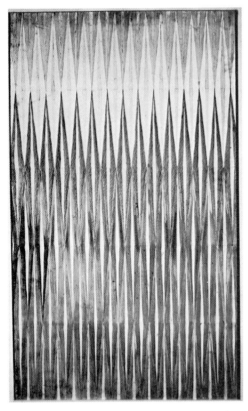

13. Morgan Russell, *Synchromy Number 3: Color Counterpoint,* 1913. Museum of Modern Art, N.Y.

12. Giacomo Balla, *Iridescent Interpenetration*, 1912. Lydia and Harry Lewis Winston collection (Mrs. Barnett Malbin); photo Joseph Klima, Jr.

14. Alberto Magnelli, *Painting*, 1915. Coll. Mlle. Blankart, Zürich.

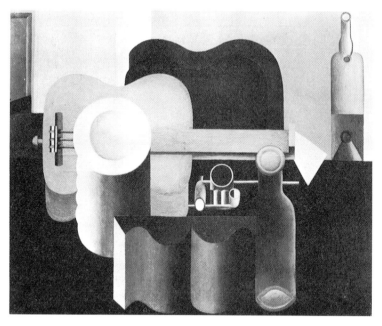

15. Charles-Edouard Jeanneret (Le Corbusier), *Still Life*, 1920.
Museum of Modern Art, N.Y., Van Gogh Purchase Fund.

16. Jacques Lipchitz, *Man with a Guitar*, 1915. Museum of Modern
Art, N.Y., Mrs. Simon Guggenheim Fund.

17. Umberto Boccioni, *Development of a Bottle in Space*, 1912.
Museum of Modern Art, N.Y., Aristide Maillol Fund.

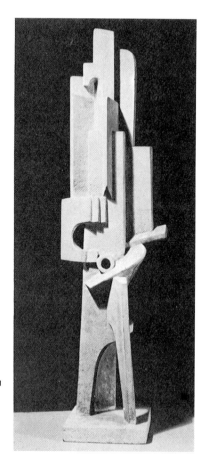

II/The Non-Objective World in Russia

In Russia the break from Cubism, both in painting and in sculpture, was catalyzed partly by Futurism—the manifestos were read in Moscow and Marinetti lectured to Russian Futurists in Moscow and St. Petersburg in 1914—and partly by Kandinsky's *Concerning the Spiritual in Art* which was written in German in 1910 and translated in part into Russian in 1912. The Russians were then prepared to make their jump into completely non-objective art.

Vladimir Tatlin, in Moscow, in 1913, made and exhibited such configurations as Boccioni had described—hanging reliefs of wood and iron *(Fig. 18)*—and, at that time, he coined the word "constructivism." Both work and word were inspired by the three-dimensional developments from collages Tatlin had seen in Picasso's Paris studio earlier that year *(Figs. 19 & 20)*; but Picasso, while occasionally flirting with an art without subject, stuck to Cubism. It was Tatlin's colleague, Alexander Rodchenko, who used the term "non-objectivism" (later adopted by Malevich) and made drawings with compass and straight edge only *(Fig. 21)*—an echo of the constructions of Euclid's geometry.

In 1913—the year "modern" art hit New York in the Armory Show—Malevich had designed for a Futurist opera a backcloth painted with a single black and white square. He had followed this with his penciled squares, and then a fully painted one *(Fig. 22)*, shown in the "Target" exhibition in Moscow. Meanwhile, he was formulating "Suprematism," and, as he later wrote: "Trying desperately to liberate art from . . . the representational world, I sought refuge in the form of the square." He acknowledged a debt to Futurism—"the expression of the rhythms of our time . . . Already pointing toward abstract art, [it] generalizes all phenomena and thereby borders on a new culture—*non-objective Suprematism*."[11]

Working with such simple forms as the square, the triangle, and the cross, Malevich had leaped in a few months to a complete grasp of non-objective art. This major step was to take the somewhat older and more mystical Piet Mondrian years to accomplish.

Suprematism was non-objective, non-social, non-utilitarian. Malevich "compressed the whole of painting into a black square on a white canvas." He said: "I felt only night within me and it was then that I conceived the new art, which

18. Vladimir Tatlin, *Corner Construction*, 1914–15. Photo Taurgo.

19. Pablo Picasso, *Guitar in Sheet Metal*, 1912. From Zervos' *Pablo Picasso*, Vol. 2 (Paris, Edition Cahiers d'Art, 1942), plate no. 337.

20. Pablo Picasso, *Study for a Construction*, 1912. Museum of Modern Art, N.Y., gift of Edward M. M. Warburg.

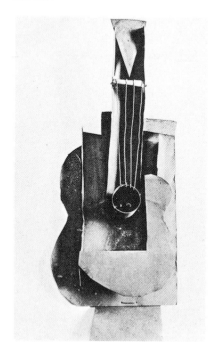

21. Alexander Rodchenko, *Line Construction*, 1920. Museum of Modern Art, N.Y.

22. Kasimir Malevich, *Suprematist Composition: Red Square and Black Square*, 1914–16?. Museum of Modern Art, N.Y.

I call Suprematism. . . . The square of the Suprematists . . . can be compared to the symbols of primitive men. It was not their intent to produce ornaments but to express the feelings of rhythm." He thought that art transcended religion and that Suprematism was the most spiritual and pure form of art. Furthermore, he believed that its purest example was a square drawn with a pencil *(Fig. 23)*. "To the Suprematist the visual phenomena of the objective world are, in themselves, meaningless; the significant thing is feeling, as such, quite apart from the

19

23 Kasimir Malevich, *Basic Suprematist Element the Square*, 1913. Photo Taurgo.

environment. . . . The Suprematist does not observe and does not touch—he feels."[12]

Despite the strength of these statements, Malevich admitted that he felt "a kind of timidity bordering on fear when I was called upon to leave the 'world of will and idea' in which I had lived and worked and in the reality of which I believed. But the blissful feeling of liberating non-objectivity drew me into the 'desert' where nothing is real but feeling, and feeling became the content of my life. This is no 'empty square' which I had exhibited but rather the sensation of non-objectivity." Like Plato, he thought the world of the senses to be illusion; reality lay beyond.

His geometrical images, including the *White on White* squares (1918), remained the purest non-objective statement of that time. His Suprematism he defined as: (1) A generalization of all phenomena; (2) "The Suprematist straight line (dynamic in character)"; (3) "The dynamic Suprematism of the plane"; (4) "Static Suprematism in space—abstract architecture (with the additional element of the 'Suprematist square') . . . a plastic feeling rendered on the canvas can be carried over into space"; (5) "The [black] square = feeling, the white field = the void beyond this feeling."

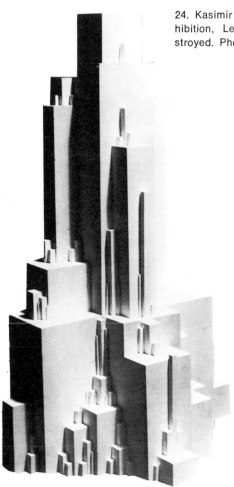

24. Kasimir Malevich, *Architectona*, 1924–26. Sculpture exhibited INCHUK Exhibition, Leningrad, June 1926—present whereabouts unknown, possibly destroyed. Photo Dumont-Schauberg, Cologne.

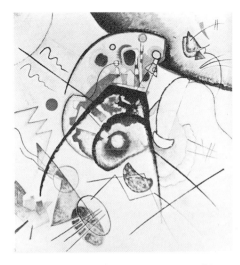

25. Wassily Kandinsky, *Backward Glance*, 1924. Photo courtesy of Marlborough-Gerson Gallery, N.Y.

The impact of Malevich's art *(Fig. 24)* and theories was immediate. Naum Gabo has said in an interview with the author that, returning to Russia in 1917 after a three-year absence, he found Suprematism without question the dominant art philosophy in the avant-garde circles of Moscow.

Wassily Kandinsky, though a Russian and destined to become famous as an abstract painter, was not directly involved in these Moscow experiments. He was absent during most of those years but his *Concerning the Spiritual in Art* had been widely read and its doctrine of "inner necessity" had provided his countrymen with a further impetus toward non-objective art.

26. Wassily Kandinsky, *Square*, 1927. Photo courtesy of Marlborough-Gerson Gallery, N.Y.; photo O. E. Nelson.

Inner necessity originates from three elements: (1) Every artist, as a creator, has something in him which demands expression. . . . (2) Every artist, as the child of his time, is impelled to express the spirit of his age. . . . (3) Every artist, as a servant of art, has to help the cause of art. . . . From the point of view of inner need, no limitation [of form] can be made. The artist may use any form which his expression demands; his inner impulse must find suitable external form.[13]

Kandinsky had apparently envisioned abstract art as early as 1908. In his autobiographical *Rückblick*, he tells how he had returned to his studio at twilight to see unexpectedly on his easel a strange but beautiful painting. "The painting lacked all subject, depicted no identifiable object and was entirely composed of bright color-patches. . . . One thing became clear to me—that objectiveness, the depiction of objects, needed no place in my paintings, and was indeed harmful to them."[14] He realized later that it was one of his own lying on its side.

For Kandinsky *(Figs. 25 & 26)*, a triangle had "its particular spiritual perfume," and "the impact of the acute angle of a triangle on a circle produces an effect no less powerful than the finger of God touching the finger of Adam in Michelangelo." His paintings of 1921, after he returned to Russia for a time, show the influence of those he had earlier influenced. In the end, he borrowed more from Constructivism than he gave to it. His poetic nature shaped an art full of mood and symbolism which later served as a prophecy, or at least as a prototype, for Abstract Expressionism, the very opposite of Constructivism. He was a romantic.

The idea of a "pure" art form was thus presented from several directions. The geometrical basis for a representational art which Cézanne had offered the Cubists was, as theory, soon obsolete, though great art was still to come from it. A clear and durable theoretical basis for non-objective art was to be set forth in Russia, then emerging from the 1914–18 war into revolution.

By 1920, after the Revolution, the artistic lines had been drawn in Moscow. Discussion of projects and philosophies of art was very open, though there was controversy. On one side were those who believed that the Workers' art should serve the masses, should be comprehensible to all, and should use industrial materials and techniques. This position was urged by Tatlin *(Fig. 27)*, Rodchenko *(Fig. 28)*, and later by Lissitzky *(Fig. 29)*, who had met Malevich in 1919, but had swung to the "Object" ideology the next year. Tatlin, in Gabo's view, was not a thinker; he had neither the background nor the training for "constructive" work; he played with experiments but was clumsy and technically uninformed.[15] Antoine Pevsner later recalled in a 1956 interview that, despite all his utilitarian theories, Tatlin never produced a design that could be executed.[16] However, Tatlin and his followers so successfully tied their aesthetic position to Marxism that to attack them seemed an attack on dogma. In fact, Tatlin's official position was so strong that he was commissioned to design the huge *Monument to the IIIrd International*.

On the other side were those who saw in non-objective art a pure poetry freed from ideology, as was urged by Malevich. He had published his "Suprematist Manifesto" in 1915, was already famous (having exhibited with the "Blaue Reiter" group in Munich), and was painting pictures more spare and austere than any the world had ever seen. Supporting him were the two Pevsner brothers, recently returned to Russia from wartime exile. When they reached Moscow in 1917, all of the excited talk had been of Suprematism. The younger and more active, Naum, called himself Gabo. It was he who, in 1920, made the spirited announcement:

> The realization of our perceptions of the world in forms of space and time is the only aim of our pictorial and plastic art. . . . We construct our work as the universe constructs its own, as the engineer constructs his bridges. . . . In creating things we take away . . . all accidental and local, leaving only the constant rhythm of the forces in them.[17]

This was part of the "Realist Manifesto" written by Gabo, subscribed to by Pevsner, which was posted on Moscow's walls during the first flush of its political revolution and in the midst of civil war. It defined clearly the limits and possibilities of non-objective art, mostly in terms of sculpture but applicable to painting, with such simplicity and clarity that its precepts are still viable two generations later. It defines the heritage and obligations which a present generation of artists continues to extend.

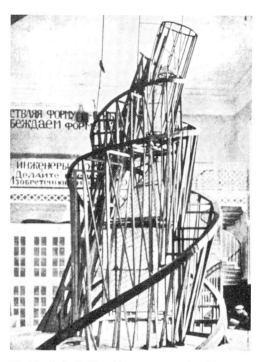

27. Vladimir Tatlin, *Monument to the IIIrd International*, 1920.

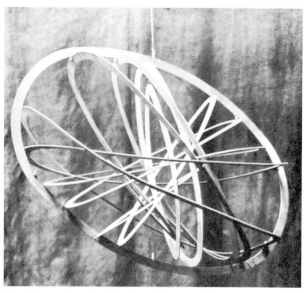

28. Alexander Rodchenko, *Construction*, 1921. Photo Taurgo.

29. El Lissitzky, *Construction Proun*, 1919–23. Museum of Modern Art, N.Y.

The Manifesto's title is misleading, and it misled the Soviet cultural officials of the time, who permitted it to be printed on some of their scarce paper because it was "realist." It was, in fact, a *constructivist* manifesto and that word is used in the text. "Realist" is an imported word in the Russian language, presumably from the French *réaliser* meaning "to achieve." Gabo said that he had in mind what could be touched and felt and was physical, in opposition to Malevich's metaphysical ideas.[18]

> We all called ourselves constructors. . . . Instead of carving or moulding a sculpture of one piece we built it up into space. . . . The word realism was used by all of us constantly because we were convinced that what we were doing represented a new reality.[19]

Gabo had been questioning established values and working out his own ideas of art since 1910, and these interests had accompanied him when he was sent to Munich to study engineering. He had attended Wölfflin's lectures on art history and, in 1912, prompted by him, had gone on a trip to Italy in secrecy and penury. When he saw his family again in 1914, he impressed them with his interest, knowledge, and originality in discussing art. Gabo was familiar with Cubism and Futurism and declared then that neither could be the style of the future. He had made contact in 1913 with the "Blaue Reiter" in Munich—Mikhail Larionov, Natalia Goncharova, and Malevich had exhibited with this group in 1912[20]—but did not meet Kandinsky until his return to Russia in 1917. He had read *Concerning the Spiritual in Art* in 1913, and did not concur with all Kandinsky wrote about identification of color with sound, though he liked his ideas and also those of Wilhelm Worringer, from whose *Abstraction and Empathy* Kandinsky had drawn much.

It was in the next three wartime years, in self-imposed exile in Norway with a younger brother, Alexei (Antoine joined them in 1916), that Gabo pondered the principles he was to expound in the Manifesto and which have guided his work ever since. Of that period Alexei has written: "He spoke to me much about the meaning of line in sculpture, and that its function was not to delimit the boundaries of things but to show the trends of hidden rhythms and forces in them."[21]

In 1915 Gabo made his first space-revealing study of a head *(Fig. 30).* Italian Renaissance sculpture had repelled him because the interior space was buried in the mass. He rejected also the showing of form by a series of profiles as Picasso and the Futurists had undertaken to do. (Gabo values these early heads so much that he has recently reconstructed one three feet high, from 1916; now he would like to realize it on a ten-foot scale, like the great Indian and Egyptian monuments.) The heads of 1915 and 1916 have been mistakenly considered Cubist because of their geometry; but Gabo was seeking to reveal interior space, not to create a stylized exterior form.

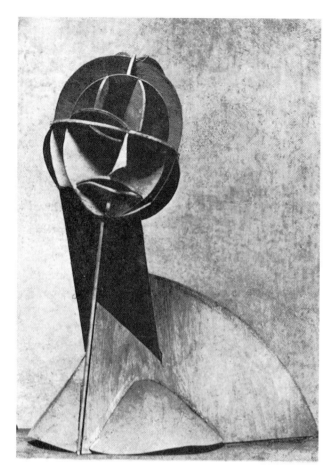

30. Naum Gabo, *Constructed Head No. 1*, 1915. Coll. the artist; photo E. Irving Blomstrann.

31. Naum Gabo, *Two Cubes*. From *Gabo* (Harvard Univ. Press, Cambridge), p. 168.

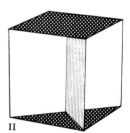

I   II

In his later essay, "Sculpture: Carving and Construction in Space," he described and illustrated this difference *(Fig. 31)*:

> . . . two cubes which illustrate the main distinction between the two kinds of representation of the same object, one corresponding to carving and the other to construction. . . . The first represents a volume of mass; the second represents the space in which the mass exists made visible. Volume of mass and volume of space are sculpturally not the same thing. Indeed, they are two different materials . . . both concrete and measurable.

Up to now, the sculptors have preferred the mass and neglected or paid very little attention to such an important component of mass as space. . . . We consider it [space] as an absolute sculptural element, released from any closed volume, and we represent it from inside with its own specific properties.

I do not hesitate to affirm that the perception of space is a primary natural sense which belongs to the basic senses of our psychology.[22]

On his return to Russia in 1917, Gabo assumed a position of leadership and also began to teach. He has recalled:

My period of testing ended in Norway. When I arrived in Russia at the beginning of 1917, I already knew I wasn't going to do any more heads. . . . Then I began making constructions which were architectonic. . . . I transferred myself to the middle of the construction, to be in the middle of space. . . .[23]

In 1920 an exhibition was arranged in a music shell in the open air, on a boulevard in Moscow. Its focus was the ideas of Gabo, but it included Antoine Pevsner and several others. Pevsner showed three Cubist and one abstract painting; only Gabo showed sculpture. It was for the opening of this exhibition on August 5 that Gabo wrote the Manifesto which Pevsner asked to sign. In five terse and ringing clauses, Gabo rejected (1) color as accidental and superficial, (2) the descriptive value of line in favor of line as direction of static forces, (3) volume in favor of depth as the only pictorial and plastic form in space, (4) mass in sculpture in favor of the same volume constructed of planes, and (5) the thousand-year-old delusion of static rhythm in favor of "kinetic rhythms as the basic forms of our perception of real time."

The Manifesto was expanded by Gabo in later writings; for example, it had not dealt with materials. Though it has been said that Gabo is so interested in space that he would like to control it with no material at all, and he did not see in Constructivism an applied art for the workers—as did Tatlin—he has, in fact, welcomed industrial materials and uses them.

In sculpture, as well as in technics, every material is good and worthy and useful, because every single material has its own aesthetical value. In sculpture as well as in technics the method of working is set by the material itself.[24]

Alexei writes of this time:

This manifesto was a major event in Moscow. To understand this one must imagine Moscow in 1920. Civil war was raging throughout the country, there was a war with Poland on our borders, and there was famine in the city, which was in fact under martial law. And suddenly, on the morning of August 5th, posters appeared at every street corner, in the spots reserved for government orders and decrees, with the heading "the realistic manifesto". One should note that in former years the people had grown accustomed to the word "manifesto" as denoting some announcement by the Tsar of some proclamation of royal favours to the people. Naturally, the people of Moscow rushed to read this manifesto under the impression that it was a government decree. Large crowds of people gathered at all the crossroads where the manifesto was displayed and in some parts meetings even sprang up. . . . But intellectual circles in Moscow read it, understood it and discussed it. News that the artists had also organized an exhibition on the Tverskoy Boulevard, in the open air, attracted crowds to the boulevard, and it was a long time, not until nightfall in fact, before people finally dispersed. Discussions of the contents of the manifesto were carried on in the street and then continued behind the walls of student residences and in the lecture halls of *Vkhutemas*. Everyone knew that Gabo was the author of the manifesto and he alone at this time had to beat off the attacks of critics and elucidate what he meant to those who were interested.[25]

Three or four months after these events, there was a gala meeting of artists, students, critics, and others. Among those present were the poet Vladimir Mayakovsky, the Futurist writer Ossip Brik, Tatlin, Malevich, and, of course, Gabo and Antoine Pevsner. There were speeches on the topic of the evening, "buildings in space, and architecture." Brik referred to Gabo's exhibition; and Tatlin's *Monument to the IIIrd International*, which had already been rejected, was discussed. Mayakovsky and Brik defended it, the latter saying that it went beyond such previous constructions as the Eiffel Tower. To that Gabo answered that it was impractical and badly engineered, but that it had value as a fantasy, which should be preserved as a model. At this point, Malevich rose to the defense of Suprematism. Then, when students asked, "Where do we go now?" he told them to study the Constructivist exhibition, for it continued the ideas of Suprematism. Alexei reports:

Gabo's speeches at public meetings and the teaching he gave in his studio brought about the end of the reigning art movement of the time, known as Suprematism, and Malevich himself admitted at a public meeting that it was necessary for Suprematism to adopt the new Constructivist ideology being preached by Gabo.[26]

Despite this, Gabo reports—in a conversation with the author—that Malevich defended Suprematism to the end, and attacked Gabo's heads, which he did not understand, though he admired his other work; Malevich was fanatical about the necessity for art to be abstract.

As though anticipating and rejecting in advance the subjective, introverted, and improvised art which was to come, Gabo called for awareness and precision:

The school of Constructive art is known to be the first movement in art which has declared the acceptance of the scientific age and its spirit as a basis for its perceptions of the world outside and inside human life. It was the first ideology in this century which for once rejected the belief that the personality alone and the whim and the mood of the individual artist should be the only value and guide in an artistic creation. It was also the first manifestation in art of a totally new attitude towards the artist's task of what to look for. It has accepted the fact that what we perceive with our five senses is not the only aspect of life and nature to be sung about; that life and nature conceal an infinite variety of forces, depths, and aspects never seen and only faintly felt which have not less but more importance to be expressed and to be made more concretely felt through some kind of an image communicable not only to our reason, but to our immediate everyday perceptions and feelings of life and nature.

The Constructive ideology . . . calls for the highest exactitude of means of expression of all the fields of human creation—it holds that, as in thought so in feeling, a vague communication is no communication at all.[27]

Gabo himself is both aware and precise; vagueness is foreign to his art and his writing. Less metaphysical than Malevich, he has also been more coherent, objective, and lucid. He has been broader and more flexible than Mondrian and has no mystical notions of "pure" art as a panacea.

By 1920, then, Gabo was the major Russian exponent of non-objective art. Two years later he showed eight works, including his famous *Kinetic Construction* of a vibrating spring, at the great Russian exhibition in the Galerie Van Diemen in Berlin, organized by David Sternberg, the Commissar of Education. Tatlin, Malevich, Lissitzky, Rodchenko, Pevsner, Kandinsky, as well as Chagall, the two Burliuks, and Archipenko also showed several works each and were singled out for comment in the preface to the catalogue.[28] Although conservative Russian artists were shown, it was the Constructivists who made history in this first large-scale export of their new art to the outside world.

In 1921, Pevsner, Kandinsky, and Malevich had found their studios suddenly closed without explanation. Gabo had, in the meantime, foreseen curbs on free expression in Soviet Russia and late in 1921 he asked for permission to leave. Having received his passport quite easily, with the understanding help of the Commissar, Lunarcharsky, he went to the Berlin exhibition and did not return. Pevsner, who did not attend the exhibition, followed him the next year; and even after Pevsner went on to Paris nine months later, the brothers maintained their contact. Alexei writes of their relationship *(Figs. 32 & 33)*:

Gabo, who was living in Berlin at the time, often visited him [Antoine] in Paris and encouraged him to take up Constructivist sculpture. Gabo instructed him, supplied him with themes, and left his models behind so that Antoine might study their structure. He also permitted him to repeat variations on them and taught him how to handle metal and plastic materials.[29]

Antoine, who continued primarily as a painter until 1923, has implied a collaboration with his brother in the development of Constructivist art which is misleading. In the early twenties he was copying Gabo's "constructions" as exercise, yet he said in an interview in 1956:

> We were both concerned with the problem of depth, trying to create depth in space. It was then that we began to develop together our concept of Constructivism based on a philosophy of space and time. We sought a means of using the void and freeing ourselves from the compact mass.[30]

There is no other evidence to justify the first person plural. In an exchange of letters with Gabo at the time, Pevsner blamed the misrepresentation on the press.

32. Antoine Pevsner, *Torso*, 1924–26. Museum of Modern Art, N.Y.

33. Naum Gabo, *Construction in Space*, 1923. Coll. the artist.

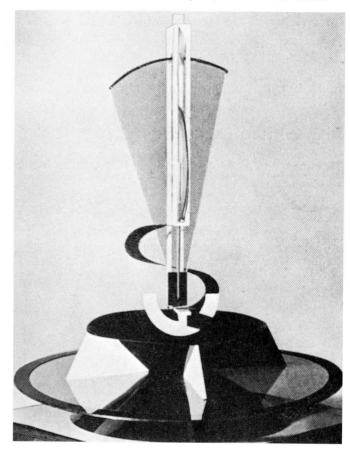

There is at least one example of a Gabo work actually having been reproduced in Paris over Pevsner's name. In *L'Histoire de l'Art Contemporain*, Christian Zervos reproduces a 1923 work of Gabo as a 1928 Pevsner.[31]

Pevsner was adopted by the French, chose to become a French citizen, and eventually developed his own deservedly appreciated style. That he became more famous than his brother, however, and in areas in which Gabo's contributions were more significant, can only be explained by the capacity of Paris at that time to confer fame. Pevsner was honored by extensive exhibitions, mostly in Paris, as a French artist, while his more isolated brother was largely ignored in official art circles.

Although Gabo supplied the intellectual backbone of Constructivist art, it is his sculpture which makes the important contribution both to art and to history. Recognition of this has been slow, and it was not until 1965 that a comprehensive exhibition of his work was seen in Europe. It opened at the Stedelijk Museum in Amsterdam in April, traveled to Mannheim, Duisburg, Zürich, and Stockholm that year, and went to the Tate Gallery, London, in March 1966.

Even after he had a worldwide reputation, Gabo met resistance in Rotterdam when he was invited to undertake what he considers his most important work —in front of Marcel Breuer's Bijenkorf department store building in Rotterdam. He tells how, after the bombing, there was careful planning of the reconstruction of the city.[32] The plans called for uniform symmetrical projections from the long façades of new buildings. When Breuer presented his designs, the city planners immediately jumped on his failure to provide for this "bulge" in his façade. He refused to change; they refused to make an exception. To break the impasse, the store owner asked if they would allow a sculpture instead of a "bulge" in the building. They said "possibly . . . let us see it." He sent for Gabo, who made a model to the scale of Breuer's model; they accepted it, though not without debate.

At their meeting, the town planners of Rotterdam wanted to know if the sculpture would be symmetrical. Gabo got up and facing them asked, "Am I symmetrical?" "Yes," they said. Then he made a quarter-turn and asked, "Am I symmetrical now?" "No." "Well, that is the way I am going to make it." According to Gabo, a committee member wrote into the contract that the design would have "asymmetrical symmetry."

The next problems were to get the structure approved by the engineers and then find a builder. The engineers were skeptical and said the structure would have to be secured by stays which, for Gabo, would ruin it; he was confident it would stand. They said it must be tested by the Royal Institute as there were no formulae for making calculations for such a design. So Gabo made a larger model which was tested in a wind tunnel and measured for deflections under various stresses, requiring a long, frustrating, and, for the store owner, expensive wait. Finally they found the design perfect, conforming exactly to technical requirements in an uncanny way; they asked only for a very slight, scarcely discernible thickening of the lower structure.

There was no firm that knew how to make such an object or was willing to undertake it. Gabo took the initiative and called a meeting of a bridgebuilder, a factory builder, an aircraft builder, and a shipbuilder. He explained how he had systematically arrived at his forms by successive rotations of two degrees at regular stages, and had built out from a pipe core with square plates at intervals, and then had surfaced the whole structure with sheet metal. They understood and showed wonder at a sculptor working in this clearly technical way; yet they were unwilling to try it on a large scale because it was so foreign to their usual practice.

Finally the shipbuilder, a young man of thirty-five, said, "I understand it and I will build it." This he did, with Gabo constantly supervising the progress of the subtly-curved forms, calling sometimes for a little more or a little less twist of the structure with the hydraulic presses or a bit more grinding down of the final surfaces, to make sure that the curve flowed without interruption, sometimes even guiding the workman's hand to the spot to be ground.

It was a century since Delacroix had written: ". . . art is no longer what the vulgar think it to be, that is, some sort of inspiration which comes from nowhere, which proceeds by chance. . . . It is reason itself, adorned by genius, but following a necessary course and encompassed by higher laws."[33]

The eighty-foot Rotterdam construction *(Figs. 34 & 35)* is to date the greatest Constructivist monument. Gabo has occasionally worked on other large-scale pieces; the two largest in America are one hanging in a stairwell in the Baltimore Museum *(Fig. 36)*, and a wall relief in the U.S. Rubber Company building in Radio City, New York (1956).

Famous as Gabo gradually became elsewhere, he was scarcely known in his native Russia after his departure in 1921, and it was only by accident that his brother, Alexei learned of his later career.

> In 1959, Alexei Pevsner visited the American exhibition in Moscow, read the introduction to the catalogue written by Lloyd Goodrich, and found Naum Gabo's name, mentioned as an American artist not represented in the exhibition. He immediately wrote a letter to Goodrich asking for Gabo's address. The letter was forwarded to Gabo and so, after twenty-three years, Gabo and Antoine Pevsner re-established contact with their brother, Alexei, in Moscow.[34]

A visit by Gabo to Moscow provided a long-overdue family reunion, and prompted Alexei to add his memoir to the scanty history of early Constructivism. This also

35. Gabo, view from below *Rotterdam Construction.*

34. Naum Gabo, *Rotterdam Construction*,
Bijenkorf stores, 1957.

led to the rediscovery of some early work which had survived in the Pevsner family cellar for over four decades.

Despite Gabo's historical role and growing reputation, his sculpture is meagerly distributed throughout the world's museums. Yet he has revolutionized our view of sculptural and architectural space. Herbert Read wrote: "The Constructivist idea in art has not changed since it was first formulated by Gabo—it is one of those irreducible concepts that do not change, and that even tend to a theoretical exclusion of the personal elements in style."[35]

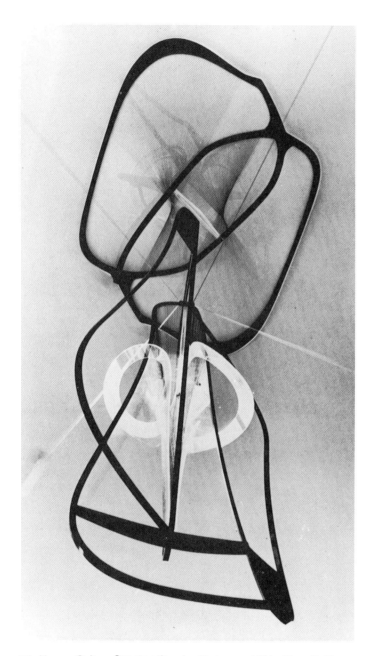

36. Naum Gabo, *Construction in Stairway*, 1951. The Baltimore Museum of Art, Sadie A. May collection.

III/Constructivism and De Stijl

Within two years of the first Russian adventures and quite independently, in Holland, Piet Mondrian, a former Cubist, had transposed nature into his "plus and minus" pictures. By 1914 he was painting compositions *(Fig. 37)* that were severe abstractions from landscape. Although they seemed non-objective, he gave them such titles as *The Sea, Façade*, and *Scaffolding*, and they contained obscure symbols from his deeply-held theosophical beliefs. He envisioned an art of relationships which later became generally known as "Neo-Plasticism."[36] Mondrian also continued to paint flower studies for a living, and he wrote, as late as 1924, that "without the flowers, I wouldn't be able to [eat]."[37] By 1915, however, he had transformed the detail he observed in nature to conform to what he saw as a universal law. This freed him from the appearance of nature but not from its mystical appeal. The surface was still painterly—he learned to paint flat from Van der Leck in 1916. "My technique, which was more or less Cubist, hence still more or less pictorial in nature, was influenced by his exact technique."[38] The next year he began painting in simple, crisp, rectilinear abstract shapes.

He met Theo van Doesburg and together in 1917 they founded the group they called "De Stijl," which began publishing in Leyden a magazine by that name. Mondrian used this vehicle to set forth his ideas of a relational art. By 1921 he had perfected the style by which he was to be known—a black grid on a white ground, with rectangles of the primary colors and proportions of line and interval, adjusted through preliminary work with strips of paper.

In Russia, Suprematism and Constructivism were coalescing and their leading figures were temporarily in positions of official responsibility. Word and example of their achievements had reached Germany, where the Bauhaus was soon to offer hospitality. Mondrian's work, however, was destined for earlier fame and influence because of his long sojourn in Paris, then the center of the art world.

Van Doesburg, a persuasive talker who had once considered being an actor, was also a great traveler. He proselitized vigorously in Berlin, Paris, and Weimar, where he met and must have impressed Le Corbusier, Mies van der Rohe, Moholy-Nagy, and Walter Gropius, the Bauhaus director.

Despite van Doesburg's success as missionary, Mondrian broke his ties with

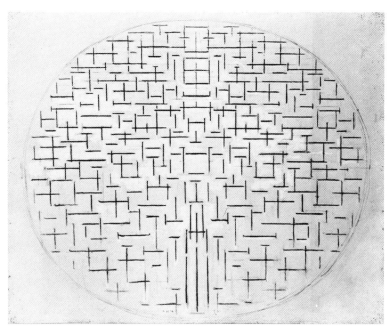

37. Piet Mondrian, *Pier and Ocean*, 1914. Museum of Modern Art, N.Y.

De Stijl in 1924. Furious in his uncompromising purity with van Doesburg's introduction of diagonals into his painting *(Fig. 38)*, Mondrian wrote: "After your arbitrary correction of Neo-Plasticism, any collaboration of no matter what kind has become impossible for me."[39] At the time it was uncertain whether Mondrian or van Doesburg was the mainspring of De Stijl; history, however, has decisively declared for Mondrian.

Of the epoch of the twenties Mondrian wrote: "Constructivism was continued in Paris and London where it became homogeneous with Neo-Plasticism, however, there always remained differences in viewpoints,"[40] which would have included his insistence on vertical-horizontal, pure color as the means of expression, ideas of social harmony through art and, always, a certain mysticism. From then on, "Constructivist" was applied to both, "Neo-Plasticism" only to the Dutch. Oskar Schlemmer could write in his diary in 1925: "The state of art shows that the three tendencies, Cubism–Futurism–Expressionism, have been condensed to two: Constructivism–Verism,"[41] his term for representation of the visible world.

"Constructivist" had thus come to cover both painting and sculpture, and had spread to absorb many of the ideas of Suprematism and De Stijl. It was no longer confined to, nor especially concerned with, what was constructed or made by joining industrial materials, nor to pure geometry or a predominance of empty space. The essential character of Constructivist art was not in style or material or technique, but in the *image*. This image required of the artist a radical shift from ideas held for thousands of years. Now the image itself was *real*. Gabo summarized it as "we do not make images of . . ."

The image in Constructivism, after forty years of manifestos, of additions, modifications and personal development by many artists, and of simplifications by critics and historians, still has these characteristics:

1. The subject of the work of art is the image itself—

> . . . it [is] impossible for our consciousness to perceive or arrange or act upon our world and in our life in any other way but through these constructions of an ever-changing yet coherent chain of images—conceptions. . . .
>
> I maintain that these consciously constructed images are the very essence of the reality of the world which we are searching for.[42]

38. Theo van Doesburg, *Countercomposition of Dissonances XVI*, 1925. Haags Gemeentemuseum, The Hague.

Further—

> The elements of a visual art such as lines, colors, shapes, possess their own forces of expression independent of any association with the external aspects of the world.[43]

2. The image does not depend on any recollected experience, event, or observed object, nor on any kind of association or suggestion, nor on projection of experience onto an evocative form. The image does not result from "emotion recollected in tranquility," nor from fantasy, from "automatic" gestures, or from any kind of trance or emanation from the subconscious. However, it need not be regular nor geometric.

3. The image is premeditated and deliberate and precisely adjusted.

4. The choice of the nature of the image is within the authority and free will of the artist. The artist may choose geometry, intuition, or a combination of both; he may delegate his determination to some mathematical expression, to chance, or even to a computer. Yet the initial choice which determines the character of the eventual image is made by the artist.

5. There is no intentional "illusionism" such as perspective or modeling; no chiaroscuro; color is flat, or, if shaded, gives no illusion by this of volume, space, or suggestion of mood.

6. The technique is not part of the image, thus there is no surface "treatment" —ars est celare artem. "No handwriting, no interesting surface." "Construction, not expression." Constructivist work, therefore, usually appears clean, pure, effortless, without élan, sense of speed, or urgency. The clean, quiet qualities are not a purpose but a by-product. From them comes the "untouched-by-human-hand" look. Industrial materials are used frankly, without any attempt at enhancement, so that they reveal their own qualities as steel, brass, plastic, cement; preoccupation with materials for their own sake would be digressive.

7. There are no romantic motives for, and no romantic inferences from the image.

8. There are no symbols.

9. It is consequent on the above that the image has not been "abstracted" from forms in nature (as in Cubism), or made to echo them (biomorphic abstraction). Yet this does not rule out the visual environment as a source of images, e.g., the square and cube can be found in iron pyrites, the circle in the sun and moon, the rhombus in other crystals. Irregular shapes, too, can be borrowed from the environment, or from tradition, which is a reservoir of all forms. It is the shape, however, that the Constructivist takes, and the object and its associations are left. The shape becomes a figure (in the sense of figure and ground), free of symbolic representation.

10. It is corollary that the image appear as though it had been arrived at independently of human thought; it is premeditated but no process shows.

Many, but not all the same qualities are found in De Stijl. Mondrian's canon was more restricted—neither responding to nor reacting against the Constructivism of his time, which he did not know when he formed the group—and he wrote extensively to explain it.[44] He was profoundly influenced by the theosophical writer, Schoenmakers, both in the formation of his thought ("Style—the general despite the particular"), and actual phrases, especially "nieuwe beeldung" (the "new configuration"), which Mondrian immortalized.[45] The writings began with a series of essays in 1917, in the first number of *De Stijl*. We have Mondrian's own definition of Neo-Plasticism, from a short unpublished essay which he wrote in 1926 (Seuphor considers it the best formulation). The following are the essentials of the image in Neo-Plasticism:[46]

1. Flat plane.

2. Primary colors plus black, white, and gray.

3. Equilibrium must be established between large, empty space and small, colored surface. Color finds opposition in non-color—i.e., in white and black.

4. Equilibrium is achieved through the proportions of the plastic means (the plane, the line, the colors).

5. No symmetry.

6. A social implication; equilibrium, through a contrasting and neutralizing opposition, annihilates individuals as particular personalities and thus creates the future society as a real unity. *The balanced relation is the purest representation of universality*."

7. It is clear elsewhere that Mondrian insisted on vertical-horizontal relations only, though they could appear on a format tilted at forty-five degrees. (There is a painting in the Philadelphia Museum with a diagonal grid but the composition is vertical-horizontal.)

"Elementarism" was devised in 1924 by van Doesburg who, while retaining the right angle, forsook the strict vertical-horizontal axes of Neo-Plasticism. In 1926 he announced, "Elementarism [as a reaction against] the too dogmatic application of Neo-Plasticism." In a manifesto in *De Stijl* he proposed a heterogeneous, deliberately unstable expression, with inclined planes which would increase the dynamic effect and introduce surprise. In this he was followed by a fellow Dutchman, César Domela, and a German, Friedrich Vordemberge-Gildewart.

In 1930, van Doesburg, who in the meantime had toyed with Surrealism as well, went further. He published, in a unique issue of what was intended to be a periodical called *A.C.* (for "Art Concret"), his "Commentaries on the Basis of Concrete Painting," in which he tried to go beyond Mondrian in an extension of

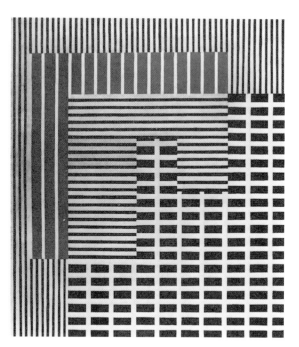

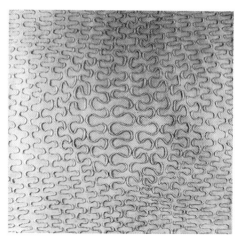

40. Wladyslaw Strzeminski, *Unist Composition*, 1934. Museum Sztuki, Lodz, Poland.

39. Henryk Stazewski, *Composition*, 1930–32. Museum Sztuki, Lodz, Poland; courtesy Galerie Chalette, N.Y.; photo O. E. Nelson.

41. El Lissitzky, *Abstract Gallery*, 1926–27. Landes Museum, Hannover; courtesy Mrs. Alexander Dorner.

Constructivist and Neo-Plastic ideas. He first made clear the distinction between "nature forms" and "art forms" (non-objective images), and called for "pure painting in constructing the spirit-form." He called it "concrete" in contrast with "abstract"

> because nothing is more concrete, more real, than a line, a color, a surface ...a woman, a tree, a cow are concrete in the natural state, but in the context of painting they are abstract, illusory, vague, speculative—while a plane is a plane, a line is a line, nothing less, nothing more.

Jean Arp for a time favored van Doesburg's terminology, as did Kandinsky after 1938. But van Doesburg's theory added little to what Gabo, Mondrian, Auguste Herbin, and a number of others had already done, and scarcely presaged the later use of the term "Concrete Art" by Max Bill.

In 1922 a Polish colleague of Malevich, Wladyslaw Strzeminski, had assembled a Suprematist group in Lodz, which called itself "Blok." A survivor today is Henryk Stazewski *(Fig. 39)*, who is still active as a non-objective painter in Poland. Strzeminski sharpened and narrowed his theories to a system he called "Unism" *(Fig. 40)*, which he described in 1932 in *Abstraction-Création*, the publication of the Parisian exhibiting group. He condemned the division of a painting through linear and rhythmic emphases, oppositions and contrasts, and intensified contours. Instead he tried to secure an optical integrity by uniform, all-over painting, which not only had no subject, but went beyond Malevich in having no image either.

> Line divides—the purpose ought not to be the division of the picture, but its unity, presented in a direct way: optically. So one must renounce the line. One must renounce rhythm, because it exists only in the relations of independent parts. One must renounce oppositions and contrasts, because only separated forms can establish oppositions and contrasts. One must renounce division because it concentrates and intensifies the forms around the contour—and cuts the picture into sections. . . .[47]

A later corroboration of his theories is to be found in the painting of Jackson Pollock, Mark Tobey, Jean-Paul Riopelle, Piero Dorazio, and other painters employing tiny divisions of surface or deliberate non-composition.

With the departure of Gabo and Pevsner from their homeland, the Russian phase of Constructivism had ended. Gabo last saw Malevich, much depressed, in Berlin at the time of the latter's Bauhaus exhibition in the late twenties.[48] In the meantime, the Russian developments and differences had been shown to the world in the comprehensive Galerie Van Diemen exhibition in Berlin. The Russian Revolution had triumphed, Lenin was secure; artists and writers, after snatching the ideological victory from the debacle of their armies and the liquidation of the class that had led them, were hopeful of a golden age. Germany, also emerging from defeat, seething with discontent on the brink of Communism, was temporarily socialist and ready for new cultural, as well as political, ideas, while inflation drained off vested wealth.

As the West grew more hospitable, the East grew more hostile. Owing partly to Lenin's antipathy to modern art (he had lodged in Zürich and ate at the nearby Cabaret Voltaire, where he witnessed the activities of the Dadaists in 1917), partly to his doctrine of Social Realism, partly to the continuing power of the old academic Russian artists, Constructivism's official fortunes declined, and the artists had to recant or leave.

In 1922 Lissitzky, having obtained permission to install the Constructivist section of the Van Diemen exhibition, came to Berlin. While there he edited, with Ilya Ehrenburg, a polyglot Constructivist magazine called *Veshch, Objet, Gegenstand*. He also made contact with De Stijl and the architect Mies van der Rohe and established with Moholy-Nagy a Berlin Constructivist group ("G"). In 1926 he was invited to the Kestnergesellschaft in Hannover. During his two-year stay there he designed for the Provinzial Museum an "Abstract Gallery" *(Fig. 41)*—the first of its kind—and published his "Story of Two Squares" in *De Stijl* magazine. He returned to Russia in 1928, worked on typography and layout, and emerged to design the dining room in the Soviet Pavilion of the 1939 World's Fair in New York.

In 1927, Malevich was allowed to go to Germany to supervise the publication of his *Non-Objective World*, describing his theories of teaching, written mostly in 1919–20 (surprisingly, it did not appear in English until 1959). He returned to Russia to die in obscurity in 1935 and to be buried in a Suprematist coffin he had designed, with his arms folded in the form of a cross.

Tatlin and Rodchenko remained in Russia, compliant, doing official photography, typography, and commercial art. They died in 1952 and 1956 respectively, their early contributions overlooked.

IV/The Bauhaus and Constructivism Between the Wars

The Bauhaus had opened under the architect Walter Gropius in 1919 in Weimar as a "Guild of Craftsmen without class distinction," which meant no distinction between artist and artisan. Gropius *(Fig. 42)* soon appointed Kandinsky *(Fig. 43)*, Paul Klee *(Fig. 44)*, Lyonel Feininger *(Fig. 45)* in painting; Gerhard Marcks in sculpture; Oskar Schlemmer in theater; Marcel Breuer in architecture; Herbert Bayer in graphic design; and, in the all-important Foundation Course, Johannes Itten, who was soon replaced by Josef Albers and László Moholy-Nagy *(Fig. 46)*. Everyone explored techniques, tools, and materials, as well as expressive ideas.

The theories of De Stijl were introduced to an already receptive atmosphere in Weimar, through the visits of van Doesburg in 1921, who founded a "De Stijl" section in the city but was not welcomed by Gropius in the school.[49] The Constructivist ideas came mostly through Moholy-Nagy, and exercised considerable influence on the students. The Bauhaus published Mondrian's essays from *De Stijl* in 1925, and Malevich's *Non-Objective World* in 1927. Primary colors became a Bauhaus mark. Faculty and students had been prepared for a machine aesthetic also, which appeared with the Russians in Berlin, where the Bauhaus faculty, already familiar with De Stijl, found its Constructivist equivalent. The two main branches of non-representational art—Dutch and Russian—met and merged in the hospitable German school. Once absorbed into the curriculum, they were, in the next fifteen years, to be propagated throughout the world.

The avid Bauhaus response to the Russians and the Dutch and the rapid assimilation of both, show that similarities exceeded differences. The 1919 proclamation of the Bauhaus had said: "Proficiency in his craft is essential to every artist"; it made no mention of design or theory. Then, in 1924, it became both more proletarian and more doctrinaire: "Manual training in workshops actively engaged in production, coupled with sound theoretical instruction in the laws of design." A visual vocabulary was also adopted: "Red . . . evokes in us other emotions than does blue or yellow [De Stijl colors]; round forms speak differently to us than do pointed or jagged forms."[50] Every Bauhaus applicant was given a questionnaire devised by Kandinsky, with a triangle, square, and circle to be filled in with red, blue, and yellow, after which the choice of color for the shape had to be explained.

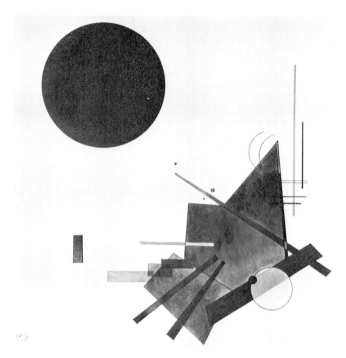

42. Walter Gropius, *Model for Chicago Tribune Competition*, 1923. Courtesy the artist.

43. Wassily Kandinsky, *Black Relationship*, 1924. Museum of Modern Art, N.Y.

44. Paul Klee, *Portal of a Mosque*, 1931. Coll. Mr. and Mrs. Ralph F. Colin, N.Y.; photo Soichi Sunami.

45. Lyonel Feininger, *Gelmeroda VIII,* 1921. The Whitney Museum, N.Y.

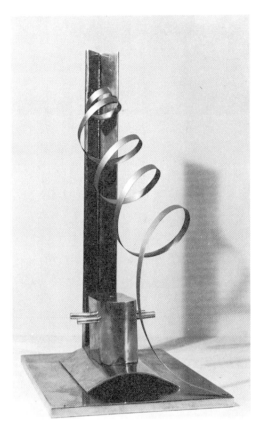

46. László Moholy-Nagy, *Nickle Construction*, 1921. Museum of Modern Art, N.Y.

47. Josef Albers, *Growing*, 1940. San Francisco Museum of Art.

From his early days as a Bauhaus teacher of drawing, design, and color, to his retirement from Yale in 1960, Josef Albers was the great pedagogue of the Constructivist aesthetic. An account of his teaching and career, which have spanned the whole evolution of Constructivism, is a part of its history.

In 1920, after a thorough academic training in Berlin, Essen, and Munich, Albers *(Fig. 47)*, at the age of thirty-two, started as a student "from the beginning" at the Weimar Bauhaus in the Foundation Course under Johannes Itten.

When Itten left the Bauhaus in 1923, he and Moholy-Nagy were asked to teach the course together. Of this, Albers says:

> If a general denominator could be found for all three *Vorkurs* teachings— Itten taught for four years, Moholy for five years, I for ten years—all three aimed at the development of a new, contemporary visual idiom.
>
> And this, with time, led from an emphasis on personal expression and individualistic graphic and pictorial representation of material, to a more rational, economic and structural use of material itself.
>
> It led to the recognition of, beside its outer appearances (matière), its inner capacities and practical potentialities; and so, to a more impersonal presentation. Or, in pictorial terms, from collage to montage.[51]

"Design" is a threadbare word, worn thin in teachers' colleges, automobile factories, and advertising studios. Yet Albers made a poem of it:

> To design is
> to plan and to organize, to order, to relate and to control.
> In short it embraces
> all means opposing disorder and accident.
> Therefore it signifies
> a human need
> and qualifies man's
> thinking and doing.[52]

Although not of the first Constructivist generation, he nevertheless recognized its importance at once and became an important interpreter. His reputation soared only when he ceased to teach; but he had always created pictures with strict order, meager means, and great refinement *(Fig. 48)*. He was an austere teacher yet fundamentally a humanist, who was always concerned with human values.

> After too much non-teaching, non-learning, and a consequent non-seeing— in too many art "activities"—it is time to advocate again a basic step-by-step learning which promotes recognition of insight coming from experience, and evaluation resulting from comparison . . . growth [of ability] is not only a most exciting experience; it is inspiring and thus the strongest incentive for intensified action, for continued investigation (search instead of re-search), for learning through conscious practice. . . . In the end, teaching is a matter not of method but of heart.[53]

The Bauhaus ideas were summarized by Alfred Barr of the Museum of Modern Art in New York: in aesthetics "it bridged the gap between the artist and the industrial system . . . it broke down the hierarchy which had divided the 'fine' from the 'applied' arts"; in pedagogy, "it differentiated between what can be taught (technique) and what cannot (creative invention), and brought together more artists of distinguished talent than any other art school of our time"; in art, "it developed a new and modern kind of beauty,"[54] which it found in De Stijl and Constructivism, whose artists frequently visited the school and were in close contact with its faculty.

Despite the fact that the pedagogical ideas of the Bauhaus seeped into art schools and polytechnic teaching in the United States, England, and postwar Germany, they made virtually no impression on art training in France, Italy, or Spain. However, Constructivist thought and images, Bauhaus designs, and a bare machine aesthetic, often debased, were diffused into all levels of visual culture in Europe, America, and industrialized regions of the Orient, from official architecture to mass-produced household objects, from elegant book design to *mise en page* of the popular press. The famous Bauhaus, about which little was really known beyond its name, received undeserved blame for the corruptions of the style, though it is also fair to say that, apart from Albers, Max Bill, Marcel Breuer and the painter Fritz Winter, it did not produce a major artist, designer, or architect. Its effect seems to have been on the mass rather than on the individual.

48. Josef Albers, *Kinetic VII*, 1945. Coll. the artist.

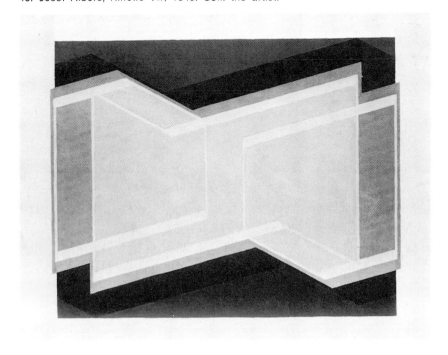

50. Theo van Doesburg and Sophie Taeuber-Arp, *Restaurant l'Aubette*, 1928. Photo Taurgo.

51. Auguste Herbin, *Rain*, 1953. Photo courtesy Galerie Denise René, Paris.

49. Jean Arp and Sophie Taeuber-Arp, *Duo Collage*, 1918. Coll. Mr. and Mrs. Burton Tremaine, Meriden, Conn.

Only fourteen years had elapsed between the founding of the Bauhaus in 1919 and its forced closing in 1933, when it was condemned as a dangerous source of independent thought and degenerate art. By the time Hitler's Brown Shirts forced the doors to shut, most of the faculty had already fled. Bauhaus teachers and the artists they knew spread their ideas, whether native or borrowed, to the West, first in Europe, then to the New World. The second dispersion was wider, more drastic, and even more fruitful than the earlier one from Russia. While Constructivism was not dependent solely on the Bauhaus for its spread, it was the teachers from Dessau who succeeded in transmitting the ideas to the Americas.

Sophie Taeuber-Arp, a Swiss, had developed independently a kind of Constructivism of her own and had collaborated with van Doesburg and her husband, Jean Arp (Figs. 49 & 50), who, until his death in June 1966, hovered between Non-Objectivism and Surrealism. In 1926–28 they had designed the interior of the Restaurant l'Aubette in Strasbourg, bringing together in one environment the summary of the two fused styles, De Stijl and Constructivism.

"Cercle et Carré," a society for discussions and exhibitions, was founded by Michel Seuphor, a friend of Mondrian, together with the painter, Joaquín Torrès-Garcia, in Paris in 1930. As an isolated stronghold of the then-unfashionable abstract art, it welcomed the followers of De Stijl or Constructivism.

Dispersion widened the circle and encouraged cross-fertilization. Thus a second generation of geometric artists became known. This included Ben Nicholson, Jean Hélion, Jean Gorin, Auguste Herbin (Fig. 51), Henryk Stazewski, Alberto Magnelli, Camille Graeser, Friedrich Vordemberge-Gildewart, Otto Freundlich, Josef Albers, from time to time Albers' Bauhaus colleague Paul Klee, and Willi Baumeister. In 1932 "Abstraction-Création" was founded in Paris by Herbin, Georges Vantongerloo, Seuphor, Gleizes and others; Pevsner, who had remained in Paris since 1927, and Gabo joined immediately.

By 1937 it was possible for the well-informed director of the Kunsthalle in Basel, Georg Schmidt, to put on an exhibition with this list on the catalogue's title page: "Constructivists: van Doesburg, Domela, Eggeling, Gabo, Kandinsky, Lissitzky, Moholy-Nagy, Mondrian, Pevsner, Taeuber-Arp, Vantongerloo, Vordemberge U.A."—four Russians, four members of De Stijl, two Bauhaus professors, the Swiss wife of Arp, and a designer of abstract geometrical films. Included in the exhibition were Tatlin, Malevich, and Rodchenko from Russia, Van der Leck from Holland, Hélion and Gorin from France, Calder from the U.S., and Hans Richter from Germany. Constructivism had become truly international.

Inevitably some history was lost in these mergers and simplifications, which led to later confusions and popular misconceptions. A sign of health and vigor in an art movement is its capacity to generate differences, to define its orthodoxies and its heresies, and to spawn splinter groups. The verbal accompaniment as artists tried to define new positions sometimes clarified, and sometimes added to the confusion. Different contexts, ignorance, and misuse endowed old words with new meanings, and still other meanings in their next incarnation. Among the manifestos published between 1913 and 1953 were declarations on Futurism, Rayonnism, Suprematism, Constructivism, "Realism," "Unism," "Art Concret," and "Konkrete Kunst," all having something to do with ideas close to Constructivism.

Thus, by the late thirties, Constructivism and Neo-Plasticism had become a worldwide force. Yet their followers were, paradoxically, obscure as well as famous. Every Western nation had well known non-objective artists who were, nonetheless, ignored by critics and shunned by collectors and museums; it was not only the dictators who were against this kind of art. It seemed to many to be dull, dry, and already outdated.

V/The New World and New Thought

As war threatened, many artists left the continent, often moving on to London where important Constructivist developments might have been expected. Among those artists in the late thirties or early forties were Gabo, Mondrian, Gropius, Kurt Schwitters, Moholy-Nagy, Breuer, Oskar Kokoschka, and an ambitious young patron, Peggy Guggenheim. However, for subtle reasons of history and temperament, none of the ideas took root in London at that time. Ben Nicholson, who had met Mondrian earlier, was the only English artist one could call non-objective. In 1937 he edited, with Gabo, an abstract art review called *Circle* which had little impact at that time; it was not until around 1950 that the ideas of Constructivism were to have wider recognition in England.

Meanwhile, there was more fertile ground in America, and mostly in the United States, though Max Bill was to have a profound influence in Brazil and Argentina. Among a limited but substantial group of patrons and artists, the way had been prepared. One of these was Katherine Dreier, who recognized, bought, and exhibited abstract art. She had met Mondrian in 1925, and her "Société Anonyme" arranged an international exhibition of modern art at the Brooklyn Museum the next year. A decade later the "American Abstract Artists" were organized and had their first exhibition in 1937. That same year, the "Guggenheim Museum of Non-Objective Art" was established in a private house in New York with works by Kandinsky, Robert Delaunay, Moholy-Nagy, Nicholson, Vieira da Silva, Lyonel Feininger, Jean Xceron, Klee, Juan Gris, Léger, and other twentieth century artists. Another important event was the publication of Alfred Barr's *Cubism and Abstract Art* in 1936 for the Museum of Modern Art, in conjunction with an exhibition of the same name.

It was in the academies of the New World that the welcome was warmest for both men and ideas. The names were known and their ideas fairly well understood in the circles that were equivalent to those left behind in Europe. Teaching positions became available along with support for the propagation of the ideas.

Albers came to America in 1933, the first immigrant from the Bauhaus. On the recommendation of the architect Philip Johnson, he was invited to the newly-founded Black Mountain College in North Carolina, for which Gropius later designed buildings. Albers accepted and, despite repeated invitations to older and more famous educational institutions, remained there until 1949. When he declined an invitation to teach in Chicago, in favor of Black Mountain, that position was offered to his colleague, Moholy-Nagy, who accepted it in 1937, founding a daughter Bauhaus called "The Institute of Design." It is interesting to note that in Moholy's 1947 book *Vision and Motion*, which includes an account of the Bauhaus, Albers' name does not appear.

Of the other Bauhaus members, Herbert Bayer withdrew to Aspen, Colorado; Feininger settled in New York; Breuer and Mies van der Rohe embarked on active architectural careers in America; while Gropius, who had left in 1928, came to Harvard in 1937, after having lived in Berlin and London. Gabo, after sojourns in Berlin (1921–32), Paris (1932–36), and London (1936–46), also came to America in response to an invitation from Harvard; he then settled in rural Connecticut.

Mondrian, long a resident of Paris, went to London in 1938, where Gabo and Nicholson found him a studio next door to theirs. Then, in 1940, the bombings drove him to New York. Though his work had profoundly influenced the façades of buildings, packaging, *mise en page*, and fabric design, it found few patrons *(Fig. 52)*. In the same year that Mondrian arrived in New York, the "American Abstract Artists" picketed the Museum of Modern Art, though it had shown his work in 1933, Pevsner's in 1934, 1936, and 1939 and purchased paintings by both. Enthusiasm for the influence of Mondrian was to come later. In 1942, he was recognized more widely in New York with the Dudensing Gallery's one-man show —the first and only of his life—and in 1945, a year after his death, the Museum of Modern Art installed a Mondrian retrospective. Three years later, this museum exhibited Gabo and Pevsner in a two-man show. For some time thereafter, it tended to leave comprehensive exhibitions of nonobjective art to the twelve-year-old Guggenheim Museum. Among New York art dealers, Rose Fried pioneered with "The White Plane" exhibition of Americans and Europeans.

Many European artists besides those mentioned had emigrated to America when war broke out in 1939. Among those who attended Mondrian's funeral in Brooklyn in 1944 were Léger, Chagall, Kurt Seligmann, Moholy-Nagy, Amadée Ozenfant, Hans Richter, Bayer, Max Ernst, Duchamp, Jean Xceron, Archipenko, and Siefried Giedion. Others who had also crossed the Atlantic were André Masson, André Breton, George Grosz, Jacques Lipchitz, and Hans Hofmann. Once in America, these artists, instead of huddling as a group of exiles, spread out across the country and the seminal ideas they brought with them germinated. These ideas made a climate of artistic activity from which both the émigrés and the natives derived benefit. But it was also a climate of refuge and exile. The ideas these men brought over were cherished and nurtured but they did not take root at once; it was to be many years before they flourished.

During the war years, artists were drawn off into the army or to factories. Art was secondary to survival; personal liberty declined everywhere. Construc-

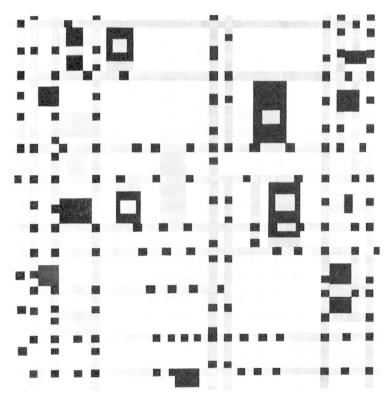

52. Piet Mondrian, *Broadway Boogie-Woogie*, 1942–43. Museum of Modern Art, N.Y.

tivism, in both Europe and America between 1939 and 1945 (longer in Germany and Italy), was in a state of hibernation. After the peace there was a sudden mood of liberation, a desire to try everything possible. The young generation in Italy and Germany, where art development had been suspended by Mussolini and Hitler, were impatient to make up for lost time. In the Allied countries, they sought new adventures and reform of prewar postures. It was evident that a profound change of direction was due. It had seemed, with the prewar generation, that the limit in abstraction had been reached. There had been predictions, as early as the thirties, that the mainstream of art would soon return to its old bed and even, some hoped, back to a Courbet "naturalism." In 1945 one could say that Cubism had freed Western art from illusion and that Constructivism and De Stijl had gone on to free it from allusion. The next turn, however, was to be by no means a turn back.

The new turn was Abstract Expressionism. Gathering momentum in the fifties, it looked like a further liberation—this time, paradoxically—from disciplines which had long been admired in the artist: preconceived purpose, sensitive adjustment, and composed order. There were two forms of abstraction available:

53

geometric, typified by Mondrian, with memorial exhibitions (1945–47) in New York, Amsterdam, and Basel; and expressionist, typified by Kandinsky, with memorial exhibitions (1945–48) in New York, Pittsburgh, and several Dutch cities. It was Kandinsky's idea of "inner necessity" rather than Gabo's idea of the "real," or Mondrian's "balanced relations," which was to dominate for a dozen years an art world in which Constructivist art, though continuing to be vigorously developed privately, almost vanished from public view. This was true not only of the production of art works, but also of patronage. Collectors everywhere in the postwar years turned first to the school of Paris, then to German Expressionism, Tachism, and Abstract Expressionism, in that order. As Abstract Expressionism rose, Constructivism—though equally well known—virtually went underground. The only exceptions were the American schools, which had rapidly adopted what they thought was Bauhaus pedagogy in preliminary courses, and then were torn between academic tradition and Expressionist fashion in later ones.

Acclaimed was impulsive gesture; attacked vigorously were art history, criteria of quality, and every kind of academic study. An abstract expressionist avant-garde developed in both Paris and New York, each with its own heroes such as Pierre Soulages, Georges Mathieu, Karel Appel, Hans Hartung, Roger Bissière, Jean Fautrier, Sam Francis in Europe, and in America, after the death of Gorky in 1948, Pollock, Willem de Kooning, Robert Motherwell, Franz Kline, Mark Rothko, and Clyfford Still.

The new style flourished in the American art schools, where Raymond Parker's dictum "Craftsmanship is optional" was followed but not understood. The movement did not favor chaos, yet it called for an expression so permissive and vehement that it seemed nihilistic, recalling Blake's famous declaration: "Sooner murder an infant in its cradle than nurse unacted desires." The abstract pictorial gestures made an art of vigor, not of rigor. They were also supremely autobiographical, not as self-portraiture, but as unguarded revelations of the psyche, like handwriting.

The movement attracted major talents and many converts who, like Philip Guston, sometimes turned their back on a fame already won as figurative artists, matching in renunciation Botticelli's willingness to throw his lovely pagan paintings on Savonarola's bonfire. These artists talked and wrote.[55] In America especially, there flowed from them eloquent, concise, clear, sometimes even witty comments and self-revelation. Enough writing was done, supported by analytical thought (often about ethics rather than aesthetics), to make one wonder if it were not, after all, a "literary" movement. In spite of Parker's statement: "The artist's acts as artist are confined to the studio," the spectator often learned from the artist's words how to view his work. The artist's explication in talk was also helpful to the critics, who then provided an official art vocabulary. These words, in turn, helped artists to sharpen their purpose, define orthodoxy, and condemn heresy. Key terms were: Abstract Expressionism (Robert Coates, 1949), Action Painting (Harold Rosenberg, 1952), *Art Autre, Art Informel* (Tapié, 1952), Tachism (Pierre Guéguen, 1953), to which other critics have added such characterizations as "psychic improvisation," "psychogram," and "pictorial gesture."

The masters of this school rose to fame and fortune with extraordinary rapidity; throughout the world they eclipsed other contemporary art. In spite of their solipsist creed, however, there soon began to appear dismaying uniformity in the product; only the very best retained their individuality. In youthful passion the Action Painters had glimpsed eternal verity; ten years later they were stirring the cinders of an all too brief infatuation.

Meanwhile an expressive figurative art continued, as a background, if not quite an underground, movement. Artists like Morandi, Sutherland and Tamayo, or Moore, Manzu, and Marini held their own. Nicholas de Stäel *(Fig. 53)* developed a trivalent art which combined characteristics of Action Painting, geometrical abstraction, and a view of nature; Jean Dubuffet rang the changes on an obvious

53. Nicholas de Stäel, *Les Martigues*, 1952. Coll. Mr. and Mrs. Taft Schreiber, Beverly Hills, Calif.

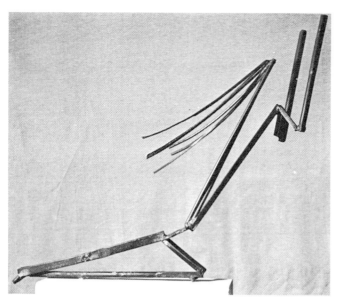

54. Julio Gonzalez, *Prayer*, 1932. Coll. Rijksmuseum Kröller-Müller, Holland.

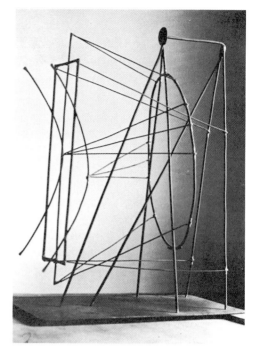

55. Pablo Picasso, *Rod Construction*, 1928. Photo Brassai, Paris.

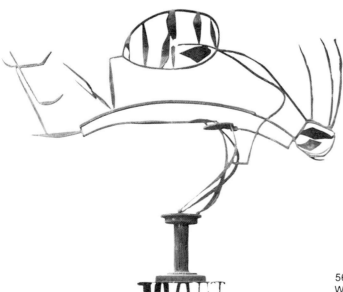

56. David Smith, *Australia*, 1951. Coll. Prof. William S. Rubin.

imagery painted with non-art materials he called "Art Brut"; and a northern California school used a traditional *alla prima* brushwork on a trancelike view of nature, where all is seen and nothing understood. Some naïvely thought figurative art to be a new discovery. Tobey hovered close by, between figuration and abstraction, respected but detached.

In contrast with the somewhat orgiastic outbursts of international Tachism, and partly in reaction against it, a stern geometrical abstraction became the choice of an increasing number of younger artists. There was also a sudden growth of interest in the third (and even the fourth) dimension.

There had been no counterpart of Abstract Expressionism in sculpture. It was impossible to translate the ideas of Action Painting into the obdurate materials employed in sculpture, which now took a different direction from painting. As a consequence, sculpture, with its many technical problems, was, during the ascendency of Abstract Expressionism, kept in the shade until the sixties, though the number of sculptors was increasing. Changes were wrought, nevertheless, and a foundation was laid for a great expansion of ideas as to what sculpture is, even going beyond the ideas about space and materials advanced by the Futurists and Gabo, though still deriving much from their revolutionary thought.

For centuries, sculpture had depended entirely on modeling and carving—until 1913, that is, when Picasso's three-dimensional collages inspired Tatlin. Even then, these constructions added only nailing and gluing to the repertory, though the forging of iron had been a highly developed craft for two thousand years and had been used for figurative sculpture outside of Europe.

Julio Gonzalez, the Spanish friend of Picasso, began, because of poverty, to make sculpture with a welding torch and scrap iron, which became more and more abstract *(Fig. 54)*. He forged his first iron sculptures in 1926–27 and passed on his knowledge to Picasso who made only occasional use of it *(Fig. 55)*. "To project and design in space with the help of new methods, to utilize this space, and to construct with it, as though one were dealing with a newly acquired material—that is all I attempt" (from catalogue of Gonzalez exhibition at Stedelijk Museum, Amsterdam, 1955). In 1932 he joined "Cercle et Carré." Sculptors before Gonzalez knew less about forging than a medieval armorer. His advances, later developed by David Smith *(Fig. 56)*, Robert Jacobsen, and the generation which followed them, confirmed the Russian idea that industrial materials *were* proper for art.

Gabo and Pevsner had been interested from the start in industrial materials that were new to the artist. Gabo joined plastics, laced strings elegantly, and soldered metal, but he employed no welding. His techniques were continued at the Bauhaus, but the welding of metal was also ignored there. Later, at the Institute of Design in Chicago, where so much was made of the exploration of techniques and materials, this basic technique received only the most cursory attention. Even Calder, in spite of his technical training, distrusted all soldering and until recently did no welding. He joined mechanically, by riveting, crimping, and lacing.

Yet it is the welded steel joint which has made possible the development of the space sculpture envisioned in the "Realist Manifesto." Appearing first in art about 1930, it has been developed mostly since 1945. It has permitted the sculptor to out-distance the architect and even the bridgebuilder in his penetration and enlivening of space. With the directness of the welded joint and the strength of steel, powerful salients into the newly perceived space have become possible. Ships' rigging, cranes, circus tents, and umbrellas were antecedents of this kind of penetration of space.

David Smith has exerted great influence. Though concerned through much of his life either directly with subject matter or with suggestive association, he came in the last few years of his life to geometrical images of monumental simplicity and scale. He piled up freely associated compositions of rectangular stainess-steel boxes, reminiscent of the Malevich constellations of squares, almost half a century before. Smith, himself a commercial welder, had recognized early the possibilities opened up by the welded sculpture of Gonzalez; this he passed on to a whole generation of younger sculptors in America, and, eventually, in Europe as well.

This extension of the third way of making sculpture—that is, by joining— begun by the early Constructivists and by Gonzalez, then vastly expanded by Smith's imaginative use of industrial techniques, has made possible cantilever, counterpoise, and penetration into space hitherto undreamed of in sculpture. Its use is as characteristically twentieth-century as the skyscraper.

VI/Postwar Developments

The last Constructivist exhibition before the war had been at the Galerie Charpentier in Paris in 1939. The first postwar decade saw an "Art Concret" exhibition in 1945 (Galerie Drouin) of abstract work done secretly during the Occupation, and the founding in 1946 of the Salon "Réalités Nouvelles" by Frederic Sidès, with the collaboration of Herbin, Gleizes, and Pevsner (Fig. 57)—the word "real" again being used as the antonym of "virtual," "ideal" or "apparent." It was comparable to the prewar "Abstraction-Création" group for the numerous abstract artists. There was also an important exhibition of early masters of abstraction at the Galerie Maeght in 1949.

Yet Paris was not fertile soil for Constructivist art. It was against the grain for Denise René to establish a gallery devoted to a Constructivist philosophy in her apartment in the rue la Boétie in 1946, where she showed Arp, Herbin, and Gorin, but otherwise had to depend on foreigners. Similarly, in her first exhibition of "Mouvement" in 1955 (Fig. 58), Marcel Duchamp was the only Frenchman; the dominant figure was the Hungarian, Victor Vasarely.

Many expatriate artists such as Vantongerloo, Magnelli, Vasarely, Ellsworth Kelly (who met Arp, Vantongerloo, and Seuphor there), Dewasne, Schöffer and Cairoli chose to live in Paris, and active groups of young artists could prosper there. In spite of this, it cannot be said that France's contribution to "Constructivist" thought, either before or after the war, went beyond hospitality to the artists; the ideas were not taken up.

The same was true of England until 1951, when abstract art began to be seen in sufficient quantity to affect the younger artists, whom the war and the subsequent currency regulations had prevented from seeing it elsewhere. Victor Pasmore, at that time, turned his back on success as a representational painter to begin a new struggle as an abstract one, with additional ventures into three-dimensional reliefs. He read Charles Biederman's compendious book, *Art as the Evolution of Visual Knowledge*, begun in 1938, in which Biederman called for a a "non-mimetic" art of right angles in relief space (Fig. 59), which was to win some staunch adherents in England and Holland.[56]

There then appeared quite suddenly an English school, using Biederman's

57. Antoine Pevsner, *Construction dans l'Oeuf*, 1948. Albright-Knox Art Gallery, Buffalo, N.Y., gift of The Seymour H. Knox Foundation, Inc.

58. Exhibition "Le Mouvement," 1955. Photo courtesy Galerie Denise René, Paris. Hanging from ceiling—Calder, *Mobile*; on wall—Agam, *Contrepoint 2 voix*; on near pedestal—Jacobsen; on far pedestal—Tinguely.

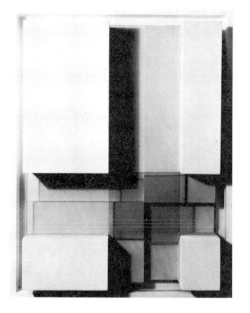

59. Charles Biederman, *Structurist Relief #14*, 1938. Coll. the artist.

60. Anthony Caro, *Prospect*, 1964. Coll. Edwin Janss; photo courtesy André Emmerich Gallery, N.Y.

verbal variant "constructionist," which included Kenneth and Mary Martin, John Ernest (an American), Anthony Hill, and Gillian Wise—all accepting the confinement of relief. Peter Stroud, in a letter to the author, was less compliant: "For me Biederman was the temporary means of coming to terms with the essentials of Cubism. From 1958 to 1960 I worked loosely within the framework of his constructionist aesthetic; but I soon found its limitations imposed too many restrictions on my work." A related but less clear style appears in the forged and welded work of Robert Adams.

These artists had little to do with another much younger group, emanating chiefly from St. Martins School in London. There they had profited by the teaching and example of Anthony Caro *(Fig. 60)*, in the years 1953–64, who had responded sympathetically to the technical directness and imaginative exploration of industrial steel shapes by David Smith, while both were teaching at Bennington College in Vermont. The younger sculptors used sheet steel, and sometimes plywood, for cutout flat shapes and simplistic box structures, with color of such sleek surface quality and primary intensity as to contradict both the material and the structure.

61. Max Bill, *Construction*, 1937 (executed 1962). The Joseph H. Hirshhorn collection; photo John D. Schiff.

A counterpart in two dimensions, though not from the same influences, was the geometrical painting of optical phenomena by Bridget Riley, Peter Sedgley, Jeffrey Steele, and Michael Kidner. These two British schools (they were not exactly groups) appeared after 1960. Most of the artists were then in their early thirties.

In Switzerland the dominant figure was Max Bill, who had enrolled at the Bauhaus in 1927 and graduated as an architect. Ideas of a "Concrete Art," as opposed to "Abstract," first noted by van Doesburg in 1930, were assimilated by Bill *(Fig. 61)*, then clarified, extended and expounded as "Konkrete Kunst" in 1953.[57] These ideas were further propagated during Bill's visit to Brazil and Argentina in 1951, with an exhibition of his work in São Paulo, and resulted in an influx of South Americans to Europe where they continued to work in diverse non-objective styles, some of them achieving fame. These South Americans include Jésus-Rafaël Soto, Almir Mavignier, Carlos Cairoli, Tomas Maldonado, Martha Boto, Gregorio Vardánega, Mary Vieira, Marino di Teana, Abraham Palatnik, Luis Tomasello, and Julio le Parc.

Max Bill assisted in the founding of the Hochschule für Gestaltung, another daughter Bauhaus, in Ulm in 1952 where he served as Rector until 1956, when he returned to Switzerland; he was succeeded by his former disciple, Tomas Maldonado. Bill organized "Konkrete Kunst" exhibitions in 1944, 1949, and 1960. Richard Lohse and Camille Graeser, his elders by six and sixteen years respectively—also working in Zürich—used parallel ideas of mathematical relationships, but they stemmed more directly from Constructivism.

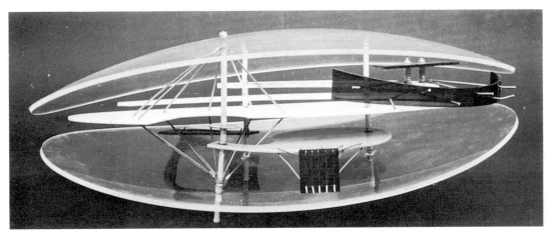

62. Constant, *New Babylonian Construction*, 1959. Courtesy Rijksmuseum Kröller-Müller, Holland.

The label and some of the ideas of "Konkrete Kunst" spilled southward to Milan, where a movement calling itself "MAC" (Movimento Arte Concreta) was formed in 1952, mostly under the influence of Bruno Munari, who had been a Futurist, then had begun working with actual movement as early as 1938—only six years after Calder's start. Munari proposed among other things a synthesis of plastic arts by combining mobility and transformability, but he influenced younger artists in northern Italy less through such theories than through his example. The absorption of Constructivist thought in Italy was through him, through the spatial ideas of the Italo-Argentine, Lucio Fontana, and through more recently transplanted anti-aesthetic ideas from northern Europe, which readily took root in the mildly Marxist ground of the industrial cities. Quite independent of these, but extending the Constructivist vocabulary, was the work of Piero Dorazio and Arturo Bonfanti.

In Denmark and the Low Countries there was—except for Richard Mortensen, long an expatriate in Paris—very little interest in Constructivist art until a decade after the war. In spite of the hovering spirit of De Stijl, energy there as elsewhere went into an equivalent of Action Painting, focused in a group called "Cobra" (for Copenhagen, Brussels, Amsterdam), which flourished from 1948 to 1950. Only in the later fifties was the rectilinear tradition revived, in the table architecture and wall reliefs of Joost Baljeu; in the sculpture-architecture of Constant *(Fig. 62)*; the metal sculpture of Carel Visser, André Volten, Robert Jacobsen (a European counterpart of David Smith); and, in Sweden, in the angular compositions of Olle Baertling.

There had been no German Constructivist artists during the Bauhaus days and they were slow to appear after the war. By the late fifties, however, the sculptor Hans Uhlmann, a former engineer (born in 1900), was working in an austere geometrical style in Berlin *(Fig. 63)*; the sometimes Constructivist Norbert Kricke (born in 1922) was working in the Rhineland; and Brigitte Meier-Denning-hof (born in 1923), a pupil of Moore and later of Pevsner, was in Paris. But more adventurous work was being done by others, such as the "Zero" group in Düsseldorf (the "0" being considered "a zone of silence" from which new sounds will emerge), a group of painters in Hamburg, several younger Munich artists in a group called "Effekt," and individual artists in the Ruhr cities.

In the United States, the history of these two decades is more complex. It comprised early practitioners such as Burgoyne Diller and Ad Reinhardt, Mondrian converts like Fritz Glarner (he called his painting "relational" from Mondrian's phrase), Ilya Bolotowsky, Harry Holtzman, Charmion von Wiegand, Naum Gabo himself; the exiles from the Bauhaus in painting, architecture, graphic design and

64. Alexander Calder, *The Crab*, 1962. The Museum of Fine Arts, Houston, Texas.

63. Hans Uhlmann, *Steel Sculpture*, 1963-64. Shown at "Documenta III," Kassel; photo Gnilka.

65. John McLaughlin, *J-1957*, 1957. Courtesy Landau Gallery, Los Angeles, Calif.

pedagogy; and an apparatus in American colleges (rather than art schools) which preserved and propagated the ideas of all of these with more enthusiasm and effect than did museums and critics. There were outstanding constructors in metal who emerged during this time—Richard Lippold, José de Rivera, and especially David Smith. Calder, already famous for his mobile constructions, which were too lyrical and subjective to be considered Constructivist, later made an important contribution with his "stabiles" *(Fig. 64)*.

The "American Abstract Artists," who had protested the New York Museum of Modern Art's hostility to abstract art in 1940, continued to work doggedly through this postwar epoch. They had recruited Mondrian himself, and had exhibited Albers, Herbert Bayer, Fernard Léger, Moholy-Nagy, and Jean Xceron. They ignored the rise to fame and the power of the "New York School" of Abstract Expressionism; consequently, they were independent of the many reactions against it. One such reaction, deriving from Dada, came to be known as "Pop Art"; another was called "Hard Edge"—or, by the critic Clement Greenberg, "post-painterly abstraction," a bow to the distinction between "linear" and "painterly" styles noted by Wölfflin in his *Principles of Art History*. These developments had been taking place on both sides of the Atlantic; "Hard Edge" was a local recrudescence of a continuing general phenomenon. This kind of edge had been painted for a generation by the "American Abstract Artists" and by many others elsewhere. It's introduction is a case history of a typical art term.

The phrase was suggested by Jules Langsner, the critic, at a 1958 gathering in Claremont, California, during the preparation of the catalogue of four non-figurative Los Angeles painters: Karl Benjamin, Lorser Feitelson, Frederick Hammersley, and John McLaughlin *(Fig. 65)*.[58] But "the term was too new for the artists to accept as a description," Langsner says.

> I had been describing the paintings by these artists as "Hard Edge" in my reviews, but never had isolated the term to separate them from such painters as Albers in an article devoted exclusively to the difference. However, in 1958, I was already using the term in conversation and did so in conversations with Laurence Alloway in both Los Angeles and London. When the show went to the I.C.A. (London, March–April, 1960), the title was changed to "West Coast Hard Edge," with the consent of myself and the artists involved.[59]

The term was apt enough to spread rapidly. It apeared in Switzerland in 1962 as the translation for "Kalte Kunst" (Cold Art).

"Hard Edge" describes only one factor of many in an artist's style and is misleading if used for the style itself. It refers to a characteristic long present under other names, including Suprematism. As if to emphasize that there are no rules, Malevich had, in 1916, painted *Yellow Quadrilateral on White (Fig. 66)* with three hard edges and one soft.[60]

Though Americans had learned from the European exiles and had themselves made outstanding contributions to modern art in individual cases—such as Calder and David Smith *(Fig. 67)*, or Tobey and Pollock—their development of Constructivist art lagged behind the Europeans. Even at his most non-objective, the American artist tended to call the observer's attention, through the work, to the artist, rather than to efface the artist so that the contemplation of the work itself was, for the observer, terminal. The American was later in coming to the use of movement, optical phenomena *(Fig. 68)*, light, chance, and other manifestations of nature, and less thoughtful about the relation of the artist and the spectator. "The Responsive Eye" exhibition at the Museum of Modern Art in 1965, and the various kinetic art exhibitions confirmed this. While Action Painting had flowed eastward, the flow of Constructive thought was toward the West.

66. Kasimir Malevich, *Yellow Quadrilateral on White*, 1916–17. Stedelijk Museum, Amsterdam.

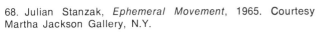

68. Julian Stanzak, *Ephemeral Movement*, 1965. Courtesy Martha Jackson Gallery, N.Y.

67. David Smith, *Voltri I*, May 25, 1962. The Joseph H. Hirshhorn collection.

VII/The New Generation

After 1960 Europe saw a wave of fresh thinking in the arts, not as a creed or compact body of doctrine, but rather as a coincidence of points of view among artists working in relative isolation in different countries on similar problems. These artists were young, mostly born in the twenties or later, and had no recollection of World War I. They were born into a world where both abstract art and Communism were a commonplace and tolerated part of the environment, and there were no inhibitions about the materials allowable in an art object. Partly through the Bauhaus (though contact was not direct), partly through exposure, they were familiar with the ideas of Constructivism and could see art as object-without-status and artist as non-hero. They came into contact with a profoundly different kind of public from the connoisseurs who had been won to Impressionism and Cubism. They shared a growing disillusionment with the structure of the art market and its emphasis on rarity, publicity, and the star system.

These young artists sometimes worked within the tradition of Constructivism. More usually, they had roots in it but pushed further and in a great many directions, including all the aspects considered in Part II of this book. They saw art as continual discovery rather than as an isolated discrete element for contemplation by connoisseurs. Much of what they made could be thought of as non-art—as Dada had been—but it was made with a seriousness Dada never pretended to have.

This outlook permitted enormous diversity in style and wide geographical distribution. Constructivist tendencies appeared in Japan, Argentina, Brazil *(Fig. 69)*, Venezuela, and throughout Western Europe, including Poland, Yugoslavia, and Spain. Possibly *because* of the very diversity, there was no great comprehensive exhibition in Western Europe of these developments which, within a short time, came to be known as the "New Tendency." It involved depersonalization of the work; group activity and a cult of anonymity; borrowings from science; use of new materials and techniques; use of direct stimuli such as light, sound, and movement; a dialogue with the spectator who assumes the role as a responsive (rather than educated) organism to be stimulated; and a generally anti-aesthetic iconoclastic attitude.

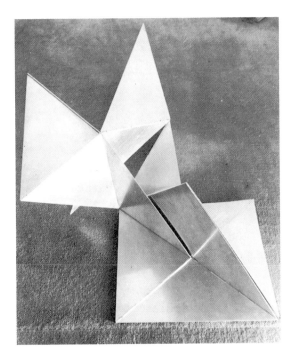

69. Lygia Clark, *Town*, 1961. Coll. the artist.

The ideas themselves appeared first in the monochrome paintings of Yves Klein (born in Nice, 1928) which he has said were exhibited in London in 1950.[61] These attempts to depersonalize color and at the same time render it "metaphysical"—therefore, for Klein, blue—were shown in Paris in 1955; the first comment was by Karl G. Hultén in the *Stockholm Tidnigen*, October 1957, and then in the London *Architectural Review* (122, 1957, p. 206). Similar ideas appeared in 1957 in the "achromatic" painting of Piero Manzoni (born in Milan, 1933), when he showed a completely white picture. The influential statements by these two against Tachism were sanctified by the premature deaths of both, Klein in 1962, and Manzoni in 1963. They were then virtually canonized and their works were included in all significant exhibitions of the "New Tendency."

In March 1960, Udo Kultermann, at that time director of the Städtisches Museum in Leverkusen, wrote in the catalogue for the exhibition, "Monochrome Malerei":

The exhibition . . . attempts an international resumé of the tendencies directed toward a new type of creation. . . . [Opening sentence of the preface] . . . The title of the exhibition is to be considered merely a name attempting to indicate a fact which cannot be defined. . . . Tachist art, which has become dangerously official, is opposed by an artistic activity which is working almost entirely underground. . . . This new artless art is the creative expression of

69

a society and will find its fulfillment in a creative self-restraint and in the conquest of art through new tasks demanded by life.[62]

In the same catalogue appears a statement by an exponent of achromatic art, Enrico Castellani:

> An artistic tendency which, due to its very essence, is impossible to define in terms of pre-existing schools or movements is certainly not a phenomenon which can be ignored. . . . The only possible compositional criterion in our works will be that of a refusal of a choice between heterogeneous elements.[63]

After Kulterman, the next museum recognition was, surprisingly, in Zagreb, where the director of the Galerija Suvremene Umjetnosti, Matko Meštrović, mounted an international exhibition ("Nove Tendencije"), in October 1961, of twenty-nine artists consisting of ten Germans, eight Italians, three Swiss, three Yugoslavs, two French, two South Americans, and one Austrian.

The "Groupe de Recherche d'Art Visuel" (GRAV), founded in Paris in 1960, professed views largely coincident with those of the "New Tendency." Three of the members were invited and attended the Zagreb exhibition; the following year, they adopted the term as their own. There was a general meeting of artists who shared these views in Paris in January 1963, under "GRAV" leadership. In July of that year an extensive exhibition in Frankfurt, called "European Avant-Garde," was subtitled: "Arte Programmata, Neue Tendenzen, Anti-Peinture, Zero." In his foreword to the catalogue, William Simmat wrote:

> There is evidence that this art is based on a great tradition. . . . These styles are not riddles and in the future will not prove to be any more difficult to understand than other differing styles. . . . No one dare overlook it without being overlooked himself.

From then on exhibitions became more frequent and the term more common. The phrase was introduced to the United States by the author, in the summer of 1964.[64] There were additional exhibitions in Zagreb in 1963 and 1965.

A few galleries were sympathetic, and Denise René in Paris had been particularly quick to recognize the "New Tendency" in her limited group exhibitions. In London, Signals Gallery, McRoberts and Tunnard, and New Vision Center Gallery put on exhibitions of aspects of the "New Tendency" in 1964, as did the Royal College of Art with an "Arte Programmata" exhibition, which later was circulated in the United States by the Smithsonian Institution. In Amsterdam, the Stedelijk Museum has shown much of this new work, under the heading "NUL" *(Fig. 70)* or "Zero" *(Fig. 71)*; while in Germany, the galleries Schmela in Düsseldorf, and D in Frankfurt, showed some of these artists early. Also the 1964 Biennale in Venice recognized "New Tendency" artists for the first time; and, since 1965, large group exhibitions have become frequent in Germany, Belgium, Italy, the U.S., and even in France through the Paris Biennale.

70. Henk Peeters, *Water-Ceiling*, 1965.
Shown at Halfmannshof, Gelsenkirchen;
photo Knorr.

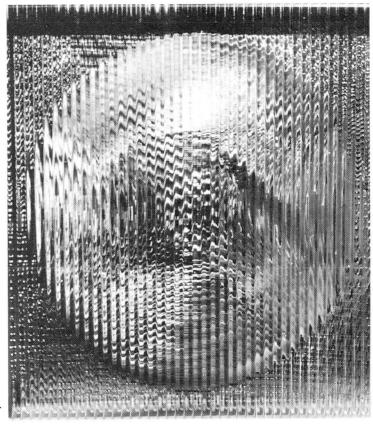

71. Heinz Mack, *Light Rotor*, 1960. Coll.
the artist.

The first showings in New York had been at the Contemporaries Gallery in 1963; then frequently at the Howard Wise Gallery since 1964. In Switzerland, they have been shown at the Bern Kunsthalle, by Suzanne Bollag in Zürich and Gallery Aktuell in Bern.

A notable characteristic of the "New Tendency" was the work in groups or teams. Groups have always been a disease of the young; the most active of these artists were born after 1930. Groups tend to dissolve as members achieve success and fame, or change purpose, or lose their fire, like "The Club" in New York or "Konkrete Kunst" in Switzerland. With maturation, individual differences sharpen, horizons broaden; there is more money for the successful ones and they travel.

In the United States, isolated figures, such as Richard Anuskiewicz and John Goodyear *(Fig. 72)*, coincided with some of the European tendencies; the five Yale artists, whose work was shown at the Galerie Chalette (December 1960–January 1961) as "Structured Sculpture," betrayed some of the tendencies but were not really a group and had little awareness of what they were doing, or their relationship to the Europeans. The American artist has tended to work alone and to shun groups. So far, the nearest American equivalent is the "Anonima" group of Ernst Benkert, Edwin Mieczkowski, and Francis Hewitt.

At the 1963 meeting in Paris, artists from several countries had formally adopted the title "Nouvelle Tendance, recherche continuelle," later abbreviated to "NTrc." Yvaral, son of the painter Vasarely and a member of "GRAV," has written to the author:

> Nouvelle Tendance—recherche continuelle—is an international movement which was born at the time of the first "Nove Tendencije" exhibition in Zagreb in 1961. It comprises about sixty young searchers working in the same ideal.
>
> Its principal characteristics are: primacy of research, depersonalization, open communication and collective work, and development of a group of visual ideas held in common which could lead to anonymous work.
>
> NTrc does not recognize the paternity of any artistic movement in particular. . . . Its most fundamental characteristic is to remain free of a definitive formula, and equally, to ensure continual evolution.
>
> Finally, NTrc considers "continuous research" to be: indeterminate works, multipliable works, aloofness at the production level, clarification of the problem in hand, activation of the spectator, and appraisal in the most precise terms of the creative act and the act of plastic transformation.

. . . . . .

The term "oltra la pittura" [beyond painting], was given by the Galleria Cadario [Milan] to an exhibition devoted only to members of NTrc. But there is not a gallery fully devoted to NTrc; Cadario, Bussola in Turin, Ad Libitum

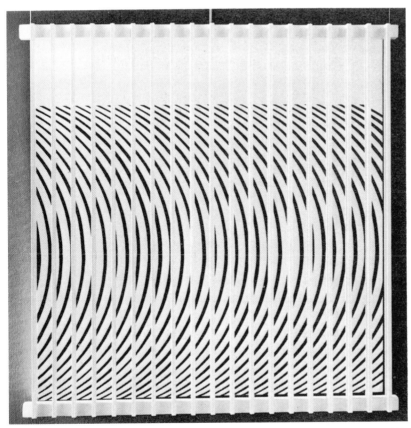

72. John Goodyear, *Black and White Wave*, 1964. Coll. Sylvia Pizitz, N.Y.;
photo O. E. Nelson.

in Antwerp, one in Venice, and Denise René in Paris, are the only private galleries which have exhibited in part the works of the "New Tendency."

As far as the museums are concerned, one must certainly list Zagreb, perhaps Leverkusen, and certainly the Musée des Arts Décoratifs in Paris in April, 1964. . . .

"Zero" and "NUL," whose spirit is a little touched with Neo-Dada, are slightly earlier movements than NTrc. Several of their members joined NT at the start but strayed later, their positions being too far from the general spirit of NTrc and one can say that there is no affinity with the exhibitions called "Zero" and "NUL."

The artists who now clearly identified themselves with "NTrc" were, naturally, some time in coming to a clear view of their direction. The idea of depersonalization, which had existed since Malevich, offered scope to talents an art of expressive gesture could not employ; the non-aesthetic, the indeterminate works, the emphasis on the spectator were new developments. In their Paris pamphlet of 1962, "GRAV" wrote:

> The New Tendency does not have a definite character. . . . [It is] against the sterile situation which now produces, day after day, thousands of works labelled lyrical abstraction, formless art, Tachism, etc., and also against the fruitless extension of a lagging mannerism based on the geometric forms . . . of Mondrian and Malevich. Again, once the positive aspect of the Neo-Dada or New Realist's irreverence for traditional considerations of beauty is noted, one sees the contradiction between their anti-art and their effort to baptise the object anew. It is evident that the New Tendency, although reacting against these currents, contains certain qualities derived from them. One sees in it the refinements of Concrete Art or Constructivism, as well as hints of Tachism and ties to Neo-Dada.
>
> But the New Tendency is, above all, a search for clarity. One must therefore be concerned with indeterminate work, with visual values, with more precise terms for valuation than "the creative art," with what is basic to a new view of the artistic phenomenon.

"Gruppo N" in Padua, like other Italians before them, wrote manifestos. In theirs of 1962, they listed their topics for study: ". . . from a conceptual point of view a universal hypothesis is needed which will include all the variables in the object-spectator relationship." They listed such variables as: "variability of the system object-spectator; reciprocal variation of the position object-spectator; variation in relations to the environment and to light; psychological situation and perception time of the spectator; psychological perception in all its aspects: perception capacity of the retina, peripheral vision, eye movement, perception at the level of the retina and cortex, focus, visual acuity, color perception."

Their "working hypothesis" included optical phenomena, movement (no "normal" condition; past, present, future presented simultaneously), instability, indeterminacy, objectification, "spectator as organism," "visual information" as a term preferable to "art," chance, programmed works, achromatism, anonymous works, and group activity ("solitude leads to subjective art").

Complete group anonymity is an extreme position. Sometimes the group agrees, more flexibly, on a set of objectives and then marks out distinct areas of research—still depersonalized in style, but easily identifiable, as in "GRAV." This brings their cooperation close to the anonymous teamwork of scientists, and in some cases—among which were the two groups, "Gruppo N" and "Equipo 57" —works were collectively signed with the name of the team.

The "NTrc" seemed to be repeating, consciously or not, one of the postures in the historic Moscow debates between 1917 and 1920. Rodchenko had described the artist as a technician who uses the tools and materials of modern production to make "laboratory art [which emerges as] object."[65]

74

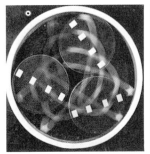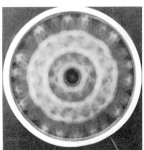

73. Gianni Colombo, *Rotooptic*, 1964. Coll. the artist.

74. Luis Tomasello, *Atmosphère Chromoplastique No. 111*, 1964. Courtesy Galerie Denise René, Paris.

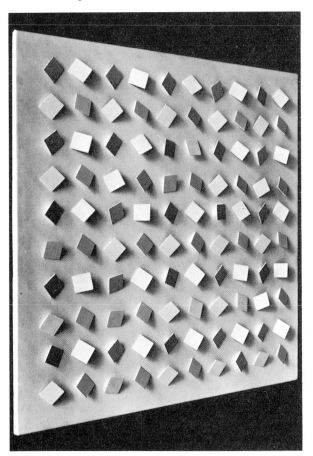

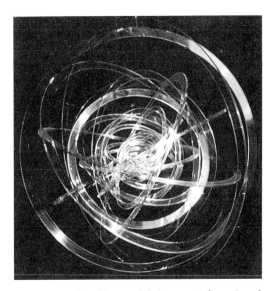

75. Gregorio Vardánega, *Déplacement Asynchronique d'un Cercle à l'Infini*, 1962. Coll. the artist.

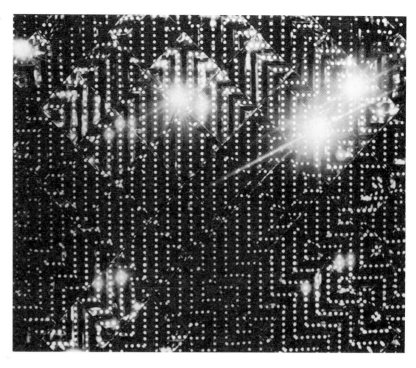

76. Martha Boto, *Labyrinthe Diagonal*, 1965. Coll. the artist.

As with the Futurist manifestos of fifty years before, the words were more impressive than the works; the artists often seemed to be novices in the studio where they extended the Bauhaus exercises but failed to endow them with a weight commensurate with the hypothesis. Not only in Italy was there this flavor of the "Foundation Course"; it could be tasted everywhere. Nor was this, of itself, bad. "Art," said David Smith, "is what an artist makes." The *artists* among these artists will make an art to outlive and, possibly, to refute the manifestos.

The basic thinking was international. The representation at the meeting in Paris, January 1963, was: "Gruppo N"—Biasi, Chiggio, Costa, Landi, Massironi; "Gruppo T"—Anceschi, Boriani, Colombo *(Fig. 73)*, De Vecchi, Varisco; "GRAV"—Garcia Rossi, Le Parc, Morellet, Sobrino, Stein, Yvaral; the Munich group—von Graevenitz, Kammer, Muller, Pohl, Staudt, Zehringer; the Düsseldorf group—Mack, Piene, Uecker; the Holland group—Peeters, Armando, Schoonhoven; "Equipo 57"—Duarte, Duart, Ibarrola, Serrano, Cuenca; Demarco, Garcia Miranda, Tomasello *(Fig. 74)*, Cairoli, Cruz-Diez, Dada Maino, Debourg, Vardánega *(Fig. 75)*, Boto *(Fig. 76)*, Mari, Munari, Dorazio, Gerstner, Talman, Diter Rot, Getulio, Mavignier, Yayoi Kusama, Knifer, Picelj.

By 1966, the artistic tendencies had ripened and clarified; group activity was fading. "Gruppo N" in Padua, the most vehement, fell apart first; "GRAV" in

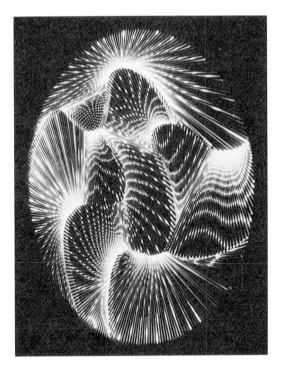

77. Equipo 57, *V.5.*, 1963. Photo courtesy A. Duart.

Paris gave up its communal studio, as the members began serially to have one-man exhibitions at the Howard Wise Gallery and to travel widely. Anonymity is not every artist's dish; and who can remain anonymous in his one-man show? The "Zero" group also showed severally in that same New York gallery, spent longer times away from Düsseldorf, but maintained intimate contact with one another. "Equipo 57" *(Fig. 77)* ceremoniously held a terminal exhibition in Bern in 1966, with this melancholy note from Duart, the one member outside Spain:

> This retrospective is the last manifestation of "Equipo 57" as such. For reasons of personal and contradictory choice its members decide by majority vote to continue their work individually.
> This does not deny the durability of our works and our collaborative experience; and this form of work and investigation remains, in my opinion, the most valid for our time.[66]

The dissolution of these "New Tendency" groups has occurred for many reasons. Quite apart from any pressures exerted by dealers, there has been ideological maturation. Experiment is not art; discovery and invention are that and no more; newness is irrelevant to art, in which there is change rather than progress. Purity can be a vice. Much great art is impure; the impurities, like trace elements in soil, strengthen it.

As the artists grew older, their styles became more personal and tended to consolidate in the direction of more successful communication with the public. Depersonalization is, after all, but another form of the piety of Fra Angelico. As with him, the personal, however unsought, will appear.

The "New Tendency" in Europe discovered itself and attempted to give itself a structure and a manifest creed. This awareness gave it definition and direction. It was, however, neither isolated nor exclusive nor did it have a monopoly on its ideas. Similar thoughts were appearing either through a sort of osmosis or biogenesis, or as response to forces and stimuli which had become identical in widely separated parts of the world as culture became more industrialized, more mass-produced, and more uniform. Two examples of this concurrence are: delegating extensive fabrication to others, and employing titles as an element of style.

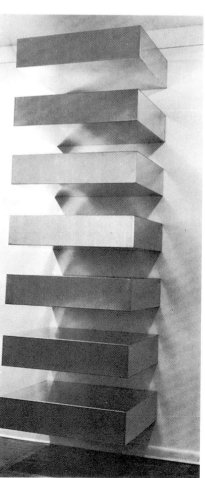

78. Donald Judd, *Untitled*, 1965. Coll. Henry Geldzahler; photo courtesy Leo Castelli Gallery, N.Y.

79. Hans Breder, *Cubes*, 1966. Coll. Mr. and Mrs. David Steine, Nashville, Tenn.

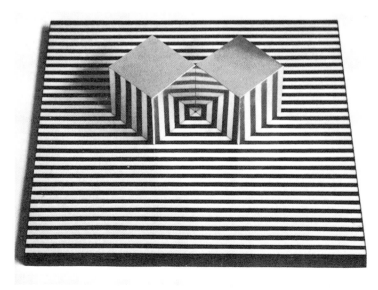

A frequent comment on present-day Constructivism is that the artists repeat; they plagiarize themselves; they manufacture a product. To be sure, some artists are tautological from meagerness of resources or from market pressures. Some strong and independent artists, however, are attacking the very principle of rarity and uniqueness in art. There is growing interest in multiple works, not just prints and plural casts of bronzes, but in very diverse works designed to be produced in quantity, such as those of the "Edition MAT" in 1962, and those exhibited at the Multiples Gallery in 1966 and in the Stedelijk Museum in 1967. There is also a belief, special to our time, that an artist must develop exhaustively all the possibilities of minute differences within a particular idea. This procedure, while resembling science, is not borrowed from it; the scientist, as soon as a new door is open, passes through. But an artist will linger and examine every aspect of the room, even when the doors are open. So it is to be expected that Heinz Mack will make a series of round glasses, Uecker will continue to use nails, Dorazio will make nets of colored straight lines, Mavignier will paint only dots, Poons only spots, and Albers need never leave the square.

An artist is supposed to be the most individualistic of men. It is a surprise, then, to find him surrendering to someone else entire fabrication of the geometrical sheet metal or plywood boxes which were exhibited in the Jewish Museum in New York in 1966, as "primary structures." This raises several questions: Is it art? Is it original? Is it commercial reproduction? Is the consent or command of the artist enough to authenticate it? Is it the craftsman's statement or the artist's?

Artists have used apprentices or journeymen helpers from time immemorial, as the guild system or their affluence permitted. There is a long tradition of "works made in the studio of" and, of course, sculptors such as Rodin or Arp had the stonecutting on large pieces done entirely by skilled artisans, who worked from plaster or clay models fashioned by the artist. Some, like Rubens, distinguished in their prices between shop work and those entirely by their own hand. In our day a hired craftsman may work from a small maquette or from a drawing, even from a telephone call, and in metal or wood or plastic—any material—with power tools, often making more than one of a kind. Sometimes this is done with continuous control by the artist, sometimes from more or less detailed instructions, sometimes with a complete delegation of control to the craftsman, who may even incorporate his own fancies, like a figured bass or a cadenza in music.

There seem to be three possible reasons for this delegation:

1. To speed the work and increase production and, presumably, the income from it. The artist quite possibly does not touch the work and its quality may fall.

2. To relieve the artist of time-consuming hack work or the need to know

esoteric techniques; this frees him for more creative effort, but leaves control in his hands. The quality of the work may rise.

3. Deliberate resort to anonymous fabrication techniques in order to depersonalize the work and deprive it of every touch of the artist's own handwriting—for aesthetic reasons. The nature of the work changes, irrespective of quality. The remoteness of the maker is part of the artist's intention, so the quality depends on the remoteness.

Mary Vieira would fall into the first category, Vasarely or Len Lye would fall into the second, Donald Judd *(Fig. 78)* into the last.

There are different degrees of delegation (often depending on affluence), and there is considerable difference in the way a style lends itself to this kind of fabrication. Calder is said to give a tiny maquette to the machine shop; Vasarely has a crew manufacturing colored circles and squares to be applied; Judd has a sheet metal shop make boxes of the commonest galvanized sheet iron and aluminum, with techniques as close to industry as possible. As a means of depersonalizing the object, such making-by-others corresponds to the use of chance or mathematics as a determinant of the composition of a painting.

Though titles of works of art are sometimes omitted by the makers and ignored by connoisseurs, one finds them still in use today in a variety of ways other than summarizing the content of the work; for example, as (1) identifying inscriptions, (2) vivid literary allusions or poetic figures of such power that roles are reversed and the painting or sculpture becomes an illustration of the literary idea, (3) enigmatic and, possibly, deliberately obscure and frustrating titles, sometimes a slightly sadistic *jeu d'esprit* by the artist, (4) provocative or evocative words, which direct the thought of the observer without fixing it on a particular interpretation—David Smith's *Tank Totem* or *Agricola*, (5) meaningless words attached arbitrarily almost like a code designation, (6) opus numbers as in music, (7) date of execution, (8) a group of words which combine their associative power with the visual image to make a new total, greater than the sum of the parts, (9) an inventory of the formal components of the work—*Thirty Systematically Arranged Rows of Color Tones* or *Cubes (Fig. 79)*.

The differences between these ways of labeling indicate differences in point of view on the part of the artist. Even with an abstract work, an evocative title gives a figurative overtone to the image; it commemorates, not the idea the artist had before he made the work, but how it struck him afterward—a self-imposed Rorschach test where the artist's projection is part of his Gestalt. Some titles are witty, some romantic, some nostalgic, some frightening, some—especially in recent Constructivist art—conceived with the neutrality of a parts catalogue. Sometimes, the title is as important as the picture. Paul Klee is the master of the combined verbal and visual image, each intensifying the other. This is psychic collage and, as in all good collage, each component is transfigured. Klee's titles are part of his style.

The tradition of titles is strong and durable. A romantic attitude toward them clings to otherwise purely Constructivist works like musk. Albers, in his long series of *Homage to the Square*, often attaches an associative qualifier for each color experience, such as *Blue Promise* and *Late Forest*. Mondrian's last two works which omitted black lines, *Broadway Victory* and *Broadway Boogie-Woogie*, suggest an imminent shift away from purely relational painting. Titles, therefore, are biographical footnotes and miniature manifestos.

A further extension of Constructivist thought in the last decade, which appears sporadically and by implication in the "New Tendency," and more consciously elsewhere, is a resort to nature, but with a difference. Nature as landscape, still-life, or portraiture is ignored; but nature, as a great fount of physical phenomena, inexorable laws, and orderly relationships, is investigated by the artist and made the vehicle for his statement. Forces such as gravity, or energy such as light, serve as stimuli for the observer, supplanting those projections of the *appearance* of the natural world which formerly had made the face of art. Thus nature, as aerodynamics, mathematical relationships, probability, chance, or magnetic lines of force is turned, by the artist's hand, to confront the observer. The artist himself then withdraws, sometimes covering his tracks by the use of an *alter fabricator* as his *alter ego*, and a title which reads like a science textbook.

These artists have created new space in and around the óbject, which itself exhibits new kinds of surface; they exploit the peculiarities of the human optical system itself, instead of that system's record of the world outside; they use randomness, indeterminacy, exact repetition and self-perpetuating diversity as expressive means; they divide a surface into minute autonomous particles and render infinitesimal differences as active contrasts. While neither mathematical nor scientific, they borrow the material (not the method) of mathematics and science and set them up as "found objects" in contexts of their own making.

These are aspects of nature as viewed by artists in our time, just as artists of other times have had their visions of it. One may quote André Maurois quoting Gide to describe Balzac: "The true formula of all art is 'God proposes and man disposes.' Nature supplies the materials, the artist shapes them."

NOTES

1. This is confirmed by the following anecdote told by one of the most famous of them, who characteristically asked to remain anonymous:

    In 1933, the summer before our leaving (Germany), we were on an island in the Baltic Sea. There, at the beach, another summer guest, not known to us, approached us because he had heard of us being modern painters. Though we and our name were unknown to him, he asked whether he could see some of our work. I happened to have with me a few linocuts which I wished to show to a friend. I lent those prints to him, and he returned them the next day, telling me his conclusion from one of them. He was a neurologist. He concluded that I was the oldest of four children in our family; that I liked the best the youngest of the four (my little sister); that we children felt distant from our parents (we had a stepmother); and that, of the parents, the mother "had the trousers on," which was very true. My conclusion to his conclusion was: "One has to be careful, probably."

2. Fritz Schmalenbach, *Jugendstil*, trans. by the author, (thesis, Münster-Wurzburg, Germany, 1934), pp. 31–32.

3. Plato, *Philebus*, trans. by William Arrowsmith.

4. *Cézanne Letters* (to Emile Bernard, 1904), John Rewald, ed. (Oxford, Cassirer, 1941 and 1944), p. 234.

5. Camilla Gray, *The Great Experiment: Russian Art 1863–1922* (New York, Abrams, 1962), p. 126.

6. Albert Gleizes and Jean Metzinger, "Du Cubisme," *Modern Artists on Art*, trans. by Robert L. Herbert (Englewood Cliffs, N.J., Prentice-Hall, 1964), p. 7.

7. Michel Seuphor, *Abstract Painting*, trans. by the author (New York, Abrams, 1961), p. 45.

8. Umberto Boccioni, "Technical Manifesto of Futurist Sculpture," in Joshua Taylor, *Futurism*, Museum of Modern Art, New York (1961), p. 132.

9. Werner Haftmann, *Painting in the Twentieth Century*, Vol. I (New York, Praeger, 1960), p. 114.

10. Boccioni, *op. cit.*

11. Kasimir Malevich, *The Non-Objective World*, trans. by Howard Dearstyne (Chicago, Ill., Paul Theobold and Co., 1959), pp. 61–68.

12. *Ibid.*, pp. 68, 94, 67. The following quotations by Malevich are from the same source.

13. Wassily Kandinsky, *Concerning the Spiritual in Art* (New York, Wittenborn, 1947), pp. 52–53.

14. Wassily Kandinsky, "Text Artista," *Wassily Kandinsky Memorial* (New York, Guggenheim Foundation, 1945), p. 61; see Peter Selz, *German Expressionist Painting* (Berkeley, Calif., Univ. of California Press, 1957), p. 341, n. 3.

15. Conversation with the author, June 1963.

16. Antoine Pevsner, "Propos d'un Sculpteur," *L'Oeil*, (number 23, November 1956).

17. Naum Gabo, "Realist Manifesto," *Gabo* (Cambridge, Mass., Harvard Univ. Press, 1957), pp. 151–152; signed by Naum Gabo and Noton [Antoine] Pevsner, 2nd State Printing House, Moscow (August 5, 1920).

18. We find then, in 1920, the prominent use of four words in Russian art ideology with very distinct meanings: Suprematist, Constructivist, Realist, and Constructive. Malevich remained Suprematist while recognizing Gabo's thought as an extension of it. A Constructivist group led by Tatlin (according to Gabo, they also called themselves "Productivists") issued a manifesto in answer to Gabo's insisting on the "Communist expression of materialistic Constructivist work." While entitling his manifesto "Realist," Gabo employed "construct" as an operative word nine times in his text and "real" only twice—"Space and time are the only forms on which life is built and hence art must be constructed." Then, as now, he insists on the adjective "constructive" as contrasted with "constructivist" which he considers to imply a limiting credo and dogmatism.

19. Interview with Ilya Bolotowsky and Ibram Lassaw, "Russia and Constructivism," *Gabo, op. cit.*, p. 158.

20. Selz, *op. cit.*, p. 213.

21. Alexei Pevsner, *A Biographical Sketch of My Brothers, Naum Gabo and Antoine Pevsner* (Amsterdam, Augustin and Schoonman, 1964), p. 14.

22. Naum Gabo, Ben Nicholson, and J. L. Martin, eds., *Circle* (London, Faber & Faber, 1937).

23. Naum Gabo, *Studio International* (London, April 1966), p. 129.

24. *Circle, op. cit.*

25. Alexei Pevsner, *op. cit.*, p. 24.

26. *Ibid.*

27. Naum Gabo, "Art and Science," *Gabo, op. cit.*, pp. 180, 181.

28. David Sternberg, "An excerpt from the Foreword to the Catalogue of the First Russian Exhibition in Berlin, 1922," *Gabo, op. cit.*, p. 155.

29. Alexei Pevsner, *op. cit.*, p. 47.

30. Antoine Pevsner, *op. cit.*

31. Christian Zervos, *L'Histoire de l'Art Contemporain* (Paris, Editions Cahiers d'Art, 1938). The same piece is correctly given in *Gabo, op. cit.*, p. 366, fig. 24.

32. Conversation with the author, June 1963.

33. Eugène Delacroix, *Journal*, trans. by Walter Pach (New York, Covici, Friede, 1937), p. 194.

34. Willem Sandberg, Introduction to Alexei Pevsner, *A Biographical Sketch of My Brothers*, *op. cit.*

35. Herbert Read, *A Concise History of Modern Sculpture* (New York, Praeger, 1964), p. 112.

36. In 1920, Mondrian had prepared a pamphlet for publication in French by *La Galerie l'Effort Moderne* of Léonce Rosenberg, who could not read Dutch. The editor printed

it as written with a note that the French was "a little peculiar" (Michel Seuphor, *Piet Mondrian*, p. 156). Mondrian's title was "La Néo-Plasticisme," later anglicized to "Neo-Plasticism"—a regrettable mistranslation. "Plasticism" does not exist in English, and "plasticity" means something quite different from "beeldung," which in Dutch concerns two-dimensional forms. This word was rendered into German in the *Bauhausbücher* in 1925 as "Gestaltung" which means "configuration" or "shape," and is considered far more accurate.

37. Michel Seuphor, *Piet Mondrian, Life and Work* (New York, Abrams, 1956), p. 207, n. 18.

38. *Ibid.*, p. 130.

39. *Ibid.*, p. 149.

40. Anthony Hill, "The Constructionist Idea and Architecture," *Ark* (number 18, November 1956), p. 26.

41. Catalogue for Konstruktivisten exhibition, Städtisches Museum, Schloss Morsbroich, Leverkusen (June 1962), p. 1.

42. Naum Gabo, *Of Divers Arts* (Bollingen Series XXXV 8; New York, Pantheon Books, 1959), p. 28.

43. Gabo, "The Constructive Idea in Art," *Gabo, op. cit.*, p. 163.

44. "For three years he did more writing than painting," reports Seuphor in *Piet Mondrian, op. cit.*, p. 156.

45. See n. 36.

46. Seuphor, *Piet Mondrian, op. cit.*, pp. 166–168.

47. Wladyslaw Strzeminski, *Abstraction-Création* (number 1, Paris, 1932), p. 32.

48. At that time, Malevich was saying he would leave his work in Germany as it was no use, he thought, to take it back to Soviet Russia.

Later, in 1929, Gabo had an exhibition in Hannover and either then or later in the 1930s, the director of the Landes Museum, Alexander Dorner, who acquired two works of Gabo and had them installed in the Museum, showed Gabo all the work of Malevich carefully put into separate drawers, oil paintings on canvases taken out of their frames, drawings on cardboards, which Dorner wanted Gabo to see that they were preserved. Gabo did not count them but Dorner told him that these were all that were in the exhibition in the Bauhaus.

In the winter of 1936–37, Dorner arrived in London; he visited Gabo there and told him that he had packed all the work of Malevich in boxes and had given them to Hugo Herring (the architect, and their mutual friend) for safekeeping. Dorner proposed to create a trust consisting of three men, himself, Gabo, and Siegfried Giedion, the Swiss historian; in case Giedion should refuse, Mies van der Rohe would be asked. The trust would be created in order to care and keep watch of these paintings for the time when Hitlerism should pass, and in case anything should happen to Herring. Gabo accepted the idea.

After 1946, when the war was over, Willem Sandberg, director of the Stedelijk Museum in Amsterdam, learned that Malevich's work was still preserved in Herring's house. He spoke about it to Gabo and together with Mies van der Rohe, they decided to write to Herring and propose that he lend it for an exhibition in the U.S. and Holland.

Herring was agreeable but asked for some money for the loan to pay for his services as custodian. The Trustees (now Sandberg, Gabo, and Mies van der Rohe) decided to pay 12,000 Deutsche marks for each month's duration of the exhibition. But later, a woman involved with Herring's household, declared that according to

84

German law, Herring being custodian for twenty-five years had become the owner; they decided that, instead of lending Malevich's work for exhibition, they would sell it.

Gabo urged Sandberg to find the money and buy the work for his Museum, so that it should not be lost between the art dealers. Sandberg understood the importance of having the work in one place and succeeded in acquiring it. He agreed with Gabo that if Russia, at some future date, should wish to buy Malevich's paintings back, the Museum's director would make it possible, of course at a price.

After counting the number of paintings and drawings, it transpired that more than fifteen were still on extended loan in the Museum of Modern Art, New York, lent by Dorner for an exhibition before the war. Gabo and Sandberg were in friendly conferences with Alfred Barr, the director of the MOMA, and he confirmed that according to American law, the custodian of abandoned property does not acquire the property; therefore, Gabo and Sandberg decided to leave the work in Barr's custody, considering him as good a guardian as any Trustee.

This is how the situation, with regard to Malevich's work left in Europe, now stands. (Notes by the author from a conversation with Gabo on May 9, 1966; corrected and expanded by Gabo.)

49. Gropius, in a letter to the author, August 1, 1966:

"I would like to give you the following details: My design of the Chicago Tribune Tower has certainly nothing to do with van Doesburg. When you look at my early buildings which became landmarks in Germany, the Fagus Factory, Alfeld, 1911; and the Factory and Office Building at the Werkbund Exhibition, Cologne, 1914, you will see that the character of my buildings had been developed already before I even knew the name of van Doesburg and De Stijl in Holland. If the work of the students in the Bauhaus in the early time shows another note, this is because I did not impose on the students any preconception of style, but let them find their way themselves, giving them only objective physiological and psychological facts.

"I met Lissitzky and Gabo for the first time in 1923 in Weimar where they came to see our Bauhaus Exhibition and had a Dada meeting together with Moholy-Nagy from the Bauhaus. Moholy-Nagy was the only Constructivist who taught in the Bauhaus. Any appointments of new faculty members of the Bauhaus, I discussed with my friend, Adolf Behne, a writer on art and architecture who was well acquainted with progressive art and particularly with the Sturm Gallery run by Herward Walden. Through him I also became acquainted with Moholy-Nagy. It is not true that Feininger was 'instrumental in bringing news of the Russians to the Bauhaus.' Feininger was very much against Constructivism and was not interested in it."

50. Herbert Bayer, Walter Gropius, and Ilse Gropius, eds., *Bauhaus, 1919–1928* (Newton Centre Mass., Charles T. Branford Co., 1959), pp. 16, 22, 27.

51. Letter to the author, June 1964.

52. Josef Albers, *Despite Straight Lines* (New Haven, Conn., Yale Univ. Press, 1961), p. 75. Another view into this subject by Albers (*Ibid.*, p. 76) is:
Art is to present
vision first,
not expression first.
Vision in art is to reveal
our insight—inner sight,
our seeing
the world and life.
Thus art is not an object
but experience.
To be able to perceive it
we need to be receptive.
Therefore art is there
where art seizes us.

53. Josef Albers, *Interaction of Color* (New Haven, Conn., Yale Univ. Press, 1963), pp. 71, 73.

54. Alfred H. Barr, Jr., statement on dust jacket, *Bauhaus, op. cit.*

55. Much of the writing, including the quotations of Raymond Parker, appeared in *It Is*; five issues were published in 1958–60; a sixth came out in 1965 (New York, Second Half Publishing Co.).

56. Charles Biederman, *Art as the Evolution of Visual Knowledge* (Red Wing, Minn., Charles Biederman, 1948).

57. Max Bill, Catalogue for Konkrete Kunst exhibition, Helmhaus, Zürich, (June 8, 1964).

58. Jules Langsner, Catalogue for "Four Abstract Classicists," Los Angeles County Museum, Calif. (1959).

59. Letter to the author, May 1963.

60. The "edge" had been a preoccupation since the beginning of abstract art. It was hardened consciously between 1912 and 1920, first with the replacement of chiaroscuro by collage, then in the Ingres-style figure drawings of Picasso, reaching a full development in his *Three Musicians*. Juan Gris was then its great exponent, influencing the "Section d'Or" movement of Gleizes and Metzinger, and the "Purism" of Le Corbusier. Mondrian made his "edges" as hard as he could, as did the Constructivists. The Bauhaus was a "Hard Edge" academy in that it followed Albers rather than Kandinsky. Klee used hard line when it suited him, as did Arp, Stuart Davis, Glarner, Bolotowsky, Reinhardt, and Hélion.

61. Catalogue for Yves Klein, the Jewish Museum, New York (1967); this date is given for private exhibition in London of monochrome painting, including all pink and all orange. Concurred in by Karl G. Hultén, Catalogue for Yves Klein, Modern Museum, Stockholm (1966).

62. Catalogue for "Monochrome Malerei," Städtisches Museum, Schloss Morsbroich, Leverkusen (March 18, 1960), pp. 2–3.

63. *Ibid.*, pp. 4–5.

64. George Rickey, "The New Tendency (Nouvelle Tendance—recherche continuelle)," *College Art Journal*, XXIII 4, p. 272.

65. Camilla Gray, *op. cit.*, p. 244.

66. Angel Duart, Catalogue for "Travaux sur l'interactivité de l'espace, 1957–1965," Kunsthalle, Bern (March 12, 1966), p. 22.

PART TWO

The Heirs and Their Work

Introduction

By the 1960s Constructivist ideas had been evolving for more than forty years—from the space structures of Gabo and the vertical-horizontal grids of Mondrian to the use of light, chance, movement, repetition, optical phenomena, and spectator participation in objects which were not claimed to be art.

The early artists in Russian had experienced repression, then exile; those in Germany, hospitality and understanding from the Bauhaus then expulsion by Hitler, dispersal through Europe in the shadow of war, flight westward to France, England, and finally the United States. There was conversion of a slowly widening circle of non-objective painters and sculptors who grouped together with them in Paris, London, and New York.

The 1920s had been a time of experiment with materials, styles, and art theories, which were digested by the Bauhaus. In the thirties there were new recruits in Europe and even America. There were countertheories, repudiations, and defections. Some new schools were founded by old teachers. There were the beginnings of fame.

In the forties there was war. By the time it had ended and a civilian pattern of life had been restored, the world had changed: a new generation had come of age; millions returned to a strange homeland while others remained in exile. A piece was missing from every survivor's life. Art as personal expression had been suppressed under dictatorships and diminished elsewhere; exiled artists had carried their ideas to great distances among strangers thereby changing in some degree the art, the new country, and themselves. In 1950, after five years of recovery, a thirty-year-old German or Italian artist could not really remember pre-Hitler times. He had grown up in cultural hibernation. Yet in Europe, and also in America, the young postwar generation had tremendous boldness, energy, and resourcefulness. Having no immediate forebears whom they acknowledged, they could look backward and choose their ancestors.

The choice had been between Cubism, Surrealism, Expressionism, and—for a handful of strong, disciplined spirits—Constructivism or Neo-Plasticism; these were the last known positions. Each won some devotees. In the mid-fifties, one style became very fashionable—Abstract Expressionism. It dominated the art world for a decade or more and eclipsed the Constructivists, who had continued to work quietly, including any newcomers who had—against the trend—chosen to join them.

By 1960, however, a strong undercurrent of Constructivist art had begun to make itself felt among the postwar generation. Some of these artists knew the Bauhaus tradition, though not directly; some had developed a deep respect for the work of Mondrian, Malevich, Gabo, Albers, and lesser masters; others were looking for the antithesis of Abstract Expressionism and found it in the hard, precise, preconceived geometry of the Constructivist idiom and its implication of impersonality. The techniques of Constructivism had, with a few exceptions, been conventional, and the vigorous and imaginative younger generation had set out to extend them: with new ideas of space in both painting and sculpture; new images or no images at all, borrowing from mathematics and science; rejecting color as a sentimental indulgence or adopting it as a force; and trying out every technical means no matter how unpromising.

These reactions and developments were found in Europe, the United States, South America, and Japan. European artists became aware of a common trend which coalesced in 1963 into a federation of groups, called the "New Tendency." This developed an orthodoxy which alienated some sympathizers. There were groups in Japan, Argentina, Brazil, the United States, and also many artists working independently.

The legacy of Constructivism, as it broadened and deepened after the war, is the main subject of this book. Only twelve aspects have been selected for discussion, while other interesting developments like programmed art, "primary" structures, color as displeasure, combining sight with sound, or preconception with impulse, have been by-passed. Though far from definitive, the twelve topics are characteristic and provide some access to this continuing component of twentieth-century art.

I/Classic Order

Geometry is inherited from the Classical world. It is a precise and logical ordering of thoughts about space arising from the human experience of it. It is not surprising, therefore, that artists in the twentieth century, in search of order, turned to geometry. The painting of Malevich and Mondrian and of the non-objective artists who followed, is a thoughtful ordering of forms found in geometry. It is precise; it employs the geometer's tools—the compass and the straight edge—yet it is not tied to logic. It makes a human, not a mechanical, statement.

The Constructivists yield to Kandinsky's "inner necessity." Rodchenko, Lissitzky, van Doesburg, Sophie Taeuber-Arp used geometrical forms for spiritual ideas. They took the square and the circle as ready-mades, comparable to those of Duchamp (as Nicholson did later), and then apportioned their space with the eye, not the ruler.

Putting an idea into strict form, whether free or ruled, is Classicism, and this strictness is characteristic of Constructivism. Though driven by "inner necessity," the artist nevertheless obeys an outer necessity which is imposed by deliberate choice and by his will. With this force and this guidance, he constructs a work. Greek ideas of unity, moderation, and the ideal are implicit. As the work proceeds, there are a preconceived plan, adjustment, and refinement of proportions. In painting, the flat figure-ground concept is retained; in sculpture, the monolith or column or mass, even if hollowed out or boxed, still stands—a dichotomy of volume and void. In painting, conventional materials are applied by conventional means.

Loyalty to these ideas does not mean imitation or dull, second-rate, subservient work. There is still room for the "inner necessity," for originality, for valid development and elaboration, for depth.

This Classicism is in contrast with two other kinds of "necessity": romantic, which is also inner but which relies on overwhelming compulsion rather than on discipline to establish its ragged form; and experimentalist, where the urge is bred of curiosity and the reward is wonder, not art.

Abstract artists in the thirties responded to one or another of these compelling forces; a few chose to adopt the Classical idiom of Constructivism and to work within its limitations. They include Vantongerloo, Nicholson, Diller, Herbin, Vordemberge-Gildewart, Stazewski, Magnelli, and Xceron after his Cubist period. These, and many others, have made their own personal interpretation of Constructivist thought.

After them have come younger artists, who conform, define, and elaborate. They are disciples rather than imitators, and the strong ones have become leaders in their time. They have polished the style, and sometimes, perhaps too tastefully.

The technical advantage available to artists in the last twenty years that their predecessors lacked, namely industrial techniques of joining, such as welding, has extended enormously the sculptors' means of making form in space. Nevertheless, many sculptor-welders have continued to compose in a conventional, though personal manner—as Gonzalez often did—establishing a relationship of part-to-part and space-to-space in a single figure against a limitless ground, retaining the essentials of a classic order, a three-dimensional equivalent of a black square on a white ground, a monolith which may be metal instead of stone, a space laced with lines, or a wooden box.

1. Ben Nicholson, *White Relief*, 1936. Coll. The Lillian H. Florsheim Foundation for Fine Arts, Chicago, Ill.

2. Fritz Glarner, *Relational Painting No. 89*, 1961. Coll. Sheldon Memorial Art Gallery, The Univ. of Nebraska; photo Rudolph Burckhardt.

Nicholson's *White Relief (Fig. 1)*, executed while Mondrian was living next door in London and Gabo was helping him to edit *Circle,* has qualities of both Constructivism and De Stijl but is also a personal statement of great authority and refinement.

Among the painters who have maintained a relatively orthodox Constructivist sytle in individual ways are Fritz Glarner and Ilya Bolotowsky. Glarner has been devoted to Mondrian for over a quarter century, keeping the general vertical-horizontal format and the primary colors plus black, white, and gray. But he has introduced wedge-shaped instead of strictly rectangular elements into his painting, liberties which his master would not have sanctioned. His *Relational Painting No. 89 (Fig. 2)* derives from Mondrian but departs from the master, in the converging lines and the suggestion of overlaps and deepening space. Furthermore, there is no grid dividing the painting.

93

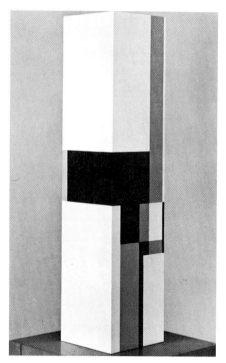

3. Ilya Bolotowsky, *Dynamic Diamond*, 1960. Courtesy Grace Borgenicht Gallery, N.Y.; photo O. E. Nelson.

4. Ilya Bolotowsky, *Column #2–White, Blue, Black, Grey*, 1962. Courtesy Grace Borgenicht Gallery, N.Y.; photo O. E. Nelson.

5. Kasimir Malevich, *Suprematist Composition (Airplane Flying)*, 1914. Museum of Modern Art, N.Y.

Although closely related to Mondrian, Bolotowsky's *Dynamic Diamond (Fig. 3)* adds to Mondrian's style a spiral movement and the progression in scale from the tiny rectangle toward the outside. *Column #2 (Fig. 4)* has the same centrifugal progression in a flat painting wrapped around a column. Edges of the painting are not allowed to coincide with edges of the column.

This is the early Malevich *(Fig. 5)*, very soon after he painted his initial square. The proportions, the intervals between the rectangles, the tipping, the tapering of one form, are highly personal, intuitive decisions; the forms are geometry, the composition is spiritual. Mondrian's *Untitled (Fig. 6)*, shows full maturity of the Neo-Plastic style.

Diller was the earliest (1934) American convert to De Stijl and was faithful to it until his death in 1965, after thirty years as a disciple of Mondrian. He worked within narrow limits, devoting a whole lifetime to the development of three themes, on which he worked concurrently or, rather, dialectically, as he reacted from one to the other. Two pages of Diller's *Notebook (Fig. 7)* set this out clearly; they give the essence of the themes, and show his debt to Mondrian. The paintings *(Figs. 8–10)* show how these are developed.

6. Piet Mondrian, *Untitled*, 1921. Coll. Mr. and Mrs. Pieter Sanders, Schiedam, Netherlands.

7. Burgoyne Diller, *Notebook*. From catalogue of exhibition of Burgoyne Diller, 1961, Galerie Chalette, N.Y.; by permission of Mme. M. Chalette Lejwa.

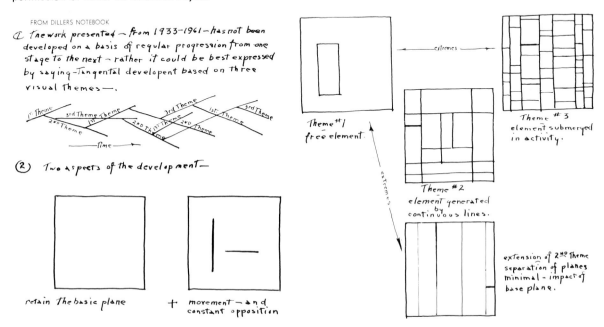

8. Burgoyne Diller, *First Theme*, 1962. Galerie Cha-lette, N.Y.; photo O. E. Nelson.

9. Burgoyne Diller, *Second Theme*, 1938–40. The Metropolitan Museum of Art, N.Y. Purchase 1963, George A. Hearn Fund.

10. Burgoyne Diller, *Third Theme*, 1946–48. The Whitney Museum, N.Y.; photo Walter Rosenblum.

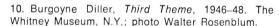

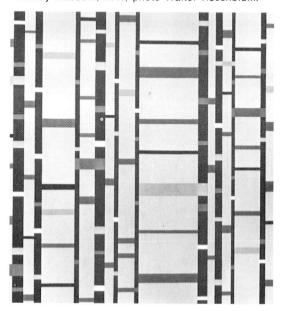

In his later years, Diller worked also in three dimensions, developing the same themes with precisely finished formica solids, sometimes larger than a man *(Figs. 11–13)*. Sensitive to proportion, he pondered deeply each dimension, each space, each opposition and despite the apparent narrowness of his themes, his work was never repetitive or stale. He emerges as one of the very strong Americans of the epoch.

96

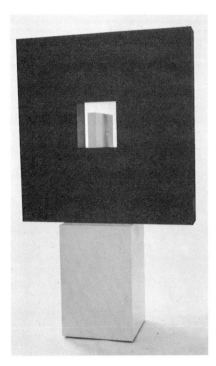

11. Burgoyne Diller, *Color Structure #2*, 1963. Galerie Chalette, N.Y.; photo O. E. Nelson.

12. Burgoyne Diller, *Color Structure VI*, 1962. Galerie Chalette, N.Y.

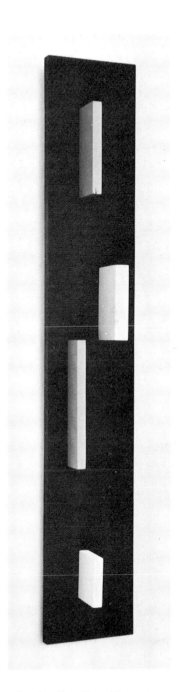

13. Burgoyne Diller, *Construction: Four Elements on Black Ground*, 1962. Galerie Chalette, N.Y.; photo O. E. Nelson.

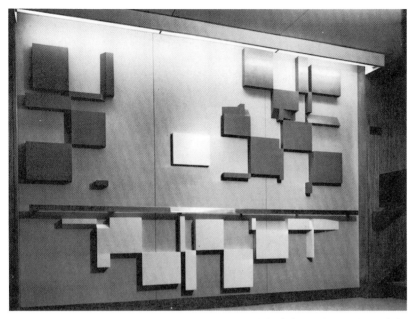

14. Mary Martin, *Relief on First Class Staircase, S.S. Oriana*, 1960. Photo John Maltby.

15. Gudrun Piper, *Square Follows Yellow,* 1963. Coll. the artist.

In England, Mary Martin *(Fig. 14)* uses rectangles of uniform height in a positive-negative design where the spaces of wall become part of the statement as they alternate with the solids. Piper *(Fig. 15)* and Mahlmann *(Fig. 16)* use the same devices of positive-negative space in relief, both paintings based on developments from the square, both suggesting overlap and transparency, both suggesting extension beyond the frame. Thépot in *Grey Diamond (Fig. 17)* builds simple flat shapes from back to front, using gently the overlap and transparency, sensitive shape and proportions, developed through the previous half century. Kenneth Martin's *Tunnel in the Air (Fig. 18)* is the intuitive placement of simple geometrical elements with repetition and contrast.

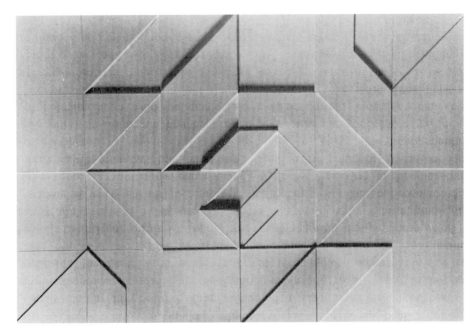

16. Max Mahlmann, *Relief 13*, 1963. Photo Ingeborg Sello.

17. Roger-François Thépot, *Grey Diamond*, 1959. Coll. Mendel Art Gallery, Saskatoon, Canada; photo Jean-Pierre Leloir.

18. Kenneth Martin, *Tunnel in the Air*, 1965. Photo John Webb.

19. Carel Visser, *8 Blocks*, 1965. Rijksmuseum Kröller-Müller, Holland.

20. André Volten, *Architectonic Construction*, 1958. Rijksmuseum Kröller-Müller, Holland.

21. Marino di Teana, *Balance, Mass, Space*, 1961. Galerie Denise René, Paris.

Visser *(Fig. 19)* derives directly from De Stijl as does Volten *(Fig. 20)*. They both work now in the climate of Biederman, emphasizing a vertical-horizontal balance. Marino di Teana in *Balance, Mass, Space (Fig. 21)*, uses vertical-horizontal elements but in a freer way with small linear elements, a single curved form, oblique cuts. His use of the reflecting qualities of the stainless steel lighten the mass.

22. Mary Vieira, *Plan-Projection-Cross I/I*, 1958–59. Outdoor sculpture collection, city of Zürich.

23. Robert Adams, *Screen Form (maquette)*, 1962. Photo courtesy Rosslyn Studio, London.

Vieira's *Plan-Projection-Cross I/I (Fig. 22)* comes out of her contact with Max Bill and through that from De Stijl. Four horizontal blocks of equal height cluster around four vertical blocks, progressing in height toward the tallest. Adams' *Screen Form (Fig. 23)* ties together two unequal planes, one of irregular shape, with a cluster of lines that by length and placement achieve stability. There is an echo of Malevich.

24. Berto Lardera, *Human Spiral #1*, 1960. Coll. the artist.

Lardera's curves, frets, and holes removed him from the austere tradition. There is a hint of banners and pageantry, a three-dimensional emblem on a field of space. His geometry is personal, yet the form is controlled and unsentimental. *Human Spiral #1 (Fig. 24)* is out of the Constructivist tradition which, though usually geometrical, need not be.

Liberman's *Rhythm (Fig. 25)* is a Constructivist image which has been personalized. The welded structure, which looks robust, wobbles easily enough to impart a feeling of insecurity. The vertical divider of the upper circle is not vertical, but slightly askew suggesting either whimsy or imperfect control.

25. Alexander Liberman, *Rhythm*, 1964. Museum of Art, Rhode Island School of Design.

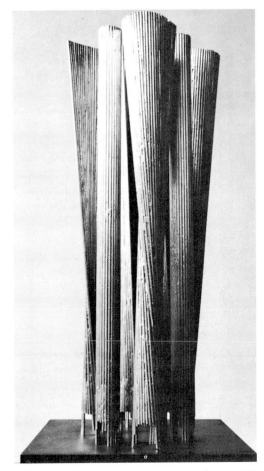

26. Brigitte Meier-Denninghoff, *Attika*, 1965. Courtesy Marlborough Fine Art, Ltd., London: photo Martin Matschinsky.

In Meier-Denninghoff's *Attika (Fig. 26)*, all traces of Henry Moore (whom she worked for) have gone, but the debt to Pevsner is apparent. She works with the same material—bronze rods soldered together—and develops surface and mass from bundles of lines, some of which also suggest a gentle rotation. Space is sometimes enfolded and hidden; the total form is essentially monolithic.

103

For twenty years David Smith had used I-beams, angles, bars, and plates—a natural consequence of his industrial experience—in conjunction with objects. He alternated between highly suggestive or downright figurative assemblages and geometric non-objective forms, the latter sometimes depending on existing industrial shapes for their geometry, sometimes on simple solids or silhouettes which he made up in quantity and assembled freely. These sculptures are typical of David Smith's last years. *Eleven Books, Three Apples (Fig. 27)* show the power of his work and the positive preference for geometric forms. They also show what is sometimes thought a weakness in a sculptor—a tendency to design flat or in profile; they all have a "front" which is more interesting than the side. The group contains *Cubi IV* on the right, *Cubi V* on the left, *Cubi VIII* in the center, all of 1963 *(Fig. 28)*.

27. David Smith, *Eleven Books, Three Apples*, 1959. Coll. Storm King Art Center, Mountainville, N.Y.

28. David Smith (foreground, left to right), *Cubi V*, January 18, 1963; *Cubi VIII*, March 21, 1963; *Cubi IV*, January 17, 1963. The Estate of David Smith, courtesy Marlborough-Gerson Gallery, N.Y.

II/New Ideas of Space

Painting from Giotto to Cézanne, from Cézanne to Cubism, and into the diverse styles of the mid-twentieth century, can be seen by historians, critics, and now by artists themselves, as a manifestation of different ideas of space. Our generation has discussed space more than line, color, light, surface treatment, or meaning. Even in the anti-planning, anti-adjusting credo of Action Painting, a coherent space order was allowed, and almost welcomed.

The early Constructivists had worked in space already established by the Cubists—as in Picasso's *Girl with a Mandolin (Fanny Tellier) (Fig. 9, p. 12)*—that had been shallow, controlled by a previous understanding of perspective, and finite. Though not singled out as such, this space was also an "object" ranking with the guitar, fruit, bottle, or person inhabiting it. As soon as these objects were removed, whether by Kandinsky, Malevich, or any other non-objective pioneer, the space around the substituted non-objective shapes also lost its finiteness, was no longer susceptible of measurement, but nevertheless kept its identity as the sea different and separate from the island. This surrounding space, however, can appear to protrude as well as recede from the picture plane. The early squares, rectangles, and circles, which Malevich said "can be compared to the primitive signs of the first man," were islands in space, the classical figure-ground relationship.

There are other space relationships, besides figure-ground and volume-void. Morgan Russell, in 1913, made paintings which no longer seemed like an abstract object laid in an empty box; his forms covered all the surface; there was no background. Macdonald-Wright followed with an effect of low relief in shallower space *(Fig. 1)*; and Giacomo Balla, in the previous year, had nearly succeeded in flattening the space completely, with the regular rectilinear pattern of his *Iridescent Interpenetration (Fig. 12, p. 15)*. Mondrian, by dividing his surface with lines from edge to edge, increased the ambiguity between figure and ground, without eliminating either. Only at the very end of his life, in the complex *Boogie-Woogie* paintings *(Fig. 52, p. 53)*, without the grid of black lines, did he really equalize figure and ground.

Cubist sculpture lagged behind painting but it caught up as soon as non-objective ideas crystallized. The Cubist carvings of Lipchitz, Zadkine, Archipenko,

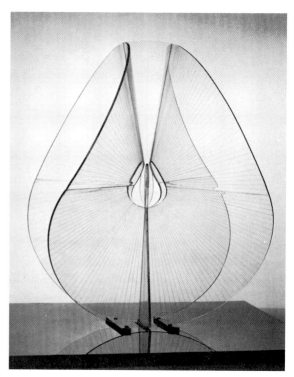

1. Stanton Macdonald-Wright, *Abstraction on Spectrum*, 1914. Nathan Emory Coffin collection, Des Moines Art Center.

2. Naum Gabo, *Translucent Variation on Spheric Theme*, 1951 version of 1937 original. The Solomon R. Guggenheim Museum, N.Y.

3. Henry Moore, *Two Forms,* 1934. Museum of Modern Art, N.Y., gift of Sir Michael Sadler.

the Cubo-Futurist modelings of Boccioni, the early montages of Picasso, and the early table architecture of van Doesburg and Vantongerloo, were conceived as a mass standing in a void. Gabo, however, discovered interior space. He worked all his life with transparent materials which reveal it, using plastic floating planes and rods *(Fig. 2)*. Later, to fix the surface of the plastic and give it direction, he scored lines on it, which eventually gave way to stretched strings. He laid the foundation for a half century's development of space sculpture. A decade later, Henry Moore *(Fig. 3)* and Barbara Hepworth cut holes in the mass to define interior space—a much less adroit access to the interior. The Russian brothers were sensitive both to the space and to the possibilities inherent in joining new (to the sculptor) materials. Yet the constructions of Gabo and Pevsner, with their revealed interior spaces, were still monolithic in concept. The space was retained within a clear and perfect outline, although less massive than before, and interior and exterior space were clearly marked. There was no exchange across the frontier.

The new ideas of space include: the manipulation of space as a plastic material which can be molded, cut, divided, bent, squeezed, interrupted, compartmented, expanded, contracted, and arranged, just as clay, wood, stone, or metal may be; elimination of any difference in kind between interior and exterior space in sculpture; no dominance of figure over ground in painting; no dominance of volume over void, of positive over negative; a free flow of space by such means as alternations of positive-negative; use of very meager material to occupy and energize much space; the avoidance of isolated, composed, monolithic structures; and indeterminate works suggesting infinite extension.

The shift from the archaic figure-ground concept in painting to the idea that space is a continuum, spreading out beyond the canvas, requires either that the canvas be seen as a window onto the continuum, a segment of which the painting renders visible, or that the canvas be active to the edges, without a neutral zone. Each artist in each painting establishes the conditions of this visibility. The painting and the space are fully and mutually involved; the painting is not a diagram of a non-space seen against space. The figure is as much space as the ground; both are interchangeable; neither stops at the edge of the canvas. Similar reciprocation is possible in three dimensions.

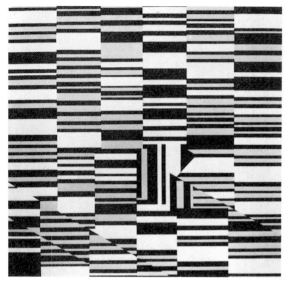

Fruhtrunk's *Pleating (Fig. 4)* denies the figure-ground relationship by equitable division into light and dark; at the same time, he suggests undulation, recession, transparency, and overlapping by varied width and sharp interruption of stripes. The surface of the canvas becomes a dynamically interwoven space of indeterminate depth. Albrecht *(Fig. 5)* attempts a similar continuity by more primitive means —the implied folding of a band across the canvas with quasi-illusionist suggestion of solids.

4. Günter Fruhtrunk, *Pleating*, 1962. Coll. the artist.

5. Joachim Albrecht, *Composition 7*, 1963. Photo Ingeborg Sello.

6. Richard Mortensen, *Opus Rouen*, 1956. Galerie Denise René, Paris.

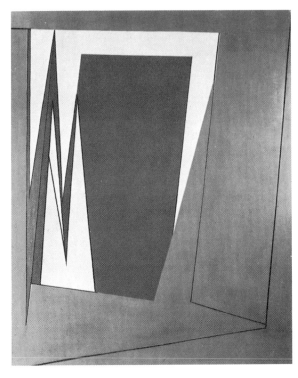

7. Richard Mortensen, *Cormeilles*, 1956. Aarhus Kunst Museum, Denmark; photo Etienne Bertrand Weill.

8. Equipo 57, *Interaction C15*, 1961. Photo courtesy A. Duart.

9. Francisco Sobrino, *Unstable Transformation 26*, 1962. Palais des Beaux-Arts, Brussels.

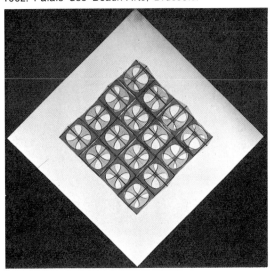

In *Opus Rouen (Fig. 6)*, and to a lesser extent in *Cormeilles (Fig. 7)*, Mortensen also implies folding but with ambiguous overlappings and other perspective devices. The Equipo 57 circles in three tones of *Interaction C15 (Fig. 8)* can be read as white on black or black on white, but not as gray on either—that is always the middle term. The swelling and diminishing forms interlock like a jigsaw puzzle. Diminishing size suggests a tunnel-space but hard contours and active design contradict this. Sobrino's *Unstable Transformation 26 (Fig. 9)* is a carving of space as much as a carving of plastic.

Dewasne and Baertling produce similar image-ground situations, with very different images, where any part of the design can be seen as advancing or receding from the rest.

109

10. Jean Dewasne, *The Strange Max*, 1965. Photo Geoffrey Clements, Cordier and Ekstrom, Inc.

11. Olle Baertling, *Mural in New City Center*, Stockholm, 1959–60. Photo Lennart Olson.

12. Yenceslav Richter, *Center of Glass*, 1965. Photo Branko Balić.

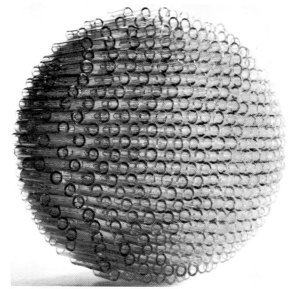

Repeating curvilinear contours in *The Strange Max (Fig. 10)* are a device familiar to Dewasne through Northwest American Indian and Peruvian art. Baertling's entrance hall mural in the New City Center, Stockholm *(Fig. 11)*, leads the eye through emphatic but ambiguous space situations. "The wall material [of the Haymarket Building lobby] was to be marble. . . . The painter rejected entirely the idea of material effects and instead he proposed to put in lines of force through the medium of colour. . . . He brought out the lines of force through energetic diagonals and violently contrasting colours so that the architectural inward movement is almost explosively accentuated. The left-hand triangles in blue, yellow and red dominate the black and red and the cold white and yellow of the right-hand fields."[1]

Gabo's spheric theme is seen above *(Fig. 2)*. Yenceslav Richter in *Center of Glass (Fig. 12)* achieves similar occupancy, definition, and revealing of space in his sphere of glass tubes as does Morellet with his *Sphere* of aluminum rods *(Fig. 13)*. Enzo Mari's cube in a sphere, *Structure No. 696 (Fig. 14)*, contrasts the two basic shapes and presses the paradox of making the finite sphere transparent and the cube a grid where each face is superimposed on the other faces and any movement of the spectator transforms their relationship. In *E, No. 6 (Fig. 15)*, Equipo 57 establishes curved surfaces with straight lines (hyperbolic paraboloid), and these surfaces in turn establish volumes and voids which are interchangeable and theoretically continuous, like a crystal

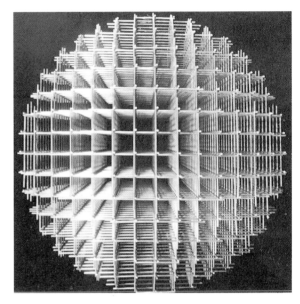

13. François Morellet, *Sphere*, 1962. Coll. the artist.

14. Enzo Mari, *Structure No. 696*, 1962. Photo Uco Mulas.

15. Equipo 57, *E, No. 6*, 1963. Photo courtesy A. Duart.

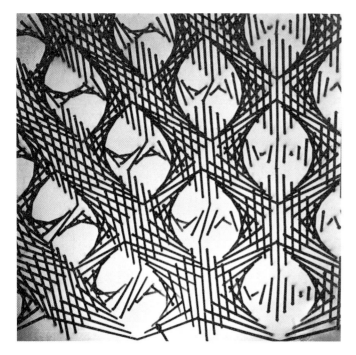

16. Yvaral, *Space Plan*, 1961. Coll. the artist.

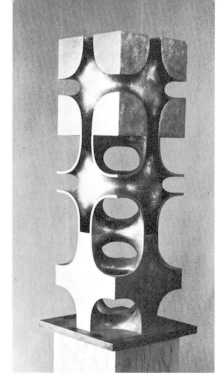

17. Erwin Hauer, *Inversion of Volumes*, 1966. Coll. the artist.

18. David Hall, *Izzard*, 1966. Coll. Mr. & Mrs. Roger Sonnabend, Boston, Mass.

structure. Yvaral, using a similar system in a detail of *Space Plan (Fig. 16)*, permits it to grow outward but limits it sharply in the third dimension. Hauer's *Inversion of Volumes (Fig. 17)*, makes the surface continuous metal, instead of linear grids, emphasizing the subdivision of space, which flows along the surfaces instead of through them; interior space is thus revealed through holes as in Moore.

David Hall's folded planes in space *(Fig. 18)* exploit the relation of directional emphases, insidedness and outsidedness, enclosure, compression, release of space and modulation of light. In addition the proportion and tapering of the planes suggest perspective which contradicts experience. These structures

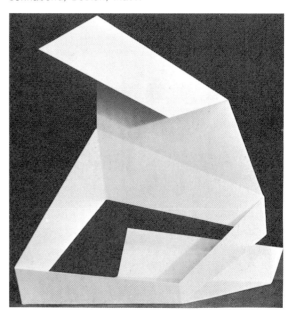

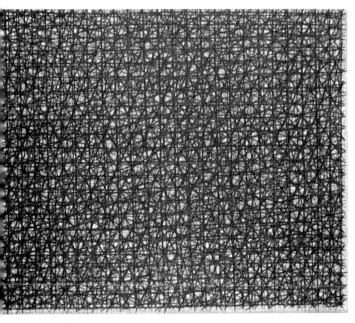

19. Piero Dorazio, *Study*, 1961. Gallery Springer, Berlin.

21. Christian Megert, *Object*, 1964. Copyright Ravssev, Bern.

20. Michel Seuphor, *Inhabited Silence*, 1958. Coll. the artist.

are a three-dimensional realization of ideas inherent in Albers' ambiguous drawings and a planar extension of Baertling's acute-angled rods.

Dorazio's *Study (Fig. 19)* requires the eye and mind to penetrate the grid of painted lines to the deep but indeterminate space he creates behind the canvas. Seuphor's *Inhabited Silence (Fig. 20)* leads into a more definite space by controlled intervals between lines and the consequent surface undulation which finally disappears into an almost solid-black space. Megert's *Object (Fig. 21)* creates the illusion of infinite recession into solid-black space by means of mirrors set face-to-face.

113

Vardánega and Lippold create lines drawn in space not with ink but with light. Vardánega's *Crystal Structure (Fig. 22)* is made of slabs of Plexiglas through which light flows from the bottom to be emitted from the edges. Lippold's huge sculpture *(Fig. 23)* in the Pan American Building in New York City, is constructed of stretched, polished gold and steel wire made visible by light reflected from it. Riley in *Straight Curve (Fig. 24)* draws curved lines across a linear grid with varying intervals (the black-white diagonals add to the optical dazzle quality, but do not, in themselves, affect the space); the broadening and narrowing, together with the curvature, are in effect a perspective device which warps the surface, pushing it in and out in space. Equipo 57

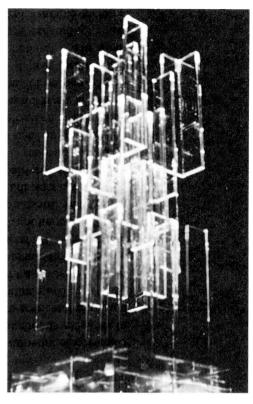

23. Richard Lippold, *Flight*. Commission for Pan American Building, N.Y., 1963.

24. Bridget Riley, *Straight Curve*, 1963. Photo courtesy Richard Feigen Gallery, N.Y.

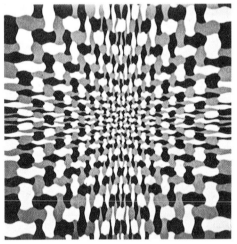

25. Equipo 57, *Development A*, 1961. Photo courtesy A. Duart.

26. José de Rivera, *Construction #76*, 1961. The Joseph H. Hirshhorn collection; courtesy Grace Borgenicht Gallery, N.Y.

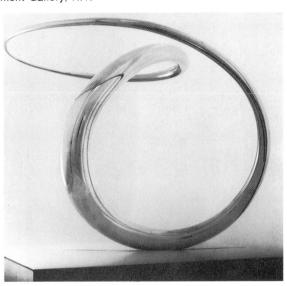

achieves a similar shrinkage and expansion with the strong suggestion of deep recession and squeezing created in *Development A*, a 1961 *gouache (Fig. 25)*.

The strings of Gabo and Moore introduced a linear element into sculpture, which had been thought of as an art of mass. Calder had anticipated this kind of linear design in 1926 with his early wire figures. Picasso, too, had made an abstract wire construction in 1928. Since this pioneer work, several artists have developed the idea further and have become specialists in linear constructions in space. José de Rivera vitalizes both interior and exterior space with a swelling and tapering endless loop. *Construction #76 (Fig. 26)*, because it can never be fully seen in profile, carries the viewer irresistibly into the third dimension, enfolding environmental space. Baertling's *Asama (Fig. 27)* is abrupt and juts uncompromisingly into space so that there is no idea of a containing envelope—his space goes continually outward. Norbert Kricke retains ideas of the loop and combines them with outward push in his *Large White (Fig. 28)* but, later *(Fig. 29)*, he combines a dense and active core with an energetic, even explosive, movement outward into the surrounding space.

27. Olle Baertling, *Asama*, 1961. Coll. the artist.

28. Norbert Kricke, *Large White*, 1955. Coll. Gerd and Ursel Hatje, Stuttgart; photo Anton Stankowski.

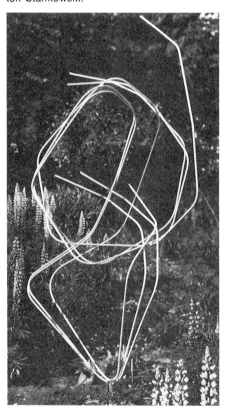

29. Norbert Kricke, *Large Reux*, 1961–63. Coll. Baroness Alix de Rothschild, Château de Reux, Normandy, France.

III/Reliefs

In the twentieth century the difference between painting and sculpture has diminished, sometimes even disappeared. In very early times it was found that painting and sculpture could be combined as relief, which suggested the third dimension with forms raised only slightly above the surface. Almost every culture has made relief sculpture in some form, from China to Mexico, from Alaska to Polynesia.

After the invention of Cubism, however, relief, though still hybrid, took a different turn. Cubist painting suggested objects set out in a shallow box; collage desanctified the painted surface; the next step was the gluing of solid objects onto the picture plane, thereby actually realizing the previously implied shallow space. Picasso's sculpture in 1913, soon after his early collaboration with Braque, gave the initial push to Tatlin. Half a century later we have the 3-D collage of such artists as Cornell, Rauschenberg, Arman and Spoerri, or quasi-sculpture in the paintings of Burri and Fontana.

Besides these somewhat Dada assemblagists, there were other artists working quite differently in relief, following the Constructivist tradition of non-objective geometrical designs, tightly organized in the special layer of shallow, close-to-the-wall, vertical space. Geometrical constructions of this sort had been made by Arp and Sophie Taeuber-Arp, and in the horizontal plane by Malevich. Van Doesburg *(Fig. 1)* built table architecture in collaboration with the architects Oud, Wills, and van Eesteren. Vantongerloo also made such constructions *(Fig. 2)*. All architecture can be thought of as a study of this shallow space in relation to a plane —the ground. The recent, non-objective, relief sculpture is a kind of architecture applied to a wall, where it does not require a helicopter to be fully seen. In his *Abstract Gallery (Fig. 41, p. 42)* in Hannover, Lissitzky used metal ribs applied to the wall to make light and space a part of it.

Several English artists have been especially concerned with relief space. One of them, Victor Pasmore, who fifteen years ago turned from brilliant success as a figure painter to non-objective art, makes clear—in a letter to the author—that relief is no longer a hybrid, but a new form:

> . . . It is a fallacy to regard the relief as necessarily or exclusively a transition between painting and full three-dimensional sculpture . . . between a painted

1. Theo van Doesburg, *Maison de Campagne (maquette)*, 1923. Courtesy Mme. Nelly van Doesburg.

2. Georges Vantongerloo, *Interrelation of Masses*, 1919. Courtesy Max Bill; photo Ernst Scheidegger.

square and a sculptural cube there is nothing. A square cannot be rendered in relief. In the square and the cube, therefore, we have two distinctly different forms involving different sensory experiences. Thus, although painting and sculpture may be related and concerned with the same problem, they are in themselves uniquely different manifestations of this problem—the same goes for relief. The relief is a unique form with its own individuality.

Pasmore, the Dutch artist Joost Baljeu, and several of their colleagues had been interested in the theories of Charles Biederman, one of whose terms was "spatial plane." Biederman had written:

What is required, then, is that the rectangle of the canvas become an actual non-illusionistic plane from which actual planes gradually emerge into the full reality of structure. This means an art of relief; a development from the limited symmetry of painting gradually into the full-dimensional symmetry structure of reality.[2]

He had some doctrinaire views and it is not surprising that other artists should diverge from his path, even if starting from the same point; he himself moved on from his original position. In an essay in *Structure*, he developed a lengthily argued assertion that "symmetry" is the key to making "non-mimetic" art, and that relief constructions on a plane are best for this because they permit multiple "centers of symmetry" to be established by the artist and observed by the spectator, moving before the relief in an "arc of symmetry." Biederman calls the maker of such objects the "Structurist, the new artist." How limited these recent views have become is demonstrated by his assertion that the movement of the spectator in front of the relief is "the only true problem of 'motion' in art at the present time." In contrast with Pasmore, whose clear and common-sense view accepts the differences between painting and relief while not granting relief any special sanctity, Biederman now considers painting "obsolete."

The London artist, Anthony Hill, also believes his views are due entirely to Biederman. He describes in great detail (1) a plane parallel to the wall before which stand (2) smaller planes parallel to this, "stratifying" the space, and (3) at right angles to them (the "orthogonal" relationship), still further planes or narrow rectangular prisms, making three layers of space. Hill then asserts that:

> The orthogonal constructional relief is a unique space/form domain that has no obvious counterpart in our environment (which removes the temptation to imitate the environment). . . . The relief is the real plastic object par excellence, it uses the dimensions of everyday objects and yet is not to be confused with them.[3]

Peter Stroud, another English painter who wanted to get rid of the profile reading of image, writes: "In relief painting the sense of distance is reduced and a common space is established where the viewer's life-space and the aesthetic space of the art work become one."[4]

In spite of the arbitrariness of Biederman's views, repugnant to those outside the group, the interest in relief space is widespread, and its manifestations very diverse, by no means limited to orthogonal designs. Doubtless, relief sculpture has advantages in regard to storage, shipping and exhibition, which make it attractive to young artists. But many also find it—as Pasmore proposes—a special province of its own. Artists with Constructivist tendencies have found this relief space very stimulating. Only a few of them limit their design to the orthogonal scheme outlined above by Hill, and some include relief among a number of other interests.

Gorin's *Composition No. 59 (Fig. 3)* and Cairoli's *Spatial Contrast (Fig. 4)* project from a wall but remain close to it, as had Biederman himself in his typical *Structurist Relief (Fig. 5)*. They limit themselves to line, square, and rectangle. Cairoli, in his work, has emphasized the dual nature of relief space: a structure parallel to the wall and a pushing outward from the wall into space; a single line binds the two together.

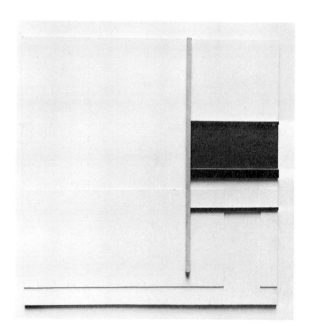

3. Jean Gorin, *Composition No. 59*, 1959. Kazimir Gallery, Chicago; photo Kurt Blum.

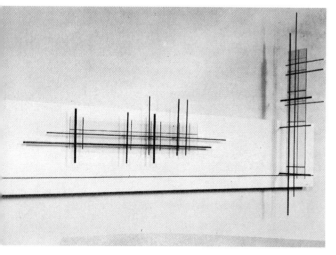

4. Carlos Cairoli, *Spatial Contrast*, 1957. Photo Yves Hervochon.

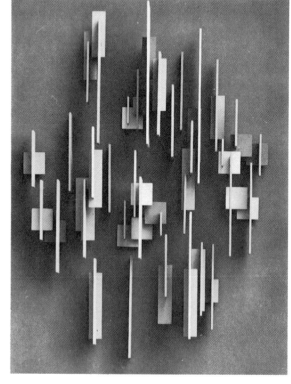

5. Charles Biederman, *Structurist Relief*, 1954. Photo Phil Revoir.

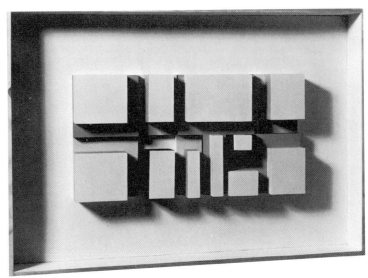

6. Mary Martin, *White-faced Relief*, 1959. Coll. the artist.

7. Victor Pasmore, *Projection Relief in White, Black, and Umber Red*, 1962. Coll. the artist.

The English school, Mary Martin, Stroud, Pasmore, Hill, and Wise acknowledge Biederman's influence, yet work more in terms of surface than he. Martin in *White-faced Relief (Fig. 6)* makes much of the negative space. Pasmore's *Projection Relief (Fig. 7)* presses out with powerfully bent lines into space above the surface. Joost Baljeu, who also designs houses, goes further forward into deep space creating, in his *Synthesist Construction (Fig. 8)*, a sculpture in full three dimensions growing from the wall. Stroud's relief painting *Extendar I (Fig. 9)* is also an ambiguous image. It can be read as steps seen from above or below and is rendered as neutral as possible in its design and the way it is painted, except in his invasion of the space in front of the picture plane. He writes to the author, "Two problems have concerned me recently: firstly that of finding an image of minimal identity; secondly a means of breaking down this image in an anonymous way."

In Hill's *Relief Construction (Fig. 10)*, the vertical-horizontal system of Mondrian is projected out into the relief space from the white panel, which is itself projected from the black square, which in turn is projected from the wall. The emphasis is on the long and short horizontals, which alternate contrapuntally to the left and right.

8. Joost Baljeu, *Synthesist Construction*, 1964. Rijksmuseum Kröller-Müller, Holland.

9. Peter Stroud, *Extendar I*, 1966. Photo courtesy University of Vermont.

10. Anthony Hill, *Relief Construction*, 1960. Coll. Dr. Michael Morris, London; photo Cooper.

11. Gillian Wise, *Two Part Construction on Three Planes*, 1965. Coll. the artist.

12. André Volten, *Relief Welded on Plywood Multiplex*, 1957. Rijksmuseum Kröller-Müller, Holland.

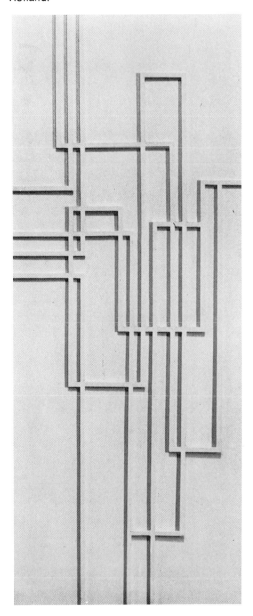

In Wise's *Two Part Construction on Three Planes (Fig. 11)*, the relief space in front of the wall is defined and isolated by the upper layer of plastic. The intermediate layer divides this volume and is compartmented by the incised lines. Further compression and division of the confined space is achieved with the opaque square in the vertical plane and the two small transparent horizontal ones.

Volten's uniformly low relief *(Fig. 12)* retains the vertical-horizontal characteristics of De Stijl in a design reminiscent of Greek key motifs, though these are more complex and irregular. No rectangle repeats any other, no horizontal aligns with any other. Like Peter Stroud's, this essentially two-dimensional design is raised just enough to invade the spectator-space.

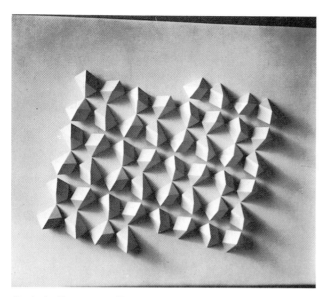

13. Luis Tomasello, *Reflection No. 60*, 1960. Photo courtesy Galerie Denise René, Paris.

14. Enrico Castellani, *Supertive*, 1961. Galleria dell'Ariete, Milan; photo C. Lini.

Very low relief is intensified by its reaction to light, which sharply separates whatever is raised or lowered from the plane. The evenness of the plane is important. Tomasello's *Reflection No. 60 (Fig. 13)* creates a very active alternation of masses and spaces in which the empty squares and crosses derive from the square and triangular facets of the solids, with both plane and solids defined by the light falling on them. The membrane of Castellani's canvas, *Supertive (Fig. 14)*, is pressed and pulled into the third dimension; and von Graevenitz in *6 Variations (Fig. 15)* alternates convex and concave hemispheres in patterns based on symmetrical variations of a plus and

15. Gerhard von Graevenitz, *6 Variations*. Coll. the artist.

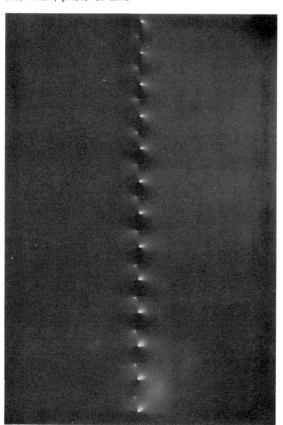

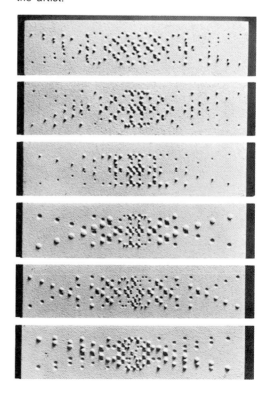

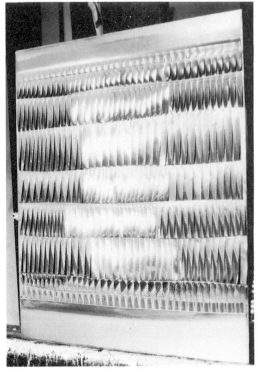

16. Heinz Mack, *Light-Relief*, 1962. Coll. the artist.

17. Zoltan Kemeny, *Involuntary Speed*, 1962. Photo Walter Drayer.

18. Yaacov Agam, *Cycle*, 1963. Coll. W. H. Weintraub; photo courtesy the artist.

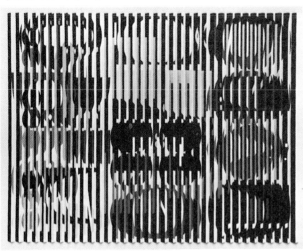

minus theme. Heinz Mack, in contrast with the others *(Fig. 16)*, destroys the plane completely by turning every strip to or from the light, depending on the viewer's position, into positive and negative strips that reverse in relation to the lights and to each other.

In a kind of metal collage, Kemeny assembled repeating shapes on the surface to establish secondary images, sometimes explicit and regular, sometimes faintly suggested. In *Involuntary Speed (Fig. 17)* the blocks of brass delineate two overlapping spirals. Agam, in his typical work, *Cycle (Fig. 18)*, cuts into the panel V-shaped grooves on the sides of which segments of several designs are painted

125

so that they appear and disappear as the observer passes by; head-on, one sees the designs mixed. In *Relief Rélations Pures (Fig. 19)*, Soto places metal squares in the relief space, three or four inches in front of the striped panel; the dazzling moiré effect of the edge against the lines causes the squares to lose their space relation to the plane and to float above. Louise Nevelson, having used relief space for years for assemblages of "found" wooden objects, now *(Fig. 20)* cuts a slice of space, in effect a wall, free standing, into which she inserts—as back-to-back relief— geometrically precise cylinders and cubes.

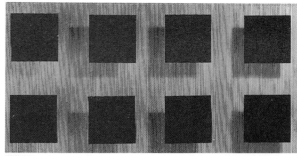

19. Jésus-Rafaël Soto, *Relief Rélations Pures*, 1965. Rijksmuseum Kröller-Müller, Holland.

20. Louise Nevelson, *Atmosphere and Environment I*, 1966. Museum of Modern Art, N.Y.; photo Ferdinand Boesch.

IV/Tangents and Pressures

Stability of composition was thought desirable in the Renaissance, with comfortable space surrounding the subject. The subject was given a pyramidal form with a broad, stable base. The corners of the rectangular format were closed, with no strong lines leading the eye outside the frame. These solid stable ideas were disturbed somewhat by the imbalances, inversions, and elongations of Mannerist composition. By the time Michelangelo reached the end of his four-year work on the Sistine ceiling, he had altered profoundly the relation between a figure and the space it occupied. The Prophet Jonah, the last of the series, appears too large to be contained in his niche, and presses out against the sides of his allotted space.

Such touching and pressure produce tense, exciting situations in non-objective as well as figurative art. In fact, where there is no distraction of subject matter or narrative, these situations may be even more disturbing. Paul Klee discusses such disturbances in his *Pedagogical Sketchbook*.[5] Van Doesburg also had something of this sort in mind when he introduced the diagonal and sought instability in painting.

Contemporary artists find a variety of ways of generating tensions and pressure which excite the spectator, often subtly, just as very intense color might. Among their devices are:

1. Close cropping of the format so that the picture seems squeezed in a tight fit or suggests a detail of a larger work.

2. Top-heaviness or other imbalance which seems to contradict the logic of our normal experience with gravity, vertical-horizontal references, the horizon line, space and perspective.

3. Tangential situations where shapes just touch the frame or each other.

4. Situations where shapes seem to *press* against the frame or each other.

5. Situations where masses just miss the frame or each other, leaving narrow —and therefore highly charged—gaps between.

6. Lines or contours which approach each other or the frame without making contact.

7. Squeezing of space within the picture by wedging, implication of weight, swelling, shrinking, etc.

8. Emphasis on acute angles.

9. Internal tensions where forms appear to have been pulled and stretched.

10. Interruption of linear elements or modification of other elements as lines cross them.

Such devices become a special kind of stimulus, similar to, but distinct from, optical phenomena. It is part of the developing tendency in art to activate the spectator in an immediate way. Similar tangents and tensions occur in sculpture, though more rarely. Squeezing situations tend to be hidden. If a frame or precise format is used, it becomes part of the sculpture and so pressure against it is internal. Every mature artist is aware of these situations, either avoiding or devising them. Arp was a master of them; his wife used them occasionally. A colored sheet construction of Ellsworth Kelly, meeting its curving reflection on a polished floor, gives the essence of one situation in a compound of painting and sculpture.

1. Jean Arp, *Configuration with Two Dangerous Points*, 1932. Gallatin collection, Philadelphia Museum of Art.

In Arp's *Configuration with Two Dangerous Points (Fig. 1)* the dangerous points are the points of contact; when the forms are close, there is pressure between them, increasing as the distance lessens. When they touch, the situation is suddenly altered, as with an electric contact. This in turn suggests a tense unresolved situation, an idea of forces at work—possibly anxiety. These are qualities as positive as intense color or black and white optical phenomena.

Sophie Taeuber-Arp's work links all the forms with contact of a point against a line, which has different qualities from point-to-point, curve-to-curve tangents. In her *Parasols (Fig. 2)*, the space between the forms is under pressure and is as palpable as the cut-out wood reliefs. Mortensen, in *Whale (Fig. 3)*, does not permit contact but brings points into close relation with other points or contours.

2. Sophie Taeuber-Arp, *Parasols*, 1938. Rijksmuseum Kröller-Müller, Holland.

3. Richard Mortensen, *Whale*, 1962. Galerie Denise René, Paris.

4. Max Mahlmann, *Turning Cubes*, 1959. Photo Sergej Kischnick.

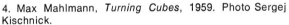

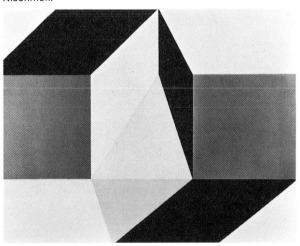

In Mahlmann's *Turning Cubes (Fig. 4)* tensions are created on the perimeter of the picture where a vertex of lines falls on the edge on each of the four sides and also on five separate points within the composition.

129

5. Victor Pasmore, *Black Development*, 1963–65. Photo John Pasmore.

6. Arturo Bonfanti, *Composition 122*, 1962. Coll. the artist.

7. Arturo Bonfanti, *Sculpture in Wood*, 1966. Coll. the artist.

8. Ellsworth Kelly, *Blue Green Red II*, 1965. Photo Geoffrey Clements.

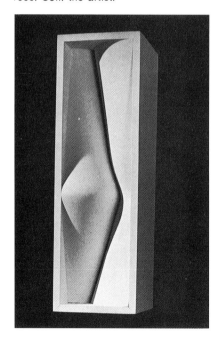

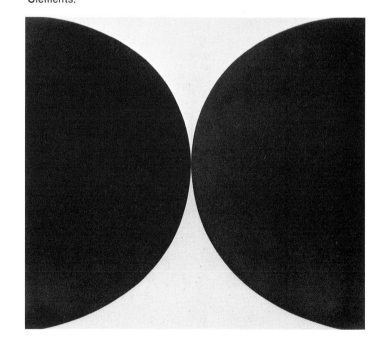

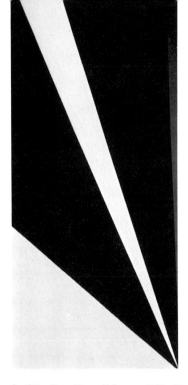

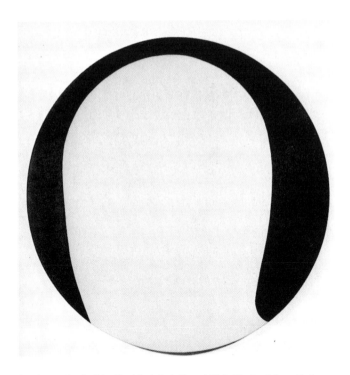

9. Olle Baertling, *Primus*, 1955. Photo Lennart Olson.

10. Leon P. Smith, *Untitled Painting*, 1954. Photo Oliver Baker Assoc.

Related to tangential situations are those where the space is squeezed. Pasmore *(Fig. 5)*, through contact of points, curves, and lines and also by a mortise and tenon alternation, compresses and energizes the white space. Bonfanti *(Fig. 6)* leans one form against another or lays one form on top of another in situations which, through close cropping, appear to be intensely magnified details of larger compositions. His *Sculpture in Wood (Fig. 7)* shows a similar situation in three dimensions. The convex and concave forms confined by the narrow box press together and squeeze out of the format. The swelling form in the center is tangent to the edge and the frontal plane. The space between the forms is under pressure and finally vanishes in the depth of the composition.

Though not preoccupied with tangential situations, Kelly's interest in form leads him to expand shapes at the expense of the surrounding space until they touch or rest on the edges of the canvas or each other *(Fig. 8)*. He does not see them extending through the limits of the canvas into the void. The pressure of the form against the edge is emphasized in shaped canvases and also in polyptychs where each form is a separate canvas. Touching goes fully into the third dimension in his cut-out forms of metal where the image is tangent to its reflection on a polished floor.

Baertling in *Primus (Fig. 9)* makes contact at the vertex of the long, narrow triangle, in situations similar to Mahlmann's, squeezing space between the lines. Leon Smith's forms derive from the interlocking design of the hidecover of a baseball. In one *(Fig. 10)* the pressure is from the outside; the other *(Fig.*

131

11) reverses it. In David Smith's *Structure (Fig. 12)*, straight lines touch the curves. Points touch each other or just cross. Space is compressed between curves and gravity is suspended.

Feitelson *(Fig. 13)* and Lundeberg *(Fig. 14)* sometimes squeeze, sometimes make contact in ambiguous situations with the convex curves pressing outward and the concave receiving the thrust. These two also imply a close-up view of a larger situation, with the action continuing beyond the picture—an idea used also in the cinema. The squares and triangles of Hill's *Low Relief Construction (Fig. 15)* are brought into the most ticklish situation possible, with the barest contact between the figures. The tension is heightened by the idea of instability and collapse. But there is reassurance in the large regular hexagonal empty spaces which repeat down the right side of the panel.

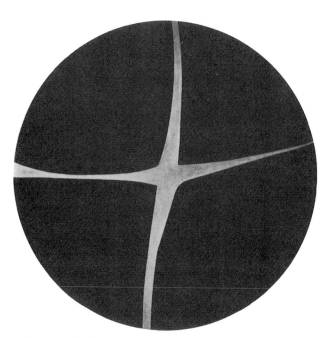

11. Leon P. Smith, *Flower Opening*, 1960. Photo Walter J. Russell.

12. David Smith, *Structure*, 1962. Coll. Estate of David Smith, courtesy Marlborough-Gerson Gallery, N.Y.

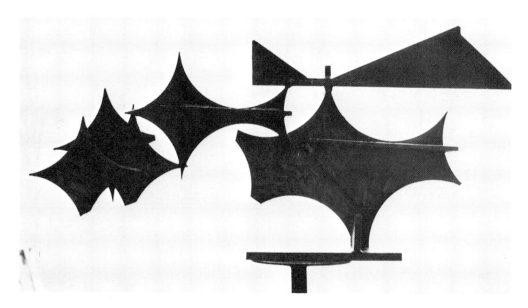

13. Lorser Feitelson, *Magical Space Forms*, 1962. Photo Lutjeans.

14. Helen Lundeberg, *Shadow of the Bridge*, 1962. Los Angeles County Museum; photo Lutjeans.

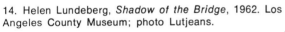

15. Anthony Hill, *Low Relief Construction*, 1955–57. Coll. the artist.

133

1. Robert Delaunay, *First Disc*, 1912. Coll. Mr. and Mrs. Burton Tremaine, Meriden, Conn.

2. Jasper Johns, *Target with Four Faces*, 1955. Museum of Modern Art, N.Y., gift of Mr. and Mrs. Robert C. Scull, N.Y.; photo Rudolph Burckhardt.

V/The Centered Image

Artists have long used very simple shapes as images, from the obelisk, the pyramid, the cylinder, the cube, the five- or six-pointed star, the hexagon and octagon in ancient art, to the cross, the post or pylon, the explosive splash, the free form, the square, in contemporary painting and sculpture. These are not only "pure" images, but they are regular and are independent of outside reference for orientation—they have no top, bottom, or side. In these images, some contemporary artists have found a hub for their painting, which will not be read from left to right like a book, or in any other ordered sequence. It can, in fact, be read from back to front or front to back along an axis at right angles to the picture plane. By their very simplicity such images, starkly placed, require contemplation.

The solitary centered image has frequently displaced the age-old compositional principle of irregular dynamic equilibrium. The image is often symmetrical. Symmetry can be seen as the most obvious platitude or as the least probable selection among infinite choices. As with ancient Stonehenge, Yang and Yin, calendar stones, rose windows, *tondi*, and shields called "targets," the greatest attraction has been the magic of the circle.

The first "centered" paintings were Delaunay's *Circular Rhythms* and *First Disc (Fig. 1)* done about 1912. His widow, Sonia, continues to work with similar motifs. Kandinsky painted the circle almost exclusively from 1923–26, and lectured on it for a year at the Bauhaus. Sophie Taeuber-Arp also was enchanted with the circle. Jasper Johns brought it abruptly into contemporary consciousness in 1957 as an anti-aesthetic gesture together with his commonplace images of flags, alphabets, and numbers *(Fig. 2)*. He did not stay with the "target" image, but, having made his hit, passed on to painterly paintings in which the geometrical images were occasionally recalled in the circles he scraped on wet paint.

Kenneth Noland, however, was the first to make the "target" his sole preoccupation, working with the same image but with a different purpose. He had seen the impact of De Kooning on New York painting and the reaction from it of Rothko, Still, and Newman. Rothko, for example, had sought containment and centering of the image, though his preoccupation with the character of the edge diminished the rhetoric of the shape. Noland devoted himself to the shape, working always with eloquent clear color. The centered image, without color, is only skeletal; the color fleshes it out and gives vitality to the flow of space forward and back. The stripes of his colleague, the late Morris Louis, were not far from the "target"—the "target" having been cut and laid out flat—Newton's color wheel in reverse. Then in 1962–63, Noland moved to the chevron image, which was still centered, still expanded in bands, still symmetrical—with the crux now at the bottom of the canvas from which it pushes and pulls at the space both within and without the picture. Albers used bilateral symmetry in his New Mexican adobe façade series of the forties *(Fig. 3)* and in his irrational space drawings *(Fig. 4)*.

It is natural to include Albers' work among the "target" paintings, for the square in its regularity is only a step removed from the circle. The square has much in common with the circle: uniformity, symmetry on four axes, possibility of repetition in widening concentric bands; both are perfect images mechanically producible (with straight edge and compass), independently of the

3. Josef Albers, *4 Greens, 2 Grays* (part of *Variants of a Theme*), 1948–55. Coll. the artist.

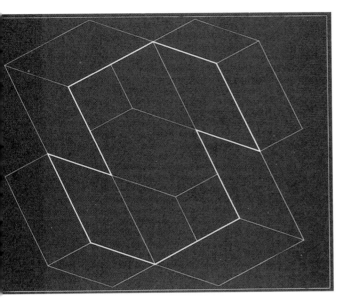

4. Josef Albers, *Structural Constellation*, 1958. Coll. the artist.

5. David Smith, *Circle, Two Legs*, 1963. Coll. Estate of David Smith, courtesy Marlborough-Gerson Gallery, N.Y.

artist's personality. Long used in decoration, they were brought into "fine art" by Malevich and Rodchenko and propagated by the Bauhaus.

In sculpture, the single simple column is an equivalent three-dimensional centered image. It presumably comes from the human image rather than from geometry. It appears in De Vries, Pomodoro, Wotruba, the *Cubi* series *(Fig. 28, p. 104)* of David Smith, and also in Diller and Glarner. Smith used a still more uncompromisingly centered image in three-dimensional space in various annular designs in flat steel *(Fig. 5)*, at their purest a simple ring on a post, but often listing asymmetrically because of arbitrary shapes in the ring or tabs tacked onto its circumference. Like Picasso, he could make a virtue out of eclecticism; there is no doubt that he was as willing to pick up ideas as he was steel scrap from the middens of his neighbors and use them with uncompromising bluntness and power. For Smith the circle could have been an *objet trouvé* picked up from Euclid, from astrologers, from traffic signs, or even from his friend Kenneth Noland.

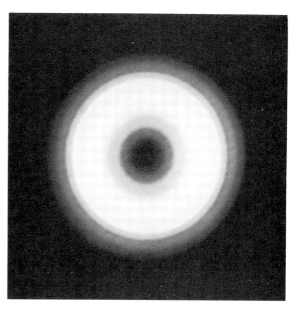

7. Peter Sedgley, *Pace*, 1966. Photo Brompton Studio.

6. Tadasky, *Untitled*, 1964. Courtesy Kootz Gallery, N.Y.

Tadasky in an untitled painting of 1964 *(Fig. 6)* employs an optical effect with an active advance and recession at right angles to the picture plane. Sedgley in *Pace (Fig. 7)* uses the circle in a journey through the spectrum and back again, unfortunately lost in black and white.

Kenneth Noland, who had begun to paint circles before Johns' "target" appeared, saw it as "corroboration." He had sought the "vacant center" after an "exploration of chaos," put the canvas on the floor to eliminate outside references to up-down, left-right, and gravity, then painted circles: "The centers are not positions but centers of pulsation." In *Rhyme (Fig. 8)* the outside edges are ragged, and edges are important to Noland; he considers them one of the deep problems in painting—"the extension of space and the energy depend on the edge." Surprisingly, Pollock

8. Kenneth Noland, *Rhyme*, 1960. Coll. Richard Brown Baker; photo courtesy André Emmerich Gallery, N.Y.

9. Richard Anuskiewicz, *The Well at the World's End*, 1961. Coll. Miss Beverly Woodner, London.

10. Kenneth Noland, *Tip*, 1961. Courtesy André Emmerich Gallery, N.Y.; photo Eric Pollitzer.

was an influence in wanting to eliminate illusion, and because his paintings seemed to turn in at the edges. Such reflections have set Noland aside from the many other users of the centered image.

The circle is not the only centered image, and one must expect departures from the circle and variations on it. Anuskiewicz's great concave illusion *(Fig. 9)* begins such a departure. It is a complex painting, combining play with

139

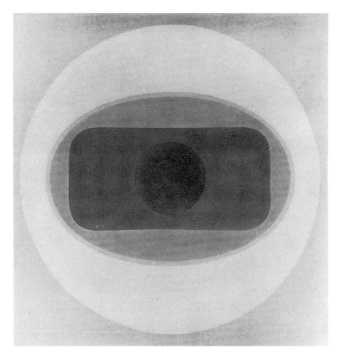

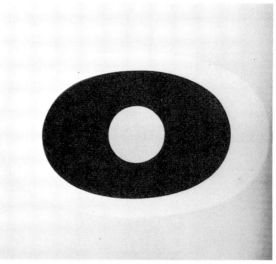

12. Kenneth Noland, *Lebron*, 1961–62. Coll. Prof. William S. Rubin; photo John F. Waggaman.

11. Kenneth Noland, *Hover*, 1962. Fogg Art Museum, Harvard Univ., Louise E. Bettens Fund Purchase; photo John F. Waggaman.

space with optical phenomena. Noland himself in his 1961–62 paintings *(Figs. 10–12)* moves into the ellipse and a suggestion of the swastika.

Noland goes on to chevrons and a full canvas in 1962. In dispensing with the neutral space around the image, he loses the important edge. The canvas now has a strong vertical orientation and the axis perpendicular to the canvas is lost, as in *Blue-Green Confluence (Fig. 13)*, where the color harmonies are subtle

and have a moodiness which contrasts the vigor of the geometric design. In *Let Up (Fig. 14)*, the rhomboid shape can be seen as half a chevron or a simple segment of a stripe motif, in which the value gradation of the stripes produces the illusion, in each one, of a concave surface.

Grosvenor's *Transoxiana (Fig. 15)* is probably the largest chevron in the world. It has other qualities besides size. It emphasizes the basic character of the chevron emblem, which

13. Kenneth Noland, *Blue-Green Confluence*, 1963.
Coll. Mr. S. I. Newhouse, Jr.; photo Eric Pollitzer.

14. Kenneth Noland, *Let Up*, 1966. Courtesy André
Emmerich Gallery, N.Y.; photo Geoffrey Clements.

15. Robert Grosvenor, *Transoxiana*, 1965. Courtesy Park Place Gallery, N.Y.; photo
Geoffrey Clements.

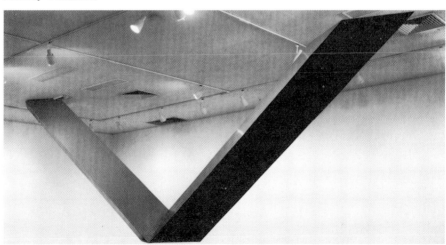

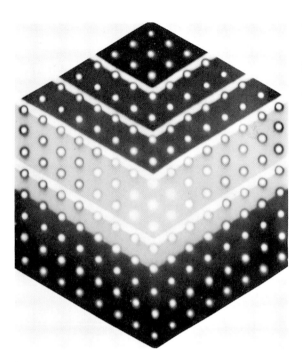

17. Josef Albers, *Far Off*, 1958. Courtesy Sidney Janis Gallery, N.Y.

18. Frank Stella, *Cato Manor*, 1962. Coll. Ferus Gallery; photo Rudolph Burckhardt.

16. Peter Sedgley, *Tilt*, 1965. Photo courtesy Brompton Studio.

derives from rafters. Cantilevered from one end, it floats in space. *Tilt (Fig. 16)* by Sedgley, superimposes optical effects on a centered chevron design, tied by the title to the illumination of pin-ball machines.

Like Noland's "target," Albers' square *(Fig. 17)* is a catalytic agent for energizing space, isolating and containing color. With this un-

20. Richard Anuskiewicz, *Knowledge and Disappearance*, 1961. Coll. Warren D. Benedek; photo O. E. Nelson.

19. Frank Stella, *Marrakech*, 1964. Coll. Mr. and Mrs. Robert C. Scull, N.Y.; photo Rudolph Burckhardt.

changing format, Albers says he is at last free from the problems of composition and can speak with color only. Stella has various forms, and these two, *Cato Manor (Fig. 18)* and *Marrakech (Fig. 19)*, are square and square transposed. If each segment of *Marrakech* is turned 90°, it becomes concentric squares.

Anuskiewicz's *Knowledge and Disappearance (Fig. 20)* combines inescapable illusionism (as Bridget Riley sometimes does to create a forced recession) with a space axis perpendicular to the canvas, micro-elements, and optical phenomena. These three conspire to build up a power effect, but with great prodigality of means.

VI/Mathematics and Concrete Art

Thomas Hobbes, born the year of the Spanish Armada, who later was to see Galileo and to know Descartes, loved mathematics at first sight:

> He was forty years old before he looked on geometry which happened accidentally: being in a gentleman's library Euclid's *Elements* lay open, and it was the 47th Proposition, Lib. I. So he reads the proposition. "By God," says he, "this is impossible." So he reads the demonstration of it, which referred him back to another which he also read, *et sic deinceps*, that at last he was demonstratively convinced of that truth. This made him in love with geometry.[6]

Hobbes went on to apply mathematical principles to politics as some contemporary artists have to aesthetics. He proposed an irrevocable contract with the sovereign Leviathan, who would then give man security by leading him out of the "state of nature," where otherwise his life would be "solitary, poor, nasty, brutish, and short."

Some artists have sought, in the authority and order of mathematical laws, a similar relief from the responsibilities of personal freedom. Instead of deciding how to put a painting together, the artist submits it to a mathematical formula, which he then obediently carries out. Mathematics is to be found not only in the candid squares and circles of Malevich and Herbin, and the ruler and compass drawings of Rodchenko, but in hidden plots in the pyramids, in the ground plans of Gothic cathedrals, in the "golden section" of the Greeks, and in Hambidges' revelations of "dynamic symmetry." However, the use of a square (intuitively selected and placed) as image differs in kind from a mathematical scheme for the entire order of a composition. Such schemes are as much a part of the Constructivist heritage as the geometrical images. They are hinted in Pevsner's developable surfaces and appeared very early in the work of Vantongerloo, who wrote:

> We see then that we may construct a work of art with the given of geometry. . . . There is no need to express art in terms of nature. It can perfectly well be expressed in terms of geometry and the exact sciences.[7]

While Mondrian was seeking an equilibrium in precisely adjusted relations, Vantongerloo sought mathematical relations which could be translated whole into

1. Georges Vantongerloo, *No. 89 Y = X⁴ − 11X² + 10*, 1935. Photo courtesy Max Bill.

2. Antoine Pevsner, *Developable Column*, 1942. Museum of Modern Art, N.Y.

visual equivalents and, if complex enough, could be considered art *(Fig. 1)*. His explanation began thus: there is a difference between ratio and proportion—x:y is a ratio; x:y = a:b is proportion. One must have comparable ratios in order to have proportion. One must have proportion to have art. "The pyramid . . . is not a work of sculpture but . . . a pure crystal."[8]

By Vantongerloo's canon, Max Bill's "concrete" works (*Harmony 1:2:3, Compression 4:3:2:1, Hexagonal Surface in Space with Complete Circumference, Integration of Four Similar Color Pairs*), with their related proportions, would then be considered sculpture, but his Moebius strip would be merely another "pure crystal." Bill, however, would not allow such a distinction. He has been the intellectual leader in the movement in design to substitute mathematical reasoning for human imagination. In his work as painter and sculptor, quite apart from his writing, such crystals as Vantongerloo's pyramid are raised to the status of works of art. Bill sees mimetic art including Cubism, as van Doesburg did, to be anarchical and chaotic; and he would apply this to Constructivism also. Instead of intuition in art, he would have mathematical order, and he looks to mathematics to provide the content of the work.

> I am of the opinion that it is possible to develop an art which is fundamentally based on a mathematical approach. . . . The primordial element of all visual art is geo-metry, the correlations of the divisions on a plane-surface or in space. . . . The mathematical approach in contemporary art is not mathematics in itself and hardly makes any use of what is known as exact mathematics. It is primarily a use of processes of logical thought towards the plastic expression of rhythms and relationships. . . .[9]

While Bill argues for mathematics as "power," as authority, his compatriot and elder, Richard Lohse, also from Zürich, uses mathematical ratios in a less doctrinaire way to establish rhythmic proportions in an otherwise intuitive and lyrical situation. His preset proportions seem to be a catalyst rather than a source of power, and he writes: "An impersonal medium is the primary condition for full and varied development." For Lohse, the work of art is a complex of "logical sequences" with an "endless series simultaneously controlled"; "form is anonymous." He continues, "This form of art can be called Constructive in the widest connotation of the word" and (echoing Russian ideologies of 1917) "is a democratic art." The extension from early Constructivism lies in measuring and controlling the elements of the design in a mathematical order which "objectifies the components." Preconception is complete; there is no invention, selection or adjustment once the painting is launched. "The elements of the picture can no longer be evolved in the course of the work but for themselves constitute the genesis of the picture. . . . Method is unvariable. . . . Method is the picture."[10] Lohse's long titles describe the method.

A third Zürich artist, Camille Graeser, had been associated with Sophie Taeuber-Arp, who taught in Zürich and died there, and with van Doesburg. He later came into contact with Max Bill and in the fifties introduced deliberate mathematical content with such titles as *3e—2e* into his painting.

Permutations and systematic combinations can give the illusion of freedom and invention to what is actually submission to narrow rules. Some of Albers' students at Yale became preoccupied with explorations of series based on simple graphs, so dutifully adhered to that no room was left for the infinite variation and combination which Lohse felt was necessary. The Yale studies were developments in the tradition of Pevsner, with good understanding of material and craftsmanship, but less intuition, and with a helpless dependence on the formula. Though Pevsner made curves in his *Developable Column (Fig. 2)* by piling up straight lines, his choice of curves was intuitive, and he denied a direct mathematical borrowing.

Artists who employ mathematical relationships in the organization of their work have spoken of the beauty and interest of mathematical models but at the same time have disavowed them, asserting that they are not influenced by mathematics. "If I paint a problem in physics, I shall violate the plastic principle as much as if I had painted a story."[11]

The dilemma between the mathematical model as image—whether a square or a hyperbolic paraboloid—and mathematical thought as process continues among younger artists. The former appears in so-called "primary" structures, the latter in the diagrammed compositions of Riley and Poons. Both are extensions, yet, at the same time, dilutions of Bill's concept of Concrete Art. Joost Baljeu writes:

> The question left unanswered was whether an art using pure plastic means is based on environmental reality or whether its stimulus is to be found in the geometric character of these very means. . . the problem results in two distinct approaches: the one trying to extend the understanding of visible reality through pure plastic means (the heritage of Mondrian), the other developing the pure plastic means via a scientific translation of reality (mathematics, arithmetics, statistics and so on). . . .[12]

The whole purpose of mathematics as determinant may be self-defeating. Lohse's painting seems rich, almost lush; he is a lyrical painter for whom numbers are a catalyst. Bill's painting is exquisitely finished, yet it renounces grace and sensitivity. It is in sculpture that his ideas, carried out against the resistance of stone, have grandeur. No matter how determined the self-effacement, therefore, the character of the artist emerges.

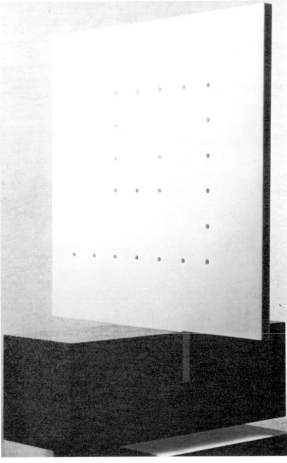

3. Georges Vantongerloo, $x^2+3x+10=y$, 1934. Coll. The Lillian H. Florsheim Foundation for Fine Arts, Chicago, Ill.

4. Max Bill, *Twenty-two*, 1953. Coll. The J. L. Hudson Gallery, Detroit, Mich.; photo courtesy Staempfli Gallery, N.Y.

In $x^2+3x+10=y$ *(Fig. 3)* an ordinary quadratic equation provides the theme and the proportion. The way these are applied, however, are the invention of the artist.

Of "the mystery of mathematical problems . . . the square in all its stability . . ." Max Bill writes, "these phenomena . . . are not formalism, for which they are often mistaken; they are not only form signifying beauty, but thought, idea, cognition transmuted into form. . . . They pertain to the structures of the world-order and are part of that overall picture . . . this is not mimeticism but a new system conveying elementary powers in a way which renders them perceptible through the senses."[13]

Bill's *Twenty-two (Fig. 4)* contains just that number of holes drilled in the marble slab.

5. Max Bill, *Endless Loop I*, 1947–49. The Joseph H. Hirshhorn collection; photo courtesy Staempfli Gallery, N.Y.

6. Max Bill, *Construction With and Within a Cube*, 1960. Coll. Mr. and Mrs. Julius Epstein; photo John D. Schiff, courtesy Staempfli Gallery, N.Y.

They make a spiral like a Greek fret and are placed so that they suggest but do not quite correspond to the ancient "golden section" or "divine proportion." The proportions are not those of a logarithmic spiral, but are based on a 1:2:3:4:5:6 relationship of spaces on each leg of the spiral. His *Endless Loop I (Fig. 5)* is a variation on the topological figure called Moebius strip, a paradox which, mathematically, has only one surface and one edge. *Construction With and Within a Cube (Fig. 6)* is a precise and full description.

Although Bill's influence is most apparent in Switzerland, it was effective earlier in South America, where several talents were receptive enough to learn from him but strong enough to remain independent. Mary Vieira, however, remained obedient. The parts of her *Square+ Movement=Space 1/3 (Fig. 7)* in stainless steel are movable and virtually carry out the equation of her title.

150

7. Mary Vieira, *Square+Movement=Space I/3*, 1953–58. Coll. Galerie Denise René, Paris; photo Peter Heman.

9. William Reimann, *Orb*, 1963. De Cordova Museum, Lincoln, Mass.

8. Karl Gerstner, *Carro 64*, 1956–61. Coll. the artist.

Gerstner uses, for almost infinite and random diversity, the permutation of a few very simple elements. His *Carro 64 (Fig. 8)* is a permutable painting consisting of sixty-four cubes (forming a square) locked in a frame, which differ in color. The spectator may unlock the frame, redistribute the cubes and lock them up again; the work is thus based partly on the permutations he permits, and partly in each instance on the combination the spectator chooses.

Max Bill was a student of Albers at the Bauhaus. Progression and permutation of fixed or systematically developing elements interested both. It would be natural to find ideas consonant with Bill's among Albers' students in America. Some have digested and developed Concretist ideas quite exhaustively, as for example, William Reimann *(Fig. 9)*, and

151

10. Deborah de Moulpied, *Palamos*, 1965–66. Photo Sybil Wilson.

11. Erwin Hauer, *23 x 32*, 1958. Coll. the artist.

Deborah de Moulpied *(Fig. 10)*. The aluminum forging of Hauer *(Fig. 11)*, composed of uniform repeating elements of this twisted form becomes a relief surface of circles in two sizes, octagons, and Maltese crosses, much as Arab craftsmen had done in wood and plaster five centuries earlier. Carlberg in *Variations, Module #1 (Figs. 12–14)* uses identical elements assembled in different ways to produce differently repeating cellular structures.

152

12. Norman Carlberg, *Module #1*, 1957. Coll. the artist.

13. Norman Carlberg, *Variation A, Module #1*, 1957. Coll. the artist.

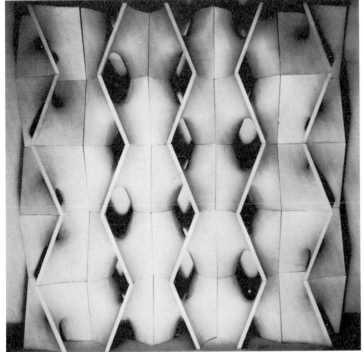

14. Norman Carlberg, *Variation B, Module #1*, 1957. Coll. the artist.

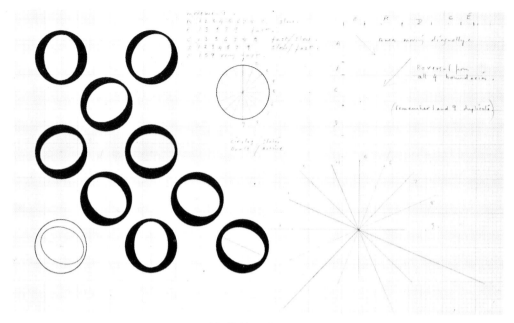

15. Bridget Riley, *a working drawing*, 1964. Photo courtesy Richard Feigen Gallery, N.Y.

Both Poons and Riley lay out grids for the distribution of their spots or stripes or dots, which are based on precise mathematic intervals and rotations, as these working diagrams show. In Riley's drawing *(Fig. 15)*, these are not the letter O, but an ellipse rotating on its axes inside a circle. She plans nine positions and also advances along the diagonals. Poons plans the distribution and posture of his dots in the most careful way *(Fig. 16)*. On a prearranged grid he advanced and rotated the constellation of dots in a strict system sufficiently complex to convince the spectator that the system was random rather than controlled and systematic.

Lippold: "Obviously it is to space that I have given most of my heart" (Lecture, Arts Club of Chicago, 1953). In his detail of the working drawing for the bronze and stainless steel sculpture *(Fig. 17)*, executed for The Four Seasons restaurant in the Seagram Building, each rod is precisely positioned on a grid with the sequences running diagonally, according to the length of the rods, as they hang from the ceiling.

16. Larry Poons, *Untitled pencil drawing*, 1964. Coll. Mr. and Mrs. Robert A. Rowan, Pasadena, Calif.

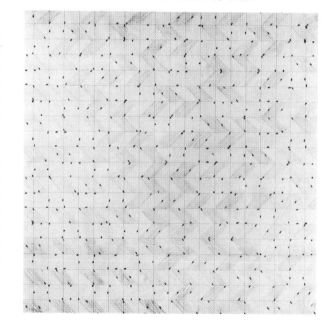

18. Richard Lohse, *Progressively gradated groups with the same number of colours, 1955/57/III.* Coll. the artist.

Although they do not subscribe wholeheartedly to Bill's theories, Lohse and Graeser are both concerned with mathematical relationships. A complete explanation is contained in the lengthy title of Lohse's *Progressively gradated groups with the same number of colours 1955/57/III, 50x50 cm.* (Fig. 18)

Colours: yellow, red, pale blue, blue, orange, green, violet, black, white.

The structural basis consists of nine vertical bands progressing from left to right in continuously diminishing progression. Two symmetrically equal group gradations run from top and bottom left, progressively increasing and diminishing as far as the fifth band, there combining in a square in order to move further in a symmetrical diminishing progression towards the two squares at top and bottom right. The basic colour motif is stated by the central group which crosses the square in the fifth band. Both group gradations above and below have the same number of colours as those of the central group.

155

Thirty systematically arranged rows of colour tones 1950/55, 60x60 cm. (Fig. 19)

Colours: gradated tones of the primaries yellow, red, and blue.

In contrast to "Systematically arranged rows of colour in fifteen repeated tones 1950/54" the formal and colour organization is here determined by the last row on the right. The precondition is that all thirty colours with their nine hundred locations are harmoniously related in each configuration.

This system has the possibility of unlimited variations each of which permits of a new formal and chromatic composition.

Graeser's *Energy in the Row (Fig. 20)* is made up of three T-forms of decreasing size, each has a vertical shank in black; the first has a red horizontal bar on the left, and blue (passing under the white) on the right; the second, in exactly the same proportions, has the bar under the white on the left, starts as red on the right and passes under the white; the smallest T is then easily discerned on the far right. These T-forms create an equilibrium of vertical and horizontal emphases against a yellow ground. The two white squares are neutral and are balanced against the large yellow square at the lower left, the squares increasing in size from right to left just as the T-forms have.

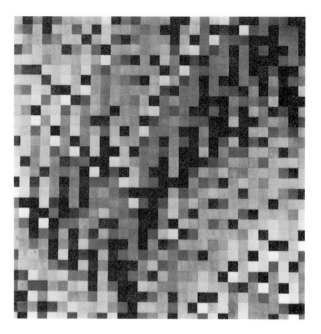

19. Richard Lohse, *Thirty systematically arranged rows of colour tones 1950/55.* Coll. the artist.

20. Camille Graeser, *Energy in the Row,* 1952. Coll. the artist.

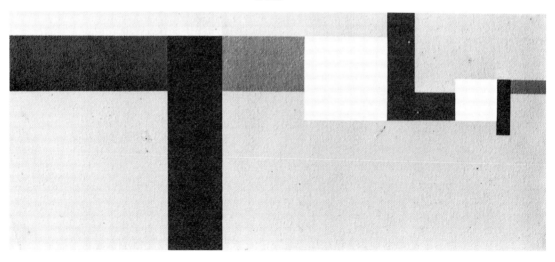

VII/Chance

Chance is an elusive concept. It has other names—luck, hazard, accident, risk, and even fate (which can be thought of as the opposite of chance). It is related to probability but it can also mean the improbable. In nature's order, much is arranged by chance, and it has its own laws—for example, "normal distribution" —in which normality *is* pure randomness, meaning without interference. Such randomness without interference now serves the artist.

The early Constructivist spurned chance. He would have resented its invasion of his design and its subversion of his complete control. Yet there is a way of allowing chance to participate, of planning hazard, of granting a limited autonomy to fortune. Chance, planned or allowed and not interfered with, supports the idea of impersonality. With the reaction against Action Painting and Tachism —the most personality oriented forms of art we have ever had—the elimination of the personality of the artist becomes an artistic objective. Natural phenomena replace composition; chance replaces free will; chance is a manifestation of natural law. Decisions as to form, as to the disposition of components, even the choice of hue and placement of color, can be put by the artist outside his authority and personal preference, and submitted to that other law. Abdicating authority in favor of chance, he can choose not to choose.

This kind of delegation to chance appeared as early as 1915 in the non-objective work of Jean Arp (he had by this time met Kandinsky who was seeking non-objectivity in a different direction)—collages made by letting scraps of torn paper fall onto a surface, to be glued down where they lay.

Recently, chance has become a determinant in more concise ways, as in a "graph paper" painting of Morellet where "the principle of the picture in blue and red squares is probability: 50% red squares, 50% blue of the same intensity are unequally distributed over the surface by a combination based on chance." He gave to each color an even or uneven number, and their distribution was determined by the numbers arrived at by chance in the telephone book. Ellsworth Kelly, who removes from his image the recollection of the observed phenomenon from which it came, was at one time also interested in letting chance determine the placement of elements in certain paintings, set up like a graph; the number of squares at a certain point on the Y axis was determined by him, their position on the X axis by chance.

While the most obvious manifestation of chance is kinetic art where, as parts move, any instant gives a unique set of formal associations, it can become a factor also in stationary art. The observer can be made the instrument through which chance asserts itself, either by giving him components to rearrange as he wishes, or possibly by using the observer's voice or his mere presence as a signal to be amplified and fed into a kinetic work.

The participation of chance has fascinated many artists who have welcomed the richness of disorder and recognized, like Arp, that random processes are but another instance of order. Just as laws of probability make a predictable order out of chance, so the laws of chance can provide for the artist a visual order completely independent of either imitation of nature or the limitation and bias of his own invention. Herman de Vries seeks this kind of order; and von Graevenitz builds a kind of roulette into the rotating micro-elements of his panels. The wind does it for Le Parc's suspended squares. A planned disorder appears in another form in Megert's assemblages of fractured mirrors, which reflect disjointed segments of the environment of the enormous room, and set the stage for an unpredictable plot.

The use of chance recasts the artist in the role of stage manager for a play in search of an author. Chance itself then becomes both the subject of the work and the means.

1. Jean Arp, *Collage with Squares Arranged According to the Law of Chance*, 1916–17. Museum of Modern Art, N.Y.

Of such works *(Fig. 1)*, Arp has said:

In 1915 Sophie Taeuber and I made the first objects in paint, embroidery, and glued paper, derived from the simplest of forms. They are probably the first manifestation of that sort. These pictures are *"Réalités"* in themselves without cerebral significance or intention. We rejected anything that was copied or descriptive in order to allow the "Basic" and the "Spontaneous" to react in full freedom. Since the arrangement of the design, the proportion of these designs and their colors seemed to depend only on chance, I declared that these works were offered "according to the laws of chance," just as in nature, chance seemed to me only a limited part of a requirement to be inscrutable, to have their makeup undecipherable.[14]

159

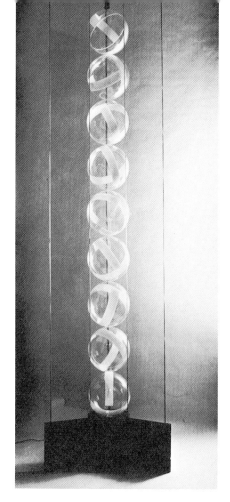

2. Bruno Munari, *Nine Spheres in a Column*, 1962. Coll. Olivetti; photo Mulas.

Munari's *Nine Spheres in a Column (Fig. 2)* are rotated in random directions by a motor from the bottom, thereafter by friction. The bands on the spheres make the motion legible.

Stimulus for this painting *(Fig. 3)* was a street light reflection on the river Seine in which the image, though denser at the center, appeared to be splintered at random by the wavelets. In order to paint this without subjective interpretation, Kelly divided the painting surface into forty equal parts vertically and eighty horizontally, and numbered this grid. Forty pieces of paper, were placed in a box. Beginning with the left vertical column, one number was drawn from the box and marked to be painted black; the number then was returned to the box. Next, two numbers were drawn from the box for the second column; then three numbers for the third column and so on until all forty units (at the middle of the painting) were all black. This was then repeated beginning at the extreme right veritcal column, working toward the center. Thus Kelly planned an image whose detailed configuration lay outside his control and contained no interpretive bias. *Seine* is a work that moves

3. Ellsworth Kelly, *Seine*, 1951. Coll. the artist.

from white to black to white in one direction only: horizontally, and represents only a slice of the light reflection. Later Kelly made works in which the black was centered and moved to white in all directions.

Herman de Vries' *Random Objectivation with Decreasing Density (Fig. 4)* and *Random Objectivation (Fig. 5)* were "based on statistical tables for agricultural, biological, and medical research."

Objectification is important as part of my occupation with "visual information" . . . the term more appropriate to the new conception than

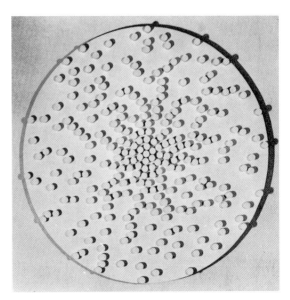

4. Herman de Vries, *Random Objectivation with Decreasing Density*, 1965. Coll. A. Blumenthal, Baltimore, Md.

5. Herman de Vries, *Random Objectivation*, 1963. Coll. the artist.

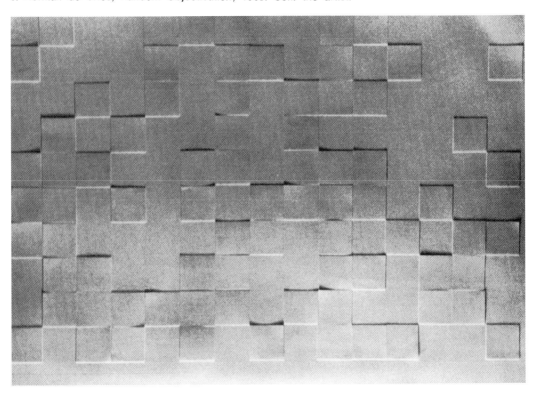

the term "art." As an extreme consequence of my objectification I tried to eliminate the personal—not the human!—... by way of the random method. [He then describes a method of choosing random numbers where the digits are distributed in their "probable" frequency and goes on]... I gave a "value" to each digit... a colour, gluing on a square or leaving it out and, in this way I obtained results which were acceptable for the spectator and gave the impression that they were intended as art. ... all compositions are of equal quality if they are sufficiently large, i.e., made with more than 20 or 30 numbers. The "random objectifications" ... I started in 1962. ... The choice of the depersonalized act is as important as the creative act itself.[15]

"Programmed art" is an Italian phrase describing motor-driven kinetic works which follow a predesigned sequence—a composition in time, like music. Random factors can be built into the program as in Mari's *Ogetto a Composizione Autocondotta No. 748 (Fig. 6a & b)* where the rotation is preset, the tumbling of the blocks is random. Colombo's *Floating Structuration (Fig. 7)* is an endless plastic ribbon pushed up into a space confined between two glass plates, where it is convoluted into an infinitely diversified design; the feed is constant, the form is random.

6a & b. Enzo Mari, *Ogetto a Composizione Autocondotta No. 748*, 1959–64. Coll. the artist.

7. Gianni Colombo, *Floating Structuration*, 1961. Coll. the artist.

  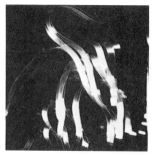 

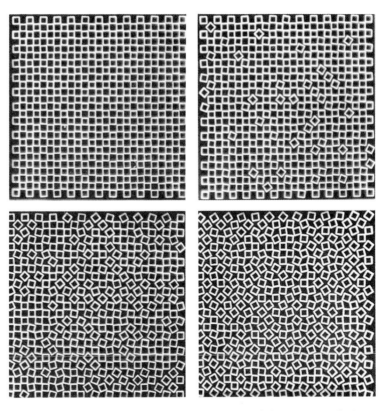

8. Gerhard von Graevenitz, *Regularité-Irregularité V*, 1962–63. Coll. the artist.

9. Gerhard von Graevenitz, *Object with White Moving Discs*, 1965. Photo courtesy University Art Museum, Univ. of Calif., Berkeley.

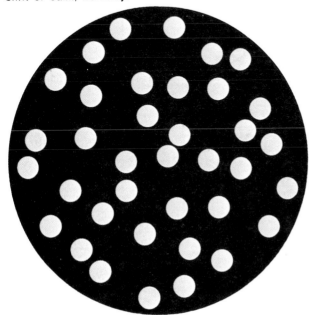

Von Graevenitz says, of his *Regularité-Irregularité V (Fig. 8)*: "There is no 'normal' condition because there are so many elements and each element in varying positions, so the arrangements are innumerable and complex. Because the human memory is not good enough to remember a certain arrangement, the movement seems to the spectator unpredictable." His *Object with White Moving Discs (Fig. 9)* also rotates slowly; at the same time, each circle rotates about a point very close to its circumference, giving the illusion that the white circles are being displaced in random fashion across the black surface.

163

10. Bruno Munari, *Articulated Sculpture*, 1960. Coll. the artist.

11. Dieter Hacker, *Eat Picture*, 1965. Coll. the artist.

Redistribution of parts can renew a work which is stationary between movements. Chance leaves, after each adjustment, a new variation within the theme—a found situation instead of a found object. Sometimes chance intervenes through the movement of the spectator himself. This had always been present in walking by or through sculpture, architecture, parks, or natural landscape, but here is the result of his direct intervention in the redistribution of parts.

164

12. Yasuhide Kobashi, *Colony VI*, 1961. Courtesy Allan Stone Gallery, N.Y.; photo Rudolph Burckhardt.

13. Karl Gerstner, *No. 10*, 1963–64. Coll. the artist.

Munari in *Articulated Sculpture (Fig. 10)* constructed interlocking angles of metal so articulated that every time the object is picked up and set down, its configuration will be different. Hacker's *Eat Picture (Fig. 11)* is subtractive—the observer consumes the peppermint and chocolate tablets. In this work of Kobashi *(Fig. 12)* the perforated wooden elements are moved back and forth on the horizontal wires to create a three-dimensional structure according to the wish of the spectator.

In Gerstner's *No. 10 (Fig. 13)* a plastic lens of a special conformation comes between the spectator and a striped pattern. Violent distortions of the stripes result and these change widely with very slight movement of the spectator's head.

165

Talman's *Untitled work (Fig. 14)* is composed of partly painted spheres that can be rotated to all white, all dark, or any distribution between. The fifteen elements in Agam's *Transformable Painting (Fig. 15a & b)* may be plugged into any of the six hundred and twenty-one holes. The spectator chooses his own composition among the millions of permutations, of which the artist will have seen very few.

Transformable paintings are works which can undergo a number of successive transformations by . . . transplantation of various pictorial elements, or rotation . . . on an axis. . . . Certain contemporary scientific philosophical approaches have a close affinity with the attitudes and convictions which underlie Agam's creative work. For example, Heisenberg's postulations of indeterminacy, i.e. that it is impossible to measure at the same time the speed and the mass of a particle, presupposes that the habitual ways in which we describe reality rest on the insecure foundations of hints and appearances.[16]

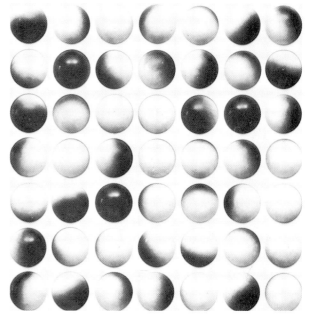

14. Paul Talman, *Untitled work*, 1964. Courtesy Byron Gallery, N.Y.

15a & b. Yaacov Agam, *Transformable Painting*, 1963. Photo Marc Vaux.

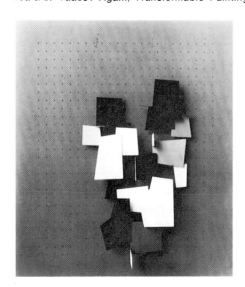

VIII/Micro-Elements

Since Plato there has been a widely accepted idea that a work of art should be *one*. Even if subdivided, the harmony of the parts should be directed toward unity of the whole. In the twentieth century hints of a nonunified art began to appear quite early, for example, in Balla's *Iridescent Interpenetration (Fig. 12, p. 15)* and in the Rayonnist paintings in Russia. Some paintings of van Doesburg and Sophie Taeuber-Arp were cellular rather than architectonic, while the anticompositional ideas of Strzeminski were perhaps the most radical departure of all.

It was not until after the Second World War, however, that one found a conscious philosophy, among numerous artists, of an art based on repetition. Overall division of the surface appeared in the calligraphy of Klee and André Masson. Dubuffet made formless, granular surfaces the outstanding characteristic of his "texturologies" of 1957, though doubtful or nebulous images were allowed to show through the surface or to be suggested by it. Similarly, in Mark Tobey's white writings and knitted lines, there could be seen landscapes and the ruins of ancient empires; in Pollock's web of repetitious accidents and controlled variation in density and color appear emblems like the *Blue Poles*. Deliberately uniform cellular structures, however, often in black and white or monochrome, often geometrically arrived at, began to appear in the fifties in several parts of Europe simultaneously. Their homogeneity extended further the "no personal handwriting" principle of Constructivism; composition could be dismissed as a personal gesture like a signature, merely writ larger and sustained longer, while a cellular surface was anonymous.

Use of these subdivisions or "micro-elements" involves the following:

1. Subdivision into units large enough to be separately identified.

2. Units small enough and numerous enough to appear "countless." (If too small they become *texture* and the balance between the one and the many is lost.)

3. Enough uniformity to make a generally homogeneous surface or mass.

4. Positive-negative interlock or interchange of figure-ground or volume-void.

5. In sculpture, space used as a plastic material.

6. In painting and relief sculpture, the picture or panel is a segment of a continuum; any other segment would do as well.

This repetitiveness, with its implicit conflict between individualism and uniformity, is old in art as it is in society, but it takes on a special appositeness today. Repetition has ceased to be an embarrassment for the artist. With the example of the scientist beside him, the artist can advance from one work to the next in small steps, exploring exhaustively the behavior of his motif under slightly altered conditions. Within the work, the piling-up of identical elements can produce a cumulative effect which, as with a choir, is more than the sum of its parts.

The hints of social symbolism are inescapable, though none of these artists is consciously concerned with it and none of these images is a diagram of society. But just as analogies with nature are apparent in non-objective art, so the use of micro-elements gives a special significance to the creation and control of the "innumerable" elsewhere. This art suggests comparison with monolithic states, the balance between the individual and the majority, the anonymity of the "one" in the modern state, the relation of the solitary artist to his seething environment, and his search for identity. It is not coincidence, therefore, that so many sculptures of Kemeny look like cities, though whether it is his thought or ours is impossible to tell. The painstaking addition of unit to unit or, conversely, the piecemeal separation of part from part, slowly takes on monumental and even universal significance.

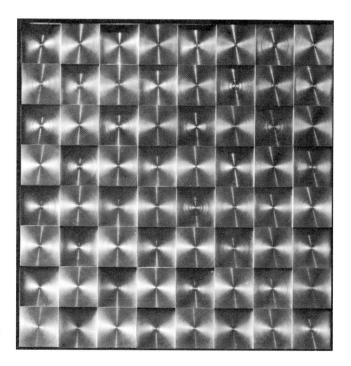

1. Karl Gerstner, *64 Squares*, 1962. Coll. the artist.

2. Yvaral, *Accélération Optique*, 1962. Coll. The Contemporaries Gal., N.Y.

3. Joel Stein, *Reseau de Réflexion*, 1963. Coll. the artist.

4. Dieter Hacker, *Cubes*, 1963. Coll. the artist.

The square format is arbitrary and neutral —an impersonal and insignificant container for the cell. It is the repetition within the square which is the essence of the statement. With absolutely uniform means, variety in sameness appears: in Gerstner's *64 Squares (Fig. 1)* the light rays on the machined surface change their angle according to the relation of the square to the light source; in Yvaral's *Accélération Optique (Fig. 2)* and Stein's *Reseau de Réflexion (Fig. 3)* a similar deviation results from light falling on strings and metal ribs; in the *Cubes (Fig. 4)* of Hacker, the artist rotates the cube into its four positions and

169

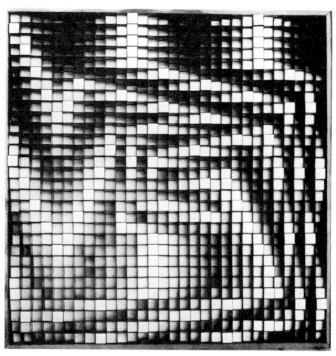

5. Luis Tomasello, *Réflexion No. 83*, 1961. Coll. Mr. and Mrs. Henry A. Markus, Chicago, Ill.

6. Enzo Mari, *Struttura No. 729*, 1963. Coll. the artist.

also makes each cube reversible; Tomasello uses identical cubes in *Réflexion No. 83 (Fig. 5)* but changes their angle of reflection in a regular way, to produce subsquares (also the underside of each cube is colored brightly so that each white projection is surrounded by a halo of reflected color). Mari in *Struttura No. 729 (Fig. 6)* secures variety by raising or lowering the floor of each cell in a systematic way —so that it receives more or less light from above. The light-dark variations produce a secondary image similar to moiré, but by different means.

In these reliefs each artist raises and lowers the surface in a regular way to gain or lose light. The elements do not vary; only their relation to light does. Reinhartz does this in *63/2 (Fig. 7)* with raised squares whose edges are brightly colored. The movement of the spectator broadens or narrows the zigzag band. Even when he cannot see the band, the raised surfaces will reflect some of its color. Von Graevenitz in his 1962 panel *(Fig. 8)* alternates convex and concave hemispheres in cast plaster. Castellani does the equivalent on his *Beige Surface (Fig. 9)* with cloth stretched

170

7. Karl Reinhartz, *63/2*, 1964. Coll. the artist.

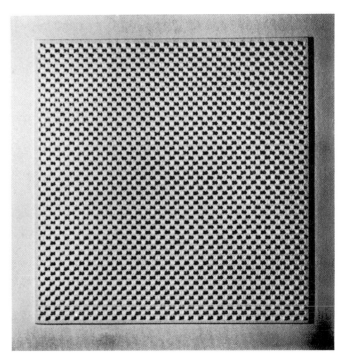

8. Gerhard von Graevenitz, *Untitled*, 1962. Coll. the artist.

9. Enrico Castellani, *Beige Surface*, 1961. Coll. Galleria dell'Ariete, Milan.

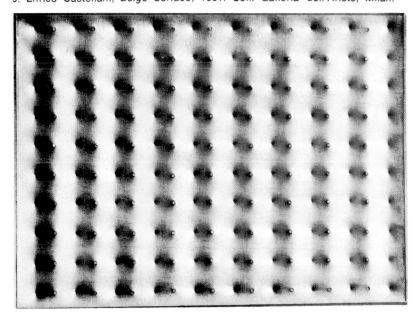

10. Luis Tomasello, *Atmosphère Chromoplastique No. 134*, 1964. Coll. Galerie Denise René, Paris.

11. Günther Uecker, *Light Forest (detail)*, 1959. Photo Reiner Ruthenbeck.

12. Günther Uecker, *White Cloud*, 1964. Coll. Howard Wise Gallery, N.Y.; photo Ulrich.

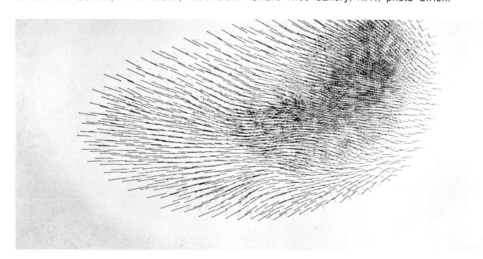

13. Yasuhide Kobashi, *Colony XXVII*, 1963. Coll. Allan Stone Gallery, N.Y.; photo Rudolph Burckhardt.

over protruding rods and nailed down between the rows. Tomasello in *Atmosphère Chromoplastique No. 134 (Fig. 10)* secures a rich result simply from slicing each cylindrical knob at 45°. The regular placement of these oblique surfaces gives the secondary light-dark check.

Uecker's nails are driven uniformly in *Light Forest (Fig. 11)* yet not with absolute regularity—they have the homogeneity of a dense growth in nature. Like a forest, the nail heads produce a new surface which floats above the solid surface. In *White Cloud (Fig. 12)*, the density varies from crowded to sparse to empty, in an analogy, but not imitation, of varying distributions in nature.

In *Colony XXVII (Fig. 13)* Kobashi builds a comparable mass from innumerable ceram-

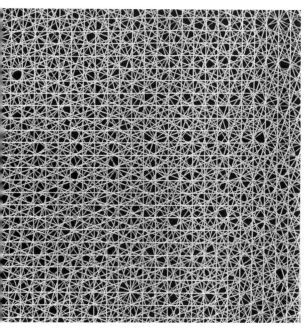

14. François Morellet, *Grillage 0°-18°-36°-54°-72°*, 1961. Coll. the artist.

15. Helge Sommerrock, *I/3*, 1962. Coll. the artist.

ic cylinders. Morellet in *Grillage 0°–18°–36°–54°–72° (Fig. 14)* and Sommerrock in *I/3 (Fig. 15)* arrive more mechanically at their distribution, the former by placing layers of metal mesh on one another, each with its axis turned, and the latter by dividing the surface into squares and diagonals and then coloring the resultant triangles brilliantly with five different Daglo colors. In the works by Zehringer *(Fig. 16)* and Gruppo N *(Fig. 17)*, circular rings and lenses, within which images are displaced ac-

cording to the position of the viewer, break the regularity. Dorazio in *Olandese II (Fig. 18)* draws straight lines with a colored brush across the canvas in many directions (comparable to Morellet's mesh) and thereby builds up an illusion of deep space penetrated by interstices. Le Parc in *Déterminisme et Indéterminisme (Fig. 19)* makes actual (and variable) interstices by hanging plastic squares to swing in the breeze at the end of nylon threads.

174

16. Walter Zehringer, *Lenses*, 1965. Coll. the artist

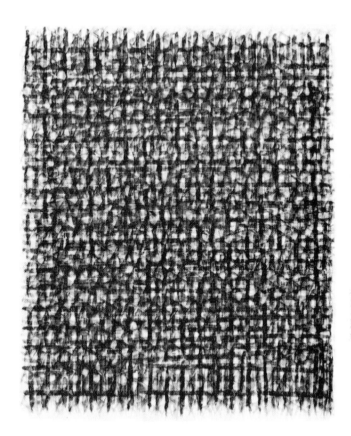

18. Piero Dorazio, *Olandese II*, 1961. Coll. the artist.

17. Gruppo N, *Struttura Ottico-dinamica*, 1962. Photo courtesy M. Massironi.

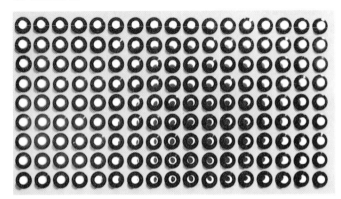

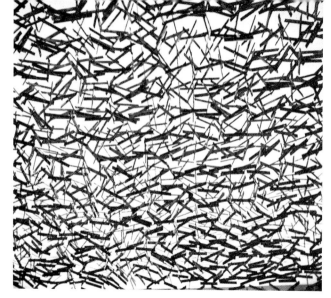

19. Julio le Parc, *Déterminisme et Indéterminisme*, 1960–61. Photo courtesy Groupe de Recherche d'Art Visuel, Paris.

20. Almir Mavignier, *Three Squares*, 1965. Coll. the artist.

The purest poet of micro-elements is Almir Mavignier. He is the "dot" master, devoting himself to the multiplication of round dots of varying size over immaculate surfaces—nothing else, except an occasional adventure with ruled lines. This would seem narrow and monotonous, but Mavignier succeeds in opening up worlds in which the dot is the normal but diverse inhabitant. In *Three Squares (Fig. 20)*, by subtle methodical changes among the dots, he creates secondary images of a simple but monumental kind. The detail of *Black-White-Red (Fig. 21)* shows one of his techniques of application. Using this method of repetition with slight change, Richter *(Fig. 22)* and Kemeny *(Fig. 23)* balance the emphasis between the uniform character of each cell (copper tubing, plastic squares, raised dots of paint) and the secondary image brought about by very slight changes between the cells—in Kemeny by interruption, in Richter by raising or lowering the surface, in Mavignier by color change.

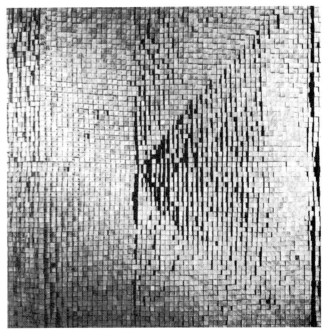

21. Almir Mavignier, *Black-White-Red (detail)*, 1962. Coll. the artist.

22. Yenceslav Richter, *System Sculpture*, 1964. Photo Branko Balić.

23. Zoltan Kemeny, *Study from Nature*, 1962. Coll. Landes Museum, Hannover; photo Walter Drayer.

24. Jan Schoonhoven, *Untitled*, 1962. Coll. the artist.

25. Henk Peeters, *Cotton-wool balls behind transparent nylon*, 1962. Coll. the artist.

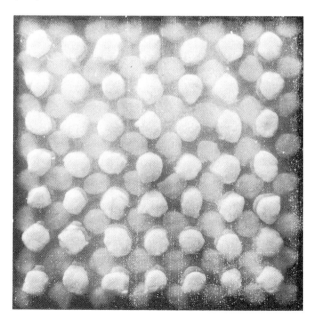

The plaster offering of Schoonhoven *(Fig. 24)*, irregular and clumsy in detail, becomes homogeneous and regular in multiplication. Peeters *(Fig. 25)* produces a diagonal rectilinear checkerboard by rigid orderly placement of puffs of cotton.

178

IX/Optical Phenomena

Artists have long ignored the peculiarities of human vision. The eye has been merely a window onto a world where every object had local qualities. Yet the eye has qualities of its own; there is a world inside the window also. In recent times, the responses to outside stimuli which take place in the eye and brain have begun to interest artists. For example, the eye responds in a direct and selective way to certain color situations, line arrangements, and patterns of alternating black and white patches or stripes, as immediately as a finger does to heat and cold. These sensations are in the mechanism of the optical system itself and are not an interpretation or evaluation of the source of the stimulus. In fact, the eye may be so shocked that attempts to interpret the stimulus may be futile.

In another type of situation, the eye may read the evidence and interpret it clearly but wrongly. This is optical illusion. Again, the eye may be baffled, confused, and frustrated by ambiguous visual situations. Such responses, generated in the observer, become—under a skillful manipulator—a means of direct access to the observer as an organism. Artists now see this access as an opportunity for a new kind of intimate artist-spectator interchange. They are beginning to explore the range of the eye's responses, sometimes borrowing from science, sometimes unsystematically duplicating, on their own, what science has long been aware of, sometimes pursuing variations of a discovery science has noted and left behind.

These phenomena are as old as the human eye and have occasionally in the past been examined as curiosities. It is only in this century, however, that they have been added to the artist's repertory of means. Their timeliness is due partly to awareness of science and materialistic explanations of human behavior, partly to an abstract art freed from memory. Even then, the first generation Constructivists and the De Stijl group only rarely showed interest in optical effects, possibly because they were hostile to any kind of trickery, magic, or illusion, and were especially wary of color effect as mere "surface quality."

Color phenomena are but a small part of the stimuli which can excite the human optical apparatus. Yet color itself is so deep a subject, as Albers has shown, that it cannot be adequately illustrated by a small quantity of plates produced by normal printing techniques. Its optical use by such artists as Vasarely,

Reinhardt, Anuskiewicz, Poons, Sedgley, Kidner, and Liberman must be mentioned; but only through the works themselves can the individual techniques be appreciated.

The primary source for the artistic use of optical phenomena is not the teaching of Albers about color but the painting and influence of Vasarely *(Fig. 1)*. Having explored optical phenomena since 1935, Vasarely wrote a number of explicit manifestos between 1955 and the present day. Younger artists have been influenced by these in their choice of visual means and directions for research. They also shared his concern for social usefulness and the relation established by the work between the artist and the spectator. A great deal of Vasarely's painting has been black and white and involved with what he calls *"cinétisme"*: optical effects of instability that suggest movement *(Fig. 2)*. This is achieved by alternating positive-negative shapes, which are interrupted in such a way as to imply secondary shapes that are never, in fact, realized. This leads through ambiguity and frustration to an uncertain but intense response from the observer.

There is, of course, no guarantee that the use of such phenomena and physical sensations makes art. As always, it is the artist who makes it. The optical properties of lines (distinct from their descriptive function as maps or depictions), and of such relational situations as convergence, tangents, superimposed grids, and ambiguous or multiple images are hard to explain but, explained or not, they become extraordinarily powerful tools in the hands of an experienced and sensitive artist. These stimuli alone are pointless harmonic demonstrations. Used as a means, they can intensify a strong design, although they cannot rescue one that is weak or banal. Just as a logarithmic spiral can be a motif in Concrete Art, so the artist can, from a neutral aesthetic position, present (though not portray) optical phenomena as an aspect of reality.

Many stimuli for the retina and optic nerve are unpleasant. Tranquillity and security are affected by visual orientation, and optical phenomena may assault the eye rather than delight it. A work by Bridget Riley or Anuskiewicz can make one feel dizzy or sick: beauty and ingratiation are not their purpose; sensation is. The phenomena, lying outside taste or beauty, intend to be neither pleasant nor unpleasant.

1. Victor Vasarely, *Étude*, 1932–42. Galerie Denise René, 1955 catalogue, Paris.

2. Victor Vasarely, *Échiquier*, 1935. Kunst Museum, Bern, 1964 catalogue, Switzerland.

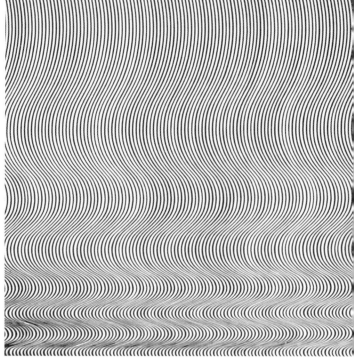

4. Bridget Riley, *Fall*, 1963. Photo courtesy Richard Feigen Gallery, N.Y.

3. Bridget Riley, *Blaze I*, 1962. Photo courtesy Richard Feigen Gallery, N.Y.

Alternation of white and black in controlled quantity is the principal means of achieving an unstable effect of "dazzle." Bridget Riley employs this device and also the effect of repeated zigzags to give the illusion of folding and ambiguity in the reading of the space in her *Blaze I* (Fig. 3). As *Fall* (Fig. 4) shows, the zigzag device need not be rectilinear to produce instability. (Some observers even see color appearing in the black and white stripes.)

5. Tadasky, *Untitled*, 1965. Photo Kootz Gallery, N.Y.

6. Marina Apollonio, *Dinamica Circolare 6S*, 1966. Coll. the artist.

7. Victor Vasarely, *Tau-Ceti*, 1955–65. Coll. the artist.

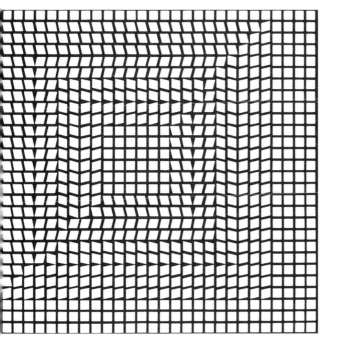

Tadasky's painting *(Fig. 5)* is limited to concentric circles of alternating light and dark lines, the quartering of which intensifies its contrasts and also introduces an ambiguous space effect. Apollonio's *Dinamica Circolare 6S (Fig. 6)* similarly combines stripes and curves within a circle into a combination of dazzle with illogical space. In Vasarely's *Tau-Ceti (Fig. 7)*, the difference in the surround of a square and a rhombus gives a reading of concentric squares woven into the unstable surface which is difficult to interpret in any single way.

8. Jeffrey Steele, *Lavolta*, 1965. Coll. the artist.

In his deceptively complex *Lavolta (Fig. 8)*, Steele uses the sharp alignment of steps by which each side of his bulging squares is reduced to set up a grid effect underlying the two systems of crosses generated by the black and white design. The bulging diminishes toward the outside. The painting reads white against black on the vertical-horizontal, the opposite on the diagonal.

Optical phenomena can also be used to warp space, to bend it, fracture it, force it back or forward from the picture plane. Vasarely was a master of this as these two examples show.

In this early painting *(Fig. 9)* the curvature of the lines combined with narrowing of the stripes force the illusion of convex and concave surfaces in addition to the dazzle of the black-white. The gray painting of 1965 *(Fig. 10)* uses similar curvature combined with subtle value differences for the illusion of a cavity.

Gruppo N's *Strutturo ottico-dinamica (Fig. 11)* combines the optical effect of black and white alternations with the space illusions brought about by the narrowing of the horizontal and vertical bands and the consequent perspective effect of diminishing size.

9. Victor Vasarely, *Japet*, 1956. Palais des Beaux-Arts, Brussels, 1960 catalogue, Paris.

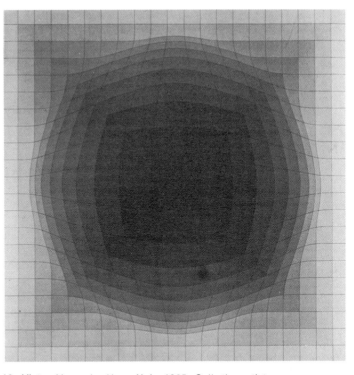

10. Victor Vasarely, *Vega-Noir*, 1965. Coll. the artist.

11. Gruppo N, *Strutturo ottico-dinamica*, 1963. Photo courtesy M. Massironi.

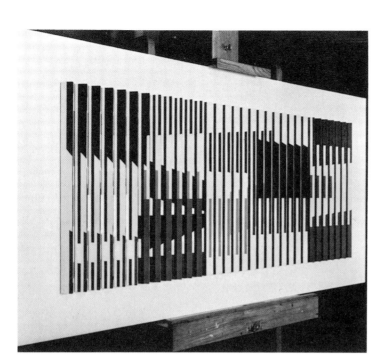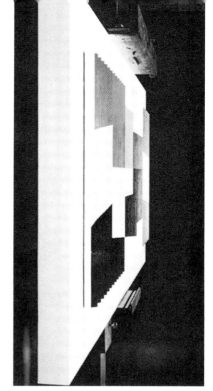

12a & b. Yaacov Agam, *Homage to J. S. Bach*, 1965. Marlborough Fine Art, Ltd., London.

13a & b. Carlos Cruz-Diez, *Physichromie #214*, 1966. Coll. Mr. and Mrs. George Rickey.

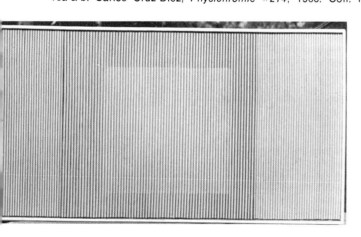

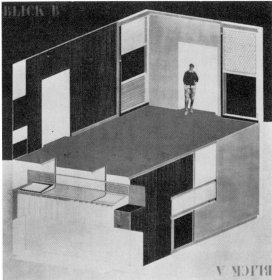

14. El Lissitzky, *Abstract Gallery*, 1926–27. Landes Museum, Hannover.

15a. b, c. Lissitzky, Agam, Cruz-Diez.

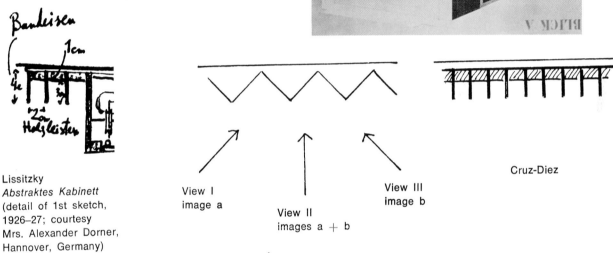

Lissitzky
Abstraktes Kabinett
(detail of 1st sketch,
1926–27; courtesy
Mrs. Alexander Dorner,
Hannover, Germany)

View I
image **a**

View II
images **a** + **b**

View III
image **b**

Agam
Transformable Painting

Cruz-Diez

A master of the idea of transformation is Yaacov Agam, yet he does not employ strictly optical phenomena. His transformations are a mechanical invention to substitute one image for another, although in these still photographs of *Homage to J. S. Bach (Fig. 12a & b)* this transformation is only partially shown. The same is true of Cruz-Diez whose typical device, as in *Physichromie #214 (Fig. 13a & b),* involves the use of separating strips to eclipse an image at certain angles, rather than Agam's pleated surfaces. With both, the images themselves are simple, non-objective geometrical paintings, with no special assault on the retina.

This device was used forty years ago by Lissitzky in his *Abstract Gallery (Figs. 14 & 15a, b, c),* where two of the walls were composed of strips of steel projecting 3 cm. from the surface, 3 cm. apart. The strips were painted black on one side, white on the other. The wall changed from black, through a mixed gray, to white, as the spectator advanced into the room.

Moiré is the commonest of the devices em-

187

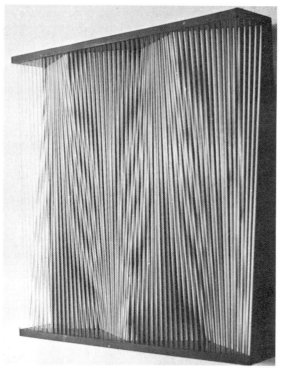

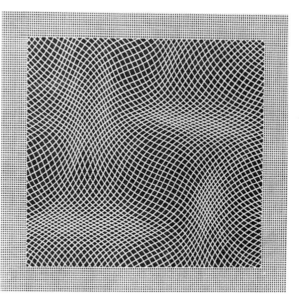

16. Yvaral, *Acceleration No. 5 Series A*, 1962. Coll. the artist.

17. Julian Stanzak, *Trespassing*, 1966. Courtesy Martha Jackson Gallery, N.Y.; photo O. E. Nelson.

18. Michael Kidner, *Orange, Violet and Pink*, 1964. Photo Hugh Gordon.

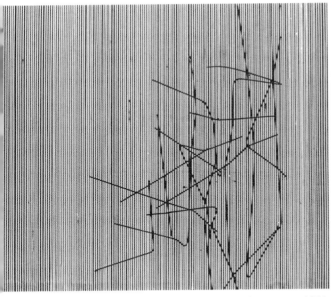

19. Jésus-Rafaël Soto, *Vibration Structure*, 1964. Coll. Signals Gallery, London; photo Clay Perry.

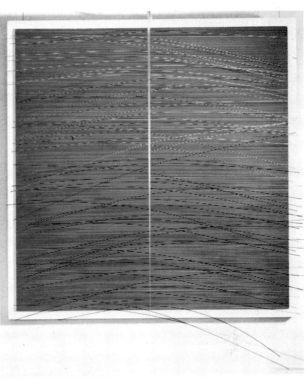

20. Jésus-Rafaël Soto, *Courbes Immatérielles—Vert*, 1966. Nancy Sayles Day collection, Museum of Art, Rhode Island School of Design.

ployed for optical impact. It originated in the Orient and came to Europe in the Middle Ages. Two layers of ribbed silk were pressed together with the ribs very slightly crossed, which gave a watery effect. When two thin lines are seen crossing one another, a thickening—like a bead—appears at the intersection where both lines gain by the width of the other at that point. This bead appears to move along the lines as the point of intersection changes. When grids of many parallel lines are superimposed, successive intersections become a secondary pattern which changes as the spectator moves.

Yvaral in his *Acceleration No. 5 Series A (Fig. 16)* uses plastic cords which cross at a very acute angle over a shallow space; and in Stanzak's *Trespassing (Fig. 17)* both *moirage*

and the secondary patterns are evident on a flat plane. Kidner superimposes three layers of tapered stripes, but on only one plane, all at acute angles, in his *Orange, Violet and Pink (Fig. 18)*.

Soto's interest in retinal responses began around 1951 or 1952 and he was using moiré in 1954. Now he hangs wires in front of a pin-striped ground; where a freely hanging wire crosses the ground a bead appears on the wire, running up or down it as the observer or the wire moves. His *Vibration Structure (Fig. 19)* is a stationary work with wires fixed in front of the panel—the spectator moves. In *Courbes Immatérielles–Vert (Fig. 20)* the wires (the upper are white, the lower black) hang by threads and swing gently in moving air.

Wilding so controls the moiré phenomenon,

that he makes a precise repeating secondary design which alters its configuration as the observer moves. He has worked with optical phenomena since 1951 and with moiré since 1955. These two examples *(Figs. 21 & 22)* of his oeuvre demonstrate a control of the secondary image produced by overlapping grids of unmatched variety and precision.

21. Ludwig Wilding, *Kinetic Structure 5–63*, 1963. Coll. the artist.

22. Ludwig Wilding, *Interference of 2 structures in 3 dimensions*, 1961. Coll. the artist.

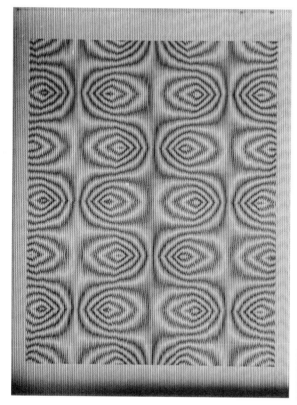

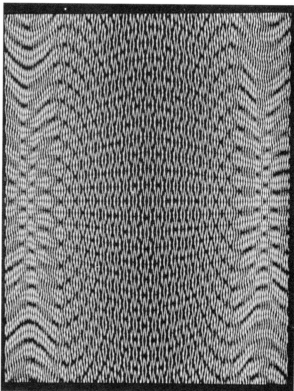

X/Movement

Before the twentieth century, artists interested in movement had been content either to show it arrested, like a snapshot, or to suggst or imply it by a skillfully contrived composition or posture, as in Leonardo's *Battle of Anghiari*. Boccioni wrote in 1912:

> We cannot forget that the tick-tock and the moving hands of a clock, the in-and-out of a piston in a cylinder, the opening and closing of two cog-wheels with the continual appearance and disappearance of their square steel cogs, the fury of a flywheel or the turbine of a propeller, are all plastic and pictorial elements of which a Futurist work in sculpture must take account. The opening and closing of a valve creates a rhythm just as beautiful but infinitely newer than the blinking of an animal eyelid.[17]

The Futurists, borrowing from Cubism and the multiple exposures of the cinematograph, tried to portray movement itself. Gabo saw how limited this was:

> Futurism has not gone further than the effort to fix on canvas a purely optical reflex. . . . It is obvious now to every one of us that by the simple graphic registration of a row of momentarily arrested movements one cannot recreate movement itself.[18]

He called for a kinetic art as the basic form for our perception of "real time." In the meantime, Tatlin had proposed movement in his famous design for the *Monument to the IIIrd International* in 1920; he had built a wooden model but was not technically adept enough to go further *(Fig. 27, p. 24)*.

Gabo declared in a conversation with the author: "There are statics and dynamics, then there are kinetics."

> Constructive sculpture is not only three-dimensional, it is four-dimensional insofar as we are striving to bring the element of time into it. By time, I mean movement, rhythm: the actual movement. . . .[19]

Though foreseeing clearly the potential of kinetic sculpture, Gabo made only three works. *Kinetic Construction No. 1 (Figs. 1 & 2)* was to demonstrate to students in the school in Moscow (the same year as the Manifesto) that a single line could, through movement, become a volume, later to be compared with Brancusi's equally famous *Bird in Flight* of 1919.

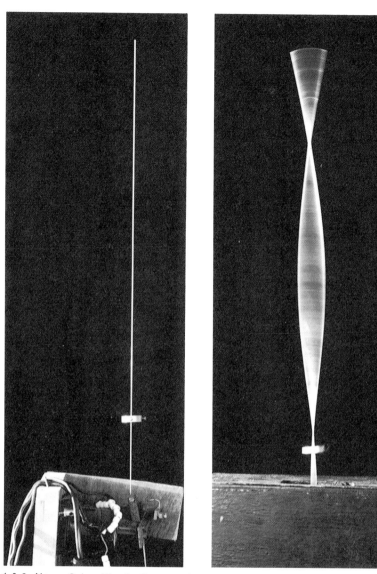

1 & 2. Naum Gabo, *Kinetic Construction No. 1* (still, and in movement), 1920. Coll. the artist; photo E. Irving Blomstrann.

Gabo's *Design for Kinetic Construction (Fig. 3)* is a notation for a structure combining a number of different motions, indicated by arrows and dotted lines to establish the choreography (Gabo's comparison) of the various movements. *Torsion (Fig. 4)* is a design for a fountain to be moved by the jets of water, corresponding to the strings in his other constructions.

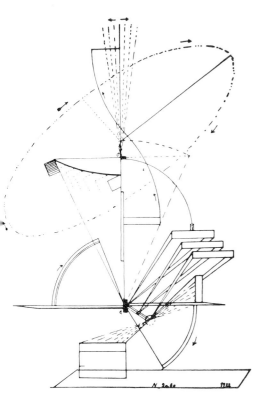

3. Naum Gabo, *Design for Kinetic Construction*, 1922. Photo E. Irving Blomstrann.

4. Naum Gabo, *Torsion* (design for a fountain), 1929–36. Coll. the artist.

He did not, at that time, go further; he realized that, with the technology of the time, the machines necessary to make the movements would be so clumsy that they would obscure the *movement itself*. He now thinks that it becomes possible with electronics. He emphasizes that the vibrating line in his pioneer work of 1920 was only an example of what was possible with a single element.

Duchamp had shown interest in movement not only as a dynamic extension of painting but also with rotating mechanical devices. His *33 West 67th Street (Fig. 5)* and *Rotoreliefs (Fig. 6)* related to his Dada interests and he did not pursue movement consistently or for long. There were, however, some mechanical sculptures made by the Futurists in 1915[20]—Giacomo Balla's *Complessi Plastici Mobili,* and Fortunato Depero's *Complessi Motorumoristi*—which were also postulated in the manifesto, "Futurist Reconstruction of the Universe." Klee was reported by

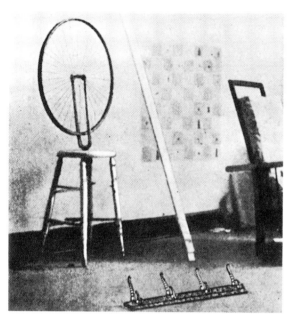

6. Marcel Duchamp, *Rotoreliefs* (original drawings for seven), 1923. Coll. Seattle Art Museum, gift of Richard E. Fuller.

5. Marcel Duchamp, *33 West 67th Street, New York,* 1917–18.

7. László Moholy-Nagy, *Light-Space Modulator,* 1922–30. Busch-Reisinger Museum, Harvard University.

Feininger to have had little mobiles in his Bauhaus studio in Dessau. It is likely that there were some others. Moholy-Nagy worked with movement in relation to light in his *Light-Space Modulator (Fig. 7)*, and studies of motion were included in the curriculum of his "Institute of Design" where students were making "kinetic" sculptures as early as 1940.

8. Alexander Calder, *Four Forms at the Fair*, 1961. Original model made for N.Y. World's Fair, 1939; done full scale at Moderna Museet, Stockholm, for Movement exhibition.

9. Alexander Calder, *Red, 1959*, 1959. The Whitney Museum, N.Y., gift of the Friends of The Whitney Museum.

These early essays were merely hints. It was Calder who succeeded in securing a place for kinetic art *(Fig. 8)*. He started making mobiles twelve years after Gabo's Manifesto, and his first exhibition of these was in 1932 at the Galérie Maeght in Paris. Although his mobiles *(Fig. 9)* have since become famous and popular and have enlarged the limits of art, his style, deriving from painterly concepts, has had little influence on the new generation, especially the more mechanically inclined. Until his "stabiles" of the last decade, Calder retained a two-dimensional outlook in sculpture devised as outline drawings, often witty, with ingratiating movement added. He seemed indifferent to the wide possibilities of a kinetic art. He discovered a new world but did not explore it.

Extension of the possibilities of movement in art has been left to younger men of different temperament. Their fresh ideas stemmed rather from the general postwar urge to burst out of traditional forms and conventions as to what was permissible in art. This urge had led, as noted, to the revival of collage and the spread of welded and other space sculpture. Young kinetic artists polarized toward either Dada or Constructivism. Such artists as Bury, the "Zero" and "NUL" groups, and, of course, Tinguely still retain a flavor of Dada. Schöffer, the "Groupe de Recherche d'Art Visuel" who were influenced by Vasarely, the Italians, and the South Americans who had heard and seen Bill, are more Constructivist. In the United States, there are both kinds of artists.

Ideas were plentiful in the fifties and there were also some hands adept enough to carry them out. In Paris in 1955, Denise René exhibited a group of seven, in addition to Calder: Agam, Bury, Duchamp, Jacobsen, Soto, Tinguely, and Vasarely. By 1961, it was possible to gather together the work of seventy-five artists for an international exhibition in Amsterdam, Stockholm, and Copenhagen. By 1965, no single exhibition could satisfactorily represent the range of activity and do justice to the artists. It was already necessary to subdivide the field; here are some of the devices:

1. All kinds of motor-driven devices using speeds from imperceptibly slow to fast enough to blur vision, and employing planned and unplanned variable speed, interruptions, reversals, etc.

2. Every kind of leverage, linkage, gear trains, belts and power transmission, and control device one can think of.

3. Liquids as power, as the design medium, as a special material to flow fast or slow, to drip, to evaporate, to mix or not mix with each other, or to produce foam and flow in a different guise, to refract light, to vibrate in surface patterns, to ride between air locks through tubing or to form and break in waves.

4. Air to bubble through water, to make an invisible jet to support weights, or simply as wind to blow where it will.

5. Pulsating membranes and similar surfaces.

6. The kinetic spectator, whose movement before the object causes apparent change within it.

7. Objects movable and objects transformable where the spectator is a power source or the computer of a rearrangement.

8. Sound in relation to movement, either as an accompaniment to movement observed or as aural evidence of movement unseen.

9. Movement of materials or structures to reveal their essential character, such as flow of water or foam.

10. Movement as an intensifier of the significance of objects taken out of context and translated into a kinetic, and often frenzied world.

196

11. Movement either of abstract designs or of found or invented objects directed to the absurd. (These last two are related to Dada.)

Three other important aspects of movement are dealt with in separate chapters:

12. *Chance* as a control or product of movement.

13. *Optical Phenomena* suggesting movement on stationary surfaces (*art cinétique*), of which an early example is the cinema, still spelled *kinema* in some languages.

14. *Light* itself, used in combination with movement.

Because of its breadth, its youth, and its rapid growth, definitions of "kinetic art" have been loose and understanding of its basic characteristics is sketchy. Its relation to optical art is unclear to many, as is the difference between the kinetic object and the kinetic spectator. Many think kinetic and optical art is "scientific" and dead, whereas it is no more made by physicists and mathematicians than music is. Obviously, science plays a role in contemporary art. Its revelations are available to artists as to other men; its laws, discoveries, and devices are part of the nature that art may feed on. The extensions of kinetic art now exceed the most optimistic projections of Gabo fifty years ago. As always, not the means themselves, but what the artist does with them, make art. The means are movement itself; the end is a kind of order, a tectonic design of the movement.

10. Jean Tinguely, *Polychrome-Métaméchanique*, 1954. Coll. Mr. and Mrs. Max Wasserman, Boston, Mass.

11. Jean Tinguely, *Water Sculpture*, 1960. Coll. the artist.

12. Harry Kramer, *Dice on Four Feet*, 1964. Photo Roy Martin.

13. Robert Breer, *Crawling Objects*, 1966. Courtesy Galleria Bonino, N.Y.; photo Peter Moore.

14. Pol Bury, *Vibratile*, 1963. Photo Shunk-Kender.

15. Pol Bury, *Eighteen Stacked Balls*, 1966. Coll. Mr. and Mrs. Chapin Riley, Worcester, Mass.

Tinguely's *Polychrome-Métaméchanique (Fig. 10)* is classical in form, based on clocks of his native Switzerland, but mocking by exaggeration. Tinguely later incorporated found objects *(Fig. 11)*, combining witty comment with the outrageously absurd; he also began to employ noise as a component. Harry Kramer who has lived in Las Vegas makes caricatures of common objects such as *Dice on Four Feet (Fig. 12)*. He embellishes these with absurd little machines which turn uselessly, sometimes hitting a toy drum or a ball. Robert Breer's *Crawling Objects (Fig. 13)*, seen in the Bonino Gallery, are basic geometric shapes of Styrofoam brought by little motors to a snail's-pace kind of life.

In contrast with these three, Bury in *Vibratile (Fig. 14)* and *Eighteen Stacked Balls (Fig. 15)* seems utterly serious and a master of understatement. His wires, spheres, or blocks are meticulously fashioned, exquisitely finished and twitch so little and so slowly as to seem at first stationary—the threshold of

199

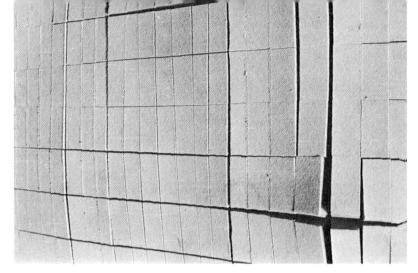

16. Gianni Colombo, *Pulsating Surface*, 1960. Coll. the artist.

17a & b. Fletcher Benton, *Yin and Yang*, 1965. Coll. Esther Robles Gallery, Los Angeles; photo Joe Schopplein.

movement. Colombo's *Pulsating Surface (Fig. 16)* of white Styrofoam is segmented and so linked that it heaves slowly and gently like a swelling ocean. The restrained movements of Colombo and Bury, so different from the large and small extravaganzas of Tinguely, Kramer, and Breer are, themselves, not without a hint of fantasy; the very slowness of Bury is surreal, and the instability of so large and solid a surface as Colombo's transports the observer into a world where his customary values no longer apply.

Motors can provide power; so can the hand, and many other forces. The electric motor is the most common. Benton uses it to transform concentric circles into *Yin and Yang (Fig. 17a & b)* and back again. Munari in *L'Ora X (Fig.*

200

18a, b, c. Bruno Munari, *L'Ora X*, 1945–63. Coll. the artist.

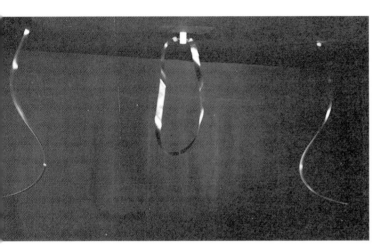

19. Len Lye, *Flip and Two Twisters*, "Trilogy," 1965. Coll. Mr. and Mrs. Howard Wise; photo Ron Chamberlain; courtesy University Art Museum, Univ. of California, Berkeley.

20. Nicolas Schöffer, *Lux 10*, 1959. Coll. the artist; photo Yves Hervochon.

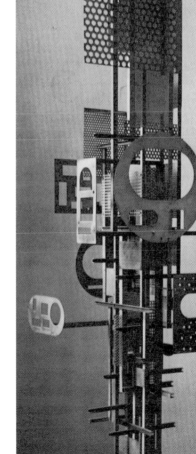

18a, b, c) uses clockwork to drive the hands on the timeless face.

The most violent movement in kinetic art comes from Len Lye. His *Flip and Two Twisters, "Trilogy" (Fig. 19)* is a contrast with both Bury and Tinguely: with the first because of the speed, the noise and the violence; with the latter, because it is simple and austere and makes no comment on the society the artist lives in. Lye lets the forces of nature speak in a direct and directed way with a programmed series of twists of ribbons of steel. The elements of Schöffer's sculpture *(Fig. 20)* are moved at different speeds and directions by motors in a manner strongly reminiscent of Moholy-Nagy in 1930.

21. Len Lye, *Loop*, 1963. Howard Wise Gallery, N.Y.;
photo Oliver Baker Assoc.

22. Walter Linck, *Construction Mobile*, 1958.
Kunst Museum, Bern; photo Mario Tschabold.

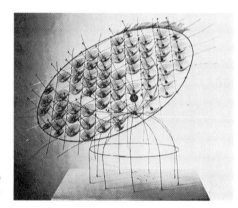

23. Günter Haese, *Roi Soleil*, 1964. Museum de
Stadt, Ulm; photo courtesy Museum of Modern Art,
N.Y.

Springs are another source of energy, less
monotonous than motors; they merely store
energy to give it out again, so their performance is necessarily intermittent, as in Len
Lye's rolling *Loop (Fig. 21)*, set in motion by
a magnetic field but with a gait determined
entirely by its springiness. Linck, in *Construction Mobile (Fig. 22)*, makes similar loops which
must be energized by the hand; Haese, in
Roi Soleil (Fig. 23), also a little surrealist,
seems to mock science as much as "Le Grand
Monarque," with a radar screen made of quiv-
ering watch springs.

The student of the anatomy of springs is
Siegfried Cremer. In *Mobile Plastik (Fig. 24)*, he
has mastered it so that he can weigh the
ends to adjust the period of oscillation in relation to the length of wire and can bend elbows
to adjust the directions into which the oscilla-
tions will naturally fall. At the same time, he
shapes the drawing in space. Though Cremer's
work is meager in material, it is mature in its
mastery of design and kinetic means.

Another form of energy in nature is magnetic
force. A few artists have chosen to use this as
their motive power. Takis—after spending
several years with springs, like his *Signal
Rocket (Fig. 25)*—has designed objects which
swing in controlled magnetic fields, such as
this large, cork ball with a magnetic core *(Fig.
26)*, which is alternately attracted and repelled. Alberto Collie goes further; in *Spatial

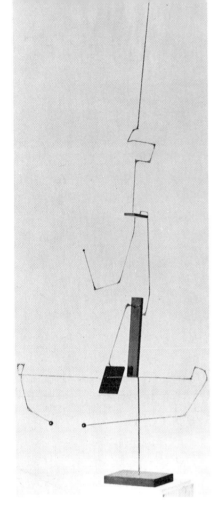

24. Siegfried Cremer, *Mobile Plastik*, 1962. Coll. the artist.

25. Takis, *Signal Rocket*, 1955. Museum of Modern Art, N.Y., Mrs. Charles V. Hickox Fund.

26. Takis, *Electromagnetic Sculpture II*, 1965. Coll. Galerie Iolas, Paris.

27. Alberto Collie, *Spatial Absolute #1*, 1964. Courtesy Nordness Gallery, N.Y.; photo Rick Levy.

28. Davide Boriani, *Magnetic Surface*, 1960–65. Coll. the artist; photo courtesy University Art Museum, Univ. of California, Berkeley.

29. Julio le Parc, *Threshold of Saturation*, 1961. Photo courtesy Groupe de Recherche d'Art Visuel, Paris.

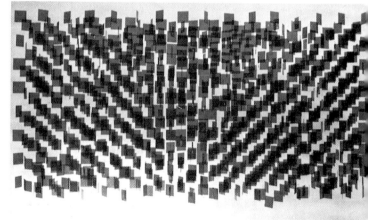

Absolute #1 (Fig. 27), the upper body floats completely freed of gravity and has to be tethered with nylon strings. Boriani's *Magnetic Surface (Fig. 28)* is a disc, divided into curvilinear compartments, containing iron filings. Behind this several magnets, moved by a mechanism from an electric motor, attract and deposit the filings. The course of the magnets is programmed so as to be always different with respect to the surface, varying continuously the image formed by the filings.

The movements of water and air are readily available, as in the great fountains of the past, yet there are surprisingly few who use them.

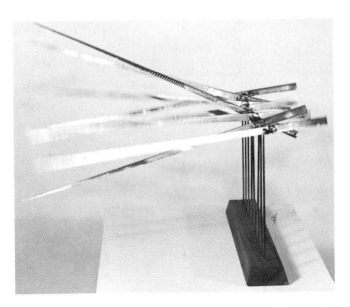

30. George Rickey, *8 Lines Horizontal*, 1966. Coll. Mr. and Mrs. Adolf Schaap; photo John D. Schiff; courtesy Staempfli Gallery, N.Y.

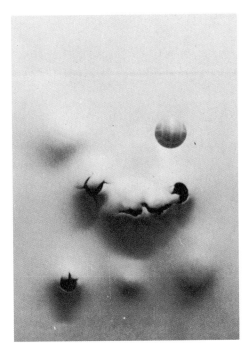

31. Willi Weber, *Space and Time*, 1965. Coll. the artist.

32. Hans Haacke, *Large Blue Sail*, 1966. Coll. the artist.

Air is also a source of power, available anywhere, and any time. Julio le Parc's *Threshold of Saturation (Fig. 29)* of translucent plastic squares, hung one below another on nylon threads, turn easily in response to light air currents, making an unstable surface. George Rickey's stainless steel blades rise and fall slowly, breaking and reforming a plane *(Fig. 30)*. In Weber's *Space and Time (Fig. 31)*, a current of air emerges from a fissure in the surface of the panel. The ball remains suspended in this current, spinning and bouncing. Haacke's *Large Blue Sail (Fig. 32)* is a piece of chiffon, lightly tethered, which floats on the air current from a fan.

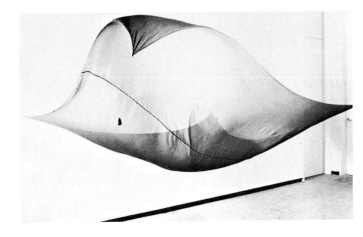

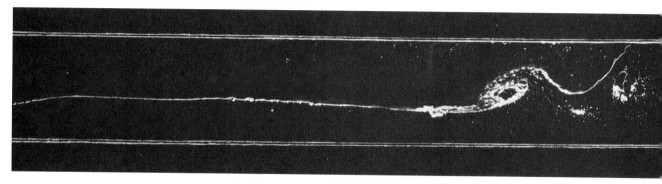

33. Hans Haacke, *Wave I*, 1964. Coll. the artist.

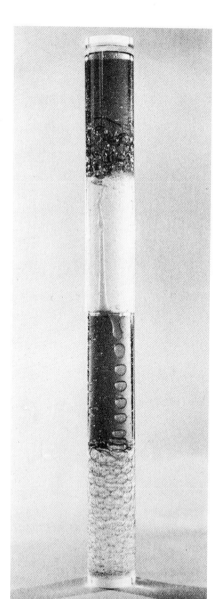

34. Hans Haacke, *Column*, 1965. Coll. the artist.

35. Sadamasa Motonaga, *Hanging Water*, 1956. Coll. the artist.

36. Norbert Kricke, *Water Forest*, 1964. Courtyard Giro-zentrale Building, Düsseldorf.

37. Lin Emery, *Aquamobile*, 1966. De Lesseps S. Morrison Memorial, Duncan Plaza, New Orleans Civic Center; photo Frank Lotz Miller.

38. David Medalla, *Cloud Canyons*, 1964. Photo Clay Perry.

Haacke's *Wave I (Fig. 33)* confines a slice of water in a long, narrow transparent box; when the box is set swinging, a wave rolls through the confined channel and breaks back on itself at each end. His *Column (Fig. 34)* of water and oil also uses other properties of liquids; when inverted, each liquid tries to pass the other and assumes the best shape it can for doing so.

The Japanese, Motonaga, in *Hanging Water (Fig. 35)*, confines water in long plastic sleeves hung between trees; when the wind blows, the water cradles rock and the brightly colored liquid sloshes back and forth on its catenary way.

Norbert Kricke makes a water forest of glass cylinders *(Fig. 36)*, where the water wells up in columns and courses down the outside. Emery in *Aquamobile (Fig. 37)*, makes a group of copper petals which fill with water and, rocking as their weight changes, spill their load into the rocking petals below and from there into the basin.

David Medalla's *Cloud Canyons (Fig. 38)* mixes air and water in a foam generator, which pushes out its froth in ever-changing, chance-dictated, always-suggestive shapes. In Agam's

Mouvement, Couleur, Sensibilité (Fig. 39), colored discs are mounted on springs and are displaced in random patterns. In Moss' *Square Peg in a Round Hole (Figs. 40 & 41)*, a steel ball is dropped into the hole at the top. "Nine spinning planes and four accented corners. Sound of sculpture is in direct contrast with exterior appearance—round sound in square peg and a four-cornered sound in round shape. Gravity and centrifugal force keep this ball in motion. Duration is about 1 min 45 sec. Many balls may be used at the same time."

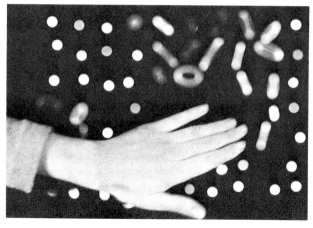

39. Yaacov Agam, *Mouvement, Couleur, Sensibilité*, 1962. Coll. the artist.

40. Joseph Moss, *Square Peg in a Round Hole*, 1965. Coll. Stanford Calderwood; photo Charles Hollandsworth.

41. Joseph Moss, drawing for *Square Peg in a Round Hole*. Courtesy the artist.

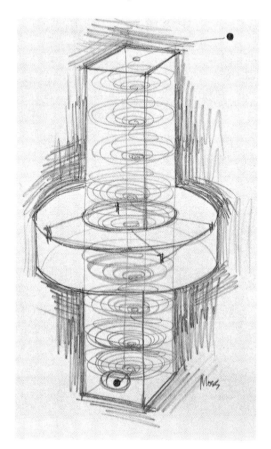

XI/Light

All art reflects light; it is by its illumination that we see art and contemplate it. Occasionally, in the past, artists have noticed the behavior of light on the surface of their work and have modified their design to exploit it. Such light-exploiting surfaces are also used on embossed paper napkins, greeting cards, confectionary boxes and, in more serious light-play, on damask, cut velvet, and tooled leather. Crystal and diamonds are cut to refract light; silver and gold are chased to reflect light as lines. In architecture, light appears in the ancient sun and shadow geometries of the Zapotecan stone walls of Mitla and Monte Alban or in eighteenth-century rusticated brickwork.

These were crafts. Awareness of light itself as a performer came slowly to painters and sculptors. Rodin divided his attention between haptic form and light-reflecting modulations of surface. The Impressionist painters did not work their surfaces to catch light, yet they succeeded in isolating the role of light. They trained themselves to see a cathedral neither as architecture nor as simply made of stone; it was made of light, the echo of the sunshine which fell upon it, and they used color to imitate that light. But they still did not take the next step: the use of light itself as a means. The glaziers of Chartres had gone further five hundred years before.

Isolation of light as an artist's material came in the twentieth century, with non-objective art, along with the use of other new materials, and with the easily controlled electric light. Gabo opened the way with constructions of transparent plastic, and continued with stretched strings which stopped part of the light to imply a surface and let part through to illuminate interior space. The behavior of light became a Bauhaus study. Moholy-Nagy worked on the idea of "light modulators" in his own plastic sculpture and, in 1930, built a machine which was, in effect, a programmed light robot used as the hero of a film, *Black, White, and Grey*. Albers also used light for inkless intaglio prints and for a mural in the graduate dormitory at Harvard *(Fig. 1)*. Gyorgy Kepes conducts research on it with architecture students at the Massachusetts Institute of Technology.

The New Zealander, Len Lye, who now lives in New York, worked first with projection of light through film as Eggeling and Richter had done, borrowing from the rapidly developing cinema techniques. All three had made abstract films in

1. Josef Albers, *America*, 1949. Wall mural, Graduate Student Center, Harvard Univ.; The Architects Collaborative, Inc., Walter Gropius, partner in charge; photo Robert Damora.

1921. Lye was the first to paint his designs directly on film in 1935—a technique adopted by MacLaren for his abstract films.

Prototypes of abstract kinetic painting with light had appeared as early as the eighteenth century, and were devoted, like Scriabin's "color organ" a century later, to producing a visual equivalent of musical composition. These attempts culminated with the invention of the Clavilux in 1919 by Thomas Wilfred—a Dane living in New York—who made a great step forward when he realized that light compositions must be made in accordance with the nature of light and not by forced analogy with music. His *Aspiration Number 145—Theme with 397 Variations* (1955), now in the Museum of Modern Art, presents to the spectator an unfolding drama projected from behind onto a translucent surface. The image is non-objective, though for many full of suggestion.

In the last ten years, light projection machines have multiplied. They have the same basic system—a source, an interceptor or modifier, and a screen. These have been exhibited by Malina, Schöffer, Abraham Palatnik, John Healey, and Vardánega.

Somewhat different are the machines of Otto Piene and Heinz Mack. Piene groups several "programmed projectors in a large dark room and fills the environment with moving abstract light particles, patterns, and from time to time, distortions of real images." Mack uses a large complex of reflecting surfaces, moved

210

partly by motors, partly by wind, on which various light beams are thrown and reflected back, providing for the observer a synthesis of the sculpture and its effect on the environment.

Other light designs are made with light and shadow from twisted ribbons (Costa and Leblanc); batteries of small rotating reflectors (von Graevenitz); coffered relief surfaces of varying depths, in which incident light is lost in varying degrees (Mari); controlled refraction by prisms and lenses (Biasi and Peeters); polarized light (Olsen and Salvadori); sunlight and shadow in outdoor situations (Hoenich and Janz); light conducted through transparent plastic (Pohl); or through combinations of slits, refractors, and reflectors (Boto); mirrors curved or flat (Le Parc, Megert, Goepfert).

Lippold, whose work has developed as linear orchestration in space, is at the same time one of the purest modifiers of light. His highly polished wires become visible through light; the reflections of the light sources travel along the wires as the spectator moves, tracing multiple paths through space. Tomasello tilts surfaces to catch and lose light. In addition, he renders visible the colored underside of each white cube through its reflection from the white panel.

The painting of Ad Reinhardt is a special case. He has worked with nonobjective images for thirty years, and latterly with rectilinear compositions in very closely related blues or reds. Since 1953, he has devoted himself to painting so dark that that the design and the colors are discernible only after the eye has become accustomed to the darkness *(Fig. 2)*. These are often casually termed "black," but they are not. They are painted with color in low values where the eye only just perceives color—marginal illumination at the threshold of vision. To employ minimal light is nevertheless the realm of light, just as Bury's minimal movement is still kinetic. In both cases the artist demands, and gets, maximum attention from the spectator for his understatement.

As with many of the new tendencies, the possibilities of design with light seem limitless. The range of opportunity and the newness are stimulating, but equally a danger. Artists labor under an *embarras de richesse*, and some of their machines are too cumbersome for free and imaginative expression. The sophistication of shop windows, theater lighting, and firework displays makes some work by artists seem clumsy and primitive. Also, it can soon become tiresome. Yet light, which has always been with us, is one of the most promising twentieth-century materials for the artist.

2. Ad Reinhardt, *Abstract Painting, Dyptych*, 1960. Coll. the artist.

3. Len Lye, *Round head*, 1963. Coll. the artist.

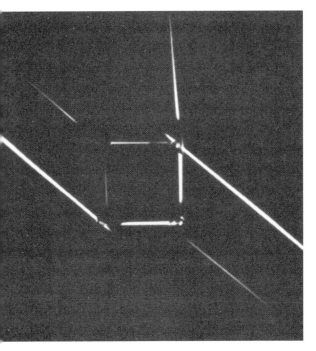

5. Otto Piene, *Milky Way*, 1965. Ceiling, Bonn Opera House; photo H. Dinnebier.

4. Alberto Biasi (Gruppo N), *Kinetic Spectral Net*, 1963. Coll. the artist.

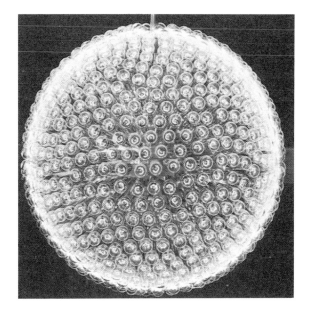

6. Otto Piene, *Onion Flower*, 1965. Foyer, Bonn Opera House; photo Hein Engelskirchen.

Five different methods of using light as an autonomous form of energy in space, with a minimum of encumbering vehicles are: Lye's whirling steel rings *(Fig. 3)* existing only by virtue of their reflections—the material has disappeared; Biasi's *Kinetic Spectral Net (Fig. 4)* produces rays of colored light from an invisible system of rotating prisms which break up pencils of light into colors and distribute them in a random crisscrossing design across a screen; Piene's *Milky Way (Fig. 5)* and *Onion Flower (Fig. 6)* consist of tiny incandescent lamps which establish volumes in space; light as lines drawn through space is reflected from

Lippold's wires in a detail from *Jersey Meadows (Fig. 7)*. Sobrino's *Unstable Transformation, Juxtaposition–Superposition A (Fig. 8)* of transparent colored Plexiglas is lit from within. It becomes a volume of light contained by the structure; different densities of shade are established by overlapping.

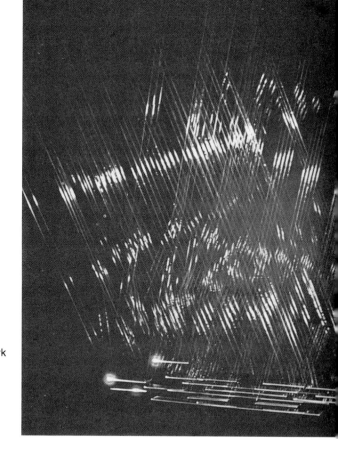

7. Richard Lippold, *Jersey Meadows*, 1964. The Newark Museum collection, Newark, N.J.; photo Hella Hammid.

8. Francisco Sobrino, *Unstable Transformation, Juxtaposition–Superposition A*, 1962. Coll. the artist.

9. Tajin Chico, *Columnar Edifice*. Photo courtesy Prof. George Kubler, Yale Univ.

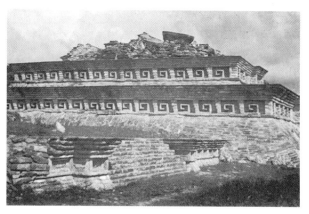

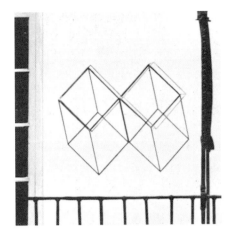

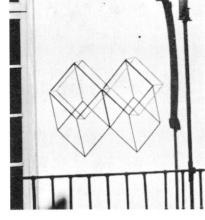

10a, b, c. Robert Janz, *Shadowline #15*, 1965. Coll. the artist.

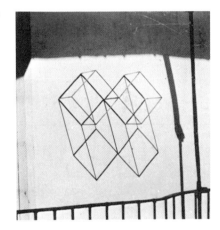

11. Gabriele de Vecchi, *Strutturazione Virtuale A*, 1964. Coll. the artist.

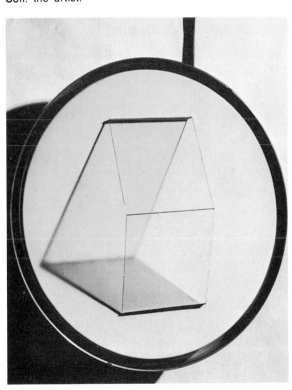

The oldest way of using light is where the absence of light—the cast shadow—becomes an equal part of the design, as in this section of wall from Tajín, near Veracruz, Mexico. *(Fig. 9)*, a mosaic of precisely shaped stones projecting from the wall far enough, under the tropical sun, to cast a shadow sharper than the stone itself. The same idea, without architectural intent, is developed by Robert Janz's orthogonal steel *Shadowline #15 (Fig. 10a, b, c)* which doubles itself on the wall with changing proportions as the sun rises and declines; De Vecchi's *Strutturazione Virtuale A (Fig. 11)* interposes a rotating translucent structure (the object moves rather than the light source) to establish an ambiguous relationship

215

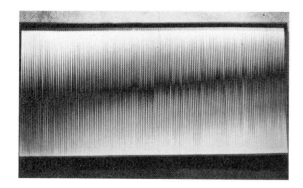

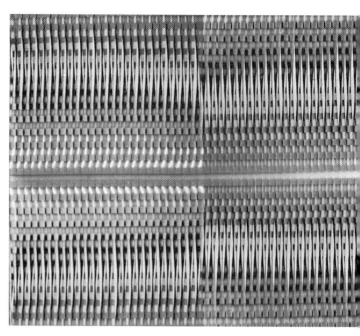

13. Walter Leblanc, *Mobilo-Statique*, 1962. Coll. V. van El-dere, Antwerp; photo by F. Tas.

12a & b. Toni Costa, *Linea dinamica vissible*, 1960–62. Coll. the artist.

14. Otto Piene, *Weiss Weiss Weiss*, 1959. Coll. Alfred Schmela, Düsseldorf; photo Hein Engelskirchen.

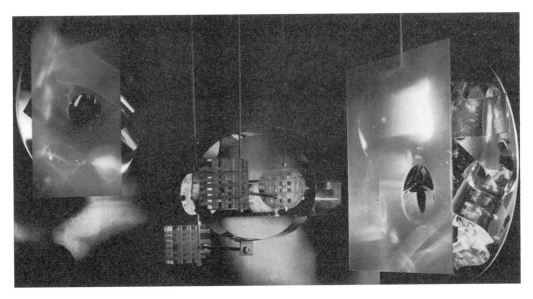

15. Nicolas Schöffer, *Suspense 2*, 1963. Photo Yves Hervochon.

16. Frank Malina, *Molecule II*, 1961. Coll. Mr. and Mrs. Daniel J. Boorstin, Chicago.

between object and shadow; Costa's *Linea dinamica vissible (Fig. 12a & b)*, and Leblanc's *Mobilo-Statique (Fig. 13)* use parallel spiral strips of white plastic which reflect and lose light and constitute a plane made of spaces. In Piene's *Weiss Weiss Weiss (Fig. 14)* the design is made by small white projections, each of which, under slanting light, casts a small shadow. Thus, modulated light fixes the shape and position of each dot on the picture plane.

Schöffer in *Suspense 2 (Fig. 15)* and Malina in *Molecule II (Fig. 16)* elaborate on the devices of Moholy-Nagy, Wilfred and their precursors by adding sound. Healey continues in

217

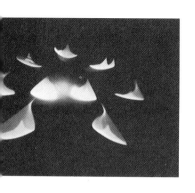

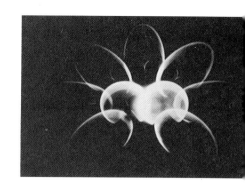

17a –e. John Healey, *Box 3*, 1964.
Coll. the artist.

18a & b. Julio le Parc, *Continuel-lumière*, 1962. Courtesy Howard Wise Gallery, N.Y.

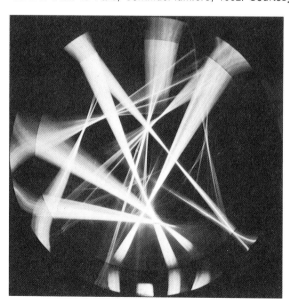

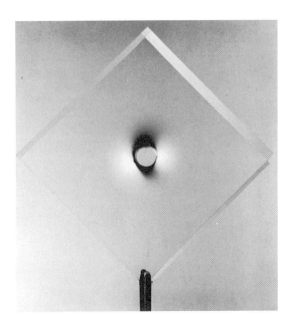

19. Uli Pohl, *PxII/155–59/61*. Courtesy Galerie Klihm, Munich.

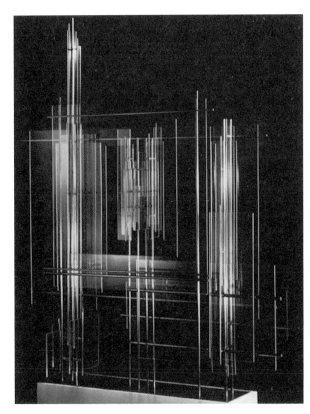

20. Carlos Cairoli, *Vertical+Horizontal=Equilibre*, 1959. Coll. the artist.

21. Karl Gerstner, *Prism Picture Red-Blue*, 1958–62. Coll. the artist.

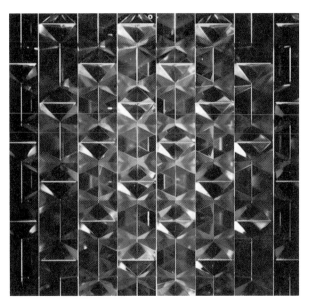

the idiom of Wilfred with silent, sharp, complex unfolding of images in black and white and color *(Figs. 17a–e)*. Le Parc, in *Continuel-lumière (Fig. 18a & b)*, modifies a moving beam by projection onto a polished cylindrical surface instead of by a transparency; this produces a complex light drawing of ever-changing spirals, beams and tangents on a circular screen.

Pohl *(Fig. 19)* uses the light transmitting, reflecting, and refracting properties of Plexiglas or Perspex to delineate the edges of geometrical form, as does Cairoli in *Vertical + Horizontal = Equilibre (Fig. 20)*. Gerstner in *Prism Picture Red–Blue (Fig. 21)* makes a relief with Perspex prisms over a mirror surface, adding

219

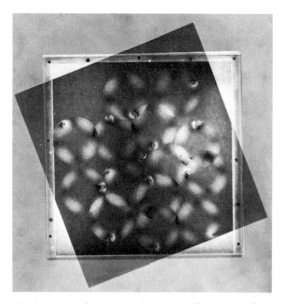

22. Marcello Salvadori, *Luminous Structure: Snow Crystals*, 1964. Courtesy Brompton Studio.

23. Christian Megert, *Untitled*, 1962. Photo courtesy Stedelijk Museum, Amsterdam.

movement to light; Salvadori in *Luminous Structure: Snow Crystals (Fig. 22)* rotates Polaroid filters against one another over a light source.

Mirrors are the oldest modifiers of light and, thereby, of space. Megert *(Fig. 23)* uses fragments of mirror to replace ordinary space with fragmented space; De Vecchi *(Fig. 24)* rotates a single triangle before two mirrors set at 90° to produce the image of a continuously warping square in space; Breder *(Fig. 25)* sets polished or transparent cubes over mirrors or stripes to mingle virtual with real images, and thus removes the barrier between the real and the looking-glass world. Mack in *Light Carousel (Fig. 26)* makes a huge montage of reflecting surfaces of great variety which, rotating under projected light beams, bounces rays onto the surfaces of the surrounding room to remove the barrier between object and environment.

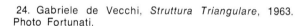

24. Gabriele de Vecchi, *Struttura Triangulare*, 1963. Photo Fortunati.

25. Hans Breder, *Interpenetration of Cubes in Space*, 1966. Coll. Mr. and Mrs. George Rickey.

26. Heinz Mack, *Light Carousel*, 1965. Coll. the artist.

27. Getulio Alviani, *L L Diag 7+2 Max 70*, 1964. Courtesy Galleria Cadario, Milan.

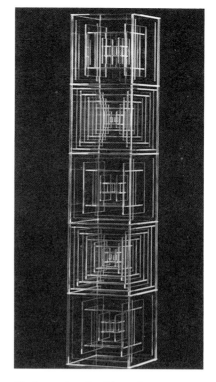

28. Leroy Lamis, *Clear Construction*, 1967. Coll. the artist; photo Richard Bruce.

29. Lucas Samaras, *Room # 2*, 1966. Coll. Albright-Knox Art Gallery, Buffalo, gift of Seymour H. Knox; photo Pace Gallery, Ferdinand Boesch.

Alviani machines surfaces of aluminum directionally. In *L L Diag 7 + 2 Max 70 (Fig. 27)*, the scratches catch and lose light systematically in such a way that they appear to be rounded forms; these forms are then composed in geometrical designs. Lamis, in *Clear Construction (Fig. 28)*, uses the properties of reflection from polished surfaces and of light refracted through a clear medium and emitted from its edges. This gives the illusion of the object being itself a light source.

In Samaris' *Room #2 (Fig. 29)*, a table and chair stand in a brightly lit room. The entire surfaces of the furniture, floor, ceiling, and walls are mirrors. One can read only corners and edges; surfaces disappear; spaces repeat ad infinitum but are punctuated by a three-dimensional lattice of illuminated edges.

XII/Color

The systematic study of color is about two and a half centuries old. Newton discovered, at the end of the seventeenth century, that light was color. Goethe made his own more subjective kind of study, at the end of the eighteenth and recorded it in his *Farbenlehre*. Statements in Delacroix's *Journal* in the middle of the nineteenth show the beginning of a wider awareness:

> The two conceptions of painting which Mme. Cavé was telling me about, that of color as *color* and of light as *light*, have got to be reconciled in a single operation.
> . . . From my window I see a man laying a floor in the gallery; he is nude to the waist. When I compare his color with that of the outer wall, I notice how colorful are the half-tints of the flesh, compared with those of inert matter. I noticed the same thing, day before yesterday, at the Place Saint-Sulpice, where a scalawag had climbed up on the statues of the fountain; I saw him in full sunlight: orange in the light, very lively violet tones for the passage from shadow, and golden reflections from the shadows turned toward the ground. The orange and violet dominated alternatively or mingled.[21]

This was written when Manet was twenty-four and Monet sixteen—eighteen years before the first Impressionist exhibition.

With increased knowledge came increased sensibility, and it was now the artist's turn to make advances. The Impressionists and their followers exploited the phenomena of color vibration and simultaneous contrast of complementaries, described by Chevreul (1786–1889), the chemist in charge of the Gobelins tapestry works. Gauguin, van Gogh, Seurat, and Signac sharpened the color sensibilities of every connoisseur who came to know their paintings; and Cézanne demonstrated to a whole generation of artists the relation of color to volume and space. Van Gogh professed emotional constants for certain colors but his response to them was clearly sensual. The Fauves, though their color seemed ferocious, broadened the range of acceptable color and led to the intense colorist effects of the mature Matisse, Rouault, and Klee. In art schools, while the study of human anatomy declined, erudition in the anatomy of color deepened and became a foundation for such colorist painters as Manessier, Afro, Rothko, Poliakoff, Francis, Morris Louis, and Noland. Eventually color theory, with its vocabulary, became part of every academy's curriculum, including the Bauhaus. The most advanced color teaching in the world now takes place at the Hochschule für Gestaltung in Ulm, where both Albers and Max Bill have taught. An alert schoolboy today knows more about color than did Newton or Delacroix.

As the properties of color became better understood, their application to expressive purposes (which had been recognized before Delacroix) was extended by such figurative artists as Munch, Soutine, Nolde, and Beckmann, and by Kandinsky in non-objective painting. A familiar anatomy of color was essential to Tachism and Abstract Expressionism.

The highly subjective nature of color has led artists interested in form to renounce it. The Cubists painted in monochrome. Malevich drew and painted the first Suprematist images in black and white, parsimoniously adding a little red, then a little yellow and blue. Gabo wrote in the Manifesto:

> Thence in painting we renounce colour as a pictorial element, colour is the idealized optical surface of objects; an exterior and superficial impression of them; colour is accidental and it has nothing in common with the innermost essence of a thing.

Mondrian adopted an arbitrary and virtually fixed system of primary color signals. One group of the Bauhaus faculty adopted similar signals, in spite of the presence of Klee and Kandinsky, for whom color was an expressive instrument of enormous range. The balance between color as meaning or emotional trigger and as a complex sensory experience has been held by Albers. His book, *Interaction of Color*, composed after a lifetime of study and produced in collaboration with his students, reveals in trenchant text and diverse, beautifully executed color plates, the spectrum of human color sensations. It was seen by reviewers as following Chevreul's theories. However, Albers proves Chevreul's basic concept of color mixture to be false. He rejects rules for color juxtaposition and, instead, presents an independent way to develop a sensitive eye. Because

> we had forgotten—but learned again—that rules to be applied to form and color design change and vanish as fashion and style do . . . therefore . . . visual development will change again . . . from retrospection to looking inward and forward, for sight, for vision.[22]

Albers demonstrates that we almost never see what a color really and physically is, and that Ostwald was right to state that it is first a psychological problem.

Though close to Constructivism all his life and a contributor to it, Albers has stood apart, recording and demonstrating the nature of color. His own painting has remained subjective and personal. Despite the apparent uniformity of his *Square*, he is a romantic, albeit a highly disciplined one. For him the problem of form lies not in the shape of the container but in what is contained, the color itself. The homage is not to the square, but to color. "Form, which includes color," he says, "demands unending performance and invites constant reconsideration."

Albers is not concerned with once more assembling old and new knowledge "about" color, nor with its physics, optics, nor with wave lengths, nor projection through lenses on our retina. All this he compares with acoustics, which cannot provide musicality, either on the creative or the appreciative side. His concern is "with what happens behind and beyond the retina with the psychological, more precisely the perceptual changes of color through interaction and interdependence." By "interaction" Albers means perceptual phenomena which "actually happen" and he relates both "action" and "actual" to "act," "actor," and "appearance," in the stage sense. Colors are actors; they constitute a cast; they perform. He teaches us to develop sensitivity to color and to its constant deceptions, and thus to recognize its perceptual (not optical) illusions. "Such recognition will enable us to make these illusions not only a deception but a means of broader color instrumentation."

Renunciation of the emotional appeal of color was reiterated by the postwar generation. "Color leads to subjective expression and response," states one recent manifesto. The same statement a decade earlier would have supported the other side. With the trend toward self-effacement, depersonalization, distrust of spontaneity, rejection of the acquired taste of an élite, color was seen as a self-indulgence or a trap. The first public renunciation, probably not thought significant at the time, was the exhibition of monochrome painting by Yves Klein in London in 1950. The impact of such painting on other young Europeans was to be enormous and to lead finally to all-white, all-black, or black-and-white exhibitions with titles as "Schwarz Weiss," "Weiss auf Weiss," "Weiss Weiss Weiss."

Achromatism was recognized as a movement in America in a "White on White" exhibition at the De Cordova Museum in Lincoln, Massachusetts, in 1965. Achromatism appears in the work of Uecker, Piene, Peeters, Tomasello, De Vries, Levinson, and Nevelson among the many shown in the De Cordova exhibition. Vasarely has lived in both camps. His black-and-white pictures have a detached, anonymous bite; his more recent color mosaics of circles, ellipses, and squares have the sonorous harmony of a romantic temperament.

Optical phenomena, with their non-aesthetic, dizzying, even nauseating, color situations, have been exploited for their direct impact on the spectator. This use of color is far removed from romantic or expressionist communication of mood or meaning. It is not only free of association, it is independent of ideas of harmonious order or any other kind of pleasure. A further step would be to rid it of any subjective bias, pleasant or unpleasant, by leaving the hue, intensity, size, or placement to chance, to mathematical formula, or to the whim of the spectator —all of which have been done (e.g., in the paintings of Lohse, Kelly, Bill).

A further use for non-associative color is for topographical effect—to separate areas as in maps. Ellsworth Kelly, Leon P. Smith, and Youngerman have used color in this way to separate figure and ground, as has been done for centuries in flags, signs, and crests. Tadasky sometimes uses it in concentric circles. Sedgley uses it inversely in his "targets" to fuse circles together which are in fact separate; Stella to separate stripes; Baertling to separate triangles, though he goes further in giving his color dissonances a special sting. George Sugarman uses topographic color in three dimensions to separate or punctuate wooden forms, as does Anthony Caro on his steel beams, while other English sculptors paint colored shapes in contradiction to the form, like the camouflaged ships of World War I.

Thus the heirs of Constructivism, after a suspicious withdrawal from color, have begun to find how rich a resource it is, that it is one more manifestation of nature which can supply them with useful tools, or simply be presented to the spectator as a force.

NOTES

1. Dr. Bo Wennberg, Catalogue for Baertling Retrospective, Modern Museum, Stockholm (1961), p. 80.

2. Charles Biederman, *Structure* (series 3, number 1; Bussum, Holland, 1960), p. 20.

3. Anthony Hill, "Movement in the Domain of Static Construction," *Structure* (series 2, number 2; Bussum, Holland, 1960), p. 59.

4. Letter to the author, July 1966.

5. Paul Klee, *Pedagogical Sketchbook, passim*, trans. by S. Moholy-Nagy (New York, Praeger, 1953). Klee's vocabulary incudes such terms as "active," "planar impact," "linear energy," "stress" and "disturbed balance."

6. Thomas Hobbes, *Leviathan* (New York, Everyman's Library, 1924), p. 8.

7. Georges Vantongerloo, *Reflections* (New York, Wittenborn, 1948), p. 9.

8. *Ibid.*, p. 18.

9. Max Bill, "The Mathematical Approach in Contemporary Art," *Structure* (series 3, number 2; Bussum, Holland, 1961), p. 65.

10. Richard P. Lohse, "Space and Principles," *Neue Grafik* (number 12, 1962).

11. Vantongerloo, *op. cit.*, p. 32.

12. Joost Baljeu, editorial in *Structure* (series 3, number 2; Bussum, Holland, 1961), p. 33.

13. Bill, *op. cit.*, p. 66.

14. Catalogue for Arp exhibition, Galerie Denise René, Paris (May, 1959), trans. by the author.

15. *NUL, 0* (series 2, number 1, Amsterdam, 1963), p. 35.

16. Catalogue for Agam exhibition, Marlborough-Gerson Gallery, New York (1966).

17. Umberto Boccioni, "Technical Manifesto of Futurist Sculpture," in Joshua Taylor, *Futurism*, Museum of Modern Art, New York (1961), pp. 131–132.

18. Naum Gabo, "Realist Manifesto," *Gabo* (Cambridge, Mass., Harvard Univ. Press, 1957), p. 151.

19. Interview with Ilya Bolotowsky and Ibram Lassaw, "Russia and Constructivism," *Gabo, ibid.*, p. 160.

20. Letter to the author from Dr. Carlo Belloli, August 1963.

21. Eugène Delacroix, *Journal*, trans. by Walter Pach (New York, Covici, Friede, 1937), pp. 248, 516.

22. Introductory text for "Interaction of Color" traveling exhibition, Smithsonian Institution, Washington, D.C.

Biographies: A Selected List

These biographies, mostly of younger artists and some groups, are limited to the salient facts of origin, training and exhibition record. Famous artists are omitted as they are amply documented in other publications as well as in the Bibliography (pp. 247–300). Bold face entries within biographies are included alphabetically. To simplify reference, the large group exhibitions—in which many of the artists are represented—are symbolized as follows:

AACI —"Art Abstrait Constructif International," Gal. Denise René, Paris, 1961.

AP —"Arte Programmata," traveling exhibit sponsored by Olivetti, 1962.

AT —"Art Today," Albright-Knox Gal., Buffalo, N.Y., 1965.

BB —"Bewogen Beweging," Stedelijk Mus., Amsterdam, 1961.

D —"Documenta," Kassel, Germany, 1955; D2—"Documenta II," Kassel, 1959; D3—"Documenta III," Kassel, 1964.

EA —"Europäische Avantgarde," Frankfurt am Main, 1963.

KK —"Konkrete Kunst," Helmhaus, Zürich, 1960.

LUB —"Licht und Bewegung," Kunsthalle, Bern, 1965.

M, M2 —"Mouvement" and "Mouvement Deux," Gal. Denise René, Paris, 1955, 1964.

N —"NUL," Stedelijk Museum, Amsterdam, 1965.

NT —"Nove Tendencije," Zagreb, Yugoslavia, 1961; NT2—"Nove Tendencije 2," Zagreb, 1963; NT3—"Nova Tendencija 3," Zagreb, 1965.

NTP —"Nouvelle Tendance," Musée des Arts Décoratifs, Paris, 1964.

OP —"Oltra la Pittura," Milan, 1963.

PB —Paris Biennale.

PIE —"Pittsburgh International Exhibition of Contemporary Painting and Sculpture," Carnegie Institute, Pa.

RE —"The Responsive Eye," Museum of Modern Art, N.Y., 1965.

SMB —San Marino Biennale.

SPB —São Paulo Bienal.

VB —Venice Biennale.

WAW —"Weiss auf Weiss," Kunsthalle, Bern, 1966.

Adams, Robert b. Northampton, England 1917. Studied Northampton School of Art. Exhibited: Réalités Nouvelles 1949; Staempfli Gal., N.Y. 1959; Mus. Modern Art, Paris 1963. SPB 1950, 1957; VB 1952, 1962. Makes welded sculpture. Lives London.

Agam, Yaacov b. Israel 1928. Studied Atelier d'Art Abstrait, Paris, 1951. Exhibited: Réalités Nouvelles 1954–55; Gal. Denise René 1955–56, 1958, 1962, 1964; Gal. Suzanne Bollag, Zürich 1959–60, 1962; Mus. Tel Aviv 1959; Gal. Chalette, N.Y. 1960; Wise Gal., N.Y. 1962; Malborough-Gerson Gal., N.Y. 1966. AACI; AT; BB; KK; LUB; PB 1959; PIE 1958, 1961; RE; SPB 1963 (Research Prize); WAW. Makes transformable paintings. Lives Paris.

Albrecht, Joachim b. Pomerania, East Prussia 1916. Studied Art Acad., Königsberg, 1934–39. Moved to Hamburg 1937; Hamburg group 1954–57; Deutsche Kunstlerbund, since 1957. Exhibited: Réalités Nouvelles 1958; Gal. Denise René 1958. PIE 1958. Edwin-Scharff Prize 1964. Geometrical painter. Lives Hamburg.

Alviani, Getulio b. Udine, Italy 1939. Exhibited: Studio F, Ulm 1962; Mus. Leverkusen; "Zero," Gal. Diogenes, Berlin; Gal. Denise René 1963; Gal. Cadario, Milan 1964. AP; AT; EA; N; NT2; NT3; NTP; M2; OP; RE; VB 1964; WAW. Concerned with light and reflection on brushed aluminum surfaces. Lives Udine.

Anonima American group concerned with optical stimuli, founded 1960 by Ernst Benkert, Francis Hewitt, and Edwin Mieczkowski in Cleveland. Exhibited: Martha Jackson Gal., N.Y. 1965.

Anuszkiewicz, Richard b. Erie, Pa. 1930. Cleveland Inst. of Art, BFA, 1948–53; Yale Univ., MFA, 1953–55. Exhibited: Mus. Modern Art, N.Y. 1961, 1963; Whitney Mus., N.Y. 1962; Janis Gal., N.Y. 1965. AT; M2; RE. Geometrical paintings with color vibration. Lives New Jersey.

Apollonio, Marina b. Trieste, Italy 1940. Studied art in Venice. Industrial designer, architect, till 1960. Painter since 1962. Exhibited: "Aktuel 65," Bern; Gal. Smith, Brussels; Gal. Del Deposito, Genoa 1965; Gal. D, Frankfurt; Gal. Del Naviglio, Milan 1966; "La Nuova Tendenza," Gal. Il Cenobio, Milan 1967. AP; NT3. Joan Miro prize, Barcelona 1966. Involved with visual research in optical phenomena. Lives Venice.

Baertling, Olle b. Halmstad, Sweden 1911. Student of André Lhote, Fernand Léger, 1948. Exhibited: Gal. Samlaren, Stockholm 1949; Réalités Nouvelles 1950–56, 1958; Gal. Denise René 1952–56, 1958, 1961–64; Mus. d'Ixelles, Brussels; Gal. Chalette, N.Y. 1960; Mus. Leverkusen 1962; Savage Gal., London; Rose Fried Gal., N.Y. 1965. AACI; SPB 1959, 1963. Guggenheim International Award 1964. Used open angles in painting and welded steel sculpture. Died 1981.

Baljeu, Joost b. Middelburg, Holland 1925. Studied Amsterdam Inst. of Design. Founder of magazine *Structure*. Exhibited: Kröller-Müller Mus., Holland. Critic and analyst of non-objective art in the Mondrian tradition. Made relief constructions. Died 1991.

Benton, Fletcher b. Jackson, Ohio 1931. Studied Miami Univ., Oxford, Ohio. Exhibited: Esther Robles Gal., Los Angeles 1962, 1965–66; Univ. Mus., Berkeley, Calif. 1966. Makes three-dimensional machines in controlled motion. Lives San Francisco, Calif.

Biasi, Alberto b. Padua, Italy 1937. Member Gruppo N, *q.v.* Exhibited: Studio F, Ulm 1963. AP; NT; NT2; NT3; OP; SMB (First Prize). Works with distribution of light, refracted through prisms. Lives Padua.

Biederman, Charles b. Cleveland, Ohio 1906. Studied Art Inst., Chicago, 1926–29. Exhibited: Pierre Matisse Gal., N.Y.; Reinhardt Gal., Paris 1936; Stedelijk Mus., Amsterdam 1962. Wrote influential book: *Art as the Evolution of Visual Knowledge*, 1949. Makes orthogonal reliefs. Lives Red Wing, Minnesota.

Bill, Max b. Winterthur, Switzerland 1908. Studied Zürich School of Applied Art, 1924–27; architecture, Dessau Bauhaus, 1927–29; organized "Konkrete Kunst," Basel, 1944. Founded Inst. of Progressive Art, 1947; cofounder Hochschule für Gestaltung, Ulm, 1950. Exhibited: Mus. São Paulo 1950; Mus. Ulm 1956; Mus. Munich; Mus. Zürich 1957; Mus. Basel; Mus. Leverkusen 1959; Mus. Stuttgart; Mus. Winterthur 1960; Staempfli Gal., N.Y. 1963, 1966; Gal. Suzanne Bollag, Zürich 1966. KK; PIE 1961; RE; SPB 1951; VB 1958; WAW. Kandinsky Prize 1949. Worked in many media; both painting and sculpture concerned with mathematics in art. Died 1994.

Bolotowsky, Ilya b. Petrograd, Russia 1907. Studied Baku; N.Y. Natl. Acad., 1924–30. Taught Black Mountain Coll., 1946–48. Exhibited: New Art Circle, N.Y. 1946, 1952; Pinacotheca Gal., N.Y. 1947; Rose Fried Gal., N.Y. 1949; Borgenicht Gal., N.Y. 1954, 1956, 1958–59, 1961, 1963–64, 1966; Whitney Mus., N.Y. 1962, 1966; De Cordova Mus., Lincoln, Mass. 1965. Influenced by Mondrian. Made geometric paintings and constructions. Died 1981.

Bonfanti, Arturo b. Bergamo, Italy 1905. Studied Art School "Andrea Fantoni," Bergamo. Exhibited: Gal. Permanente, Bergamo 1927, 1945; Gal. Ganzini, Milan 1945; Gal. Charles Lienhard, Zürich 1961; Gal. Denise René 1961–63; Gal. Lorenzelli, Milan 1962, 1964–66; Palazzo Strozzi, Florence; Natl. Arts, Antiques Festival, N.Y. 1965. AACI. Lissone Prize 1963. Painted subtle, elegantly proportioned, curvilinear shapes in muted, flat colors. Died 1978.

Boriani, Davide. b. Milan 1936. Studied Brera Acad., Milan. Founding member **Gruppo T,** *q.v.* Exhibited: AP; BB; LUB; NT3; OP; SMB 1961. Makes kinetic objects using magnets and iron filings. Lives Milan.

Boto, Martha b. Buenos Aires 1925. Exhibited: Gal. Denise René 1961, 1963–65; Mus. Leverkusen 1962; Hanover Gal., London; Mus. Tel Aviv; Kunsthalle, Bern 1965. AT; LUB; M2; OP; NT3; NTP; PB 1959; SMB 1963. Constructions using electric lights and motors. Married to Vardánega; lives Paris.

Breder, Hans b. Herford, Germany 1935. Studied Werkkunstschule, Bielefled; Hochschule fur bildende kunste, Hamburg 1957–64. To U.S. 1964 under scholarship from "Studienstiftung des deutschen Volkes." Member International Artists' Seminar, Fairleigh Dickinson Univ., summer 1965. Exhibited: Group shows in France, Switzerland, Germany 1963, 1964; Riverside Museum, N.Y.; Empire State Gallery, N.Y. 1965; Rutgers Univ., N.J.; AM Sachs, N.Y. 1966; Feigen Gal., Chicago; Whitney Museum, N.Y. 1967. Works with plastics; uses clear and reflecting surfaces to multiply the image. Teaches Univ. of Iowa; lives Iowa City, Iowa.

Breer, Robert b. Detroit, Mich. 1926. Studied Stanford Univ. Moved to Paris, 1949. Exhibited: Gal. Denise René 1950–55; Cordier and Ekstrom Gal., N.Y. 1964; Bonino Gal., N.Y. 1965–66; Univ. Mus., Berkeley, Calif. 1966. BB; M. Makes moving constructions of Styrofoam. Lives New York.

Bury, Pol. b. Hainte-Saint-Pierre, Belgium 1922. Studied Acad. des Beaux Arts, Mons, 1938–39. Exhibited: Gal. Apollo, Brussels 1955; Lefèbre Gal., N.Y. 1964–66; Univ. Mus., Berkeley, Calif. 1966. AT; BB; EA; LUB; M; PIE 1961; SMB 1963; WAW. Makes motor-driven constructions that twitch and wave slowly. Lives near Paris.

Cairoli, Carlos b. Buenos Aires 1926. Studied Natl. Acad. of Fine Arts, Buenos Aires, 1943–50; Inst. of Fine Arts, Buenos Aires, 1948–52. Exhibited: Réalités Nouvelles 1957–61; Stedelijk Mus., Amsterdam; Kunstgewerbemuseum, Zürich 1962; Mus. of Toulon 1963. Makes Plexiglas sculpture. Lives Paris.

Carlberg, Norman b. Roseau, Minn. 1928. Yale Univ., BFA, 1958, MFA, 1961. Exhibited: Mus. Modern Art., N.Y. 1959; Gal. Chalette, N.Y. 1960; Whitney Mus., N.Y. 1962; Baltimore Mus. 1966. Makes bronze, marble, and plaster three-dimensional screens. Lives, teaches Baltimore.

Caro, Anthony b. London 1924. Studied Charterhouse School; engineering degree, Christ's Coll., Cambridge; Regent St. Polytechnic, 1946; Royal Acad., 1947–52; asst. to Henry Moore, 1951–53. Taught Bennington Coll., 1963–65. Exhibited: ICA, London 1955; Tate Gal., London 1958; Marlborough New London Gal., London 1961; Emmerich Gal., N.Y. 1964; David Mirvish Gal., Toronto 1966. D3; PIE 1958; VB 1958. Makes painted steel and aluminum sculpture. Lives London.

Castellani, Enrico b. Castelmassa, Italy 1930. Studied Royal Acad., 1956. Exhibited: Gal. Pater, Milan 1958; Mus. Leverkusen 1960; Gal. Denise René 1961; New Vision Center, London; "Zero," Gal. Schindler, Bern 1962; Gal. Cadario, Milan 1963; Gal. Aktuell, Bern 1965. Monochrome reliefs with stretched fabric. Lives Milan.

Clark, Lygia b. Belo Horizonte, Brazil 1920. Studied with Roberto Burle Marx, 1947; with Fernand Léger, Paris, 1950. Founder "Grupo Néo-Concreto," 1959. Exhibited: Luis Alexander Gal., N.Y. 1963; Signals, London 1964–65. SPB 1953, 1963; VB 1962. Prize winner, 1952, 1953, 1957, 1961. Ceased painting in late fifties; began "time-space" constructions of aluminum planes hinged together. Lives Rio de Janeiro.

Collie, Alberto b. Caracas, Venezuela 1939. Boston Univ., BA, 1964; Harvard Univ. Grad. School of Design, 1965. Exhibited: Nordness Gal., N.Y. 1964. Makes floating-in-air sculptures using magnets. Lives Boston.

Colombo, Gianni b. Milan 1937. Collaborates with **Gruppo T,** q.v. Exhibited: AP; BB; LUB; OP; N; NT3; SMB 1961; VB 1964; WAW. Makes surface constructions set in motion by observer, or by motors. Lives Milan.

Constant (Constant Nieuwenhuys) b. Amsterdam 1920. Studied Amsterdam Acad. Founded "Cobra" group with Corneille and Appel, 1948. Exhibited: Gal. Breteau, Paris 1950; Stedelijk Mus., Amsterdam 1953, 1959; Salon de Mai; Réalités Nouvelles 1955; Kunsthalle, Bern 1965–66. VB 1952, 1956, 1966. Designed city of future, *New Babylon.* Spatial constructions in Plexiglas, wood and metal. Lives Amsterdam.

Costa, Toni b. Padua, Italy 1935. Member of **Gruppo N,** q.v. Exhibited: AP; NT. Lives Padua.

Cremer, Siegfried b. Dortmund, Germany 1929. Exhibited: "Anti-Peinture," Antwerp; "Zero," Gal. Schindler, Bern; Gal. Modern Art, Basel 1962; "Aktuell 65," Bern 1965; Gal. Mayer, Stuttgart 1966. BB; LUB. Makes moving linear sculptures. Lives Stuttgart.

Cruz-Diez, Carlos b. Caracas, Venezuela 1923. Studied Caracas School of Fine Arts, 1940–45. Taught, codirected, Caracas School of Fine Arts; taught design at Central Univ. of Venezuela, 1958–60. Exhibited: Gal. Denise René 1963; "Aktuell 65," Bern 1965. M2; NT2; RE; SPB 1953, 1957, 1963; VB 1962. Concerned with light and color perception and transformable works. Lives Paris.

Dewasne, Jean b. Hellemmes-Lille, France 1921. Studied art, science, music, architecture. Abstract painter since 1943. Directed Acad. Abstract Art with Pillet, 1950–52. Exhibited: Gal. Denise René 1945–56; Réalités Nouvelles 1946; Gal. Lorenzelli, Milan 1961; Cordier and Ekstrom Gal., N.Y. 1965–66; Kunsthalle, Bern 1966. PIE 1961. Kandinsky Prize. Large paintings in striking colors. Lives Paris.

Diller, Burgoyne b. New York 1906; died New Jersey 1965. Studied Mich. State Coll., Art Students' League. First American disciple of Mondrian, 1934. Head of Mural Div. of Fed. Art Project, 1935–40. Exhibited: Pinacotheca

Gal., N.Y. 1946–51; Mus. Modern Art, N.Y. 1951; Gal. Chalette, N.Y. 1960–62, 1964; Whitney Mus., N.Y. 1961. KK; SPB 1961. Practiced geometric abstraction.

Dorazio, Piero b. Rome 1927. Studied drawing, painting, architecture, Univ. of Rome, 1941–45. Published *La Fantasia dell'Arte.* Exhibited: Rose Fried Gal., N.Y. 1954; Gal. Springer, Berlin 1959; Mus. Leverkusen 1960; Tokyo Biennial 1961; NUL, Amsterdam 1962; Marlborough Gal. d'Arte, Rome 1964; Marlborough-Gerson Gal., N.Y.; Marlborough New London Gal., London 1966. D2; NT; PB 1961; PIE 1959; RE; VB 1950, 1956, 1958, 1960. Lissone Prize, 1965. Paints interlacings, hatchings, and stripes, frequently in pure colors. Prof. at Univ. of Penn. Lives Rome.

Effekt Group Founded Munich by Helge Sommerrock, Karl Reinhartz, **Dieter Hacker,** and **Walter Zehringer.** The purpose: "work with large kinetic spaces as a means."

Emery, Lin b. New York 1926. Studied Columbia and Chicago Univ., Art Students' League, Sorbonne, with Zadkine. Exhibited: Sculpture Center, N.Y. 1953, 1957, 1962; Riverside Mus., N.Y. 1958; Cordier Gal., Paris 1962; De Waters Art Center, Flint, Mich. 1965–66. Makes welded and moving sculptures powered by water. Lives New Orleans.

Equipo 57 Founded in Paris 1957, by José Duarte, Angel Duart, Juan Serrano, Agustin Ibarrola, "for plastic research and the demystification and study of various currents of abstract art." Disbanded in 1966. Other artists joining included Amata, Basterechea, Cuenca, **di Teana,** and Thorkild. Exhibited: Gal. Denise René 1957, 1959, 1962; Réalités Nouvelles 1958; Mus. d'Ixelles, Brussels 1960; Gal. Suzanne Bollag, Zürich 1962; Mus. Decorative Arts, Paris 1964; "Aktuell 65," Bern; Mus. Tel Aviv, 1965. M2; NT2; RE. Experimental painting and sculpture. Strict anonymity.

Feitelson, Lorser b. Savannah, Ga. 1898. Taught drawing by father; studied in N.Y. and Paris. Exhibited: Daniels Gal., N.Y. 1924; Los Angeles County Mus. 1929, 1944, 1959; Mus. Modern Art, N.Y. 1936, 1944; Whitney Mus., N.Y. 1955, 1962, 1965; ICA, London 1960; Ankrum Gal., Los Angeles 1962–65. RE; SPB 1955. Employed color to intensify space and form. Died 1978.

Fruhtrunk, Günter b. Munich 1923. Studied architecture 1940–41, painting with William Straube and Léger 1945–50. Moved to Paris 1954. Exhibited: Gal. Denise René 1957–58, 1960–61; Kunsthalle, Zürich 1958; Mus. Leverkusen 1959, 1962, 1963; Gal. Chalette, N.Y. 1960; Mus. Decorative Arts, Paris 1962; Goethe Inst., Paris 1966. RE. Painted interlocking, rectilinear, fretted designs usually in black and white or intense monochrome. Died 1984.

Gerstner, Karl b. Basel 1930. Graduated tech. schools Basel, Zürich; studied commercial art. Exhibited: Gal. Suzanne Bollag, Zürich 1960; Gal. Denise René 1962; Staempfli Gal., N.Y. 1965. RE. Gold Medal winner, Milan Triennale, 1953. Wants onlooker to participate in process of design. Lives Basel.

Glarner, Fritz b. Zürich 1899. Attended Acad. of Naples, 1915–18. Went to Paris 1923. Joined "Abstraction-Création" 1933. Exhibited: Kunsthaus, Zürich 1936, 1961; Mus. Modern Art, N.Y. 1951, 1954–56; Gal. Carré, Paris 1952, 1955, 1966; Tokyo Biennial 1953; Guggenheim Mus., N.Y. 1954; Mus. Modern Art, Paris, Zürich, Barcelona, The Hague 1954–55; Gal. Denise René 1961; Whitney Mus., N.Y. 1962. D; PIE 1952, 1958, 1961; SPB 1951. After death of Mondrian, modified pure Neo-Plasticism with slanted line between two parallels. Died 1972.

Goodyear, John b. South Gate, Calif. 1930. Graduated Univ. of Mich., 1952. Exhibited: Riverside Mus., N.Y. 1958, 1965; Martha Jackson Gal., N.Y. 1960, 1964; Wise Gal., N.Y.; Amel Gal., N.Y. 1964–66; Whitney Mus., N.Y. 1966. AT; RE. Optical painter uses moving grids and plastic. Lives Lebanon, New Jersey.

Gorin, Jean b. Saint-Emilien-Blain, France 1899. Studied Grande Chaumière Acad., Paris, 1916–17; Nantes, 1923. Member "Cercle et Carré" 1930, and "Abstraction-Création" 1932. Exhibited: Kunsthalle, Bern 1936, 1966; Réalités Nouvelles 1946; Gal. Pinacotheca, N.Y. 1948; Janis Gal., N.Y. 1953; Gal. Chalette, N.Y. 1959; Mus. d'Ixelles, Brussels 1960; Gal. Denise René 1960–63; Stedelijk Mus., Amsterdam 1962; Marlborough-Gerson Gal., N.Y. 1964. Neo-plastic paintings, constructions and sculptures. Died 1980

Graeser, Camille b. Genf, Germany 1892. Studied Kunstgewerbeschule, Stuttgart 1913–15. Exhibited: Landesgewerbemus., Stuttgart 1926; Kunsthalle, Basel 1938, 1956; Réalités Nouvelles 1948, 1950; Gal. 16, Zürich; Kunstmus., Bern 1951; Kunstmus., Winterthur 1958; Metropolitan Art Gal., Tokyo; Gal. Suzanne Bollag, Zürich 1959; Mus. Leverkusen 1962; Kunsthaus, Zürich; Kunstverein, Ulm 1964. AACI; KK. Made polychrone geometrical paintings, often on a mathematical plan. Died 1980.

Graevenitz, Gerhard von b. near Berlin 1934. Studied economics Univ. of Frankfurt; Munich Art Acad. 1957. Exhibited: Kunstverein, Hannover 1959; Studio F, Ulm 1960; Mus. Leverkusen; Gal. Denise René; Kunsthaus, Munich 1961; "Anti-Peinture," Antwerp 1962; Gal. Cadario, Milan 1963; Univ. Mus., Berkeley, Calif. AACI; LUB; M2; NTP; NT2; OP; RE; SMB 1963; WAW. Concerned with light and movement. Died 1983.

Grosvenor, Robert b. New York 1937. Studied Ecole des Beaux Arts, Dijon, 1956; Ecole des Arts Décoratifs, Paris, 1957–59. Exhibited: Park Place Gal., N.Y. 1962–65; John Daniels Gal.,

N.Y. 1965; Jewish Mus., N.Y. 1966. Makes sculptures of wood, polyester and steel, which extend from floor to ceiling. Lives New York.

Groupe de Recherche d'Art Visuel Formed Paris 1960. Members: **Julio le Parc, François Morellet, Francisco Sobrino, Joel Stein, Yvaral,** and Garcia Rossi. Anonymous endeavor to establish a close artist-spectator relationship by visual stimuli, precisely executed, using modern materials and technology. Exhibited: Gal. Denise René 1961, 1966; "Anti-Peinture," Antwerp 1962; Contemporaries Gal., N.Y. 1962, 1965; Gal. Cadario, Milan 1963; Wise Gal., N.Y.; Gimpel Hanover, Zürich; "54/64," Tate Gal., London 1964; Gal. Ad Libitum, Antwerp; Mus. Modern Art, N.Y. 1966. AACI; AP; AT; D3; LUB; M2; NT; NT3; PB 1963, 1965; PIE 1961; RE; SPB 1963; VB 1964.

Gruppo N Formed Padua 1959. Of original eleven, six remained in 1960, five in 1962, and four in 1963. Until group dissolved 1965, members included: **Alberto Biasi,** Ennio Chiggio, **Toni Costa,** Eduardo Landi, Manfredo Massironi. Group exhibited anonymously, issued manifestos, concerned itself with optic dynamic research. Exhibited: AP; NT; NT2; NTP; OP; SMB (First Prize).

Gruppo T Formed Milan 1959; joined NTrc in 1963. Members: Giovanni Anceschi, **Davide Boriani, Gianni Colombo, Gabriele de Vecchi,** Grazia Varisco. Use movement, optical phenomena and light. Exhibited: "Miriorama I," Gal. Pater, Milan 1959; "Miriorama II, III, IV, V, VII," Gal. Matteo, Genoa 1960; "Miriorama X," Gal. La Salita, Rome; Modern Mus., Stockholm; Hessenhuis, Antwerp 1961. AP; BB; LUB; N; NT2; NT3; NTP; OP; SMB 1961. Lissone Prize.

Haacke, Hans b. Cologne 1936. Studied Acad. Kassel, 1960; Paris; Fulbright Fellow, Temple Univ., Phila., 1961–62. Exhibited: Wittenborn Gal., N.Y. 1962; Mus. Modern Art, N.Y. 1962,

1964; De Cordova Mus., Lincoln, Mass.; "Zero," New Vision Center, London; Jewish Mus., N.Y. 1964; Wise Gal., N.Y. 1966. LUB; N. Works with water and Plexiglas. Lives New York.

Hacker, Dieter b. Augsburg, Germany 1942. Member of **Effekt Group,** *q.v.* Lives Munich.

Haese, Günter b. Kiel, Germany 1924. Private art school, Plon, 1945; studied with Bruno Goller, Edward Mataré, Düsseldorf Acad. 1950. Exhibited: Mus. Ulm; Mus. Modern Art, N.Y.; Marlborough-Gerson Gal., N.Y. 1965. D3. Works in wires, screens, gears, inspired by dismantled watches. Lives Düsseldorf.

Hall, David b. Leicester, England 1937. Studied architecture, 1954–56; Leicester Coll. of Art, 1956–60; Royal Coll. of Art, London, 1960–64. Exhibited: AIA, London 1961; Tooth Gal., London 1963; ICA, London 1964; Axiom Gal., London; Jewish Mus., N.Y.; Feigen Gal., N.Y. 1966. PB (Prize Winner) 1965; WAW. Makes painted steel structures. Lives London.

Hauer, Erwin b. Vienna 1926. Studied Acad. of Applied Arts, Vienna; Brera Acad., Milan; Fulbright Fellow, R.I. School of Design, and Yale Univ. Art School. Exhibited: De Cordova Mus., Lincoln, Mass. 1966. Makes screen designs of repeating units. Teaches Yale Univ. Art School; lives Bethany, Conn.

Healey, John b. London 1894. Educated Harrow; Univ. of London. No formal art training. Exhibited: Royal Coll. of Art Gal., London 1964; Van Abbemus., Eindhoven 1966. Works with luminous kinetic pictures. Lives Sussex, England.

Hill, Anthony b. London 1930. Studied Central School of Arts and Crafts, 1949–51. Exhibited: ICA, London; Gimpel Fils Gal., London 1951; Réalités Nouvelles 1952; Gal. Denise René 1961, 1963; Gal. Modern Art, Basel;

Kunstgewerbemuseum, Zürich; Stedelijk Mus., Amsterdam; Mus. Leverkusen 1962; Tate Gal., London; Mus. Tel Aviv 1965. AT; KK; PB 1961; SMB 1963. Makes constructions of highly polished metals contrasting with plastics. Lives London.

Jacobsen, Robert b. Copenhagen 1912. Went to Paris 1946. Exhibited: Gal. Denise René 1947, 1948, 1950, 1951, 1953, 1956; Salon de Mai 1949–61; Réalités Nouvelles 1949, 1952–62; Salon de la Jeune Sculpture 1949–53; Mus. Modern Art, Rio de Janeiro, São Paulo 1954; Mus. Modern Art, Paris; Kunsthalle, Bern; Stedelijk Mus., Amsterdam 1955, 1957, 1960–61; Mus. Rodin 1956; Mus. Mod. Art, Stockholm; Lefèbre Gal., N.Y. 1960; Kootz Gal., N.Y. 1961; Mus. Decorative Arts, Paris; Kunsthaus, Munich 1962; Gal. Creuze, Paris 1963; Gal. Chalette, N.Y. 1966. D3; PIE 1959, 1961, 1964; VB (First Prize Winner) 1966. Worked mostly in welded steel, primarily concerned with relationship of open space to metal. Died 1993.

Janz, Robert b. Holland 1932. Studied Univ. of Chicago; Maryland Inst. of Art, 1964; Fulbright Fellow, Spain, 1964–65. Exhibited: Balin-Traube Gal., N.Y. 1962; Baltimore Mus. 1963; Gal. Carlos, Zaragoza 1964; "Aktuell 65," Bern 1965; "Continuum 1," Cordoba 1966. Makes movable linear constructions involving light. Lives Spain.

Judd, Donald b. Excelsior Springs, Missouri 1928. Columbia Univ., BS; Art Students' League, 1949. Exhibited: Green Gal., N.Y. 1963–65; Tibor de Nagy Gal., N.Y.; Byron Gal., N.Y. 1965. SPB 1965. Concerned with static, spatial relations; Made large wood and metal constructions. Died 1994.

Kelly, Ellsworth b. Newburgh, N.Y. 1923. Studied Englewood, N.J.; Brooklyn; Boston Mus. School. Went to Paris 1948. Met Vantogerloo, Arp, and Seuphor in 1950. Exhibited: Réalités Nouvelles 1950, 1951; Gal.

Arnaud, Paris 1951; Gal. Maeght, Paris 1951–52, 1964; Betty Parsons Gal., N.Y. 1956; Gal. Denise René 1961–62; Jewish Mus., N.Y. 1963; Janis Gal., N.Y. 1964. KK; PIE (Prize Winner) 1964; RE. Concerned with shape and color. Lives New York.

Kemeny, Zoltan b. Banica, Transylvania, Hungary 1907; died 1965. Apprenticed to furniture maker, 1921–23; studied architecture and painting, Budapest, 1924–30. Lived Paris 1930–41; moved to Zürich 1942. Exhibited: Kunsthalle, Bern 1945; Gal. des Eaux-Vives 1945, 1947; Stedelijk Mus., Amsterdam 1950; Gal. 16, Zürich 1951, 1955; Mus. Leverkusen; Réalités Nouvelles 1958; Kunsthaus, Zürich; Mus. Modern Art, N.Y.; French and Co., N.Y. 1959; Janis Gal., N.Y.; Martha Jackson Gal., N.Y.; Gal. Suzanne Bollag, Zürich; Kröller-Müller Mus., Holland; Mus. Rodin 1963; "54/64," Tate Gal., London 1964. D2; KK; PIE 1958, 1961; VB (Sculpture Prize) 1964. Experimented with relief, light, and metal in his paintings; after 1960, only relief sculpture.

Kidner, Michael b. England 1917. Studied Cambridge Univ., 1939; Acad. Lhote, 1952–55. Exhibited: AIA, London 1960; McRoberts and Tunnard Gal., London 1964, 1966; Axiom Gal., London 1966. RE. Concerned with optical and color relationships. Lives London.

Kobashi, Yasuhide b. Okayama, Japan 1931. Studied Tokyo Tech. Univ. Exhibited: Stone Gal., N.Y. 1961, 1965; Wise Gal., N.Y. 1964; World House Gal., N.Y. 1965. PIE 1962. Works in ceramic and wood. Lives Japan.

Kramer, Harry b. Lingen, Germany 1925. Dancer to 1951. Moved to Berlin 1952; to Paris 1956. Exhibited: Loeb Gal., N.Y. 1965; Felix Landau Gal., Los Angeles 1966. D3; LUB. Makes moving wire sculptures. Lives Paris.

Kricke, Norbert b. Düsseldorf 1922. Studied Berlin. Exhibited: Kunsthalle, Düsseldorf 1955;

Kunsthalle, Bern 1955, 1960; Milan Triennale; Réalités Nouvelles 1957; Staempfli Gal., N.Y. 1959; Mus. Modern Art. N.Y.: Lefèbre Gal., N.Y. 1961. D2; VB 1964. Worked with stainless steel wires or rods, straight, in sheaves, or knotted. Died 1984.

Lamis, Leroy b. Eddyville, Iowa 1925. Studied New Mexico Highlands Univ., 1949–52; Columbia Univ. T.C., 1954–56. Began work with plastics, 1960. Exhibited: Sheldon Art Gal. 1962; Contemporaries Gal., N.Y. 1963; Staempfli Gal., N.Y.; Martha Jackson Gal., N.Y. 1965; Whitney Mus., N.Y. 1966; "American Sculpture of the Sixties," Los Angeles County Mus. 1967. RE. Makes transparent plastic boxes within boxes, usually colored. Teaches Indiana State Coll.; lives Terre Haute, Indiana.

Lardera, Berto b. La Spezia, Italy 1911. Studied Florence. Self-taught sculptor. Went to Paris 1948. Exhibited: Gal. Denise René 1948; Kunsthalle, Bern 1955; Knoedler Gal., N.Y. 1957; Helmhaus, Zürich 1960; Kunsthalle, Basel 1961. D3; NT2; SPB 1951; VB 1948, 1950, 1952, 1954, 1960. Creates space constructions in various media, mostly metal. Lives Paris.

Leblanc, Walter b. Antwerp 1932. Studied Fine Arts Acad., Antwerp. Exhibited: Mus. Leverkusen 1960; New Vision Center, London 1961; Gal. Schindler, Bern 1962; Redfern Gal., London; McRoberts and Tunnard Gal., London; Mus. Decorative Arts, Paris; Salon de Mai 1964; Gal. Suzanne Bollag, Zürich 1965. LUB; RE. Made reliefs involving light and spectator movement. Died 1986.

Le Parc, Julio b. Mendoza, Argentina 1928. Educated Buenos Aires. Moved to Paris 1958. Member of **Groupe de Recherche d'Art Visuel,** *q.v.* Exhibited: Spanish-American Biennial, Mexico 1958; Wise Gal., N.Y. 1966. AT; PB 1959; RE; SPB 1957; VB (Grand Prize Winner) 1966. Works mostly in metal, constructing mobiles, reliefs, and light-reflecting machines. Lives Paris.

Liberman, Alexander b. Kiev, Russia 1912. Studied with André Lhote, Paris, 1929–31. Exhibited: Guggenheim Mus., N.Y. 1954; Mus. Modern Art, N.Y. 1959, 1962, 1964; Betty Parsons Gal., N.Y. 1960, 1962–64; Tooth Gal., London 1961; Whitney Mus., N.Y. 1962–63, 1965; De Cordova Mus., Lincoln, Mass.; Gal. Bernard, Paris, 1963; Gal. Denise René; Robert Frazer Gal., London 1964; Gal. dell'Ariete, Milan 1965; Jewish Mus., N.Y. 1966. KK; RE. Formerly a painter, now welding sculptor. Lives New York.

Linck, Walter b. Bern 1903. Studied art schools Bern, Zürich, Berlin. Exhibited: Kunsthalle, Bern 1950, 1965; Stedelijk Mus., Amsterdam 1950; Kunstmuseum, Winterthur 1956; Gal. Bernard, Paris 1958; Kunsthalle, Basel 1959; Mus. Rodin, Paris 1963; Kunstverein, Düsseldorf 1965–66. BB; KK; LUB; PIE (Prize Winner) 1950; VB 1956; SPB 1963. Made moving sculptures with springs. Died 1975.

Lippold, Richard b. Milwaukee 1915. Studied Chicago Univ., 1933–37; industrial designer 1937–39. Taught at various colleges. Moved to New York 1944. Artist-in-Residence, Black Mountain Coll., 1948. Exhibited: Willard Gal., N.Y. 1947; Mus. Modern Art, N.Y. 1953; Whitney Mus., N.Y. 1955. Numerous architectural commissions including Metropolitan Mus., N.Y. and Lincoln Center, N.Y. Creates enormous hanging structures of polished metal wire. Lives Locust Valley, New York.

Lohse, Richard b. Zürich 1902. Studied Kunstgewerbeschwe, Zürich, 1920–24. Early contact with Klee, Moholy-Nagy, Hans Richter, Taeuber-Arp. Evolved through Cubism to vertical-horizontal non-objective designs. Organized Swiss section "Réalités Nouvelles," Paris, 1950. Contact with Pevsner, Vantongerloo, Herbin, Le Corbusier. Exhibited: Gal. Denise René 1948; Réalités Nouvelles 1948, 1950; Milan Triennale 1957; Gal. Chalette 1960; Kunsthaus, Zürich 1962. AACI; SPB 1951; VB 1958. Gug-genheim International prize 1958. Geometrical paintings using mathematical relationships. Died 1988.

Lundeberg, Helen b. Chicago 1908. Studied with Lorser Feitelson. Exhibited: Mus. Modern Art, N.Y. 1936, 1942; Paul Rivas Gal., Los Angeles 1950–61; Ankrum Gal., Los Angeles 1962, 1964; Whitney Mus., N.Y. 1962, 1965. PIE 1952; SPB 1955. Refined and austere flat compositions combining straight and curved forms. Married to Lorser Feitelson; lives Los Angeles.

Lye, Len b. Christchurch, New Zealand 1901. Studied Wellington Tech. Coll., Canterbury Coll. of Fine Arts, Christchurch. Traveled to Samoa to work on kinetic sculpture, 1920. Moved to London 1926. Made first film inscribing design directly on film, 1928. Moved to New York 1946. Exhibited: Mus. Modern Art, N.Y.; Stedelijk Mus., Amsterdam 1961; Wise Gal., N.Y. 1964–65; Univ. Mus., Berkeley, Calif. 1966. AT. Made mechanized moving sculptures. Died 1981.

Mack, Heinz b. Lollar, Germany 1931. Studied Acad. of Art, Düsseldorf, 1950–53; Univ. of Cologne, 1956. Member of **Zero.** Exhibited: Gal. Schmela, Düsseldorf 1957–58, 1960; Gal. Clert, Paris 1959; New Vision Center, London 1960; Wise Gal., N.Y.; Univ. Mus., Berkeley, Calif. 1966. LUB; NT2; KK; EA; WAW; RE; AT; NT; OP; PIE 1961; SMB 1961; AACI; M2. Lissone Prize; Guggenheim Award 1963. Concerned with light and movement, using glass, aluminum. Lives Düsseldorf.

Mahlmann, Max b. Hamburg 1912. Exhibited: Gal. Denise René 1958; Réalités Nouvelles 1958–59; Mus. d'Ixelles, Brussels 1960; Kunsthaus, Hamburg 1963; Kunstverein, Wiesbaden 1965. Geometrical paintings and reliefs. Married Gudrun Piper; lives Hamburg.

Malina, Frank b. Texas 1912. Studied Cal.

Tech. Formerly astronautical scientist; moved to France. Exhibited: Gal. Furstenburg, Paris; Kunstgewerbemuseum, Zürich 1960; Gal. Schwarz, Milan 1965. LUB; NT3. Kinetic paintings with light. Died 1981.

Mari, Enzo b. Milan 1932. Studied Brera Acad. Exhibited: Gal. San Fedele, Milan 1955; Gal. Danese, Milan 1959–60, 1962–63; Mus. d'Ixelles, Brussels 1960; Gal. Strozzi, Florence 1962. KK; LUB; NT3; RE. Makes moving and movable structures in wood, plastic and metal. Lives Milan.

Martin, Kenneth b. Sheffield, England 1905. Studied Sheffield and London. First abstract painting 1948; first mobile construction 1951. Exhibited: AIA, London; Gimpel Fils, London 1951; Redfern Gal., London 1955; Hanover Gal., London 1956; ICA, London 1960; Drian Gal., London 1960–61; "British Constructivist Art," Amer. Fed. of Arts, N.Y., and toured U.S. 1961–62; Arts Council, London; Internat. Sculpture Exhibition, Lausanne 1963. BB; KK; SMB 1963. Died 1984.

Martin, Mary b. Folkestone, England 1907. Studied Goldsmith School of Art, London. Exhibited: AIA, London; Gimpel Fils, London 1951; ICA, London 1957, 1960; Mus. Leverkusen 1961; Stedelijk Mus., Amsterdam 1962; Molton and Lords, London; Albright-Knox Gal., Buffalo 1964; Tate Gal., London; Tokyo Biennial 1965; Signals, London 1966. Made reliefs of painted wood and plastic. Married to Kenneth Martin. Died 1969.

Mavignier, Almir b. Rio de Janeiro 1926. Art studies Brazil; Hochschule für Gestaltung, Ulm, 1953–58. Exhibited: Salon de Mai 1952; Réalités Nouvelles; Mus. Modern Art, São Paulo; Kurtfried Mus., Ulm; Gal. Suzanne Bollag, Zürich 1953; Gal. Nota, Munich; Gal. Denise René 1961; Dato Gal., Frankfurt 1962; Mus. Ulm; Mus. Modern Art, Rio de Janeiro 1963. NT; RE. Specializes in color through dot concentration. Lives Ulm.

McLaughlin, John b. Sharon, Mass. 1898. Attended Univ. Hawaii. Went to Japan 1935. Exhibited: Landau Gal., Los Angeles 1953, 1958, 1962, 1966; Downtown Gal., N.Y. 1955; Los Angeles County Mus. 1959–60; Whitney Mus., N.Y. 1962. RE. Painted very simplified abstractions. Died 1976.

Medalla, David b. Manila, Philippines 1942. Studied Columbia Univ. Exhibited: Signals, London 1964–66. WAW. Makes sculptures called *Bubble Mobiles*, with foam. Editor of *Signals*; lives London.

Megert, Christian b. Bern 1936. Studied Arts and Crafts School, Bern, 1952–55. Exhibited: Réalités Nouvelles 1958; Gal. Køpcke, Copenhagen 1959–60; Mus. Leverkusen; "Nieuwe Tendenzen," State Univ., Leyden 1962; Halfmannshof, Gelsenkirchen 1965. N. Louise Geschlimann Prize 1960; Swiss Federal Fine Arts Prize 1962–63. Works with cut pieces of mirror at angles, so the image is fractured. Lives Bern.

Meier-Denninghoff, Brigitte b. Berlin 1923. Studied Berlin School of Fine Arts, 1943. Henry Moore's asst. in England, 1948; worked in Pevsner's studio, Paris, 1949–50. Exhibited: Réalités Nouvelles 1949; Marlborough New London Gal., London; Staempfli Gal., N.Y. 1963; Gal. Franke, Munich 1965; Gal. Grosshennig, Düsseldorf 1965–66. VB 1962. Architechtonic sculptures of clusters of bronze rods. Lives Paris.

Morellet, François b. Cholet, Maine-et-Loire, France 1926. Member **Groupe de Recherche d'Art Visuel,** *q.v.* Exhibited: AACI; AT; KK; M2; NT; NT2; NT3; NTP; OP; PIE 1961; RE; SMB 1961; WAW. Makes complex grids of interlaced lines. Lives Cholet.

Mortensen, Richard b. Copenhagen 1910. Studied Royal Acad., Copenhagen. Moved to Paris 1947. Exhibited: Gal. Denise René 1948–

54, 1956–59, 1960–62; Salon de Mai 1949–62; Réalités Nouvelles 1948–62; Janis Gal., N.Y. 1953; Kunsthalle, Bern 1954; Mus. Leverkusen 1954, 1956; Stedelijk Mus., Amsterdam; Gal. Chalette, N.Y. 1959–60; Tate Gal., London 1962. AT; D; D2; D3; KK; PIE 1955, 1958, 1961; VB 1948, 1960. Lissone Prize 1955. Vivid, often very freely-designed lyrical abstract painting. Lives Paris.

Moss, Joe b. West Virginia 1933. Studied West Virginia Univ., BA, 1955; MA, 1960. Exhibited: West Virginia Univ. 1955, 1963; Western Pa. Sculpture, Pittsburgh 1954–55, 1957; "Exhibit 60," Morgantown, West Virginia 1958–63; Members' Penthouse, Mus. Modern Art, N.Y., 1966. Ball moves through intricate passages in a box, defining space by sound. Teaches West Virginia Univ.; lives Morgantown.

Motonaga, Sadamasa b. Ueno, Japan 1922. Studied with Jiro Yoshihara. Member of "Gutai" group. Exhibited: Tapié exhibition, Zürich 1959. N. Makes sculptures of hanging plastic filled with transparent liquid. Lives Osaka.

Moulpied, Deborah de b. Manchester, New Hampshire 1933. Studied Boston Mus. School, 1952–56; Yale School of Art and Architecture, 1958–62. Exhibited: Gal. Chalette, N.Y. 1961; Mus. Modern Art, N.Y. 1961; Whitney Mus., N.Y. 1962. Works in plastic. Teaches Univ. of Bridgeport; lives New Haven, Conn.

Munari, Bruno b. Milan 1907. Took part in Futurist movement; pioneer kinetic artist. Organized "Arte Programmata," 1962. Exhibited: Mus. Modern Art, N.Y.; Hessenhuis, Antwerp 1959; National Mus. Modern Art, Tokyo 1960; Wise Gal., N.Y. 1965–66. AP; BB; EA; KK; LUB; NT3; OP; SMB 1961. Professional designer; influenced Italian avant-garde. Works with chance, movement, and light. Lives Milan.

Nevelson, Louise b. Kiev, Russia 1900. Moved to Rockland, Maine 1905. Studied Art Students' League, N.Y., 1929–30; with Hans Hofmann, Munich, 1931. Exhibited: Nierendorf Gal., N.Y. 1941, 1943–44, 1947; Mus. Modern Art, N.Y. 1943, 1959; Grand Central Moderns Gal., N.Y. 1951, 1954–58; Martha Jackson Gal., N.Y. 1959–61; Cordier Gal., Paris 1960; Janis Gal., N.Y.; Hanover Gal., London 1963; Pace Gal., N.Y. 1964, 1966; Whitney Mus., N.Y. 1967. D3; VB 1962. Made assembled reliefs of wooden scraps or machined metal, usually painted black. Died 1983.

Noland, Kenneth b. Asheville, North Carolina 1924. Studied Black Mountain Coll. under Albers, Bolotowsky; Paris under Zadkine, 1948–49. Lived New York 1960–63. Exhibited: Kootz Gal., N.Y. 1954; French and Co., N.Y. 1959; ICA, London 1960; Marlborough New London Gal., London 1961; Emmerich Gal., N.Y. 1961–66; Gal. Lawrence, Paris 1961. RE; SMB; VB 1964. Colorist painter of "target," chevron, and lozenge images. Lives Vermont.

NUL Dutch group founded 1961 by Armando, **Henk Peeters, Jan Schoonhoven,** and **Herman de Vries.** Counterpart of **Zero** group in Düsseldorf, just across Dutch border from Arnhem, working with similar problems and frequently exhibiting with them, though retaining a trace of surrealism. Exhibited: Gal. Chalette, N.Y.; New Vision Center, London 1960; Halfmannshof, Gelsenkirchen; Stedelijk Mus., Amsterdam 1965. EA; NT3; N; OP; SMB 1963.

Pasmore, Victor b. Chelsham, England 1908. Studied Harrow School, 1922–26. Exhibited: Zwemmer Gal., London 1929, 1934; Redfern Gal., London 1947–52, 1955; Marlborough New London Gal., London 1961; Tate Gal., London 1964; Marlborough-Gerson Gal., N.Y. 1964, 1966. BB; D2; D3; KK; PIE 1950, 1961; SMB 1963; SPB 1965; VB 1960. Winner Guggenheim International Award 1960; Marzotto Prize 1962–63. Makes reliefs, panel paintings in curvilinear abstract designs. Lives London.

Peeters, Henk b. The Hague 1925. Studied Royal Acad., The Hague. Member of **NUL**, *q.v.* Exhibited: Gal. Køpcke, Copenhagen 1960; New Vision Center, London 1960, 1962, 1963; De Cordova Mus., Lincoln, Mass. 1965. NT; NT2; NT3; N; EA; OP; SMB 1963. Swiss Prize for Abstract Painting 1960. Collages with commonplace materials, also water and light-play. Lives Arnhem.

Piene, Otto b. Laasphe, Westphalia 1928. Studied Blocherer Art School; Hochschule der Bildenden Künste, Munich, 1948–50; Staatliche Kunstakad., Düsseldorf, 1950–53; Univ. of Cologne, 1953–57. Member **Zero**, *q.v.* Artist-in-Residence, Univ. of Penn., 1964. Exhibited: Gal. Schmela, Düsseldorf 1959–60, 1962–63; McRoberts and Tunnard Gal., London 1964; Wise Gal., N.Y. 1964–66. AT; BB; D3; EA; KK; LUB; NT; NT2; NT3; OP; PIE 1961, 1964; SMB 1963; WAW. Specialist in light sculpture and projected, programmed, light manifestations. Lives Düsseldorf and New York.

Piper, Gudrun b. Kobe, Japan 1917. Studied Düsseldorf, Berlin, Italy, Munich, 1937–44. Exhibited: Stephan Gal., Vienna 1957; Gal. Denise René 1958; Réalités Nouvelles 1958; Mus. d'Ixelles, Brussels 1960; Kunsthaus, Hamburg 1963; Kunstverein, Ulm 1964; Kunstverein, Wiesbaden 1965. Concerned with cellular division of the surface. Married to Max Mahlmann; lives Hamburg.

Pohl, Uli b. Munich 1935. Studied Akad. der Bildenden Künste, Munich. Exhibited: Kunstverein, Hannover 1959; Studio F, Ulm; Dato Gal., Frankfurt 1961; Gal. Denise René; "Zero," Gal. Schindler, Bern; Gal. Ad Libitum, Antwerp 1962. AACI; AT; EA; M2; NT; NT2; NTP; OP; RE; SMB 1963. Makes sculptures of clear solid plastic. Lives Munich.

Poons, Larry b. Tokyo 1937. Studied New England Conservatory of Music; Boston Mus. School, 1955–57. Exhibited: Green Gal., N.Y. 1963, 1965; Ferus Gal., Los Angeles; Guggenheim Mus., N.Y. 1964; Janis Gal., N.Y. 1964–65; Whitney Mus., N.Y. 1965. PIE 1964; RE; SPB 1965. Makes paintings with colored ground, punctuated with a series of small, round, or elliptical areas of colored pigment. Lives New York.

Reimann, William b. Minneapolis 1935. Yale Univ., BA, 1957; MA, 1961. Exhibited: Mus. Modern Art, N.Y. 1959; Whitney Mus., N.Y. 1961–65; Gal. Chalette, N.Y. 1961; De Cordova Mus., Lincoln, Mass. 1965; Carpenter Center for Visual Arts, Cambridge, Mass. 1966. Repeating units which build up into curved masses. Teaches Harvard; lives Cambridge.

Reinhardt, Ad b. Buffalo, N.Y. 1913. Studied Columbia Coll. Self-taught painter. Exhibited: Artists' Gal. 1944; Betty Parsons Gal., N.Y. 1946–66; Mus. Leverkusen; Clert Gal., Paris 1962; Dwan Gal., Los Angeles 1962–63; Graham Gal., N.Y.; Stable Gal., N.Y. 1965; "The Hilles Collection," Boston Mus. 1966. KK; RE. Made large monochromatic paintings, often almost black. Died 1967.

Richter, Yjenceslav b. Drenova, Yugoslavia 1917. Studied Zagreb. Professional architect. Founded group EXAT 51. Architectural works include: Yugoslav pavilions, Expo 1958, Brussels; and Turin, 1961; Milan Triennale (Gold Medal) 1964. Began making sculpture 1963. Exhibited: Mus. Leverkusen 1963; Gal. Obelisco, Rome 1965. NT2; NT3; NTP; SPB 1965; VB 1963. Works with plastic; concerned with micro-elements and repetition of forms. Lives Zagreb.

Riley, Bridget b. London 1931. Studied Goldsmiths School of Art; Royal Coll. of Art. Exhibited: Young Contemporaries, London 1955; South London Art Gal. 1958; Gallery One, London 1962–63; Feigen Gal., N.Y. 1965. AT; NT3; NTP; RE. Paints geometrical works in black and white. Lives London.

Rivera, José de b. West Baton Rouge, Louisiana 1904. Worked as machinist, blacksmith, tool- and die-maker, 1922–30. Studied Chicago Studio School, 1929–30; Art Inst. of Chicago, 1930. Visited Europe and North Africa 1932. Made sculpture for Newark Airport 1937–38. Teacher and critic at Yale 1953–55. Exhibited: Mus. Modern Art, N.Y. 1956; Gal. Bernard, Paris 11961. KK. Worked in polished, stainless steel, curvilinear forms. Died 1985.

Salvadori, Marcello b. Florence 1928. Studied Rome, 1945–54. Moved to London 1955. Exhibited: New Vision Center, London 1957; Redfern Gal., London; Gimpel-Hanover, Zürich 1964; Signals, London 1964–65. Works in Polaroid plastic, foam rubber, aluminum, chemicals and other industrial materials. Lives London.

Samaras, Lucas b. Greece 1936. Studied Rutgers Univ.; Columbia Univ. Exhibited: Green Gal., N.Y. 1961, 1962, 1964; "Assemblage," Mus. Modern Art, N.Y. 1961; Dallas Mus.; San Francisco Mus.; Whitney Mus., N.Y.; "Pop and Op," Janis Gal., N.Y.; "Beyond Realism," Pace Gal., N.Y. 1965; Whitney Mus. Sculpture Annual, N.Y.; "Object Transformed," Mus. Modern Art, N.Y. 1966. Worked with assemblages of pins; recently with constructivist environments of mirrors. Lives New York.

Schöffer, Nicolas b. Kalocsa, Hungary 1912. Studied Fine Arts Acad., Budapest. Moved to Paris 1936. Exhibited: Gal. Denise René 1958, 1960, 1966; Mus. Modern Art, Paris 1959; ICA, London 1960; Mus. Decorative Arts, Paris 1963; "54/64," Tate Gal., London 1964; Jewish Mus., N.Y. 1965. AT; BB; D3; KK; LUB; M2; SPB 1961. Sought to put art object into motion, used light to modify plastic values. Died 1992.

Schoonhoven, Jan b. Delft, Holland 1914. Studied Art Acad., The Hague, 1932–36. Member of **NUL**, q.v. Exhibited: Gal. Gunar, Düsseldorf 1959; Gal. Køpcke, Copenhagen 1960; New Vision Center, London 1960, 1962; Dato Gal., Frankfurt; Gal. Schmela, Düsseldorf; Gal. A, Arnhem; Gal. Schindler, Bern; Gal. Denise René 1963; De Cordova Mus., Lincoln, Mass. 1965. EA; N; NT; NT2; OP; RE; SMB 1963. Makes reliefs. Lives Arnhem.

Sedgley, Peter b. England 1930. Studied architecture, School of Building, Brixton. Exhibited: McRoberts and Tunnard, London 1964–66: Wise Gal., N.Y.; Réalités Nouvelles; Gal. Motte, Geneva 1965; Axiom Gal., London 1966. AT; RE. Vibrant color relations in concentric circles. Lives London.

Smith, David b. Decatur, Indiana 1906; died 1965. Studied Ohio Univ.; Art Students' League. Exhibited: East River Gal., N.Y. 1938; Willard Gal., N.Y. 1940, 1943, 1946, 1947, 1950–54, 1956; Kleeman Gal., N.Y. 1952; Kootz Gal., N.Y. 1953; Mus. Modern Art, N.Y. 1957; French and Co., N.Y. 1959–60; Gerson Gal., N.Y. 1960–61; Spoleto Festival 1962; Balin-Traube Gal., N.Y. 1963; Inst. of Fine Arts, Boston 1964; Marlborough-Gerson Gal., N.Y. 1964; Kröller-Müller Mus., Holland; Fogg Mus., Cambridge, Mass.; "The Hilles Collection," Boston Mus. 1966. D3; KK; PIE 1961; SPB 1959; VB 1958. American pioneer of welded sculpture.

Smith, Leon Polk b. Oklahoma 1906. Oklahoma State Coll., BA, 1934; Columbia Univ., MA, 1938. Guggenheim Fellowship 1943–44. Exhibited: Uptown Gal., N.Y. 1941; Pinacotheca Gal., N.Y. 1942, 1946; Janis Gal., N.Y.; Rose Fried Gal., N.Y. 1949; Betty Parsons Gal., N.Y. 1958, 1960; Stable Gal., N.Y. 1961, 1963; Gal. Chalette, N.Y. 1965. PIE 1961. Paints spherical works, concerned with space. Lives New York.

Sobrino, Francisco b. Guadalajara, Spain 1932. Member **Groupe de Recherche d'Art Visuel**, q.v. Exhibited: AACI; AT; LUB; M2; OP; RE; SMB 1961; WAW. Makes constructions of colored plastic. Lives Paris.

Soto, Jésus-Rafaël b. Venezuela 1923. Studied School of Fine Arts, Caracas, 1942. Director School of Fine Arts, Maracaibo, 1947. Went to Paris. Exhibited: Réalités Nouvelles 1952–54, 1956; Salon de Mai 1954; Gal. Denise René 1955–56, 1965; Martha Jackson Gal., N.Y.; Gal. Clert, Paris; Mus. Leverkusen 1959; "Zero," Gal. Schmela, Düsseldorf 1961; Signals, London 1964–65; Kootz Gal., N.Y. 1965. AT; BB; EA; KK; M2; N 1965; PIE 1961; SPB 1957, 1959, 1963; VB 1958, 1962, 1964; WAW. Makes three-dimensional moiré constructions, with movement. Lives Paris.

Stanczak, Julian, b. Poland 1928. Studied art under British govt. scholarship, 1948; Cleveland Inst. of Art, BFA; Yale Univ., MFA. Exhibited: Martha Jackson Gal., N.Y. 1964–66; Riverside Mus., N.Y. 1965. AT; RE. Paints optical works in black and white. Lives Cleveland.

Steele, Jeffrey b. Cardiff, Wales 1931. Studied Cardiff and Newport Coll. of Art. Exhibited: ICA, London 1961; AIA, London 1962; McRoberts and Tunnard Gal., London 1964, 1966; Gabrowski Gal., London 1964. RE. Paints black and white optical works. Lives London.

Stein, Joel b. Boulogne, France 1926. Member **Groupe de Recherche d'Art Visuel,** *q.v.* Exhibited: Contemporaries Gal., N.Y. 1962, 1965. AACI; AT; KK; M2; NT; NT2; NT3; NTP; OP; PIE 1961; RE; SMB 1961; WAW. Lives Paris.

Stella, Frank b. Malden, Mass. 1936. Studied Phillips Acad., Princeton Univ. Exhibited: Tibor de Nagy Gal., N.Y. 1959; Leo Castelli Gal., N.Y. 1960, 1962, 1964, 1966; Mus. Modern Art, N.Y. 1960; Guggenheim Mus., N.Y. 1960, 1966; Gal. Lawrence, Paris 1961, 1964; Jewish Mus., N.Y. 1963–64, 1966; Kasmin Ltd., London 1964; Whitney Mus., N.Y. 1964–65; Fogg Mus., Cambridge, Mass. 1965. RE; SPB 1965; VB 1964. Stark rectilinear paintings with strong color, sometimes uses shaped canvases. Lives New York.

Stroud, Peter b. London 1921. Studied London Univ., 1947–51. Exhibited: New Vision Center, London 1957; AIA, London 1959; Drain Gal., London 1960; Mus. Leverkusen; ICA, London 1961; Marlborough New London Gal., London 1962; Kunsthalle, Basel; Guggenheim International, N.Y. 1963; Fleming Art Mus., Burlington, Vermont 1966. PIE 1961, 1964; RE. Makes relief paintings. Lives Bennington, Vermont.

Tadasky (Tadsuke Kuwayma) b. Negoya, Japan 1935. Studied Art Students' League; Brooklyn Mus. School. Exhibited: Kootz Gal., N.Y. 1964–66; Mus. Modern Art, N.Y. 1965–66; National Mus. Modern Art, Tokyo; Jewish Mus., N.Y.; Tokyo Gal.; Fischbach Gal., N.Y. 1966. AT; RE. Makes paintings of concentric circles with optical effect. Lives New York.

Takis b. Athens 1925. Moved to Paris 1954. Exhibited: Hanover Gal., London 1955, 1958; Iris Clert and Alain Jouffroy presentation, Paris 1959; Gal. Clert, Paris 1959–60; Iolas Gal., N.Y. 1960–61, 1963; Gal. Schwarz, Milan 1962; Signals, London 1964; Gal. Iolas, Paris 1964, 1966. AT; BB; KK; LUB; WAW. Makes complex sculpture machines involving magnetism. Lives Paris.

Talman, Paul b. Zürich 1932. Studied Bern. Moved to Basel 1956. Member group "Nouvelle Tendance." Exhibited: Gal. 33, Bern 1955; Kunsthalle, Basel 1961; "Anti-Peinture," Antwerp; "Zero," Gal. Schindler, Bern; Mus. Modern Art, Basel 1962; Byron Gal., N.Y. 1965. BB; EA; LUB; SMB 1961. Makes movable reliefs of black and white or colored spheres. Lives Basel.

Teana, Marino di b. Teana, Italy 1920. Moved to Argentina; became master mason 1936. Studied mechanics; changed to art school 1942; worked in Spain as sculptor 1952. Moved to Paris 1953. Exhibited: Mus. Rodin 1956; Gal. Denise René 1957; Mus. Saint-Etienne

1960. Began working with glass in addition to metal in early 1960s. Lives Paris.

Thépot, Roger-François b. Landeleau, France 1925. Member of group "Mésure." Exhibited: Gal. Breteau, Paris 1952; Réalités Nouvelles 1954–65; "Mésure," Mus. Leverkusen 1963; Roberts Gal., Toronto 1965. The Europe Prize, Ostend, 1962. Creates geometrical paintings. Lives Paris.

Tomasello, Luis b. Argentina 1915. Studied Ecole des Beaux Arts and Ecole Supérieure de peintre, Buenos Aires. Moved to Paris 1957. Exhibited: Réalités Nouvelles 1959, 1961, 1963–65; Gal. Chalette, N.Y. 1960; Mus. Tel Aviv 1960, 1965; Gal. Denise René 1962–63, 1965–66; Gal. Modern Art, Basel; Mus. Leverkusen 1962; Gimpel-Hanover, Zürich 1964. AACI; AT; BB; LUB; M2; NTP; OP; SMB 1961; WAW. Makes relief paintings of wood, exploiting light reflection. Lives Paris.

Uecker, Günther b. Mecklenburg, Germany 1930. Member of **Zero**, *q.v.* Exhibited: Gal. Azimut, Milan 1958, 1959; Mus. Leverkusen 1960; "Zero," Gal. Ad Libitum, Antwerp 1961–62, 1964; Gal. Schmela, Düsseldorf 1961, 1963; Gal. Lawrence, Paris; McRoberts and Tunnard Gal., London; Wise Gal., N.Y. 1964, 1966. AT; D3; EA; LUB; M2; N; NT2; NTP; OP; PB (Prize Winner) 1965; SMB 1963; WAW. Makes white sculptures and paintings using nails on canvas and wood. Lives Düsseldorf.

Uhlmann, Hans b. Berlin 1900. Studied Inst. of Tech., Berlin. Exhibited: Gal. Rosen, Berlin 1945; Gal. Franke, Munich; Kestnergesellschaft, Hannover 1953; Mus. Modern Art, N.Y. 1955, 1957; Kleeman Gal., N.Y. 1957. SPB 1952. Since 1950, Professor Berlin Acad. of Fine Arts. Welded sculptures in steel. Died 1975.

Vardánega, Gregorio b. Passagno, Italy 1923. Moved to Argentina 1926. Attended Acad. Fine Arts, Buenos Aires. Moved to Paris 1959. Exhibited: Gal. Allendi, Paris 1950; Gal. Galatea, Buenos Aires 1955; Réalités Nouvelles 1961; Gal. Denise René 1961, 1963; Mus. Modern Art, Basel; Mus. Leverkusen 1962; Gal. Cadario, Milan 1963; Hanover Gal., London; Mus. Tel Aviv; Kunsthalle, Bern 1965. AACI; AT; LUB; M2; NT3; NTP; OP; SMB 1963; SPB 1957. Makes constructions of plastic which respond to light. Lives Paris.

Vasarely, Victor b. Pecs, Hungary 1908. Studied Poldini-Volkmann Acad., Budapest, 1927; "Muhely" Acad. of Alexander Bortnyik, Budapest, 1928–29; moved to Paris 1930. Co-founder Gal. Denise René 1944. Exhibited: Gal. Denise René 1944, 1946–57, 1959–66; Salon de Mai 1948–63; Réalités Nouvelles 1948–63; Betty Parsons Gal., N.Y. 1949; Kunsthaus, Zürich 1950; Janis Gal., N.Y. 1952, 1965; Guggenheim Mus., N.Y. 1953, 1958; Mus. Modern Art, São Paulo 1954; Gal. Der Spiegel, Cologne 1956, 1958–59, 1961; Gal. Rose Fried, N.Y.; Mus. Modern Art, N.Y.; Gal. Schmela, Düsseldorf 1958; Mus. d'Ixelles, Brussels; Gal. Chalette, N.Y. 1960; World House, N.Y. 1961; Hanover Gal., London 1961–63; Gimpel Hanover, Zürich 1962, 1964; Pace Gal., N.Y. 1964–65; Tate Gal., London; "The Hilles Collection," Boston Mus. 1966. AACI; AT; BB; D; D2; D3; EA; KK; LUB; SPB (First Prize) 1965; WAW. Gold Medal winner, Milan Triennale; Lissone Prize 1955; Guggenheim International Award 1964. Leader in European optical and kinetic tendencies. Lives Annet-sur-Marne.

Vecchi, Gabriele de b. Milan 1938. Member of **Gruppo T**, *q.v.* Exhibited: "Anti-Peinture," Antwerp 1962; Mus. Decorative Arts, Paris 1964; Milan Triennale 1965; Vismara Arte Contemporanea, Milan 1966. AP; BB; N; NT2; NT3; SMB 1963; WAW. Makes constructions which turn and move; uses plastic and metal. Lives Milan.

Vieira, Mary b. São Paulo 1927. Studied Brazil. Moved Zürich 1952. Exhibited: Atelier Behring, Rio de Janeiro 1950; Kunstgewerbemuseum, Zürich 1954; Gal. Modern Art, Basel 1958; Helmhaus, Zürich 1960; Stedelijk

Mus., Amsterdam 1961; Gal. Denise René 1962–63; Réalités Nouvelles 1963. KK; PIE 1961; SPB (Prize Winner) 1953, 1955. Geometrical constructions in stone and metal. Lives Basel.

Visser, Carel Nicholaas b. Papendrecht, Holland 1928. Studied Delft School, 1948–49; Acad. Gravenhage, 1949–51. Exhibited: Mus. Rodin, Paris 1956, 1961; Hilversum 1959; Stedelijk Mus., Amsterdam 1960; Bertha Schaefer Gal., N.Y. 1961. PIE 1961; VB 1958. Makes abstract sculptures in iron, ferro-concrete or wood. Died 1975.

Volten, André b. Andijk, Holland 1925. Studied Arts and Crafts School, Amsterdam 1945. Exhibited: VB 1956. Makes linear forged sculptures. Lives Amsterdam.

Vries, Herman de b. Alkmar, Holland 1931. Studied architecture; self-taught painter. Began painting in 1953; "collage trouvée" in 1955; monochrome painting in 1956. Executed white collages, paintings, and objects, 1958–60. Exhibited: Stedelijk Mus., Amsterdam 1957, 1961–62; Gal. Køpcke, Copenhagen 1960; "Anti-Peinture," Antwerp 1962; Metz & Co., Amsterdam 1963; De Cordova Mus., Lincoln, Mass.; "Aktuell 65," Bern. EA; NT; NT3; WAW. White objects often assembled with the help of chance. Lives Arnhem.

Weber, Willi b. Bern 1933. Formerly surrealist painter. Exhibited: Gal. Clert, Paris; Grattacielo, Milan 1963; Städ. Gal. Biel 1964; Salon des Comparaisons, Paris 1966. LUB; PB 1965; WAW. Constructions using column of air to support objects. Lives Bern.

Wilding, Ludwig b. Grunstädt, Germany 1927. Studied Univ. of Mainz Art School; also with Willi Baumeister. Exhibited: Mus. Leverkusen 1953, 1962–63; Zimmergal., Frankfurt 1958, 1961; Duisburg; Florence; Rome 1960; Studio F, Ulm 1965; Kabinett de Greisbach, Heidelberg 1965–66. LUB; NT2; NT3; NTP; RE. Specialist in moiré. Lives Westheim, Augsburg.

Wise, Gillian b. Essex, England 1936. Studied Wimbledon Art School, 1954–57; Exhibited: Young Contemporaries, London 1957; New Vision Center, London; AIA, London 1958; Drain Gal., London 1961–62; Gal. Dautzenberg, Paris 1962; ICA, London 1963; Tokyo Biennial; Tate Gal., London 1965. Makes constructions and reliefs using plastics and metal; concerned with light and reflection. Married to Anthony Hill; lives London.

Yvaral (Jean-Pierre Vasarely) b. Paris 1934. Studied Ecole des Arts Appliqués, Paris. Cofounder **Groupe de Recherche d'Art Visuel,** *q.v.* Exhibited: with group; Wise Gal., N.Y. 1966; Univ. Mus., Berkeley, Calif. 1966. AACI; AT; BB; D3; LUB; NT2; OP; RE. Concerned with light, movement, and moiré mostly in relief situations. Lives Paris.

Zehringer, Walter b. Memmingen, Germany 1940. Member **Effekt Group,** *q.v.* Lives Munich.

Zero Group founded Düsseldorf 1957, by Heinz Mack and Otto Piene; Günther Uecker joined 1958. "Zero" means "a zone of silence for a new beginning." Exhibited: Atelier Piene, Düsseldorf 1958; Dynamo I, Wiesbaden; Hessenhuis, Antwerp; Gal. Clert, Paris; Kunstverein, Hannover 1959; Mus. Leverkusen; Gal. Seide, Hannover 1960; Gal. A, Arnhem; Gal. Schmela, Düsseldorf; Modern Mus., Stockholm; Mus. Modern Art, N.Y.; Dato Gal., Frankfurt 1961; Corcoran Gal., Washington, D.C.; McRoberts and Tunnard Gal., London 1962, 1965; Gal. D, Frankfurt; Gal. Ad Libitum, Antwerp; Gal. Schindler, Bern 1962; Gal. Diogenes, Berlin; Studio F, Ulm 1963; New Vision Center, London; ICA, London; Wise Gal., N.Y.; Mus. Modern Art, Paris; Redfern Gal., London; "54/64," Tate Gal., London; "Aktuell 65," Bern; Sachs Gal., N.Y. 1965. BB; D2; D3; EA; KK; N; NT; NT2; OP; PB 1961; PIE 1961, 1963; SMB (Prize Winner) 1963. Lissone Prize 1963; Guggenheim International Award 1964; Marzotto Prize 1964.

Survey of Museum Holdings of Constructivist Art, 1963

	ALBERS	GABO	HERBIN	LISSITZKY	MAGNELLI	MALEVICH	MONDRIAN	PEVSNER	VAN DOESBURG	VANTONGERLOO
Amsterdam, Stedelijk	1*	6*	3*	28	2	52*	14*	2	5*	1
Baltimore, Museum of Art	1	2					1	2	1	
Basel, Museum of Art	1		1				2	2	1	1
Boston, Museum of Art							1			
Chicago, Art Institute	6*	2	1				2	1	1	
Cologne, Stadt Museum										
Detroit Institute of Art				1						
Glasgow Museum and Art Gallery										
Guggenheim Museum, New York	7	7	1	2		1	7*	2	1	9
The Hague, Gemeentemuseum			1	4			154*		3	
Holland, Kröller-Müller			29				10	1	1	
London, Tate Gallery		2	1					1		
Los Angeles County Museum										
New York, Museum of Modern Art	3*	6*		3		16	13*	4*	12	3
Paris, Musée d'Art Moderne			2		2			19*		
Philadelphia Museum of Art		1		1	1		6	1	1	1
St. Louis, City Art Museum										
Toronto, Art Gallery	1						1			
Yale University Art Gallery	32	7		2	2	1	3	2	2	
Zürich, Kunsthaus	1*		1		2*		2*	1		

*one-man show

Bibliography

For convenience, there are six sections as follows: 1: *General References* (Nos. 1–80): Theoretical, Historical, National, Pictorial, Movements. II. *Special Fields* (Nos. 81–103): Architecture & Design, Painting & Sculpture. III. *Periodicals* (Nos. 104–120). IV. *Articles* (Nos. 121–223). V. *Exhibition Catalogues* (Nos. 224–282). VI. *Artists & Groups* (Nos. 283–824). While there are 824 numbered references, owing to the numerous additional notes there are over 1160 citations.

In the case of periodicals, a suggestive cross-section of those which may be considered to be "more directly concerned" and "probably lesser known" has been the objective. While it is true that almost all major magazines, for example *Cahiers d'Art*, will include related articles even though their emphasis lies elsewhere than toward Constructivism, they are conveniently accessible via the standard indexes. As Constructivist-oriented texts proliferate, their bibliographies include details in obscure documents from the "non-book" world. Sometimes this occurs with admirable comprehensiveness, as in the *Museumjournal* (Bibl. 662), or in major catalogues (Bibl. 557, 783), and even in dissertations (Bibl. 61, 70).

Since the origins of Constructivism as presented in this text have not been a paramount element in most books about modern art, it was decided to let the general references stand as a *suggestive* outline. Therefore, instead of reflecting the author's text precisely, the Bibliography hopes to parallel it.

Bernard Karpel
Librarian, Museum of Modern Art, New York

I. GENERAL REFERENCES: Theoretical, Historical, National, Pictorial, Movements

1. Alsleben, Kurd. *Asthetische Redundanz.* Hamburg, Schnelle, 1963.
   "Abhandlungun über die artistischen Mittel der bildenden Kunst." Cover by V. Vasarely, foreword by A. A. Moles. Chapters on "Symmetrie," "Kombinatorik," etc. Bibliography.

2. Alvard, Julien & Gindertaël, R. V., ed. *Témoignages Pour l'Art Abstrait.* Paris, Editions *Art d'Aujourd'hui*, 1952.
   "Propos recueillis." Introduction by L. Degand; portraits by S. Vandercam. Includes Arp, Calder, S. Delaunay, Lardera, Magnelli, Pevsner, Vasarely, and others. Color plates and selections emphasize geometric abstraction.

3. American Abstract Artists. *The World of Abstract Art.* New York, Wittenborn, 1957.
   The most recent publication sponsored by the A.A.A. An international anthology with chapters by M. Seuphor, V. Pasmore, E. Pillet, E. Buchholz, H. Richter, P. Dorazio, C. von Wiegand, S. Hasegawa, G. Kosice, N.

Gabo, W. Barnet, K. Morris, G. L. McCann Morley, G. L. K. Morris, J. Arp. Biographical notes.

4. ———. [Publications]. New York, The Association, 1938–1946.

Previous titles released by the association: *American Abstract Artists*, New York [Distributed by Witteborn], 1946 (articles by Moholy-Nagy, Léger, Mondrian, Albers); *American Abstract Artists*, New York, 1939 (collotype plates and notes on Albers, Bolotowsky, Glarner, Holtzman, Pereira, Reinhardt, David Smith); *American Abstract Artists*, New York, 1938 (text by G. L. K. Morris, "The quest for an abstract tradition," and other statements and illustrations).

5. Arnheim, Rudolf. *Art and Visual Perception.* Berkeley & Los Angeles, University of California Press, 1957.

"A psychology of the creative eye." Deals with basic elements: balance, shape, form, growth, space, light, color, movement, tension, expression. Extensive bibliography.

6. ———. *Toward a Psychology of Art. Collected Essays.* Berkeley & Los Angeles, University of California Press, 1966.

A continuation of perceptual and formal ideas in art.

7. Art Concret (Groupe). *Numéro d'Introduction du Groupe et de la Revue Art Concret.* Paris, 1930.

Actually a collective manifesto (since only one number was published) and the first use of "concrete" art. Associates: Carlslund, Van Doesburg, Hélion, Tutundjian, Wantz. Contents: "Commentaires sur la base de la peinture concrète" (pp. 2–3); Hélion, "Les problèmes de l'art concret: art et mathématiques" (pp. 5–6, 8–10); Van Doesburg, "Vers la peinture blanche" (pp. 11–12); Definitions, quotations, etc. (pp. 12, 14–16); Gérant: Jean Hélion.

8. Baljeu, Joost. *Attempt at a Theory of Synthesist Plastic Expression.* London, Tiranti, 1963. Illustrated booklet.

9. Ballo, Guido. *La Linea dell'Arte Italiana dal Simbolismo alle Opera Moltiplicate.* Rome, Edizioni Mediterranee, 1964 (2 vols.).

Latest manifestations: Castellani, Munari, etc., v. 2, pp. 327 ff. (ill.). Bibliography.

10. Barr, Alfred H., Jr. *Cubism and Abstract Art.* New York, Museum of Modern Art, 1936. (Reprint: New York, Arno Press, 1966.)

Still a major work of analysis and synthesis, emphasizing European developments. Includes catalogue of accompanying exhibition, bibliography. Biographical notes include Archipenko, Arp, Boccioni, Calder, Delaunay, Van Doesburg, Duchamp, Gabo, Gonzalez, Jeanneret (Le Corbusier), Kandinsky, Kupka, Larionov, Lissitzky, Malevich, Moholy-Nagy, Mondrian, Nicholson, Pevsner, Rodchenko, Tatlin, Vantongerloo.

11. Battcock, Gregory, ed. *The New Art.* New York, Dutton, 1966.

Includes Lucy Lippard's New York Letter from *Art International*, 1965, e.g. "Duchamp, Reinhardt, Morris," etc.

12. Belloli, Carlo. *Stenogrammi della Geometria Elementare. Lucistrutture integrative di Roger Humbert.* (St. Gallen, Tschudy Verlag, 1960.)

Die Quadrat-Bücher. Also "no. 2 delle serie Il Quadrato; impaginazione Mary Vieira."

13. Biederman, Charles. *Art as the Evolution of Visual Knowledge.* Red Wing, Minn., The Author, 1948.

A copiously illustrated tome (710 pp.) with extensive bibliography. Main sections: "Pictographs to photographs"; "Camera to cubism"; "Imitation to invention." Emphasizes potentialities arising from a science-machine culture. Complemented by his *The New Cézanne*, Red Wing, Minn., Art History Publishers, 1958 (at head of title: "From Monet to Mondrian." Includes analyses of works with artists' statements).

14. Bill, Max, ed. *5 Constructionen—5 Composition. 10 Original Grafische Blätter*, Zürich, Allianz Verlag, 1941.

Ten color plates in folio. Includes Bill, Lohse, Leuppi, Taeuber-Arp, etc.

15. Bjerke-Petersen, Vilhelm. *Konkret Kunst.* Stockholm, Rabén & Sjögren, 1956.

Insert (7 pp.) is English summary: "Non-objective art." References to Arp, Baertling, Bill, Calder, R. & S. Delaunay, Eggeling, Gabo,

Kandinsky, Kupka, Magnelli, Malevich, Mondrian, Nicholson, D. Smith, Taeuber-Arp, Tinguely, Van Doesburg, Vantongerloo, Vasarely.

16. Cabanne, Pierre. *L'Epopée du Cubisme.* Paris, La Table Ronde, 1963.
     Chronological bibliography, pp. 409–418.

17. Cagnet, Michel & others. *Atlas of Optical Phenomena,* by Michel Cagnet, Maurice Françon, Jean Claude Thrierr. Göttingen-Heidelberg, Springer; Englewood Cliffs, N.J., Prentice-Hall, 1962.
     Text also in German and French. Includes 45 plates with commentary, based on work of the Institut d'Optique et Faculté des Sciences, University of Paris. Subjects: geometrical aberrations, interference, diffraction, polarization, phase and interference contrast in transparent objects.

18. Carpenter Center for the Visual Arts. *Proportion, a Measure of Order.* Cambridge, Harvard University, Spring–Summer 1965.
     Major catalogue (111 pp.). Exhibition directed by E. F. Sekler; collaborators: H. H. Buchwald, A. B. Gregory, Jr. Bibliography.

19. Carraher, Ronald & Thurston, Jacqueline B. *Optical Illusions and the Visual Arts.* New York, Reinhold, 1966.
     "Works of art . . . define some of the ways . . . an artist may express his interest in perceptual effects. . . . The contents . . . broaden the concept of optical or geometric art." Illustrations: Vasarely, Riley, Neal, Steele, Morellet, etc. Glossary.

20. Carrieri, Raffaele. *Futurism.* Milan, Ed. del Milione, 1963.
     With manifesto and bibliography. Complemented by *Archivi del Futurismo,* Rome, De Luca, 1958–1962 (2 vols.). Exhaustive documentation.

21. Chapuis, Alfred & Droz, Edmond. *Automata. A Historical and Technological Study.* Neuchâtel, Griffon; New York, Central Book Co., 1958.
     French edition, 1949. A foreshadowing of objects and figures in motion.

22. *Circle:* International Survey of Constructive Art. Editors: J. L. Martin, Ben Nicholson, N. Gabo. London, Faber & Faber, 1937.
     Sections on painting, sculpture, architecture, "art and life." Includes: Gabo, "The construc-tive idea in art"; Mondrian, "Plastic art and pure plastic art" (figurative art and non-figurative art); Read, "The faculty of abstraction"; Le Corbusier, "The quarrel with realism"; Nicholson, "Quotations"; Gabo, "Sculpture—carving and construction in space"; J. D. Bernal, "Art and the scientist"; S. Giedion, "Construction and aesthetics"; Gropius, "Art education and the state"; Moholy-Nagy, "Light painting"; K. Honzik, "A note on biotechnics"; exhibitions; bibliography.

23. Degand, Léon. *Langage et Signification de la Peinture en Figuration et en Abstraction.* Paris, Edition de l'Architecture d'Aujourd'hui, 1956.
     Complemented by: "L'abstraction dite géométrique," *Quadrum,* no. 1, May 1956.

24. Dorazio, Piero. *La Fantasia dell'Arte nella Vita Moderna.* Rome, Polveroni e Quinti, 1955.
     Includes "la poetica dell' essenzialità: il costruttivismo" (pp. 77–83). Bibliography.

25. Edition MAT: *Multiplication d'Oeuvres d'Art.* Paris, Daniel Spôrri [1959].
     Folder (ill., port.) including Agam, Bury, Duchamp, Rot, Soto, Tinguely, Vasarely. Similar editions, in association with Karl Gerstner, Galerie der Spiegel, Galleria Schwarz, etc. also issued in 1964. Tokyo exhibition (Edition Mat, 1965) included other artists. Also see Bibl. 267.

26. ———. *Multiplizierte Kunstwerke.* Krefeld, 1960.
     "Die sich bewegen oder bewegen lessen. Ausgabe Edition Mat 1959, erweitert um 5 Künstler Josef Albers, Bo Ek, Mack, Malina, Man Ray."

27. Ehrenzweig, Anton. *The Psychoanalysis of Artistic Vision and Hearing.* London, Routledge & Kegan Paul, 1953.
     Deals with "a theory of unconscious perception."

28. Fagiolo dell'Arco, Maurizio. *Rapporto 60: l'Arti Oggi in Italia.* Rome, Bulzoni, 1966.
     Includes "la tecnica della visione" (pp. 215–251): Castellani, Accardi, Calderera, Gandini, Alviani, Boriani e Colombo, etc. Biographies, bibliography.

29. *Four Essays on Kinetic Art* [by] Stephan Bann, Reg Gadney, Frank Popper, and Philip Steadman. London, Motion Books, 1966.
     Includes essay on "colour music."

30. Golding, John. *Cubism: a History and an Analysis, 1907–1914.* New York, Wittenborn, 1959. Bibliography. Also French edition, 1962.

31. Gordon, John. *Geometric Abstraction in America.* New York, Whitney Museum of American Art (by Frederick A. Praeger, Publisher), 1962.
    With a chronology of important events in the development of geometric abstraction in America (pp. 64–65). Catalogue of exhibition mentions Albers, Anuskiewicz, Benjamin, Bolotowsky, Calder, Daphnis, de Rivera, Diller, Feitelson, Gabo, Glarner, Hammersley, Kelly, Lippold, McLaughin, Moholy-Nagy, Noland, Reinhardt, D. Smith, L. P. Smith, Stella, Von Wiegand, etc.

32. Gray, Camilla. *The Great Experiment: Russian Art, 1863–1922.* New York, Abrams; London, Thames & Hudson, 1962.
    Comprehensive history and evaluation; documents, biographies, bibliographies in English and Russian. Emphasizes the work of Malevich and Tatlin, the ideas of Suprematism and Constructivism. Important references to Futurism, Rayonnism, etc. Biographical notes on Goncharova, Kandinsky, Larionov, Lissitzky, Malevich, Rodchenko, Tatlin, and others. Also early texts by Kandinsky (1910), Malevich (1919), A. Gan (1920).

33. Gray, Christopher. *Cubist Aesthetic Theories.* Baltimore, Johns Hopkins Press, 1953. Bibliography.

34. Hertel, Heinrich. *Structure, Form and Movement.* New York, Reinhold, 1966.
    "Concerned with the relationship between biology and engineering." Translation from the German edition (Mainz, Krausskopf, 1963). Bibliography.

35. Jaffe, H. L. C. *De Stijl, 1917–1931: The Dutch Contribution to Modern Art.* Amsterdam, Meulenhoff, 1956.
    Preface by J. J. P. Oud. Translations of two essays by Mondrian (pp. 211–258). Extensive bibliography. Complemented by: *De Stijl* (Amsterdam, Stedelijk Museum, July–Sept. 29, 1951), a comprehensive catalogue (120 pp.) with many texts, especially Van Doesburg. Also recent paperback edition of 1956 title.

36. Jean Arp, Sonia Delaunay, Alberto Magnelli, Sophie Taeuber-Arp. [Album de 10 lithographies exécutées en collaboration]. Paris, Nourritures Terrestres, 1950.

37. Kassák, Ludwig & Moholy-Nagy, Ladislaus, eds. *Buch Neuer Künstler.* Vienna, "MA," 1922.
    "Unser Zeitalter ist das der Konstruktivität." Largely plates; brief preface by Kassák. "Herausgegeben von der aktivistischen Zeitschrift *MA*." Also monograph issued by the same magazine in its *Horizont* series; e.g. "Peter Mátyás," "Moholy-Nagy" (Vienna, 1921).

38. Kepes, Gyorgy. *Language of Vision.* Chicago, Theobald, 1944.
    Introductions by S. Giedion, S. I. Hayakawa. Complemented by the author's *The New Landscape in Art and Science*, Chicago, Theobald, 1956 (essays by Arp, Gabo, Gropius, Hélion, and 13 others). Both profusely and significantly illustrated.

39. ———, ed. *Vision & Value Series.* New York, Braziller, 1965 (6 vols.).
    Numerous contributions and illustrations "dedicated to the search for values common to our contemporary scientific, technological and artistic achievements." Six titles: "Education of Vision," "Structure in Art and in Science," "The Nature and Art of Motion," "The Module," "Sign Image and Symbol," "The Man-Made Object."

40. ———. *The Visual Arts Today.* 1960.
    The book edition of special number of *Daedalus* (no. 1, pp. 79–126, 1960) consisting of statements and documents by artists such as Albers, Arp, Duchamp, Gabo, Kandinsky, Mondrian, and others.

41. Kosice, Gyula. *Géoculture de l'Europe d'Aujourd'hui.* (Ed. Losange, 1959).
    Entretiens: Arp, Bill, S. Delaunay, Herbin, Le Corbusier, Mortensen, Munari, Pasmore, Pevsner, Schöffer, Vantongerloo, Vasarely, etc.

42. Kuh, Katherine. *The Artist's Voice.* New York, Harper, 1962.
    Includes interviews with Albers, Calder, Duchamp, Gabo, D. Smith and others. Chronologies.

43. Lebel, Robert, ed. *Premier Bilan de l'Art Actuel, 1937–1953.* Paris, Le Soleil Noir, 1953.
    "Le Soleil Noir. Positions. No. 3–4." Article

on sculpture by M. Clarac-Sérou. Extensive biographical review, including occasional statements, on Albers, Bill, Bodmer, Lardera, Lippold, Mortensen, Nicholson, D. Smith, Vasarely, and others.

44. Lissitsky, El & Arp, Hans. *Die Kunstismen— Les Ismes de l'Art. The Isms of Art*. Erlenbach-Zurich, Munich, Leipzig: Rentsch, 1925.
   Includes trilingual definitions of numerous "isms," e.g. prounismus. The abstract artists included represent the European avant-garde. Text probably edited by Lissitzky; picture selection by Arp.

45. *Maîtres de l'Art Abstrait*. Boulogne, Editions *Art d'Aujourd'hui*, 1953–54.
   Large serigraph color plates in two folios, signed by those artists still living. *Album I*: Arp, Balla, R. & S. Delaunay, Gleizes, Herbin, Kandinsky, Klee, Kupka, Léger, Mondrian, Picabia, Taeuber-Arp, Van Doesburg, Villon. *Album II (1954)*: Jacobsen, Mortensen, Vasarely, and 14 others.

46. Marchiori, Giuseppe. *Arte e Artisti d'Avanguardia in Italia, 1910–1950*. Milan, Ed di Communità, 1960.
   Bibliographies.

47. Merleau-Ponty, M. *Phenomenology of Perception*. London, Routledge & Kegan Paul, 1962.
   Translated from the French.

48. Metro. *International Directory of Contemporary Art 1964*. Milan, Editorial Metro, 1963.
   Introduction in English, French, Italian. Biographical notes, portrait, bibliography on "200 leading artists of today," including Adams, Agam, Albers, Arp, Bill, Calder, Chillida, Gabo, Johns, Kemeny, Kricke, Lardera, Lippold, Mack, Mortensen, Noland, Pasmore, Picasso, Schöffer, D. Smith, Tinguely, Vantongerloo, Vasarely.

49. Metzger, Gustav. *Auto-destructive art*. London, A.C.C., 1965.
   Mimeographed edition, June 1965, 32 pp. "Expanded version of talk given at Architectural Association, 24 Feb. 1965." General bibliogra-

Bibl. 44. El Lissitzky & Hans Arp. *The Isms of Art*, 1925.

phy. Complemented by *Auto-destructive art. Demonstration by G. Metzger, South Bank, London, 3 July 1961* (a single sheet with statements dated 1959, 1960, 1961). Similar manifest in *Ark* (London), no. 32, pp. 7–8: "Machine art, auto-creative art, auto-destructive art."

50. Mon, Franz, ed. *Movens.* Wiesbaden, Limes, 1960.
   "Dokumente und Analysen zur Dichtung, bildenden Kunst, Musik, Architektur." Collaborators: Walter Höllerer, Manfred de la Motte. Commentary on recent developments in all the arts according to the principle of motion. Includes chronology of kinetic art after 1900. Brief biographical notes and references, e.g. Arp, Kandinsky, Kemeny, Mack, Malevich, Mies van der Rohe, Tinguely, Vasarely. French and English summary, pp. 188–197. Reviewed in *Times Literary Supplement*, Sept. 3, 1964.

51. Munari, Bruno. *Il Quadrato.* Milan, Al'Insegna del Pesce d'Oro, 1960.
   Bibliography. Pictorial excerpt published in *Domus* no. 368, July 1960. Also issued with English insert by Wittenborn & Co., New York.

52. ———. *The Discovery of the Circle.* New York, Wittenborn [1964].
   Bibliography.

53. ———. *Discovery of the Square.* New York, Wittenborn, 1962.
   English translation of *Il Quadrato* (Milan, 1960). Bibliography.

54. ———. *Teoremi sull'Arte.* Milan, Al'Insegna del Pesce d'Oro, 1961.

55. *De Nieuwe Stijl.* Deel 1. Radaktie: Armando, Henk Peeters [etc.]. Amsterdam, De Bezige Bij [1966?]
   An international anthology including "Nieuwe Poëzie," "Nul-Zero," "Nieuw Realisme." Multilingual texts include Uecker (English, pp. 155–156); Klein (French, pp. 165–171); Mack (German, p. 172); Zero-Nul (English, pp. 173–175); Popper (English, pp. 178–180).

56. Nuremberg, Gewerbemuseums der Bayerischen Landesgewerbeanstalt. *Schwingungen experimentell sichtbar gemacht von Dr. Hans Jenny.* May 9–June 5, 1966.
   "Demonstration of structure and dynamics as determined by vibration." Includes English text.

57. Oster, Gerald. *Moiré Kit. Series B.* Barrington, N.J., Edmund Scientific Co., 1965.
   Boxed series of patterns on plastic and cardboard. Includes booklet of commentary. Lists other series "developed for scientists, experimenters, artists (especially of the Op Art school. . . ."

58. Pelligrini, Aldo. *New Tendencies in Art.* New York, Crown, 1966.
   Chapters on Constructivist and Concrete Art, the Zero group, etc.; 300 illustrations; no bibliography.

59 Periera, I. Rice. *The Nature of Space. A Metaphysical and Aesthetic Inquiry.* New York, Privately Published [by the Artist], 1956.
   By an established painter in the geometric style.

60. Poensgen, G. & Zahn, L. *Abstrakte Kunst: eine Weltsprache.* Baden-Baden, Klein, 1958.
   Extensively illustrated.

61. Popper, Frank. *L'Image du Mouvement dans l'Art depuis 1860.* Paris, University of Paris, 1966.
   Dissertation. Comprehensive bibliography (ca. 450 entries).

62. Read, Herbert. *Art Now. An Introduction to the Theory of Modern Painting and Sculpture.* London, Faber & Faber, 1933 (revised edition, 1949).
   Other titles by this poet, critic, and philosopher have included *The Meaning of Art* (1949); *The Philosophy of Modern Art: Collected Essays* (1952); *Icon and Idea* (1955). References to Constructivist art, sculptors, and theory are frequent.

63. Ritchie, Andrew C. *Abstract Painting and Sculpture in America.* New York, Museum of Modern Art, 1951.
   Discusses abstract art in general, includes catalogue of the Museum's exhibition. Brief biographical notes refer to Albers, Calder, Diller, Glarner, Lippold, etc. Plate groupings include "geometric" (pure, architectural and mechanical, naturalistic and expressionist). Bibliography (1913–1950) by B. Karpel.

64. Robertson, Bryan, Russell, John, & Lord Snowdon. *Private View: the Lively World of British Art.* London, Nelson, 1965.
   Similarly, Robertson's exhibition catalogue:

The New Generation: 1965 (London, White-chapel Gallery, 1965).

65. Rodman, Selden. *Conversations with Artists.* New York, Devin-Adair, 1957.
Reports of interviews with Reinhardt, D. Smith, S. Calder, G. Rickey, and others.

66. Rosenblum, Robert. *Cubism and Twentieth-Century Art.* New York, Abrams, 1961.
Comprehensive survey. Bibliography.

67. Schmidt, Georg & Schenk, Robert, eds. *Form in Art and Nature.* Introduction by Adolf Portmann. Basel, Basilius Press, 1960.
Trilingual text: German, French, English. Comments on and illustrates visual and structural parallels in art and science, based on exhibition organized by Swiss artists: "Kunst und Naturform." For similar pictorial affinities consult: Horst Reumuth, *Wunder der Mikrowelt* (Stuttgart, Kohlhammer, 1954); Carl Strüwe, *Formen des Mikrokosmos: Gestalt und Gestaltung einer Bilderwelt* (Munich, Prestel, 1955); C. Postma, *Plant Marvels in Miniature* (London, Harrap; New York, Day, 1961).

68. Seuphor, Michel. *L'Art Abstrait: Ses Origines, Ses Premiers Maîtres.* Paris, Maeght, 1950.
First edition (1949) based on exhibition at the Galerie Maeght, characterized by M. Ragon as "le meilleur document sur les origines de l'art abstrait. S'arrête, en fait, avant la guerre de 1939." Seuphor emphasizes "l'art non-figuratif," omitting "cubistes et semi-abstraits." Includes: "témoignages, images, textes, portraits de reproductions, notes biographiques, bibliographie." Biographical section, among others, refers to: Albers, Calder, R. and S. Delaunay, Eggeling, Gabo, Goncharova, Herbin, Kandinsky, Kupka, Larionov, Lissitzky, McDonald-Wright, Magnelli, Malevich, Moholy-Nagy, Mondrian, Pevsner, Richter, Rodchenko, Servranckx, Taeuber-Arp, Van Doesburg, Vantongerloo, Vordemberge-Gildewart; also note on the author, p. 318.

69. Sharp, Willoughby, ed. *Kineticism* [an anthology]. New York, Kineticism Press [1968?].
Publication in progress. Articles by Brett, Dorfles, Popper, Sharp, Thwaites, etc. Bibliography.

70. ————— *The Role of Physical Movement in 20th Century Sculpture* [Dissertation in progress]. New York, 1966–[1968?].
Doctoral thesis for Columbia University. Bibliography.

70a. Staber, Margit. *Konkrete Kunst.* St. Gallen, Galerie Presse, 1966.
"Serielle manifeste 66. Manifest XI, Nov. 1966." Introduction, selections from Arp, Bill, van Doesburg, Kandinsky, Lohse, Vantongerloo. Bibliography.

71. Steneberg, Eberhard, ed. *Beitrag der Russen zur Modernen Kunst.* Dusseldorf, Druck: H. Wintersheidt [1959].
Preface by E. S. List of 208 exhibits, introduced by K. vom Rath. "Die Ausstellung ist ein Teil der Frankfurter kulturellen Arbeit." Biographical notes on Archipenko, Delaunay-Terk, Gabo, Goncharova, Kandinsky, Larionov, Lissitzky, Malevich, Pevsner, and others.

72. Taylor, Joshua C. *Futurism.* New York, Museum of Modern Art, 1961.
"Biographies and catalogue of the exhibition" (pp. 141 ff). Reviewed by Dore Ashton, *XXᵉ Siècle*, no. 17, 1961. Emphasis on Balla, Severini, Carrà, Russolo, Boccioni. Chronology. Manifestos include Boccioni's "Technical manifesto of Futurist sculpture" (1911). Bibliography (1905–1961) by B. Karpel.

73. Torrès Garcia, Joaquin. *Universalismo Constructivo.* Buenos Aires, Poseidon, 1944.
A massive compilation (1011 pp., ill.). Chapters on Constructive Art, Abstract Art, Neo-Plasticism, Mondrian, Arp, etc.

74. Turin, Castello del Valentino. *Mostre: Bibliografica del Linguaggio Grafico nella Communicazione Visiva.* Sept. 8–Oct. 3, 1965.
Organized by the Institute of Science in Graphic Art, the Polytech of Turin. Catalogue: G. Brunazzi, G. Celent, E. Gribaudo. Includes Constructivist, optic, and kinetic examples at the popular level.

75. Vollmer, Hans. *Allgemeines Lexikon der Bildenden Künstler des XX Jahrhunderts.* Leipzig, Seemann, 1953–1961 (5 vols.).
Biographical notes (sometimes brief) and bibliography (sometimes pictorial) on the more recent generations. Includes Albers, Archipenko, Arp, Bill, Boccioni, Calder, Delaunay, Delaunay-Terk, Van Doesburg (under Küpper,

v. 3), Eggeling, Gabo (under Pevsner, N., v. 3), Glarner, Gonzalez, Gropius, Kandinsky, Kemény, Kricke, Kupka, Lardera, Larionov, Le Corbusier, Lippold, Lissitzky, Lohse, Magnelli, Malevich, Mies van der Rohe, Mondrian, Mortensen, Munari, Nicholson, Pasmore, Pevsner, Picasso, Reinhardt, Richter, J. de Rivera, Schöffer, Seuphor, D. Smith, L. P. Smith, Stazewski, Torrès Garcia, Vantongerloo, Vasarely, Vordemberge-Gildewart, Von Wiegand, and others.

76. Wember, Paul. *Bewegte Bereiche der Kunst. Kinetik—Objekte—Plastik.* Krefeld, Scherpe, 1963.
    Thirty-six artists illustrated, including Agam, Albers, Bury, Calder, Cremer, Duchamp, Getulio, Klein, Kramer, Lardera, Mack, Malina, Munari, Soto, Tinguely, Uecker, Vasarely. Bibliography.

77. Whythe, Lancelot L., ed. *Aspects of Form: a Symposium on Form in Nature and Art.* London, Lund Humphries, 1951.
    Texts by R. Arnheim, E. H. Gombrich, and others. Includes a chronological survey on form (pp. 229–237); selected bibliography (pp. 238–249) whose "scope has been extended beyond the visual forms of science and art, to cover mathematical, logical and symbolic forms."

78. Worringer, Wilhelm, *Abstraktion und Einfühling.* Munich, Piper, 1908; Neudruck, 1948 [other editions, 1961]. (Translation: *Abstraction and Empathy*, London, Routledge & Kegan, Paul, 1953.)
    A pioneer study of "abstraction—geometry and empathy—representation treated as dual aspects of European art, in relation to cultural and psychological factors" (L. L. Whyte).

79. Yale University Art Gallery. *Collection of the Société Anonyme: Museum of Modern Art 1920.* New Haven, Conn., Associates in Fine Arts, 1950.
    Catalogue by the trustees, Katherine S. Dreier and Marcel Duchamp, edited by George H. Hamilton. Biographies include bibliographies. References to Kandinsky, Moholy-Nagy, Gabo, Archipenko, Malevich, Calder, Torrès Garcia, Albers, Servranckx, Mondrian, Van Doesburg, Taeuber-Arp, Diller, Glarner, Holtzman, Duchamp, Pevsner, Richter, Boccioni, and others (see alphabetical index). For comprehensive record of the activity of the Société Anonyme see the exhaustive documentation in *Some New Forms of Beauty, 1909–1936: a Selection of the Collection* (Springfield, Mass., George Walter Vincent Smith Art Gallery, Nov. 9–Dec. 17, 1939).

80. *10 Origin. Lithographies Originales.* Zürich, Allianz, 1942.
    Prints in folio. Text in French and German. Artists: Arp, Bill, S. Delaunay, Kandinsky, Leuppi, Lohse, Magnelli, Taeuber-Arp, Vantongerloo.

II. SPECIAL FIELDS: Architecture & Design, Painting & Sculpture

81. Arp, Jean. *Onze Peintres Vus par Arp.* Zurich, Girsberger, 1949.
    Essays on Arp, Delaunay, Kandinsky, Magnelli, Taeuber-Arp, Vordemberge-Gildewart, etc. Also limited edition with original graphics.

82. Banham, Reyner. *Theory and Design in the First Machine Age.* New York, Praeger, 1960.
    Discusses Futurism, De Stijl, the Bauhaus, Le Corbusier, etc. Bibliographies.

83. Brion, Marcel, ed. *La Peinture Contemporaine, 1900–1960.* Paris, Baschet, 1962.
    Contributions by W. George, R. Cogniat, B. Dorival, C. Zervos, and others. Volume II covers Non-Objectivism, Purism, Abstraction, etc. Section 5 of Brion's *Art Abstrait* (Paris, Michel, 1956) also presents Abstract painting, as well as observations on Delaunay and Orphism (pp. 129–135), Malevich and Suprematism (pp. 135–144), etc.

84. Giedion, Sigfried. *Space, Time and Architecture: The Growth of a New Tradition.* Fourth edition (enlarged). Cambridge, Mass., Harvard University Press, 1962, (c.) 1941.
    "Concerned with contemporary man's separation between thinking and feeling and with the unconscious parallelism of method employed in art and science" (S. G.). Continued in his *Mechanization Takes Command* (New

York, Oxford, 1948). "How this break between thinking and feeling came about . . . [how] every generation [bridges] the gap between inner and outer reality by reestablishing the dynamic equilibrium that governs their relationship" (S. G.).

85. Giedion-Welcker, Carola. *Contemporary Sculpture: an Evolution in Volume and Space.* New York, Wittenborn, 1960.

Revised and enlarged version of 1955 edition, which was a substantial expansion of the Girsberger text of 1937. Biographical data includes, among others, Archipenko, Arp, Bill, Calder, Chillida, de Rivera, Van Doesberg, Gabo, Gonzalez, Kricke, Lardera, Le Corbusier, Lippold, Malevich, Moholy-Nagy, Pevsner, Picasso, Rodchenko, D. Smith, Taeuber-Arp, Tatlin, Vantongerloo, M. Vieira. Comprehensive bibliography by B. Karpel, pp. 355–396 (same as 1955 edition). Also European editions.

85a. Haftmann, Werner. *Painting in the Twentieth Century.* New York, Praeger, 1961.

Revised from the German edition. Vol. I: Text. II: Plates. Extensive references to major personalities, emphasizing the mature Europeans. Also popular edition, 1965.

85b. Hess, Thomas B. *Abstract Painting: Background and American Phase.* New York, Viking, 1951.

Also his essay "Introduction to Abstract" in the *Art News*, vol. 49, no. 7, pt. 2, Nov. 1950. This section of the *Art News Annual* 1951 (pp. 127–158) includes "the worlds of geometry."

85c. Hitchcock, Henry-Russel. *Painting Towards Architecture.* New York, Duell, Sloan & Pearce, 1948.

The collection of the Miller Company, Meriden, Conn. Introduction by A. H. Barr, Jr.

85d. Hitchcock, Henry-Russell & Johnson, Philip. *The International Style: Architecture Since 1922.* New York, Norton, 1932.

Complemented by: *Modern Architecture: International Exhibition.* New York, Museum of Modern Art, 1932. Text by Hitchcock, Johnson and Barr. Documentation on Gropius, Le Corbusier, Mies van der Rohe, etc.

85e. Itten, Johannes. *The Art of Color.* New York, Reinhold, 1961.

By a former Bauhaus-Meister. Translation of: *Kunst des Farbe: Subjektives Erleben und objektives Erkennen als Wege der Kunst.* Ravensburg, Maier, 1961.

85f. Joray, Marcel. *La Sculpture Moderne en Suisse* [Vol. 1]. Neuchâtel, Griffon, 1955.

Vol. II: *Schweizer Plastik der Gegenwart, 1954 bis 1959.* About 50 sculptors (with biographical notes) and 300 illustrations in both vols. e.g. Bodmer, Kemeny, Tinguely, etc.

86. Lake, Carleton & Maillard, Robert, ed. *Dictionary of Modern Painting.* New York, Paris Book Center [1955].

Translated from the French. Includes general articles (Abstract Art, Concrete Art, Suprematism, etc.) as well as major biographical coverage. Also European editions, e.g. *Knaurs Lexikon Moderner Kunst* (1955). Revised and enlarged "avec le concours de Robert Maillard": *Nouveau Dictionnaire de la Peinture Moderne* (Paris, Hazan, 1963).

87. Lozowick, Louis. *Modern Russian Art.* New York, Société Anonyme, 1925.

Published by the Museum of Modern Art— Société Anonyme, a pioneer collection of the avant-garde in America, directed by Katherine Dreier and Marcel Duchamp, now at Yale.

88. Ponente, Nello. *Modern Painting: Contemporary Trends.* [Switzerland], Skira, 1960.

Bibliographical notices include Albers, Bill, Herbin, Magnelli, Mortensen, Nicholson, Vasarely, and others. General bibliography. Also European editions.

89. Rathbun, Mary C. & Hayes, Bartlett H., Jr. *Layman's Guide to Modern Art: Painting for a Scientific Age.* New York, Oxford University Press, 1949.

Based on Addison Gallery exhibition (1947): "Seeing the Unseeable."

90. Raynal, Maurice & Others. *History of Modern Painting, vol. 3: From Picasso to Surrealism.* Geneva, Skira, 1950.

Comprehensive survey of contemporary movements, with extensive biographies and bibliographies. Also European editions and modified versions of the three-volume series entitled *Modern Painting* (1953, 1959).

91. Read, Herbert. *The Art of Sculpture.* New York, Pantheon, 1961.

Malevitch

Bibl. 87. Louis Lozowick. *Modern Russian Art.* New York, 1925.

Bibl. 593. Kasimir Malevich. [The Non-Objective World.] Munich, 1927.

Second edition of Bollingen series (1956). Partial contents: "The discovery of space"; "The realization of mass"; "The illusion of movement"; "The impact of light." Complemented, among many titles by this perceptive author, by *A Concise History of Modern Painting* (New York, Praeger, 1959; second edition, 1962). Bibliography.

92. Sauvage, Tristan. *Pittura Italiana del Dopoguerra (1947–1957).* Milan, Arturo Schwarz, 1957.
"Astratti e concretisti" (pt. III). Includes Magnelli and Munari (biographical notes et passim). Bibliography. Published by the author (pseud.).

93. Selz, Jean. *Modern Sculpture: Origins and Evolution.* New York, Braziller, 1963.
Translated from the French. Comments on "the new aesthetic" (ch. 7), lists 10 types of sculpture (p. 4). Biographical dictionary includes Archipenko, Boccioni, Gabo, Moholy-

Nagy, Rodchenko, Taeuber-Arp, Tatlin, Vantongerloo, and others. Bibliography.

94. Seuphor, Michel. *Abstract Painting. Fifty Years of Accomplishment from Kandinsky to the Present.* New York, Abrams, 1961.
Translated from the French. Refers to this work as an expansion and commentary on his *L'Art Abstrait* (1949). A valuable chronicle, based on personal associations and evaluations of painting and painters "wholly liberated from dependence on the figure" from "before 1915 to after 1940." Numerous plates including color. Also European editions. Bibliography.

95. ———. *Abstract Painting in Flanders.* Brussels, Arcade, 1963.
Collaborateurs: M. Bilcke, L.-L. Sosset, J. Walravens. Foreword: E. Langui. Also French, German, Dutch editions. Chronology, biographies, bibliography. Commentary and docu-

256

mentation: Vantongerloo, Servranckx, Seuphor, Pol Bury, etc.

96. ———. *Dictionary of Abstract Painting. With a History of Abstract Painting.* New York, Paris Book Center [1957].

Translated from the French. A history (pp. 1–113) of unusual personal memoirs and associations, including texts by Severini, Malevich, Mondrian, and a chronological table of Abstract Art (1910–1956). Dictionary (pp. 117–293). Bibliography (pp. 297–305) is supplemented by many references in the comprehensive alphabetical listings. Also European editions.

97. ———. *Sculpture of This Century.* New York, Braziller, 1960.

Unlike the "Dictionary" above, this is a longer history followed by a shorter biographical dictionary. Not restricted to specific movements or styles (438 sculptors, 411 ill.). Also European editions.

98. Solomon R. Guggenheim Museum. *Modern Sculpture from the Joseph H. Hirshhorn Collection.* New York, The Museum, 1962.

A comprehensive catalogue (246 pp., ill.) issued on the occasion of an exhibition. Biographical notes and bibliography include Bill, Engman, Gabo, Gonzalez, Johns, Pevsner, D. Smith, etc.

99. *Staatliches Bauhaus: Weimar 1919–1923.* Munich-Weimar, Bauhaus-Verlag; Cologne, Nierendorf, 1923.

Texts by Gropius and the Bauhaus artist-faculty. Numerous illustrations. Edition: 2000.

For supplementation see *Bauhaus 1919–1928* (New York, Museum of Modern Art, 1938), with bibliography; *Die Maler am Bauhaus* (Munich, Haus der Kunst, 1950); H. Peters, *Die Bauhaus-Mappe* (Cologne, Czwiklitzer, 1957), with bibliography.

100. *Témoignages pour la Sculpture Abstraite.* Paris, Editions A A & Denise René, 1956.

Published on the occasion of an exhibition at the Galerie Denise René. Preface by P. Gueguen ("le constructivisme . . . une autre révolution"); long statements by Lardera, Lippold, and Schöffer; biographical data on 12 sculptors including Arp, de Rivera, D. Smith.

101. Trier, Eduard. *Form and Space: Sculpture of the Twentieth Century.* London, Thames & Hudson, 1961.

Translation from the German (1960).

102. Wright, Willard Huntington. *Modern Painting. Its Tendency and Meaning.* New York, John Lane, 1915.

102a. Wright, Frank Lloyd. *The Life Work of the American Architect Frank Lloyd Wright.* Edited by Henricus Theodorus Wijdeveld. Santpoort (Holland), C. A. Mees, 1925.

Includes seven special numbers of *Wendingen* (Amsterdam), nos. 3–9, 1925.

103. Zevi, Bruno. *Poetica dell' Architettura Neoplastica.* Milan, Tamburini, 1953.

Commentary covers the Bauhaus, De Stijl; emphasizes Neo-Plasticism in Van Doesburg and Mondrian. Documentation on Van Doesburg (pp. 157–160).

III. PERIODICALS

104. *Abstraction, Création, Art Non Figuratif.* No. 1–5. Paris, 1932–1936.

Founded Feb. 15, 1931, these annuals are centered about the idea of "Non-Figuration." Edited by an artist or editorial committee with authority to invite sympathetic collaborators. Director for no. 1, Herbin; no. 2, Herbin; no. 3, Vantongerloo; no. 4, Vantongerloo, Béothy; no. 5, Herbin, Vantongerloo, Béothy, Gleizes, Gorin. Illustrations frequently accompanied by statements or critiques.

105. *Art d'Aujourd'hui.* Editor: André Bloc. Vol. 1–5. Paris, June 1949–Dec. 1954.

"The first review in the world entirely given to a defence of abstract art" (M. S.). Associates: Edgard Pillet, M. Bloc, L. Degand, P. Guéguen, M. Seuphor. Numerous articles, illustrations, and special numbers. Index published in final number, v. 5 no. 8. Beginning Jan. 1955, absorbed by *Aujourd'hui, Art et Architecture*, "revue bimestrielle consacrée à l'avant-garde de la création plastique" (Boulogne, Seine), edited by André Bloc.

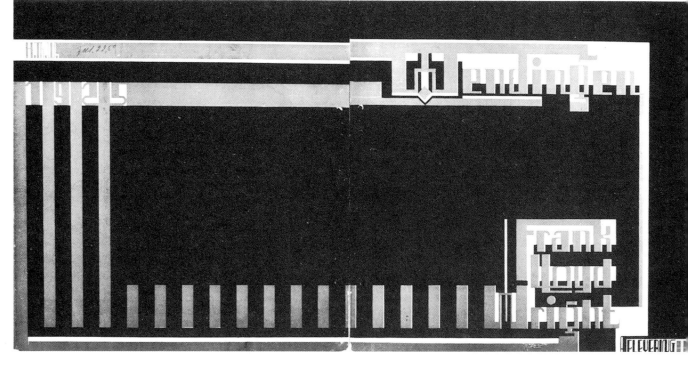

Bibl. 102a. Frank Lloyd Wright. *Wendingen*, nos. 3–9, 1925.

106. *Axis*. Editor: Myfanwy Evans. No. 1–6. London, 1935–1936.

"Quarterly review of abstract painting & sculpture," Jan. 1935–Summer, 1936. Numerous articles, e.g. Herbert Read, and illustrations, e.g. Arp, Calder, Mondrian. Evans also published an anthology on *The Painter's Object* (London, Howe, 1937), including Calder, Moholy-Nagy, and others.

107. *Cercle et Carré*. Editors: Michel Seuphor, Joaquín Torrès Garcia. No. 1–3. Paris, 1929–1930.

Three issues: March 1929, April 1930, June 30, 1930. Texts by the editors and others. Second number included catalogue of show at "Galerie 23," with article by Mondrian. In tracing the development of the avant-garde journal, Seuphor mentions that chronologically *Cercle et Carré* was followed "two years later" by *Abstraction-Création* "whose kingpins were Georges Vantongerloo and Auguste Herbin." Also continued, more literally, by *Circulo y Cuardro*: "Secunda época de Cercle et Carré . . . revista de la Asociacion de Arte Constructivo"; editor, Torrès Garcia, no. 1–7, Montevideo, May 1936–Sept. 1938.

108. *Cimaise*. Editors: R. V. Gindertael (1953–1955); Herta Wescher (1955 ff.). Paris, 1953–current.

Oriented toward abstraction and the avant-garde, international manifestations, etc. Multilingual texts. Representative authors and articles: J. Alvard, "Le manifeste réaliste constructiviste," Feb.–March, 1954; G Annenkov, "Les débuts de l'art abstrait en Russie," Dec. 1953; R. V. Gindertael, "Peintures et sculpteurs non figuratives dans l'Allemagne d'aujourd'hui," May 1955; M. Ragon, "Peinture en mouvement et sculpture animé dans le ballet contemporain," Jan.–March 1960; M. Seuphor, "Algèbres et géométries," May 1954; H. Wescher, "Les bases théoriques de l'art non figuratif," I, May 1952; II, June 1954, etc.

109. *Form*. Editors: Philip Steadman, Mike Weaver, Stephen Bann. Cambridge (England), 1966 ff.

Aims "to provoke discussion of the relations of forms to structure in the work of art, and of correspondences between the arts. Emphasis to be placed in particular on the fields of kinetic art and poetry and concrete poetry." Includes articles on Le Parc, on Van Doesburg, on Hirschfeld-Mack by Gillo Dorfles, etc.

110. *G. Zeitschrift für Elementare Gestaltung.* Editors: Hans Richter; subsequently El Lissitsky, Werner Gräff ("second series"). No. 1–5/6 Berlin, 1923–1925.

First series in newspaper format and scale, included articles by Theo van Doesburg: "Zur elementaren Gestaltung," no. 1, July 1923; "Pariser neuheiten. Motiv: Nur," no. 2, Sept. 1923. Representative article in "second" series: Hans Richter, "An den Konstruktivismus," no. 3, June 1924. Also see Bibl. 161.

111. *Graphic Design.* Editor: Katzumie Masaru. Tokyo, 1959–current.

Quarterly review published by Diamond Publishers. Partial contents: No. 3, "Max Bill's variations on a single theme" (S. Mukai); "A silhouette of Bruno Munari" (S. Takiguchi). No. 6, "El Lissitsky" (K. Masaki). No. 10, "Recent works of Camille Graeser" (M. Katzumie).

112. *NUL=O.* Editors: Henk Peeters, Herman de Vries. No. 1–3 Arnhem (Holland), 1961–1963.

No. 1, Nov. 1961; no. 2, April 1963; no. 3, 1963. "Tidschrift voor de nieuwe konseptie in de beeldende kunst." Texts in Dutch, French, English. First issue includes: O. Piene, "Licht"; H. Mack, "La structure dynamique"; G. Uecker, "Reflecktionen"; Megert, "Un espace nouveau." No. 2 includes article by Getulio, propositions of the Groupe de Recherche, etc. Also announced but unavailable: "Bibliographie de la nouvelle tendance (jusqu'au 1963)." Probably same bibliography issued in *Museumjournal*, v. 9, no. 5–6.

113. *Plastique.* Editor: S. H. Taeuber-Arp. No. 1–5. Paris, Meudon, New York, 1937–1939.

Editorial associates: H. Arp, C. Domela, A. E. Gallatin, L. K. Morris. Texts, largely devoted to abstract art, in French, German, and English. No. 1 is a Malevich number. No. 2 (1937) includes manifesto on "Dimensionisme" by Sirato with "signatures" by Arp, Moholy, Delaunay, etc. No. 3 is an American number including "Die Entwicklung der abstrakten Kunst in America."

114. *Signals.* Director: Paul Keeler. Editor: David Medalla. London, 1964–1966.

No. 1 called *Signalz, Newsbulletin of the Center for Advanced Creative Study.* Later as the news bulletin of the Signals Gallery. Emphasis on experimental artists, including kinetic and contemporary constructivists. Special numbers on Takis (I, 3–4), Lygia Clark (I, 7), Cruz-Diez (I, 9), Soto (I, 10), Otero (v. 2, no. 11, Jan.–March 1966). Articles frequently draw on relevant illustration in the field of the sciences.

115. *Spirale. Internationale Zeitschrift für Konkrete Kunst und Gestaltung.* Editor: Marcel Wyss. Berne, 1953—[196?].

More abstract documentation begins with no. 3 (1954). Lavish layout and illustrations, e.g. Albers. No. 6–7 includes Lohse, Moholy-Nagy, etc. No. 8 (Oct. 1960) is edited jointly with E. Gomringer ("Sprache"), including Gerstner, Franke, Laposky, etc.

116. *De Stijl.* Editor: Theo van Doesburg. No. 1–[90]. Leyden, etc., 1917–1932.

Avant-garde journal for art and literature, with many articles, for instance, manifesto on elementarism (1962) by Van Doesburg who wrote also as I. K. Bonset and Aldo Camini. Special numbers: *10 Jahren 1917–1928* (no. 79–84); *Aubette Nummer* (no. 87–89); *Van Doesburg 1917–1931* (dernier numéro, Jan. 1932). Moreover, with similar wide European participation, this journal sponsored *Mécano* (1922–1923) in numbers respectively titled: *Bleu, Jaune, Rouge, Blanc.*

117. *Structure.* Editor: Joost Baljeu. Series 1–6. Amsterdam, 1958–1964.

A magazine on "Constructionist Art," now largely edited by Baljeu who writes many articles. Contributors include C. Biederman, A. Hill, K. and M. Martin, Gerstner, Gorin, and others. Biographical notes on participants. Issues center respectively about "nature," "motion," "symmetry," "mathematics," "architecture," "philosophy."

118. *The Structurist.* Editor: Eli Bornstein. Saskatoon (Canada), 1960–1969 (in progress).

MAANDBLAD GEWIJD AAN DE MODERNE BEELDENDE VAKKEN EN KULTUUR RED. THEO VAN DOESBURG

No. 1 (1960–1961); no. 2 (1961–1962); no. 3 (1963). Includes articles by the editor, e.g. "Structurist art—its origins." Contributions by Biederman, Gorin, and others. Numerous illustrations. No. 9 announced for late 1969.

119. *Vernissage.* Editors: Alexander Leisberg, Heinz Rehn. Baden-Baden, 1960–current.
"Kunst-Kritik-Kontakte." Articles or illustrations include Agam, Castellani, Dorazio, Kricke, Mack, Mavignier, Megert, Moholy-Nagy, Richter, Stazewski, Strzeminski, Uecker, and others. Articles include "Zero vor 40 Jahren" and "Licht-Echt" (v. 2, no. 5–6, 1961), etc.

120. *Zero.* Editors: Heinz Mack, Otto Piene. No. 1–3. Dusseldorf [1958?–1961].
Nos. 1–2 not available for summary. No. 2 published 1959. "Vol. 3 . . . diese Ausgabe ist die letze Zero-Nummer." "Dynamo" sections on Fontana, Yves Klein, Tinguely, Piene, Mack include illustrations and multilingual texts. Briefer sections (plates or texts) on Bury, Castellani, Mavignier, Uecker, and others.

Bibl. 116. *De Stijl.* Editor: Theo van Doesburg. Leyden, 1917 ff.

IV. ARTICLES

121. Albers, Josef. "The Yale school—structured scupture." *Art in America*, no. 3, 1961.
Reproduces Engman and others.

122. Alloway, Lawrence. "Description of 'Dimensions.' " In *Dimensions: British abstract art, 1948–1957*, London, O'Hana Gallery [1957].
Followed by his "topics guide to the chronology and bibliography."

123. ———. "British Constructivism." *Art International*, March 1961.
On the Drian Gallery show, "Construction, England, 1950–60." Complemented by: "Constructivisme et architecture en Grande Bretagne," *Aujourd'hui*, v. 21, 1959.

124. Alvard, Julien. "Le manifeste réaliste constructiviste." *Cimaise*, no. 4, Feb.–March 1954.

125. Apollonio, Umbro. "Del fattore cinetico nell'arte contemporanea." *La Biennale di Venezia*, no. 42, Jan.–March 1961.
> English summary. Complemented by Swedish text in *Konstrevy*, no. 3 (1961): "Den inre rörelsen" (on motion in Futurism, Duchamp, Calder, Mondrian).

126. ———. "Ipotesi su nuove modalità creative." *Quadrum*, no. 14, 1960.
> Revised version of lecture at Fondazione Georgio Cini (Venice). English and French résumé. Illustrations: Biasi, Boriani, Colombo, Costa, Graevenitz, Getulio, Kosice, Le Parc, Mari, Mavignier, Sobrino, Soto, Varisco, Vasarely, etc.

127. "Art on the Move." *Horizon*, v. 7, no. 2, Spring 1965.
> "Optical art" with visually kinetic illustrations.

128. Badovici, Jean. "Les constructivistes." *Architecture Vivante*, no. 9, 1925.
> Incorporated into special number: *L'Architecture Vivante en Hollande—Le Groupe "De Stijl"* (Paris, Morancé, 1925). This also includes: Van Doesburg, "L'évolution de l'architecture moderne en Hollande"; Mondrian, "L'Architecture future néo-plasticienne."

129. Baljeu, Joost. "The Hegelian romantic negation in modern plastic art." *Art International*, no. 2, Feb. 1966.
> Also see Bibl. 317.

130. ———. "Mondrian or Miro." *De Beuk*, nos. 2–3, Summer 1958.
> Also issued as independent booklet (Bibl. 319).

131. ———. "The problem of reality with suprematism, constructivism, Proun, neoplasticism and elementarism." *Lugano Review*, no. 1, 1965.
> Subtitled: "Marginal notes to the dialectical principle in the aesthetics of Malevich, Tatlin, El Lissitzky, Mondrian and Van Doesburg." Footnotes (bibliography). Also see Bibl. 318.

132. Barrett, Cyril. "Mystification and the Groupe de Recherche." *Studio International*, no. 880, Aug. 1966.

133. Belloli, Carlo. "Nuove direzioni dell cinevisualità plastica totale." *Metro*, no. 7, 1962.
> "Indications for a catalogue of today's artists concerned with visual integration." Numerous illustrations of this selected international group.

134. "Bibliografico dell'arte astratta e concreta." *Spazio*, no. 2, Jan.–Feb. 1951.
> In "abstract-concrete" number (pp. 53–54), including articles by Argan, Degand, Seuphor, etc.

135. Biederman, Charles. "The visual revolution of structurist art." *Artforum*, no. 7, April 1965.
> Illustrated by the artist's works.

136. Bill, Max. "The Bauhaus idea: from Weimar to Ulm." *Architects' Year Book*, no. 5, 1953.

137. ———. "Umweltgestaltung nach morphologischen Methoden." *Werk und Zeit*, no. 11, 1956.
> Address at the Hochschule für Gestaltung, Ulm.

138. Bordier, Roger. "Propositions nouvelles: le mouvement, l'oeuvre transformable." *Aujourd'hui*, no. 2, March–April 1955.
> Supplemented in no. 4: "Quelques notes complémentaires sur le mouvement."

139. Bourgeois, Victor. "Salut au Constructivisme." *Zodiac*, no. 1, 1957.
> On architectural ideas in Russia in the 20's.

140. Bronowski, J. "The creative process." *Scientific American*, no. 3, Sept. 1958.
> Innovation in science and art. Followed with illustrated articles on innovation in mathematics (P. R. Halmos) and in physics (F. J. Dyson).

141. Cleaver, Dale. "The concept of time in modern sculpture." *Art Journal*, no. 4, Summer 1963.
> From Canova to Calder. Illustrations: Boccioni, Calder, Gabo, Tinguely.

142. Contemporary French Art. *Yale French Studies*, no. 19–20, 1958.
> Partial contents: "Notes on a new trend: multidimensional animated work" (G. Habasque); "Criticism and the history of painting in the twentieth century" (P. Francastel); "In praise of sculpture" (M. Ragon); "Painting today: principles and practitioners" (B. Dorival). Observation by Francastel: "Artists and mathematicians alone create forms."

143. Curjel, Hans. "Konfrontationen." *Werk*, no. 12, 1952.

"Formensprache um 1900 und Gestatungs-methoden des 20. Jahrhunderts." English and French résumés.

144. Degand, Léon. "L'abstraction dite géométrique." *Quadrum*, no. 1, 1956.
English résumé. Deals largely with the established European painters but includes Vasarely.

145. Degand, Léon & Gindertael, R. V. "Klar Form." *Art d'Aujourd'hui*, no. 1, Dec. 1951.
With biographical notes and critiques on 20 artists, including Arp, Calder, Herbin, Le Corbusier, Magnelli, Mortensen, Taeuber-Arp, Vasarely.

146. Del Marle, Félix. "Le constructivisme et son influence." *Art d'Aujourd'hui*, no. 3, Jan. 1951.
Also essay on "le néoplasticisme" in same special number: "Cinquante années de sculpture."

147. Demarco, Hugo R. [La couleur et la vibration]. In *Demarco*, Paris, Galerie Denise René, Nov. 1961.

148. Dorazio, Piero & Turcato, Giulio. "Conversazione sull'arte oggi e su cosa interessanti in occasione della trentatreesima Biennale di Venezia." *Metro*, no. 11, 1966.

149. Dorfles, Gillo. "For or against a structuralist aesthetic?" *Form*, (England), no. 2, Sept. 1966.

150. Dorner, Alexander. "Zur abstrakten Malerei. Erklarung zum Raum der Abstrakten in der Hannoverischen Gemäldgalerie." *Die Form*, no. 4, April 1928.
"Entwurfen von Prof. Lissitzky, Moskau."

151. Feiniger, T. Lux. "The Bauhaus: evolution of an idea." *Criticism*, no. 3, Summer 1960.
Reprinted from the *Wayne State Journal* and extracts in "The Theater of the Bauhaus" 1961. A useful corrective to standard accounts.

152. Ferebee, A. "On the move." *Industrial Design*, Feb. 1964.
Similarly: "On the move." *Arts*, Jan. 1964.

153. Fitzsimmons, James. "Space and the image in art." *Quadrum*, no. 6, 1959.
On the occasion of the 29th Biennale (Venice), discusses space in general as well as M. Bill, Chillida, D. Smith, etc.

154. Fuller, Buckminster. "Tensegrity." *Portfolio and Art News Annual*, no. 4, 1961.
On "discontinuous-compression, continuous-tensioning structure," with introduction (pp. 114, 144, 146) by J. McHale.

155. Gan, Alexei. "Constructivism." In Camilla Gray, *The Great Experiment: Russian Art*. London, Thames & Hudson, 1962.
Excerpts from his "Constructivism (Moscow, 1920) published Tver, 1922."

156. Gassiot-Talabot, Gerald. "Abstraction and construct!" *Cimaise*, no. 58, March–April 1962.
Also in French, German, and Spanish. Reviews "structures" show at Galerie Denise René and observations by Seuphor.

157. Gerstner, Karl. "Die 'Aubette' als Beispiel integrieter Kunst." *Werk*, no. 10, Oct. 1960.
On the collaboration of Arp, Sophie Taeuber, and Van Doesburg in designing and decorating the restaurant at Strasbourg. Previously published as "Rundfrage zur integration der künste," *Werk*, Aug. 1960.

158. ———. "Pendenzen 62." *Werk*, no. 1, Jan. 1962.
Numerous illustrations include Agam, Mack, Mavignier, Morellet, Vieira, and others.

159. Giedion, Siegfried. "Transparency: primitive and modern." *Art News*, no. 4, June–Aug. 1952.
On "similar methods of presentation . . . abstraction, representation of movement, transparency, simultaneity."

160. Gabo, Naum, & Others. "Naum Gabo and the constructivist tradition." *Studio International*, Apr., 1966.
Texts by Gabo, Pevsner, D. Thompson, A. Hill, J. Ernest, v. 171, pp. 125–156.

161. Graeff, Werner. "Concerning the so-called G group." *Art Journal*, Summer 1964.
On the magazine "G" (Gestaltung) founded by Richter, Lissitzky, Graeff, and others.

162. Guéguen, Pierre. "L'écriture géométrique après Mondrian." *XXᵉ Siècle*, no. 10, March 1958.
Influence of Mondrian on artists, especially Nicholson and Vasarely. Illustrates Herbin, Malevich, Mortensen, Taeuber-Arp. etc. English résumé.

163. Habasque, Guy. "Art and technique: kinetics."

XXe Siècle, no. 17, Christmas 1961.
Also in French edition. Illustrations: Balla, Delaunay, Agam, Munari, Malina, Calder, Schöffer, Kosice, Vasarely, Bury, and others.

164. ———. "Documents inédits sur les débuts de Suprématisme." *Art d'Aujourd'hui*, no. 14, 1955.

165. Halas, John. "Kinetics and automated movements." *Ark*, no. 35 [1963–64?].

166. Hélion, Jean. "From reduction to growth." *Axis*, no. 2, April 1935.
An important essay on abstract attitudes and judgments.

167. Henze, Anton. Über das Basteln in der modernen Kunst." *Kunstwerk*, no. 7, Jan. 1958.
"Basteln" includes collages, constructions, montages, mobiles, stabiles, etc.

168. Hill, Anthony. "Art and mathematics: a constructionist view." *Structure*, no. 2, 1961.
Other articles: In no. 1 (1959), "On constructions, nature and structure"; no. 2 (1960), "Movement in the domain of the static construction," etc.

169. ———. "The constructionist idea & architecture." *Ark*, no. 18, Nov. 1956.
Although reviewing the exhibition "This is Tomorrow: Group 5," includes a thoughtful survey of Constructivism, Neo-Plasticism, and De Stijl.

170. ———. "Constructivism—the European phenomenon." *Studio*, April 1966.
In Gabo number, v. 171, pp. 140–147, followed by John Ernest: "Constructivism and content."

171. Hofmann, Werner. "Das Material in der neuen Plastik." *Werk*, March 1959.

172. Hope, Henry R. "Sculpture in motion." In *Rickey: Kinetische Skulpturen*. Berlin, Galerie Springer, July 2–Aug. 6, 1962.
Text also in German.

173. Hultén, K. G. "Geschichte der Bewegungskunst im 20. Jahrhundert." *Kunstnachrichten*, v. 1, no. 6, April 1965.
Translation from exhibition catalogue: *Rörelse i Konsten* (Stockholm, 1961).

174. Jakowski, Anatole. "Brancusi." *Axis*, July 1935.
"Rotation, gyrations, cyclical movement serve as a framework for all artistic creation. . . .

Aero-dynamics affirms the power on all sides. . . ." In part, a survey of sculpture by a perceptive critic who was published by *Abstraction-Création*, and wrote "Essais" on Arp, Calder, Gonzalez, Pevsner, Taeuber-Arp, in the 30's.

175. Janis, Harriet. "Mobiles." *Arts and Architecture*, no. 2, Feb. 1948.
On mobility in sculpture as well as specific sculptors.

176. Jelinski, K. A. "Avant-garde and revolution." *Arts* (New York), Oct. 1960.
Translated from the Polish (*Kultura, Paris*). On art in Russia from the October revolution to Stalin. All illustrations are Constructivist (1921–1923). Mentions recent Polish abstraction and E. Steneberg's 1959 exhibition: "The Russian contribution to contemporary art." Complemented by "Russian art: evolution and revolution" (Nov. 1962), a review and evaluation of Camilla Gray: *The Great Experiment: Russian Art* (Bibl. 32).

176a. Kállai, Ernst. "Konstruktivismus." *Jahrbuch der Jungen Kunst*, v. 5, 1924.

176b. Kémeny, Alfred & Moholy-Nagy, L. "Dynamisch-konstruktives Kraftsystem." *Der Sturm*, v. 13, no. 12, 191?
On the "dynamic constructive system of forces." Continued by Kémeny: "Das dynamisch Prinzip der Weltkonstruktion im Zugammenhang mit der funktionellen Bedeutung des konstruktiven Gestaltens" (v. 14, no. 4).

176c. Knapp, Ernst. "Licht-Echt?" *Vernissage*, v. 2, 1961.
Illustrations: W. Strzeminski, H. Stazewski, H. Bayer. Followed by E. Steneberg: *Henryk Berlewi's mechano-faktur* [1923]. N. Braun: *Das konkrete Licht* [1925].

176d. Kozloff, Max. "Geometric abstraction in America." *Art International*, nos. 5–6, Summer 1962.
Commentary based on current Whitney show. Among many articles, for continuation see: "Abstract attrition," *Arts Magazine*, no. 4, Jan. 1965; "The further adventures of American sculpture," *Arts Magazine*, Feb. 1965, etc.

176e. Lapique, Charles. "Color into space." *Portfolio and Art News Annual*, no. 1, 1959.
A physicist-painter on physiological optics.

176f. Laposky, Ben F. "Electronic abstracts: art for the space age." *Proceedings of the Iowa Academy of Science*, Nov. 20, 1958.
Also published and illustrated in *Spirale*, no. 8, Oct. 1960.

176g. Legrand, F. C. "La peinture et la sculpture au défi." *Quadrum*, no. 7, 1959.
Illustrated by Agam, Kemeny, Linck, Lippold, etc.

176h. Leider, Philip. "Kinetic sculpture at Berkeley." *Artform*, no. 9, May 1966.
On the occasion of Selz's exhibition.

176i. Leisberg, Alexander. "Neue tendenzen." *Das Kunstwerk*, nos. 10–11, April–May 1961.
Illustrated by Castellani, Lissitzky, Mack, etc.

176j. Lippard, Lucy R. "The third stream: constructed paintings and painted structures." *Art Voices*, Spring 1965.
Also see her regular section in *Art International*, the "New York Letter."

177. Lohse, Richard P. "The influence of modern art in contemporary graphic design." *New Graphic Design*, no. 1, Sept. 1958.
Emphasizes constructivist influence. Text also in German and French. Bibliography.

178. Marchis, Giorgio di. "La IV biennale di San Marino." *Art International*, no. 7, Sept. 1963.
Illustrated by Getulio, Mari, Morellet, etc. Followed by: "Una ipotesi neo-concreta" (pp. 54–55).

179. Massat, René. "Materiology and desire for the absolute." *XXᵉ Siècle*, no. 17, Christmas 1961.
Materials in relation to styles and experiments of the 19th and 20th century. Also French edition, no. 17.

180. Michelis, P. A. "Space-time and contemporary architecture." *Journal of Aesthetics and Art Criticism*, Dec. 1949.

181. Michelson, Annette. "L'abstraction géométrique en Amérique." *XXᵉ Siècle*, no. 20, April 1962.
On the exhibition at the Whitney Museum. Reproduces two works by Kelly.

182. "Modern Art in Britain Today." *Cambridge Opinion*, no. 27, Spring 1964.
A special number with 13 contributors, edited by M. Peppiatt.

183. Morris, George L. K. "On the mechanics of abstract painting." *Partisan Review*, no. 5, Sept.–Oct. 1941.
Other articles by this artist-critic: "Life or death for abstract art?" *Magazine of Art*, March 1943; "La sculpture abstraite aux U.S.A.," *Art d'Aujourd'hui*, Jan. 1953. Also see *Plastique* (Bibl. 113).

184. "Moscow Kineticists." *Studio International*, no. 880, Aug. 1966.
On sculpture and film by D. Konecny and Lev Nusberg.

185. Newhall, Beaumont. "The new abstract vision." *Art News Annual*, 1946–1947, v. 45, no. 10, pt. 2, Dec. 1946.
Photographs as by-products of scientific and practical studies, selected to illustrate the "unseen" beauty of natural phenomena.

186. L'Objet. *Cahiers d'Art*, no. 1–2, 1936.
Special issue with numerous illustrations of natural, mathematical, and man-made objects. Article by Christian Zervos, "Mathématiques et art abstrait"; illustrations relate to shape and design in science.

187. Oster, Gerald. "Moiré optics: a bibliography." *Journal of the Optical Society of America*, v. 55, p. 1329, Oct. 1965.
Complemented by: "Optical art," *Applied Optics*, v. 4, pp. 1359–69, Nov. 1965.

188. Padtra, Jiri. "Konstruktivní tendence." *Výtvarné Umĕní (Fine Arts)*, no. 6–7, 1966.
Insert: German translation.

189. Popper, Frank. "Kinetic art and our environment." In *De Nieuwe Stijl Deel 1*, pp. 178–180, Amsterdam [1966?].

190. Potter, Ralph K. "New scientific tools for the arts." *Journal of Aesthetics & Art Criticism*, no. 2, Dec. 1951.
References to light, abstract films, music, research, etc.

191. Ragon, Michel. "Le 'constructivisme' réalise-t-il le mariage d'amour de la ligne et du volume?" *Arts* (Paris), May 1962.

192. Rambsbott, Wolfgang. "Chronologie der kinetischen Kunst nach 1900." In *Kinetische Kunst*, Zürich, Kunstgewerbe Museum, May–June 1960.
From *Movens* (Wiesbaden, 1960) "ergänzt und vervollständigt durch Kunstgewerbemuseum Zürich."

193. Read, Herbert. "Realism and abstraction in modern art." *Eidos*, no. 1, May–June 1950.

Quotes from letters with Gabo and concludes: "reality is a chain of images invented by man." Numerous articles by this poet-critic are included in various anthologies (Bibl. 62).

194. Richter, Hans. "An den konstruktivismus." *G* (Berlin), no. 3, June 1924.

195. ———. "Dalla pittura moderna al cinema moderna." *La Biennale di Venezia*, no. 54, Sept. 1964.

Includes Duchamp's roto reliefs.

196. Rickey, George. "Kinesis continued." *Art in America*, Dec. 1965–Jan. 1966.

Recent developments, illustrated (pp. 45–55).

197. ———. "The kinetic international." *Arts Magazine*, Sept. 1961.

198. ———. "Kinetic sculpture." In *Art & Artist*, Berkeley & Los Angeles, University of California Press, 1956.

199. ———. "The morphology of movement: a study of kinetic art." *Art Journal*, no. 4, Summer 1963.

Since published in "Vision and Value," ed. by Gyorgy Kepes (New York, Braziller, 1965).

200. ———. [Statement on movement]. In *George Rickey: Kinetic Sculpture*, Pittsfield, Mass., Berkshire Arts Center, June 18–July 16, 1963.

201. Rose, Barbara. "The primacy of color." *Art International*, no. 4, May 1964.

Among other complementary articles: "Beyond vertigo: optical art at the Modern," *Artforum*, April 1965; "ABC art," *Art in America*, Oct.–Nov. 1965.

202. Roszak, Theodor. "In pursuit of an image." *Quadrum*, no. 2, Nov. 1956.

Refers to his constructivist work.

203. Schöffer, Nicolas & Habasque, Guy. "Art, science et technique." *Art d'Aujourd'hui*, no. 9, Sept. 1956.

Followed (pp. 50–51) by J. Pellandini: "La photoélasticimétrie et les verms photoélastiques" (ill., col.).

204. Seitz, William, ed. "A survey of recent sculpture." *Arts Yearbook 8* (New York), 1965.

205. Selz, Peter. "Arte programmata." *Arts Magazine*, no. 6, March 1965.

Based on circulation in the U.S. of the Olivetti-sponsored exhibition, 1965–1966.

206. Seuphor, Michel. "Art construit." *XXᵉ Siècle*, no. 24, June 1962.

Illustrations and color plates from Malevich to Mahlmann.

207. ———. "Constructivist painting." *Selective Eye*, no. 4, 1960.

Translated from French essay in *L'Oeil* (1959).

208. ———. "Le monde à construire (Réflexions sur le constructivisme)." Paris, Oct. 1962.

Essay prepared as introduction for Rickey's *Constructivism: Origins and Evolution*, Braziller (1967).

209. ———. "Peintures construites." *L'Oeil*, no. 58, Oct. 1959.

Translated for *Selective Eye, IV: Modern Art —Yesterday and Tomorrow* (New York, Reynal, 1960).

210. ———. "Sens et permanence de la peinture construite." *Quadrum*, no. 8, 1960.

Extensive illustrated essay, pp. 37–58, 194–196, with English translation.

211. ———. "De Stijl." *L'Oeil*, no. 22, 1956.

The magazine and the movement, dominated by the master Mondrian.

212. Sharp, Willoughby. "Kineticism." In Amiel Gallery, *Tsai Multi-Kinetics*, New York, Nov. 1965.

Announcement includes essay and chart.

213. Steneberg, Eberhard. "Die Ungeduldigen: zum Verständis der École Russe." *Kunstwerk*, Aug.–Sept. 1959.

With English summary ("space—that is always the stimulation—not mass or things"). Also "Der revolutionäre Grossvater [USSR]," April–May 1961.

214. Sweeney, James J. "Americans 1950." In *American Painting 1950*, Richmond, Virginia Museum, April 22–June 4, 1950.

Perceptive essay on "refreshing the tradition," "new nouns," "the process of metaphor," etc.

215. Sylvester, David. "Aspects of contemporary British art: Image of Britain 2." *Texas Quarterly* (Austin), Autumn 1961.

216. Tillim, Sidney. "What happened to geometry?" *Arts* (New York), June 1959.

"An inquiry into geometrical painting in America." Illustrates and discusses Albers and Leon Polk Smith, among others. Reprinted: *Arts Yearbook 6*, ed. by J. R. Mellow, New York, *Arts Digest*, 1962.

217. Times Literary Supplement. London, Sept. 3, 1964.
Includes articles by Munari, Mon, Bense, Piene. Reviews W. E. Simmat, "Europäischer Avantgarde"; F. Mon, "Movens"; H. Heissenbüttel, "Textbuch 4"; monographs on Agam and Schöffer (Griffon); S. Lupasco, "Science et Art abstrait," etc.

218. Valensi, Henry. "Introduction au mot 'abstrait.'" *La Revue d'Esthétique*, Jan.–March 1951.
Abstraction in art and cinema. Extracts published in *Réalites Nouvelles*, no. 8 (1954), no. 9 (1955). Also included in his *Dictionnaire et Vocabulaire Technique de l'Esthétique* (Presses Universitaires de France).

219. Vallier, Dora. "L'art abstrait en Russie: ses origines, ses premières manifestations." *Cahiers d'Art*, v. 33–35, 1960.

220. Vasarely, Victor. "Ce que devrait être la critique d'art." *Les Beaux-Arts*, no. 907, Oct. 28, 1960.
Taking a work by Morellet as a point of departure, discusses fresh objectives in visual research, experiment in science and art, etc. Also issued as separate for *Morellet* (Brussels, Galerie d'Aujourd'hui, Oct. 22–Nov. 5, 1960).

221. Vordemberge-Gildewart, Friedrich. "Zur Geschichte der Stijl-Bewegung." *Werk*, no. 11, 1951.

222. Weininger, Andor. "Bauhaus und Stijl." *Form* (Dusseldorf), no. 6, 1959.
On Van Doesburg and his influence on the Bauhaus. English translation (pp. 43–44).

223. Wescher, Herta. "Collages constructivistes et successeurs." *Art d'Aujourd'hui*, no. 2–3, April 1954.
One of many articles by this prolific critic. Also see *Plastique* (Bibl. 113), *Cimaise* (Bibl. 108).

V. EXHIBITION CATALOGUES

The chronology by the author (pp. 1–6) will provide the time sequence of most events noted below. For convenience in reference, these selected shows are arranged according to place of exhibition.

224. Albright-Knox Art Gallery. *Kinetic and Optic Art Today*. Buffalo, Feb. 27–March 28, 1965.
Europeans and Americans (84 exhibits). Includes Len Lye and Nicolas Schöffer. Similar American exhibits, now widespread, include: Des Moines Art Center. *Art with Optical Reaction*. Jan. 21–Feb. 20, 1966. Foreword: T. T. Tibbs. Plastic cover, 72 exhibits, ill.

225. Amsterdam, Stedelijk Museum. *Bewogen Beweging*. March 10–April 17, 1961.
Catalog edited by K. G. Hultén. Also shown at the Moderna Museet, Stockholm as "Rörelse i Konsten," May 17–Sept. 3, 1961. This "movement in art" exhibition is documented in an unusual oblong catalogue with folding insert. Comprehensive data on many exhibitors, supplemented by essay by Hultén. Later exhibited at the Louisiana Museum, Copenhagen (1961). Among the numerous reports of these shows, note "Movement in art" [at Stockholm], *Art International*, Sept. 20, 1961; "Rörelse i Konsten" [at Stockholm], *Konstrevy*, no. 3, 1961; "Exposition du mouvement à Amsterdam (H. Richter)," *Aujourd'hui*, May 1961.

226. ———. "*Experiment in Constructie*." May 18–June 16, 1962.
Dutch and English text. Statement by Sandberg. "The new plastic expression" by J. Baljeu. Biographical notes on Baljeu, Biederman, Gorin, M. Martin, and others. Dutch postscript by J. B. Bibliography. Also shown as *Experiment in Fläche und Raum*, Zürich, Kunstgewerbe Museum, Aug. 25–Sept. 30, 1962. Minor modifications in catalogue.

227. Austin, University of Texas Museum. *Exhibition of Retinal and Perceptual Art.* April 11–May 9, 1965.
Forty-six artists, biographies, statements. Similar university shows, now widespread, include Kansas University Museum of Art, "Optics, Illusion and Art" (Introduction by B. Waller, includes B. E. Benkert, Demarco, J. Goodyear, and others), May 14–June 7, 1965.

228. Basel, Kunsthalle. *Konkrete Kunst.* March 18–April 16, 1944.
One hundred seventy-nine exhibits, plus 7 graphic albums, representing about 25 artists: Albers, Bill, Eggeling, Lohse, Mondrian, Taeuber-Arp, Vantongerloo, etc. Texts by Arp and Bill.

229. ———. *Konstruktivisten.* Jan. 16–Feb. 14, 1937.
One hundred seventy-seven exhibits; brief biographies. Artists include Eggeling, Van Doesburg, Gabo, Lissitzky, Moholy-Nagy, Mondrian, Vordemberge-Gildewart, etc. Preface by G. Schmidt.

230. Berkeley, University Art Gallery. *Directions in Kinetic Sculpture, by Peter Selz, with an Introduction by George Rickey and Statements by the Artists.* March 18–May 1, 1966.
Also shown at Santa Barbara, June 5–July 10. Exhibitors: F. Benton, D. Boriani, R. Breer, P. Bury, G. Colombo, G. von Graevenitz, H. Haacke, H. Kramer, L. Lye, H. Mack, C. Mattox, G. Rickey, Takis, Tinguely. Biographies, chronology, bibliography, and "Chronology of kinetic art" by B. Richardson.

231. Berlin, Galerie Van Diemen. *Erste Russische Kunstausstellung.* Nov. ?, 1922.
Foreword by A. Holitscher, cover by Gabo; 594 exhibits include fine and applied arts. Painters: Malevich, Pevsner, Rodchenko. Also Archipenko, Gabo, Kandinsky, Lissitzky, Tatlin, etc.

232. Bern, Kunsthalle. *Weiss auf Weiss.* May 25–July 3, 1966.
Newspaper format (16 pp.). Preface: Udo Kultermann. 118 works by Constructivist, Kinetic, Optic, and Pop artists. Biographies and portraits of 60 participants.

233. Biot, Groupe Espace. *Exposition Espace: Architecture, Formes, Couleur.* July 10–Sept. 10, 1954.
Introduction by André Bloc. Biographical notes on Arp, S. Delaunay, Gorin, Lardera, Magnelli, Schöffer, Vasarely, etc. Lists memberships, both individuals and national groups, e.g. MAC (Italy).

234. Düsseldorf, Kunsthalle. *Licht und Bewegung—Kinetische Kunst.* Feb. 2–March 13, 1966.
Katalog: K.-H. Hering (145 works). "Kunstverein für die Rheinlande und Westfalen." Preface: F. Popper. Chronology of Kinetic Art, biographical notes.

235. Eindhoven. Stedelijk van Abbe Museum. *Kunst-LichtKunst.* Sept. 25–Dec. 4, 1966.
Extensive essay by Frank Popper on the new art of artificial light, 1914–1966 (in English and Dutch). Multilingual texts. Comprehensive representation (ca. 100 exhibits) of artists and groups. Includes chart on luminescence in art.

236. Frankfurt, Galerie D. *Europäische Avantgarde.* Frankfurt-am-Main, July 9–Aug. 11, 1963.
Organized and catalogued by W. E. Simmat with preface on "Neue europäische Schule, arte programmata, neue tendenzen, antipeinture, zero." Biographies and bibliographies, statements; illustrations on 47 participants, including Bury, Castellani, Dorazio, Getulio, Mack, Megert, Munari, Piene, Soto, Uecker, Vasarely.

237. Hague, Gemeentemuseum. *Kinetische Kunst uit Krefeld.* Feb. 3–March 14, 1965.
"Eigentijdse kunst uit de collectie van het Kaiser Wilhelm Museum te Krefeld." Also shown at Eindhoven (March–May).

238. Hannover, Kestner-Gesellschaft. *Gabo. Konstruktive Plastik.* Nov. 6–23, 1930.
Included small "historical" section arranged by the artist for this early German exhibition. Extract from "Realistic Manifesto 1920." Biographical note, list of 23 works, preface by J. Bier.

239. Krefeld, Museum Haus Lange. *Ausstellung Mack, Piene, Uecker.* Jan. 1963.
Catalog by Paul Wember, with comprehensive bibliographies.

240. Lausanne, Musée Cantonal des Beaux-Arts. *Le Mouvement dans l'Art Contemporain.* June 24–Sept. 26, 1955.

Lettered on cover: "Du Futurisme à l'Art abstrait." Introduction by Guy Weelen. Biographical notes, including Bodmer, Calder, R. & S. Delaunay, Kandinsky, Kupka, and others. At the same time the association *Pour l'Art* (Lausanne) issued a whole issue (no. 43, July–Aug. 1955): "Textes et documents présentés . . . à l'occasion de l'exposition 'Le Mouvement.'" Largely includes artists' statements, 1909–1954. Earlier in the year the *Galerie Denise René* held a similar show, "Le Mouvement," Paris, April 6–30, 1955. The catalog has texts by K. Hultén and V. Vasarely. For a review see *Cimaise*, no. 6, pp. 17–18, May 1955.

241. ———. *Ier Salon International de Galeries Pilotes*. June 20–Sept. 22, 1963.
A massive catalogue (330 pp. incl. ill., col.) of "artistes et decouvreurs de notre temps," constituting "leading" artists handled by selected European galleries. References may be found to Agam, Albers, Arp, Baertling, Daphnis, Delaunay, Johns, Kemeny, Le Parc, Mortensen, Nicholson, Schöffer, Seuphor, Taeuber-Arp, di Teana, Tomasello, Vasarely, Yvaral, and others.

242. Leverkusen, Städtisches Museum. *Konstruktivisten*. June 22–Aug. 19, 1962.
Introduction by Udo Kultermann. Ninety-seven works exhibited, with acknowledgment to Galerie Denise René and others. Comprehensive representation.

243. ———. *Monochrome Malerei*. March 18–May 8, 1960.
Preface by Udo Kultermann: "Eine neue Konzeption." Multilingual texts by Gabo, Piene, Castellani, etc. Works by Dorazio, Mack, Mavignier, Megert, Piene, Uecker, etc. Brief biographies.

244. Liége. Musée de l'Art Wallon. *20 Artistes de l'École de Paris*. Aug. 20–Sept. 18, 1952.
Organized by Denise René in Sweden, Norway, Denmark, and Finland. Preface by L. Degand. Biographies. Also issued as insert for *Art d'Aujourd'hui*, Dec. 1951, in special issue on "Klar Form."

245. London, Arts Council of Great Britain. *Construction England*. [Circulated in England] April–Nov. 1963.

Forty exhibits, with notes on 14 participants (K. and M. Martin, Pasmore, etc.). Selection and introduction by Alan Bowness; references to Gabo & Pevsner (1920), influence of Biederman's book (1938). Also see his essay in *Arts* (Apr. 1961): "Construction: England, 1950–1960 at the Drian Gallery."

246. ———. *Situation: An Exhibition of Recent British Abstract Art*. London, 1962.
Circulated 1962–1963, with 18 artists (including statements). Essay by Roger Coleman (from catalog of first "Situation" show, 1960) refers to "scale, gesture, geometry."

247. London, Hanover Gallery. *Agam, S. Delaunay, di Teana, Herbin, Mortensen, Schöffer, Tomasello, Vasarely*. March 19–April 27, 1963.
With 32 pp. catalogue of plates.

248. London, Institute of Contemporary Art. *Statements: A Review of British Abstract Art in 1956*. London, 1957.
Texts, among others, by Adams, the Martins, Nicholson, Pasmore, etc. Also see their show organized for the American Federation of Arts: *British Constructivist Art*, 1962, introduction by L. Alloway.

249. London, Lefèvre Gallery. *Abstract and Concrete*. Spring, 1936.
"Nicolete Gray organized the first international exhibition of abstract art to be held in London" (C. G.). Fifteen artists including Calder, Gabo, Kandinsky, Moholy-Nagy, Mondrian, Nicholson. Installation views in *Circle* (1937, p. 280), which also lists similar abstract shows 1935–1937 (pp. 279–281).

250. London Gallery. *Constructive Art* [July] 1937.
Thirteen artists including Calder, Gabo, Moholy-Nagy, Nicholson. Review by Eric Newton, July 1937, reprinted in his *In My View* (1950, pp. 56–59).

251. London, O'Hana Gallery. *Dimensions: British Abstract Art, 1948–1957*. [Fall ?], 1957.
Sixty-five exhibits include K. and M. Martin, Nicholson, Pasmore, etc. Arranged in co-operation with the I.C.A., by L. Alloway, additional research by Toni del Renzio. Important documentation.

252. Milan, Galleria Pagani. *Stringenz: Nuove Tendenze Tedesche*. [Spring ?], 1959.

Biographical notes and illustrations: Kricke, Mack, Mavignier, etc.

253. Milan, Società Olivetti. *Arte Programmata, Arte Cinetica, Opere Moltiplicate, Opere Aperta.* May–Oct. 1962.

Organized by Bruno Munari and Giorgio Soavi for the "Direzione Pubblicita" and circulated in Milan, Venice, Rome. An international with many illustrations, emphasizing the Italians and including the Gruppo N, Gruppo T, and Gruppo di Ricerca d'Arte Visuale. Text by Umberto Eco in Italian, French, and English. Important chronology of "arte cinetica" (1914–1916), mentioning persons, events, and exhibitions.

254. Minneapolis, Walker Art Center. *The Classic Tradition in Contemporary Art.* April 24–June 28, 1953.

Biographical notes and bibliography covering the more and less prominent names in this tradition: Bolotowsky, Diller, Glarner, Kupka, Reinhardt, Servranckx, Torrès Garcia, Von Wiegand, etc. Complemented by an associated exhibition: "The Precisionist View in American Art," Nov. 13–Dec. 25, 1960. Essay by Martin L. Friedman, who describes its unifying characteristic as the "attraction of all its artists to the colossal geometry of the city and industry."

255. New York, American Federation of Arts. *British Constructivist Art.* April 12–May 27, 1962.

Organized by Institute of Contemporary Art (London); circulated in the U.S.A. Introduction by L. Alloway. Included K. & M. Martin, Pasmore, etc.

256. New York, Galerie Chalette. *Construction and Geometry in Painting: From Malevich to "Tomorrow."* March 1960.

A major catalogue: 130 pp. including 105 exhibits and biographical notes on 50 artists from 17 countries. Introduction by Dr. Madeleine Chalette-Lejwa; essay by Michel Seuphor (18 pp.). "The pioneers" include Kupka, Macdonald-Wright, etc.; "the contemporaries" include Diller, Fruhtrunk, Glarner, Servranckx, Stazewski, Thépot, Von Wiegand, etc. as well as the standard representatives of this international style. Reviewed by: Hilton Kramer, "Constructing the absolute," *Arts* (N.Y.), May

1960. Complemented by an earlier exhibition: "Structured Sculpture," Dec. 1960–Jan. 1961 (six artists including R. Engman and other Yale graduates).

257. New York, Jewish Museum. *Primary Structures: Younger American and British Sculptors.* April 27–June 12, 1966.

Exhibit and introduction by Kynaston McShine. Includes 42 participants: Anthony Caro, Ellsworth Kelly, etc. Biographies; bibliography.

258. New York, Jewish Museum. *Toward a New Abstraction.* New York, May 19–Sept. 15, 1963.

American painters; introduction: Ben Heller. Text and bibliographies. Includes Paul Brach, Al Held, Ellsworth Kelly, Morris Louis, Kenneth Noland, George Ortman, Raymond Parker, Miriam Shapiro, Frank Stella.

259. New York, New Art Center. *Masters of Abstract Art.* April 1–May 15, 1942.

Editors: Stephen C. Lion, Charmion von Wiegand. Among the texts are: Mondrian, "Pure plastic art"; Richter, "Orchestration of the form." Seventy-four exhibits (16 ill.) include Diller, Doesburg, Eggeling, Lissitzky, Malevich.

260. New York, The Contemporaries. *L'Instabilité: Groupe de Recherche d'Art Visuel.* Nov. 27–Dec. 15, 1962.

Compact expository text on perception and movement.

261. New York, Martha Jackson Gallery. *Vibrations Eleven.* Jan. 6–31, 1965.

Eleven artists including Anonima group. Statement; biographies, ports., ill.

262. New York, Rose Fried Gallery. *The White Plane.* March 19–April 12, 1947.

"The first pure abstract show, organized by Charmion von Wiegand," included 18 works by Bolotowsky, Diller, Glarner, as well as Albers, Malevich, Mondrian. Also separate mimeographed essay by C. von Wiegand.

263. New York, Solomon R. Guggenheim Museum. *Abstract Expressionists and Imagists.* Oct.–Dec. 1961.

Comprehensive general and individual bibliography. Includes Albers, Daphnis, Johns, Kelly, M. Louis, K. Noland, Ad Reinhardt, L. Smith, etc. Related recent exhibits: *Cézanne and*

Structure in Recent Painting, 1963, included Albers, Malevich, Mondrian, etc.; *Six Painters and the Object*, 1963, included Johns. Text in the former by Daniel Robbins, for the latter by Lawrence Alloway.

264. Northampton, Lillian H. Florsheim Foundation for Fine Arts. *A Selection of Abstract Art, 1917–1965*. Smith College, May 11–June 7, 1966.

Introduction by A. J. S. to a "sequence of geometric painting." Reproductions and biographies on Vantongerloo, Moholy-Nagy, Delaunay, Domela, Nicholson, Diller, Glarner, Vasarely, Pasmore, Albers, Bill, Kelly, Stella, Reinhardt, Yvaral, Honegger, G. Davis, H. Beckmann.

265. Oslo, Kunstnerforbundet. *International Nutidkunst: Konstruktivisme, Neoplasticisme, Abstrakt Kunst, Surrealisme*. Sept. 16–Oct. 2 [1938].

Organized by Arp, Taeuber-Arp, Bjerke-Petersen. Introduction by B.-P.; bibliography. Eighteen exhibitors including Arp, Van Doesburg, Kandinsky, Magnelli, Taeuber-Arp, Vantongerloo.

266. Paris, Diderot Gallery. *Structures Vivantes . . . Bury, Soto, Takis*. Paris, April–May, 1963.

Text unsigned. "Copyright by Marcel Zerbib." Similarly Redfern Gallery: *Structures Vivantes —Mobiles Images*, London, March 3–27 1964 (22 pp., ill., nineteen artists: Agam, Bury, Soto, etc., biographies).

267. Paris, Edouard Loeb. *Multiplication des Objets*. Nov. 27–Dec. 19, 1959.

"Tirage d'objets d'art multipliés au nombre de cent exemplaires numérotés et signés": Agam, Albers, Bury, Duchamp, Mack, Rot, Soto, Tinguely, Vasarely. Also related exhibitions: Galleria Danese, "Opere d'Arte Animate e Moltiplicate," Milan, Feb.–March 1960 (adds Enzo Mari, Man Ray), text by Belloli; Gallery One "Oeuvres d'Art Transformables," Feb. 1960 (artists same as Loeb's but adds Man Ray, Munari). Also shown at Kunstgewerbemuseum, Zürich, March 1960, with further modifications in exhibitors: Bo Ek, Gerstner, Malina, etc. During 1960 *Edition MAT* published another "Multiplication des Oeuvres d'Art." Also see Bibl. 25, 26.

268. Paris, Galerie Denise René. [Exhibitions]. 1954–current.

The most important gallery for the systematic exhibition of relevant "abstract" and "experimental" manifestations. Many one-man shows have already been reported in the bibliography. Some recent exhibitions are: "Premier Salon de la Sculpture Abstraite," Dec. 10, 1954–Jan. 15, 1955 (comprehensive presentation in *Art d'Aujourd'hui*, Dec. 1954); "Second Salon de la Sculpture Abstraite," April–May 1956 (published on this occasion: *Témoignages pour la Sculpture Abstraite* [Editions Art d'Aujourd'hui]); "Exposition Art Abstrait Constructif International," Dec. 1961–Feb. 1962 (essay by M. Seuphor for this comprehensive presentation of 39 artists, both pioneers and contemporaries); "Ligne Constructive de l'Art Abstrait" [Mar.] 1962 (Reviewed extensively in *Cimaise*, no. 58, 1962); "Esquisse d'un Salon," May–Sept. 1963 (includes 90 exhibitors, all illustrated, 4 installation views, texts by J. Lassaigne, J.-C. Lambert); "Hard-Edge," Paris, June (?) 1964 (biographies, multilingual texts and statements, essays by L. Alloway, M. Seuphor, T. Brunius).

269. Paris, Galerie Maeght. *Les Premiers Maîtres de l'Art Abstrait*. April–June 1949.

"First big historic show of early abstract painting." Part I: "Préliminaires à l'art abstrait (fin avril au 23 mai)"; II: "Épanouissement de l'art abstrait (27 mai–juin 30)." Organizers: Clayeux and Seuphor. Major text by the latter: *L'Art Abstrait* (Bibl. 68) issued 1949 and 1950 ("nouvelle édition"). See this for comprehensive illustrations and documentation. Complemented by related coverage in the gallery's deluxe bulletin: *Derrière le Miroir*, e.g. special numbers on Kandinsky.

270. Paris, Galerie Percier. *Constructivistes Russes, Gabo et Pevsner: Peintures, Constructions*. June 19–July 5, 1924.

An early manifestation in Paris, preceding Gabo's Hanover show by six years. Catalogue: 12 leaves, 4 plates; text by Waldemar George.

271. Paris, Galerie René Drouin. *Art Concret*. June 15–July 13, 1945.

Includes Arp,* Domela, the Delaunays,* Freundlich, Gorin, Herbin, Kandinsky,* Magnelli, Mondrian, Pevsner,* Taeuber-Arp, Van Doesburg* (excerpting texts by those marked*). Unsigned historical preface. Exhibition, assembled with help of Mrs. Van Doesburg, was first important abstract art show after the war, is limited strictly to "non figuratif" artists.

272. Paris, Galerie 23. *Cercle et Carré.* [April] 1930. "First international exhibition of abstract art." Exhibition covered in no. 2 of *Cercle et Carré* (April 1930). Introduction by Mondrian: "L'art réaliste et l'art superréaliste (la morphoplastique et la néo-plastique)." Described by the organizer and its chronicler, M. Seuphor, in his *Dictionary of Abstract Painting* (pp. 49 ff) and in his *Abstract Painting* (pp. 109 ff), who emphasizes the plastic and spiritual pre-eminence of Mondrian.

273. Paris, Salon des Réalités Nouvelles. *Réalités Nouvelles.* 1947–current.

Bibl. 272. Exhibitors at "Cercle et Carré" show, Paris, 1930. From left to right: Clausen, Florence Henry, Mme. Torrès-Garcia, Torrès-Garcia, Mondrian, Arp, Daura, Cahn, Sophie Taeuber, Seuphor, Vordemberge-Gildewart, Idelsohn, Russolo, Mme. Kandinsky, Vantongerloo, Kandinsky, Gorin.

Bibl. 659. NUL Exhibition, Stedelijk Museum, April 1965. Participants include, from left to right, Jiro Yoshihara, Hans Haacke, Michio Yoshihara, Henk Peeters, Jan Schoonhoven, Rotraut Klein-Uecker, Pol Bury, Lucio Fontana, Ad Peterson, Gianni Colombo, Mme. Fontana, E. L. L. de Wilde, Nono Reinhold, Yayoi Kusama, George Rickey, Otto Piene, Nanda Vigo, Alfred Schmela, Heinz Mack, Günther Uecker.

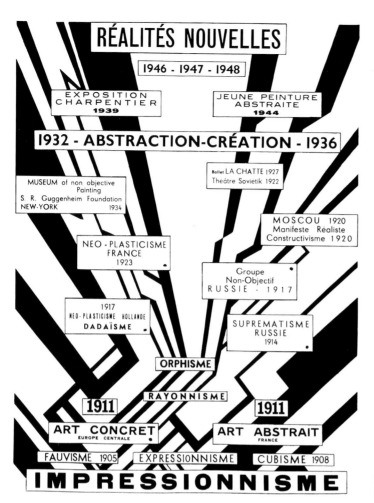

Bibl. 273. Chart from *Réalités Nouvelles*, Paris.

The annuals serve as exhibition catalogues and yearbooks of the association, with details on committees, directors, participants, texts. No. 1 (1947), no. 2 (1948), no. 3 (1949), no. 4 (1950), no. 5 (1951), etc. Numerous illustrations and significant texts by artists in Paris and from the European community, ranging from Kupka to Bolotowsky.

274. Stockholm, Moderna Museet. *Rörelse i Konsten*. May 17–Sept. 3, 1961.
Organized by K. G. Hultén with an extraordinary oblong catalogue of 233 exhibits. Includes lexicon of artists in "kinetisch konst"; also quotations from relevant statements and texts, 1675–1961. Supplementary historic survey by Hultén. References to the Futurists, biographical notes on pioneers and contemporaries from Eggeling to Malina.

275. Stuttgart, Staatsgalerie. *Kinetik und Objekte*. Feb. 21–March 21, 1965. 24 pp. ill.
Preface by J. Cladders. Seventy-three works. Also Badischer Kunstverein, April 11–May 16, 1965.

276. Tel Aviv, Museum. *Art et Mouvement: Art Optique et Cinétique*. [40] pp. ill.
Hebrew, French, and English texts. Ninety-one exhibits. Organized in cooperation with Galerie Denise René, Paris. Historical chart in French.

277. Westfälischer Kunstverein. *Tendenzen Strukturaler Kunst*. Münster, May 8–June 19, 1966.
Introduction: J. Wissman. Biographies, quotes; 78 pp., ill.

278. Wiesbaden, Galerie Roepcke. *Komplexe Farbe*. Feb. 1962.

"Ausstellung der Maler Berner, Dorazio, Graubner, Joachims, Jürgen-Fischer." Statements by the artists.

279. Zagreb, Galerija Suvremene um Jetnosti. *Nove Tendencije*. Aug. 3–Sept. 14, 1961; Aug. 1–Sept. 15, 1963; Aug. 13–Sept. 19, 1965.
"Nouvelles tendenances" with 29 exhibitors (29 ill.), including Castellani, Dorazio, Gerstner, Von Graevenitz, Mack, Mavignier, Piene, Uecker, and the "Groupe" participants. Prefaces by M. Meštrović and R. Putar. Biographical notes, brief statements. Also *Nove Tendencije 2*, (Aug. 1–Sept. 15, 1963), with texts by Meštrović and Putar. Sixty-two participants including "Equipo 57" and other "Groupes"; 50 illustrations plus portrait photos. Brief statements, e.g. Getulio, Le Parc, Picelj, Uecker, etc. With a chronology of new directions referring to artists and exhibitions, 1914–1963. No. 3, 1965: Numerous multilingual texts (180 pp.). Essay by Frank Popper: "Kinetic art and our environment," pp. 65–66.

280. Zürich, Kunstgesellschaft. *Konkrete Kunst: 50 Jahre Entwicklung*. June 8–Aug. 14, 1960.
Texts by R. W., M. Bill. "Katalog dokumentiert von Margit Staber." Manifests from "De Stijl"

and on "Konkrete Kunst," substantial quotations from the artists, quotes from Max Bense: "Asthetik und Zivilisation" (1958). Notes on many pioneers and contemporaries, including for example, Berlewi, Graeser, Stazewski, Strzeminski as well as Diller, Equipo 57, Reinhardt, Uecker, etc.

281. Zürich, Kunstgewerbemuseum. *Experiment in Fläche und Raum*. Aug. 25–Sept. 30, 1962.
Variant of Bibl. 226, with quote from Sandberg, preface by Baljeu. Biographical notes on J. Baljeu, C. Biederman, C. Cairoli, J. Ernest, J. Gorin, A. Hill, M. Martin, D. van Woerkam.

282. ———. *Kinetische Kunst. Alexander Calder. Edition MAT*, Paris. May–June 1960.
"Calder: "Mobiles und Stabiles aus den letzten Jahren." MAT: "Kunstwerke, die sich bewegen oder bewegen lassen." Wegleitung 233 with preface by H. Fischli and W. Rotzler and a "Chronologie der kinetische Kunst nach 1900" by W. Ramsbott. Text on Calder by C. Giedion-Welcker, on MAT by D. Spoerri. Biographical data and commentary on Agam, Albers, Duchamp, Gerstner, Mack, Melina, Mari, Munari, D. Rot, Soto, Tinguely, Vasarely.

VI. ARTISTS & GROUPS

Adams, Robert

283. Alloway, Lawrence. *Nine Abstract Artists*. London, Tiranti, 1954.
Statement by Adams and illustrations chosen by the artist. Footnotes. See also: "Personal statement: Lawrence Alloway and Robert Adams," *Ark*, no. 19, 1957.

284. Baden-Baden, Staatliche Kunsthalle. *Robert Adams. Eine Ausstellung des British Council*. Oct. 30–Nov. 18, 1962.
Texts by D. Mahlow, J. P. Hodin. Biography, catalogue of 29 works.

285. Gimpel Fils. *Robert Adams: Recent Sculpture*. London, Nov. 1962.
List of 40 works with plates. Chronology, 1947–1962.

286. Thwaites, J. A. "Der bescheidene Meister: die

Plastik von Robert Adams." *Kunstwerk*, no. 9, March 1958.

Agam, Yaacov

287. ———. *Yaacov Agam*. Texts by the Artist. Neuchâtel, Griffon, 1962.
Includes chronology and bibliography. Insert: Musical transforms (a 45-rpm recording). French, English and German editions.

288. ———. "Yaacov Agam propose: l'éclatement du temps et de la réalité dans les arts." *Galerie des Arts*, no. 8, June 1963.

289. Kolb, Eugene. "Agam." *Art International*, v. 3, no. 5–6, 1959.

290. Le Lionnais, T. "Une esthétique nouvelle: les oeuvres transformables." *Art d'Aujourd'hui*, v. 2, no. 8, June 1956.
Complemented by May 1961: Y. Taillandier: "Voyage dans un tableau d'Agam."

291. Marlborough-Gerson Gallery. *Yaacov Agam*. New York, May–June 1966.

Albers, Josef

292. ———. *Interaction of Color*. New Haven & London, Yale University Press, 1963.
Eighty-one large color folders and explanatory text (88 pp.) in boxed folio edition.

293. ———. *Homage to the Square: Ten Works by Josef Albers*. New Haven, Ives-Sillman, 1962.
Limited edition (250 copies) of 10 large color plates in folio. Preface by Richard Lippold.

294. ———. *Poems and Drawings*. Second ed. New York, Wittenborn, 1961.
Revised and enlarged edition of 1958 work. Bilingual text.

295. Bucher, François. *Josef Albers: Despite Straight Lines. An Analysis of his Graphic Constructions*. New York, Yale University Press, 1961.
Captions, poems, statements by the artist. Biographical notes. Bibliography revised in: New York, Museum of Modern Art, Dept. of Circulating Exhibitions, *Josef Albers: Homage to the Square* (New York, 1963, foreword by R. d'Harnoncourt, essay by K. McShine).

296. Los Angeles County Museum of Art. *Josef Albers: White Line Squares*. Los Angeles, Gemini G.E.L., 1966.
Anthology of multilingual texts, by Tyler, Hopkins, Albers. Comprehensive chronology and bibliography.

297. Welliver, Neil. "Albers on Albers." *Art News*, no. 9, Jan. 1966.
A conversation about the past and present.

Anonima Group

298. *Anonima*. Vol. 1, No. 2, New York, March 1964.
Editor: Ernst Benkert. Articles on the Anonima group; "perceptual conflict and the new abstraction" (Hewitt). No. 1, Nov. 1963, was titled *Out-In*.

299. London, Institute of Contemporary Art. *Anonima Group*. Feb. 9–March 19, 1966.
Lists group exhibitions (1962–1965). Statement on verso catalogue.

Anuskiewicz, Richard

300. ———. *A Study in the Creation of Space with Line Drawing*. New Haven, Conn., 1955.
M.F.A. thesis for Yale University.

301. Miller, Dorothy, C., ed. *Americans 1963*. With Statements by the Artists and others. New York, Museum of Modern Art, 1963.
Includes biography, port. and ill., catalogue.

302. "A Painter's Palette." *Time* (New York), July 19, 1963.

303. Sidney Janis Gallery. *New Paintings by Anuszkiewicz*. New York, Nov. 1965.

304. University of Illinois. *Contemporary American Painting and Sculpture*. Urbana, Ill., 1961.
Catalogue includes illustration and biography.

Archipenko, Alexander

305. ———. "Nature and the point of departure." *The Arts*, Jan. 1924.

306. ———. *Archipenko. Fifty Creative Years, 1908–1958, by Alexander Archipenko and Fifty Art Historians*. New York, Tekhne, 1960.
Bibliography. Appendix of international commentary, 1921–1954.

307. Galerie "Im Erker." *Alexander Archipenko*. St. Gallen, No. 17, 1962–Jan. 10, 1963.
One hundred three works (1909–1962), chronology, essay, extracts, 1913–1960; text by the artist.

308. Hildebrandt, Hans. *Alexander Archipenko: Son Oeuvre*. Berlin, Ukrainske Slowo, 1923.
Edition in Ukrainian; German; French; English; Spanish (1924).

Arp, Jean

309. ———. *On My Way*. New York, Wittenborn, Schultz, 1948.
"Poetry and essays, 1912–1947." Texts by Motherwell, Giedion-Welcker, Buffet-Picabia. Bibliography by B. Karpel.

310. Cathelin, Jean. *Arp*. Paris, Le Musée de Poche, 1959.
Chronology and bibliography.

311. Giedion-Welcker, Carola. *Jean Arp*. Documentation: Marguerite Hagenbach. New York, Abrams, 1957.
Also published as *Hans Arp*, Stuttgart, Gerd Hatje, 1957. Oeuvre catalogue by M. Hagenbach; bibliography by Hans Bolliger.

312. Soby, James Thrall, ed. *Arp.* Articles by Jean Hans Arp, Richard Huelsenbeck, Robert Melville, Carola Giedion-Welcker. New York, Museum of Modern Art, 1958.
Bibliography by B. Karpel complements Bibl. 309.

Baertling, Olle

313. Denise René, Galerie. *Baertling.* Paris, March–April 1962.
Essay by Alberto Sartoris; exhibitions, bibliography. Similarly: essays by Reutersvaerd: "Baertling, dramaturgie des formes" (Paris, 1958), "Baertling: dramaturge des espaces" (Paris, 1961).

314. Reutersvaerd, Oscar, ed. *Baertling.* Retrospective Exhibition arranged by Moderna Museet and the Swedish Institute, Stockholm. [Texts by] Teddy Brunius, Oscar Reutersvaerd, Bo Wennberg. Stockholm, Nyblom, 1961.
Preface by T. Talbroth, K. G. Hultén. Extensive bibliography.

315. Rose Fried, Gallery. *Baertling: creator of open form.* New York, Jan. 11–Feb 11, 1967.
Accompanied by Oscar Reutersvaerd booklet of the same title (Stockholm, Nyblom, 1966) with extensive documentation.

316. Schultz, Sigurd. *Baertling.* Copenhagen, Galerie Hybler, Feb.–March 1963.
Translated into French. Lists exhibitions. Bibliography (1951–1963).

Baljeu, Joost

317. ———. "Attempt at a theory of synthesist plastic expression." *Structure,* no. 2, 1962.
Comprehensive exposition (pp. 42–62) with illustrations.

318. ———. "Architecture and art." *Structure,* no. 1, 1958.
Includes, significantly, the 17 points originally used by Van Doesburg in a French lecture at Madrid (1930), slightly revised from text published in *De Stijl,* 1924.

319. ———. *Mondrian or Miro.* Amsterdam, De Beuk, 1958.
A series of four articles first published in *Structure* (1956–1957).

Benjamin, Karl

320. Esther Robles, Gallery. *Karl Benjamin.* Los Angeles, Oct. 5–24 (1960?)
Announcement with biographical notes.

321. London, Institute of Contemporary Arts. *Four Abstract Classicists: West Coast Hard-Edge.* London, March–April 1960.
Preface by Lawrence Alloway. Essay by Jules Langsner reprinted from Los Angeles Museum catalogue, 1959.

Berlewi, Henryk

322. Situation 60 Galerie. *Mechano-fakturen von Henryk Berlewi.* Berlin, Oct. 1963.
Introduction: Christian Chruxin; bibliography (1922–1963).

Biederman, Charles

323. ———. [Art and science as creation]. *Parnas* (Amsterdam), no. 6, 1957.
English text in *Structure,* 1958.

324. ——— *Letters on the New Art.* Red Wing, Minn., The Author, 1951.
Complements his "Evolution" opus (Bibl. 13).

325. Hill, Anthony. "Charles Biederman and constructionist art." *Broadsheet* no. 3, 1957.

326. Sjöberg, Leif. [Interview with Charles Biederman]. *Konstrevy,* no. 1, 1962.
Translation published in *The Structurist,* no. 3, 1962–1963.

327. Walker Art Center. *Charles Biederman: The Structurist Relief, 1935–1964.* Minneapolis, March 30–May 2, 1965.
Essay by Jan van der Marck. Extensive chronology and bibliography. Glossary on Neo-Plasticism, Constructivism, Constructionism, Structurism (p. 8).

Bill, Max

329. ———. "The mastery of space." *XXe Siècle,* v. 2, no. 1, 1939.

330. ———. "Über konkrete Kunst." *Werk,* no. 8, 1938.

331. ———. "Die mathematische Denkweise in der Kunst unserer Zeit." *Werk,* no. 3, 1949.
Also note translation: "The mathematical approach in contemporary art" (Bibl. 335).

332. ———. *Quinze Variations sur un même Thème.* Paris, Chroniques du Jour, 1938.

333. Gomringer, Eugen. ed. *Max Bill.* Teufen (Switzerland), Niggli, 1958.
   Notes on contributors. Complemented by Gomringer's later article translated for the *Architects' Year Book*, vol. 10: "Max Bill, variety and unity of the shaped environment."

334. Hill, Anthony. "Max Bill, the search of the unity of the plastic arts in contemporary life." *Typographica*, no. 7, 1953.

335. Maldonado, Tomas. *Max Bill.* Buenos Aires, Editorial Nueva Vision, 1955.
   Multilingual texts. Bibliography, pp. 133–145, complemented by pp. 87–92 in: Eduard Plüss, *Künstlerlexikon der Schweiz, XX Jahrhundert.* Frauenfeld, 1958.

336. Rogers, Ernesto N. "Max Bill." *Magazine of Art*, May, 1953.

Boccioni, Umberto

337. Argan, Giulio Carlo. *Umberto Boccioni. Scelta degli Scritti, Regesti, Bibliografia e Catalogo delle Opere a Cura di Maurizio Calvesi.* Rome, De Luca, 1953.
   Writings, pp. 39–74. Bibliography.

338. Boccioni, Umberto. *Pittura, Scultura Futuriste. (Dinamismo Plastico).* Milan, "Poesia," 1914.
   Other editions: *Estetica e Arte Futuriste*, Milan, Il Balcone, 1946.

339. ———. "Manifeste technique de la sculpture futuriste, 11 avril 1912." *Cahiers d'Art*, v. 25, 1950.
   Translated in Taylor below (pp. 129–132). Similarly: "La scultura futurista," *Lacerba*, no. 13, July 1914.

340. Carrieri, Raffaele. "Boccioni, painter of sensations." *XXᵉ Siècle*, no. 17, Christmas 1961.

341. Longhi, Roberto. *Scultura Futurista: Boccioni.* Florence, La Voce, 1915.

342. Taylor, Joshua C. *Futurism.* New York, Museum of Modern Art (distributed by Doubleday & Co.), 1961.
   Comprehensive Boccioni commentary. Includes manifestos, letters. Selected bibliography, 1905–1961, by B. Karpel.

Bodmer, Walter

343. Belloli, Carlo. "Bodmer e lo spazio—volume." In *Bodmer*, Milan, Galerie Blu, 1960.

344. Galerie Charles Lienhard. *Walter Bodmer.* Zürich, June–July 1962.
   Essay by Georg Schmidt (complemented by another for *Plastique*, no. 5, 1939), bibliography.

345. Moeschlin, Walter J. *Der Maler Walter Bodmer: Kunstmappe.* Basel, 1952.
   Foreword quoted in *Walter Bodmer—Hans Hartung.* Basel, Kunsthalle, 1952.

346. Netter, Maria. "Walter Bodmer." *Arts—Documents (Geneva)*, no. 17, 1952.
   Also her "Walter Bodmers Bilder und Drahtplastikenin," *Werk*, June 1949.

Bolotowsky, Ilya

347. American Abstract Artists. [*Yearbooks*]. New York, The Association, 1938, 1939, 1946.
   Reproductions in 1938, 1946. Biographical data, 1939.

348. Bolotowsky, Ilya. [*Statements*]. *Réalités Nouvelles* (Paris), no. 1, 2, 4, 6, 1947–1952.
   Illustration, no. 1, p. 15 (1947). Illustration, no. 2, p. 11 (1948). Article and illustration, no. 4, p. 43 (1950). Article and illustration, no. 6, p. 8 (1952).

349. New Art Circle. *Ilya Bolotowsky.* New York, Feb. 11–28, 1946.
   Another exhibition at this J. B. Neumann gallery, March 3–29, 1952; commentary by G. L. K. Morris. Similar preface in *Eight by Eight: American Abstract Painting Since 1940*, Philadelphia Museum of Art, March 7–April 1, 1945. Exhibits no. 1–8 by Bolotowsky.

350. Yale University Art Gallery. *Collection of the Société Anonyme.* New Haven, 1950.
   Catalogue by G. H. Hamilton; note by Katherine Dreier, p. 165. "The collection owns many geometric works by me. However, the reproduction is of the one non-geometric work" (I. B.).

Bonfanti, Arturo

351. Alfieri, Bruno. *Arturo Bonfanti.* Milan, Alfieri, 1966.

352. Belloli, Carlo. "'Tensioni cromo-strutturate' di Bonfanti." *Metro*, no. 3, 1961.

276

353. Galerie Charles Lienhard. *Bonfanti.* Zürich, Sept. 1961.
    Essay by Mario Valsecchi.

354. Galerie Denise René. *Bonfanti.* Paris, Feb-March 1962.
    Introduction by Carlo Belloli.

355. Galleria Lorenzelli. *Bonfanti.* Milan, June 1962.
    Extracts from critiques. Text by M. Seuphor. Similar booklet, June–July 1966.

Bury, Pol

356. Alvard, Julien. "Le voyage de Bury." *Art International*, no. 8, 1963.
    Exhibitions list. Bibliography.

357. Bordier, Roger. "Pol Bury et le mouvement." *Art d'Aujourd'hui*, no. 39, Dec. 1962.

358. Bury, Pol. *Le Boule et le Trou.* Brussels, Editions Stella Smith, 1961.
    Limited edition including "planches originales."

359. ———. *10 Cinétizations.* Foreword by Balthasar. New York, Lefebre Gallery, 1966.
    Color lithographs. Limited edition signed and numbered.

360. Lefèbre Gallery. *Pol Bury.* New York, March–April 1966.
    "Cinétizations" (March 1–12), "Moving sculptures" (March 11–April 6). Later catalogue (Oct. 12–Nov. 7).

361. Séaux, Jean. "Jeunes artistes: Pol Bury." *Quadrum*, no. 5, 1958.

Calder, Alexander

362. Agam, Yaacov. "Calder en pleine mature." *XXᵉ Siècle*, no. 20, Noël 1962.
    Also English summary.

363. Arts Council of Great Britain. *Alexander Calder: Sculpture, Mobiles.* London, 1962.
    Shown at the Tate Gallery, July 4–Aug. 12. Essay by J. J. Sweeney. Also bibliography of "statements."

364. Calder. *Derrière le Miroir*, no. 31, July 1950.
    De luxe bulletin of the Galerie Maeght, Paris. Texts by J. J. Sweeney, and others. No. 113 (Jan. 1959), another Calder issue.

365. Hultén, K. G. "Alexander Calder." In *Rörelse i Konsten*, Stockholm, Moderna Museet, 1961.
    Exhibits and illustrations, pp. 6–9, 17–18, 33, 36. Additional references in appended survey (14 pp. insert).

366. Solomon R. Guggenheim Museum. *Alexander Calder: A Retrospective Exhibition.* New York, Nov. 1964–Jan. 1965.
    Text by T. M. Messer, chronology, bibliography.

367. Staempfli, George W. "Interview with Alexander Calder." *Quadrum*, no. 6, 1959.

368. Sweeney, James Johnson. *Alexander Calder.* Second ed., New York, Museum of Modern Art, 1951.
    Bibliography by B. Karpel. First edition (1943) issued as exhibition catalogue.

Caro, Anthony

369. Alloway, Lawrence. "Interview with A. Caro." *Gazette* (London), no. 1, 1961.

370. Forge, Andrew. "Anthony Caro interviewed . . ." *Studio International*, Jan. 1966.

371. Fried, Michael. "Caro and Noland: some notes on not composing." *Lugano Review*, no. 4, 1965.

372. Lucie-Smith, Edward. "Anthony Caro at Venice." *Art and Artists*, June 1966.

373. Whitechapel Gallery. *Anthony Caro: Sculpture 1960–1963.* London, Sept.–Oct. 1963.
    Text by B. Robertson. Biography, bibliography.

Castellani, Enrico

374. *Azimuth. Rivista d'Avanguardia.* Eds: Enrico Castellani, Piero Manzoni. Milan, 1959 ff.
    No. 2 includes exhibition catalogue and Castellani text (Galleria Azimut).

375. Castellani, Enrico. [Monochromatic painting]. In Leverkusen, Städtisches Museum, *Monochrome Malerei.* Mar. 18 ff, 1960.

376. Dorfles, Gino. "Castellani, incarnazione di una nuova struttura ritmica, spaziale e luminosa." *Metro*, no. 8, 1962.

377. Galleria dell'Ariete. *Castellani.* Milan, Feb. 26, 1963.
    Essay by Gillo Dorfles.

Chillida, Eduardo

378. Bachelard, Gaston. "Le cosmos du fer." *Derrière le Miroir* (Paris), no. 90–91, Oct.–Nov. 1956.

Preface for Galerie Maeght show of works by Chillida. Additional no. 125, March 1961, with text by James Johnson Sweeney.

379. Basel, Kunsthalle. *Edouardo Chillida*. Basel, March 3–April 8, 1962.

380. Houston, Museum of Fine Arts. *Eduardo Chillida*. Houston, 1966.
Text by J. J. Sweeney. Chronology.

381. O'Hara, Frank. *New Spanish Painting and Sculpture*. New York, Museum of Modern Art, 1960.
Chillida, pp. 10, 14–16, 55, 63; bibliography.

Clark, Lygia

382. "Lygia Clark." *Signals* (London), no. 7, 1965.
Special number of Gallery bulletin, including artist's texts.

Cruz-Diez, Carlos

383. Signals Gallery. *A Decade of Physichromies by Carlos Cruz-Diez*. London, Sept. 23–Oct. 23, 1965.
Chronology. Complemented by special number of *Signals* (Bulletin), no. 9, 1965.

Delaunay, Robert

384. ———. *Du Cubisme à l'Art Abstrait*. Paris, S.E.V.P.E.N., 1957.
"Documents inédits publiés par Pierre Francastel et suivi d'un catalogue de l'oeuvre de R. Delaunay par Guy Habasque." Bibliography.

385. Francastel, Pierre. "Les 'Fenêtres' de Robert Delaunay." *XXᵉ Siècle*, no. 21, May 1963.
Complemented by *Les Delaunay*, no. 22, 1960.

386. Gilles de la Tourette, F. *Robert Delaunay*. Paris, Ch. Massin, 1950.

387. Oeri, Georgine. "Delaunay in search of himself." *Arts* (New York), March 1959.

388. Paris, Musée National d'Art Moderne. *Robert Delaunay (1885–1951)*. Paris, May 25–Sept. 30, 1957.
Preface by J. Cassou. Bibliography.

Delaunay, Sonia

389. Bielefeld, Städtisches Kunsthaus. *Sonia Delaunay, Paris*. Sept. 14–Oct. 26, 1958.
Major German retrospective of 252 works. Preface by G. Vriesen. Biographical notes and bibliography.

390. Delaunay, Sonia. "La couleur dansée: 50 ans de recherche." *Art d'Aujourd'hui*, no. 17, May 1958.

391. ———. *Sonia Delaunay*. Paris, Librairie des Arts Décoratifs, 1925.
Ses peintures, ses objets, ses tissus simultanés, ses modes." Texts by Lhote, Cendrars, Delteil, Tzara, Soupault.

392. Galerie Denise René. *Sonia Delaunay*. Paris, May 1962.
Comprehensive chronology, biography, and bibliography (14 pp.) including writings and albums.

393. Gindertael, R. V. "Sonia Delaunay et la poésie pure des couleurs." *XXᵉ Siècle*, no. 21, May 1963.

Demarco

394. Galerie Denise René. *Demarco*. Paris, Nov. 1961.
Artist's statement, biography.

Dewasne, Jean

395. Bern, Kunsthalle. *Jean Dewasne*. April 2–May 8, 1966.
Preface: H. Szeemann. Bibliography.

396. ———. *Jean Gorin—Jean Dewasne—Constant*. April 2–May 1966.
Dewasne text by D. Cordier.

397. Descargues, Pierre. *J. Dewasne*. Paris, Presses Littéraires de France, 1952.
Chronology.

398. Galleria Lorenzelli. *Jean Dewasne*. Milan, May 1961.
Text by the artist.

Diller, Burgoyne

399. Ashton, Dore. [Review of Galerie Chalette show]. *Arts & Architecture*, July, 1961.

400. Campbell, Lawrence. "The rule that measures emotion." *Art News*, May, 1961.

401. Galerie Chalette. *Diller: Paintings, Constructions, Drawings, Watercolors*. New York, May, 1961.
Mss. from the artist's notebook. In 1962 another show of "Color structures."

402. New Jersey State Museum. *Burgoyne Diller: 1906–1965*. Trenton, Feb. 11–April 3, 1966.

Note by K. W. Prescott reprints brief comments by Diller. Main essay by L. Campbell (a reprint of article in *Art News*, May 1961).

Doesburg, Theo van

403. Amsterdam, Stedelijk Museum. *De Stijl* (Catalogue 81). Amsterdam, July 6–Sept. 25, 1951.

   A comprehensive document (120 pp., ill., col.). Articles printed in the original language, many parts translated into English and French. Usefully complemented by the "De Stijl" number of the *Museum of Modern Art Bulletin*, v. 20, no. 2, 1952–1953, a modified version of the above exhibition.

404. Art of This Century Gallery. *Theo van Doesburg: Retrospective Exhibition*. New York, April 29–May 31, 1947.

   Essay by J. J. Sweeney. Comprehensive chronology and bibliography.

405. Doesburg, Theo van. "Film as pure form." *Form (England)*, no. 1, Summer 1966.

   Translated from *Die Form*, May 1929.

406. ———. *Grondbegrippen der Nieuwe Beeldende Kunst*. Edition Tijdschrift voor Wijsbegeerte, 1919.

   Two vols. translated as *Bauhausbuch Nr. 6: Grundebegriffe der neuen Kunst*. Munich, Langen, 1924.

407. ———. *Klassiek, Barok, Modern*. Antwerp, De Sikkel, 1920.

   Translated as: *Classique, Baroque, Moderne*. Paris, Rosenberg, 1921. Text dated "Leyden, Dec. 1918."

Domela, César

408. Bayer, Raymond. "César Domela." *Phoenix* (Amsterdam), no. 12, 1949.

409. Kandinsky, Wassily. *Domela: Six Reproductions en Couleurs*. Paris, Imprimérie Union, 1943.

410. Kay, Marguerite. "Domela's abstractions." *Studio* (London) Oct. 1949.

411. The Hague, Gemeentemuseum. *César Domela*. Sept. 9–Oct. 23, 1960.

   Chronology on C. D. Nieuwenhuis; bibliography.

Dorazio, Piero

412. ———. "Cartographies." In *Constructions and Paintings by Piero Dorazio*, New York, Rose Fried Gallery, April 26–May 22, 1954.

413. Galerie Suzanne Bollag. *Piero Dorazio*. Zürich, Oct. 19–Nov. 14, 1962.

   Biographical notes; chronology; bibliography.

414. Grohmann, Will. "Piero Dorazio—or a return to quality in painting." *Metro*, no. 4–5, 1961.

   Also in Kunsthalle Düsseldorf catalogue, Oct. 18–Nov. 26, 1961; bibliography.

415. Marlborough-Gerson Gallery *Piero Dorazio*. New York, Feb. 1965.

   Preface: "For Dorazio five questions" (M. Mendes). Biography, bibliography (1947–1964).

416. Santini, Pier Carlo. "Piero Dorazio." *Quadrum*, no. 6, 1959.

   Text in French.

Duchamp, Marcel

417. Arts Council of Great Britain. *The Almost Complete Works of Marcel Duchamp*. London, 1966.

   Shown at the Tate Gallery, June 18–July 31. Preface by Richard Hamilton. Exhaustive bibliography by Arturo Schwarz.

418. Lebel, Robert. *Marcel Duchamp*. N.Y., Grove; Paris, Trianon, 1959.

   Extensive bibliography.

419. Tomkins, Calvin. *The Bride & the Bachelors: the Heretical Courtship in Modern Art*. New York, Viking, 1965.

   Includes Duchamp, John Cage, Tinguely, Rauschenberg.

Eggeling, Viking

420. Hultén, Karl G. [Eggeling]. In *Rörelse i Konsten*, Stockholm, Moderna Museet, 1961.

   Includes reprint of "Aus dem nachlass Viking Eggelings" from *G* (Berlin), no. 4, pp. 2–3, March 1926.

421. Richter, Hans. "Von der statischen zur dynamischen Form." *Plastique*, no. 2, Summer 1937.

422. Stockholm, National Museum. *Viking Eggeling, 1880–1925: Tecknare och Filmkonstnar*. Stockholm, Oct. 27–Nov. 19, 1950.

   Catalogue by C. Nordenfalk and H. Richter. Texts by Richter, Arp, Tzara, Mies van der Rohe, G. Schmidt. Bibliography.

Engman, Robert

423. Albers, Josef. [Statement on structural sculpture]. In *Robert Engman: recent sculpture,* Stable Gallery, Feb. 23–March 12, 1960.

424. Chaet, Bernard. "Structural sculpture: interview [with Robert Engman]. *Arts* (New York), Sept. 1958.

425. Preston, Stuart. "Engman's geometrical shapes." *New York Times,* March 5, 1960.

Equipo 57

426. Darro (Gallery). *Equipo 57: Pintura, Escultura, Estructuras Espaciales.* Madrid, May 1960.
Preface: J. M. Moreno Galvan. Text: "La interactividad del espacio plástico en pintura" (7 pp.), dated Dec. 1959.

427. Equipo 57 (Groupe). *Interactivité de l'espace plastique.* Madrid, Gráficos Reunidas, 1957.
Manifesto "translated from the Spanish," dated Sept. 1957. Color plates of works by Basterrechea, Duarte, Ibarrola, Serrano, Thorkild. Original collaborators (10) noted on rear page.

428. Galerie d'Art Actual. *Equipo 57.* Geneva, Jan. 26–Feb. 26, 1966.
Chronology, exhibits, collections.

429. M., A. "Art and artists: violent Spaniards." *New York Herald Tribune* (Paris), Aug. 7, 1957.
Reviews Galerie Denise René show (July 5–Aug. 15).

430. Moreno Galvan, José Maria. "Alternative de l'abstraction formelle dans la peinture spañole." *Art d'Aujourd'hui,* no. 24, Dec. 1959.
Comments on "Equipo 57." Additional material in *Acento,* no. 8, May–June 1960; *Insula,* no. 164, July–Aug. 1960; and his "Introduccion a la Pintura Española."

431. Paris, Cafe le Rond-Point. *Peintures.* Paris, May 1957.
First group show of "Equipo 57," including di Teana. Includes "manifest" by Duart, Ibarrola, Serrano, Duarté.

Feitelson, Lorser

432. Langsner, Jules. "Lorser Feitelson." In *Four Abstract Classicists,* Los Angeles, Sept. 16–Oct. 18, 1959.

433. ———. "Permanence and change in the art of Lorser Feitelson." *Art International,* no. 7, Sept. 1963.

434. London, Institute of Contemporary Arts. *Four Abstract Classicists: West Coast Hard-Edge.* London, March–April 1960.

435. Longstreet, Stephen. *Lorser Feitelson, painter.* Pasadena, The Contemporary Galleries, Pasadena Art Institute, March–April 1952.

Fruhtrunk, Günter

436. Belloli, Carlo. *Fruhtrunk: Album de 10 Sérigraphies.* Dortmund, 1963.
Previous commentary in *Metro,* no. 7, Oct. 1962.

437. Fruhtrunk, Günter. [Diskussionen über die "sprachliche Struktur" zeitgenössicher Malerei.] Aug. 1963.
Typescript [3 pp.] forwarded to George Rickey. Text also in French.

438. Galerie Denise René. *Fruhtrunk.* Paris, April 1960.
Texts by F. Mathey, J. Séaux. Biographical and bibliographical notes.

Gabo, Naum

439. ———. *Gabo: Constructions, Sculpture, Drawings, Engravings.* Introductory essays by Herbert Read and Leslie Martin. London, Lund Humphries; Cambridge, Harvard University Press, 1957.
Numerous illustrations including 10 stereoscopic color plates. Bibliography by B. Karpel.

440. ——— & Read, Herbert. "Constructive art: an exchange of letters." *Horizon* (London), no. 55, July 1944.
Also published in *The Philosophy of Modern Art,* by Herbert Read (1952).

441. Olson, Ruth & Chanin, Abraham. *Naum Gabo —Antoine Pevsner.* Introduction by Herbert Read. New York, Museum of Modern Art, 1948.
A major retrospective, with bibliography by H. B. Muller.

442. Pevsner, Alexei. *Naum Gabo and Antoine Pevsner. A Biographical Sketch of My Brothers.* Amsterdam, Augustin & Schoonman, 1964.
Includes important chronological and corrective commentary, e.g. on Pevsner, p. 53.

443. Whitford, Frank. "Gabo and constructivism." *Architectural Review,* June 1966.

Gerstner, Karl

444. ———. *Carro 64.* [Switzerland, Artist's Edition, 1965?]

Numbered and signed limited edition. "Carro 64 is made of 64 accurately tooled aluminum cubes which are set in an adjustable white frame. The size is 16"×16".

445. ———. *Kalte Kunst? Zum Standort der heutigen Malerei.* Teufen (Switzerland), Niggli, 1957. Second ed. 1963.

On paintings by Albers, Bill, Graeser, Loewensberg, Lohse. Reviewed by A. Hill, *Art News and Review* (London), no. 5, Mar. 1959.

446. ———. "Picture-making today? Thoughts and comments." *Spirale*, no. 8, 1960.

Text also in German. Additional material, no. 5, 1955.

447. ———. *Designing Programmes.* New York, Hastings House, 1964.

Translated from the German (Verlag Niggli, Teufen, Suisse, 1964). Four essays, with introduction by P. Gredinger.

448. ———. *Spiegel Bilder.* Cologne, Galerie der Spiegel, 1963.

Twelve mounted plates. Preface by A. Fabri. Texts on symmetry and harmonic form. Edition: 250 signed copies.

Getulio (Getulio Alviani)

449. ———. "Lamine in alluminico." *Metro*, no. 4–5, 1961.

450. ———. "Lichtlinien." *Nul*, no. 2, April 1963.

451. Leverkusen, Museum. *Getulio.* Leverkusen (Schloss Morsbroich), Jan.–Feb. 1963.

Statement also published in *Nul*, no. 2.

452. Simmat, William E. "Getulio (Alviani)." In *Europäische Avantgarde*, Frankfurt-am-Main, Galerie d, July 9–Aug. 11, 1963.

Biography, quotation, documentation.

Glarner, Fritz

453. Ashton, Dore. "Fritz Glarner." *XXᵉ Siècle*, no. 9, June 1957.

454. Glarner, Fritz. "What abstract art means to me." *Museum of Modern Art Bulletin*, v. 18, no. 3, 1951.

An associated document is his: "Relational painting," lecture given at the art school:

Subjects of the Artist, 5 pp. (typescript), New York, Feb. 25, 1949.

455. Louis Carré Gallery. *Fritz Glarner: Peintures (1949–1962).* Paris, Feb. 18–March 31, 1966.

456. New York, Museum of Modern Art. *12 Americans.* Edited by Dorothy C. Miller with Statements by the Artists and Others. New York, May 29–Sept. 9, 1956.

457. Zurich, Kunsthaus. *Joseph Albers, Fritz Glarner, Frederich Vordemberge-Gildewart.* Zürich, April 28–June 10, 1956.

Introduction by Max Bill (pp. 7–17).

Gonzalez, Julio

458. Aguilera Cerni, Vicente. *Julio Gonzalez.* Rome, Ateneo, 1962.

Italian and English texts. Extensive bibliography.

459. Galerie Chalette. *Julio Gonzalez.* New York, Oct.–Nov. 1961.

Essay by Hilton Kramer (15 pp.). Chronology; bibliography (pp. 72–75).

460. Galerie de France. *Julio Gonzalez.* Paris. 1959.

Text by Roberta Gonzalez. Bibliography.

461. Ritchie, Andrew C. *Julio Gonzalez.* New York, Museum of Modern Art, 1956.

Also issued as Bulletin of the Museum of Modern Art (v. 33, no. 1–2). Bibliography.

462. Smith, David. "Gonzalez: first master of the torch." *Art News*, Feb. 1956.

Goodyear, John

463. Belz, Carl L. "The optic-kinetic constructions of John Goodyear." *Arts & Architecture*, Oct. 1964.

Gorin, Jean

464. Galleria Pagani. *Mostra Personale di Jean Gorin.* Milan, n.d.

Documentation to 1962. Preface by A. Sartoris.

465. ———. [Articles]. *Cahiers des Réalités Nouvelles*, 1947–1955.

Articles in no. 1 (1947), no. 7 (1953), no. 8 (1954), no. 9 (1955).

466. ———. [Articles]. *Structure*, 1958–1962.

Articles in numbers for 1958, 1960, 1961, 1962.

467. Liège, Musée de l'Art Wallon. *Jean Gorin.* Nov.

19–Dec. 18, 1960.

Introduction by M. Seuphor. Chronology to 1960. Bibliography.

Graeser, Camille

468. Curjel, Hans. "Camille Graeser." *Werk*, v. 48, no. 2, p. 68–72. Feb. 1961.

469. Graeser, Camille. "Optische Musik." In *Zürcher Künstler um Helmhaus*, Zurich, Nov. 11–Dec. 20, 1950.

470. Plüss, Edouard. *Künstlerlexikon der Schweiz, XX Jahrhundert*, pp. 375–378, Frauenfeld, 1960.

471. Schnyder, Rudolf. "Camille Graeser zum siebzigsten Geburtstag." *Neue Zürcher Zeitung*, no. 730, p. 6, Feb. 25, 1963.

Graevenitz, Gerhard von

472. Galerie Anna Roepcke. *Gerhard von Graevenitz*. Wiesbaden, Nov. 9–Dec. 5, 1962.
Text by J. Morschel. Chronology.

Groupe de Recherche d'Art Visuel

473. Centre de Recherche d'Art Visuel. *Acte de Fondation*. Paris, July 1960.
Participants: Demarco, Garcia Miranda, Garcia Rossi, Le Parc, Molnar, Morellet, Moyano, Servanes, Sobrino, Stein, Yvaral.

474. Descargues, Pierre. "Groupe de Recherche d'Art visuel." *Graphis*, no. 105, Jan.–Feb. 1963. Includes view of 1963 show: *L'Instabilité*. Text in French and German.

475. Galleria Cadario. *Mostra di Ricera di Arte visiva*. Milan, April 26–May 17, 1963.
Brief texts. Exhibitors include Gruppo N.

476. Groupe de Recherche d'Art Visuel. *Propositions générales du Groupe de Recherche d'Art visuel*. Paris, Oct. 25, 1961.
Leaflet "signed" by Rossi, Le Parc, Morellet, Sobrino, Stein, Yvaral.

477. ———. *Groupe de Recherche d'Art visuel, Paris 1962*. Paris, Galerie Denise René & le Groupe, April 1962.
Illustrated booklet: introduction by G. Habasque, "propositions générales" (1961); double spreads on the members; references to the Zagreb show (1961); Groups "N" and "T," "Equipo 57"; "nuance néo-dada" (Mack, Uecker, Piene, etc.) and "nuance tachiste" (Dorazio, etc.). The René gallery exhibited

their group show April 4–18, 1962 as "L'Instabilité."

478. ———. *L'Instabilité: recherches visuelles de Garcia, Rossi, Le Parc, Morellet, Sobrino, Stein, Yvaral*. [Paris, 1963].
"Manifestation organisée par Minvielle à Paris." Includes a "curriculum vitae collectif."

479. Habasque, Guy. "Le Groupe de Recherche d'Art visuel à la Biennale de Paris." *L'Oeil*, Nov. 1963.

480. Judd, D. "Groupe de Recherche d'Art visuel." *Arts* (New York), Feb. 1963.
Complementary English text in *Craft Horizon*, Jan. 1963: "Design in dimension."

481. Popper, Frank. "Le Parc and the group problem." *Form* (England), no. 2, Sept. 1966.

Gruppo N and T

482. Galleria "La Salita." *Mostra Miriorama 10*. Rome, April 1961.
Exhibitors: Boriani, Colombo, Devecchi, Varisco, Aneschi of "Gruppo T." Includes declaration by Fontana.

483. Galleria Pater. *Miriorama 4: Attivitá del Gruppo T.—Mostra personale di Gianni Colombo*. Milan, Feb. 9 [1960?].

484. Gruppo N. *Scritti*. Padua, Gruppo Enne, [1959–1963].
Mimeographed (15 leaves). Brief texts comprise statements, diagrams, manifests, catalogue introductions, etc. Lettered on cover: . . . nnn 2.

485. Munari, Bruno. "I giovani del gruppo T." *Domus*, no. 378, May 1961.

Haese, Günther

486. Galerie Stangl. *Günther Haese*. Munich, Aug. 27–Oct. 10, 1964.
With preface and plates.

487. Marlborough Fine Art Gallery. *Günther Haese*. New York, Nov.–Dec. 1965.
Preface: H. Pée. Biographical note.

Hammersley, Frederick

488. California Palace of the Legion of Honor. *Frederick Hammersley Paintings*. San Francisco, Nov. 3–Dec. 9, 1962.
Selected critiques, biography, bibliography.

Also La Jolla Museum (March 13–April 14).

489. Langsner, Jules. "Frederick Hammersley." In *Four Abstract Classicists*, Los Angeles County Museum, 1959.
Exhibit reviewed in *Art News*, Sept. 1959 (p. 50), *Arts* Dec. 1959 (p. 23).

490. London, Institute of Contemporary Arts. *Four Abstract Classicists. West Coast Hard-Edge*. London, March–April 1960.
U.S.I.S. version of Los Angeles show; preface by L. Alloway; artists: Benjamin, Feitelson, McLaughlin.

491. Wurdemann, H. [Exhibition in San Francisco]. *Art in America*, Feb. 1963.
Illustrates "On in" (v. 51, p. 130).

Healy, John

492. ———. *International Lighting Review*, no. 5–6, 1965.
Also issued as separate. Biographical note; comment by Hugh Casson.

493. R.C.A. Galleries. *Art in Motion*. London, n.d. [196?]
Catalogue on "Luminous pictures by John Healy," "Arte programmata, presented by Olivetti." Note on Healy by H. Casson, on Olivetti's show by Munari. Also press releases.

Herbin, Auguste

494. Galerie Denise René. *Herbin*. Paris, May–June 1960.
Includes "La réalité de la peinture non-objective: testament spirituel d'Auguste Herbin" (pp. 6, 8, 14). Foreword by J. Cassou. Extensive bibliography.

495. Herbin, Auguste. *L'Art Non-figuratif, Non-objectif*. Paris, Conti, 1949.
Introduction by P. Peissi.

496. Jakovski, Anatole. *Auguste Herbin*. Paris, Editions Abstraction-Création, 1933.
Additional data in 1932–1936 numbers of "Abstraction-Création."

497. Massat, René. *Auguste Herbin*. Paris, Collection Prisme, 1953.
Complemented by pictorial coverage in: Léon Degand, *Auguste Herbin: eine Kunstmappe über sein Leben und Schaffen*, Basel & Stuttgart, Basilius Presse (1961).

Holtzman, Harry

498. ———. "Attitude and means." In *American Abstract Artists*, [Yearbook], New York, 1938.
Part V, complemented by biographical data in the 1939 Yearbook.

499. ———, ed. *Trans/formation: arts, communication, environment*. No. 1–3. New York, Wittenborn, 1950–1952.
"Affirms that art, science, technology are interesting components of the total human enterprise but today they are treated as if they were cultural isolates and mutually antagonistic . . . [it] will emphasize the dynamic process view as against static absolutes."

500. Sidney Janis Gallery. *Post-Mondrian Painters in America*. New York, May 16–June 14, 1949.

Jacobsen, Robert

501. Galerie Chalette. *Robert Jacobsen*. New York, Nov.–Dec. 1966.
Essay by I. Meyerson. Biography, illustrations, bibliography.

502. Galerie de France. *Jacobsen*. Paris, Nov. 12–Dec. 4, 1958.
Chronology, 1912–1958; 22 exhibits.

503. ———. *Jacobsen—Sculpture, 1961–1962*. Paris, April 23–May 18, 1963.
Preface by P. Descargues; plates in folder.

Johns, Jasper

504. Heller, Ben. "Jasper Johns." In *School of New York*, New York, Evergreen Books, 1959.

505. Restany, Pierre. "Jasper Johns and the metaphysic of the commonplace." *Cimaise*, no. 55, Sept.–Oct. 1951.
Quadrilingual text.

506. Rosenblum, Robert. "Jasper Johns." *Art International*, Sept. 1960.
Complemented by: "Les oeuvres récentes de Jasper Johns," *XXᵉ Siècle*, no. 18, Feb. 1962.

507. Steinberg, Leo. "Jasper Johns." *Metro*, no. 4–5. 1962.
An extensive essay, pp. 80–109. Revised and enlarged, with bibliography, and issued as a booklet (45 pp., ill.) by Wittenborn (New York, 1963).

Kandinsky, Wassily

508. Bill, Max, ed. *Wassily Kandinsky*. Paris, Maeght; Boston Institute of Contemporary Art, 1951.

    Insert: English, German, and Spanish translation of French text. Bibliography.

509. Grohmann, Will. *Kandinsky*. Cologne, DuMont Schauberg, 1958.

    Extensive bibliography based on notes by B. Karpel.

510. Kandinsky, Wassily. *Point and Line to Plane*. New York, Solomon R. Guggenheim Foundation for the Museum of Non-Objective Painting, 1947.

    Translation of: *Punkt und Linie zur Fläche*, Munich, Langen, 1926. (Bauhausbücher, second ed., 1928). Third edition: *Mit einer Einführung von Max Bill, Bern-Bümpliz*, Benteli, 1955.

511. ——. "The value of a concrete work." *XXᵉ Siècle*, no. 5–6, 1939.

    Continued in v. 2, no. 1 (1939). Complemented by: *L'art concret*, no. 1 (1938); reprinted in new series no. 13 (1959) with English translation (pp. 105–108).

Kelly, Ellsworth

512. Ashton, Dore. "Kelly's unique spatial experiences." *Studio International*, no. 867, July 1965.

513. Betty Parsons Gallery. *Ellsworth Kelly: Painting and Sculpture*. New York, Oct. 29–Nov. 23, 1963.

    Lists exhibitions, awards, collections.

514. Goosen, E. C. "Ellsworth Kelly." *Derrière le Miroir*, no. 110, Oct. 1958.

    De luxe bulletin-catalogue of the Galerie Maeght (Paris). Entire text also in English. Additional Kelly reference in no. 41, Oct. 1951.

515. Gren, A. W. "Ellsworth Kelly." In *USA Now*, ed: Lee Nordness. Text by Allen S. Weller. Vol. 2, p. 392–395 New York, Viking, 1963.

516. McConathy, Dale. *Kelly—27 Lithographs*. Paris, Maeght, 1965.

    Catalogue for exhibition at Galerie Adrien Maeght, June 1965.

517. Washington Gallery of Modern Art. *Paintings, Sculpture and Drawings by Ellsworth Kelly*.

Dec. 11, 1963–Jan. 26, 1964.

    Includes interview with Henry Geldzahler, 1963. Similarly, interview in *Art International*, Feb. 1964.

Kemeny, Zoltan

518. ——. "Über meine Kunst." In Kestner Gesellschaft, *Kemeny*, Hannover, Feb. 12–March 24, 1963.

    Includes an essay by W. Schmied, chronology, bibliography (3 pp.).

519. Marchiori, Giuseppe. "The plastic inventions of Zoltan Kemeny." *Metro*, no. 6, 1962.

520. Otterloo, Rijksmuseum Kröller-Muller. *Reliefs: Zoltan Kemeny*. Otterloo, June 8–July 21, 1963.

    Essay by C. Giedion-Welcker. Texts by the artist: "Over mijn werk." Biography, bibliography (1945–1963).

521. Ragon, Michel. *Zoltan Kemeny*. Neuchâtel, Griffon, 1960.

    A comprehensive monograph; bibliography.

Klein, Yves

522. ——. "Fragments de la brochure d'Yves Klein." In *De Nieuwe Stijl*. Deel 1, Amsterdam [1966].

    Biographical notes. Also Dutch text, pp. 54–82.

523. New York, Jewish Museum. *Yves Klein*. New York, Jan. 25–Mar. 12, 1967.

    Texts by K. McShine, P. Descargues, P. Restany, the artist. Bibliography.

524. Restany, Pierre. "Yves Klein (1928–1962)." *XXᵉ Siècle*, no. 25, May 1963.

    Also his: "L'avventura di Yves Klein," *Domus* no. 428, July 1965.

Kosice, Gyula

525. Galerie Denise René. *Kosice*. Paris, April 1960.

    Preface by M. Seuphor. Biography and bibliography. Documentation refers to the journal "Art Madi" and the "Mouvement Madi."

526. Habasque, Guy. "Conversation dans l'atelier: Kosice." *L'Oeil*, no. 95, Nov. 1962.

    "Un reportage assez complet sur mon trajectoire" (G. K.).

Kricke, Norbert

527. Habasque, Guy. "Conversation dans l'atelier, 7: Norbert Kricke." *L'Oeil*, no. 86, Feb. 1962.

528. Krefeld, Museum Haus Lange. *Kricke*. Krefeld, Oct. 14–Dec. 16, 1962.
Essay by Paul Wember. Extensive bibliography.

529. Kricke, Norbert. "Raum und Bewegung . . ." *Das Kunstwerk*, March 1962.
Statement (p. 23) in article on Kricke; text by C. Giedion-Welcker and illustrations, v. 15, no. 9, pp. 17–24. Additional statement in: *Norbert Kricke*, Paris, Karl Flincker Galerie, Nov. 15–Dec. 9, 1961.

530. Thwaites, John. "Space sculpture and the work of Norbert Kricke." *Art Quarterly*, no. 3, Autumn 1954.
Previously *Das Kunstwerk*, no. 3–4, 1953. Complemented by: "Norbert Kricke und Yves Klein," *Art International*, no. 6–7, Sept.–Oct. 1958).

Kupka, Frank

531. Arnould-Grémilly, Louis. "De l'orphisme—à propos des tentatives de Kupka." *La Vie des Lettres* (Paris), Oct. 1921.
Later published as *Kupka*, Paris, Povolotsky, 1922.

532. Cassou, Jean & Fédit, Denise. *Kupka*. Paris, Tisné, 1964.

533. Galerie Charles Lienhard. *Frank Kupka*. Zurich, March 1961.
Four texts; bibliography (1905–1960).

534. Kupka, Frank. [Statements and texts]. 1913–1953.
Abstraction-Création, Art Non-Figuratif: no. 1, 1932, p. 23; no. 2, 1933, p. 25 (plate p. 26); no. 3, 1934, p. 28; *Art Actual International*: L'origine du mot "tachisme . . ." (excerpts unpublished notebook 1913, press critiques of 1912, 1921); *Réalités Nouvelles*, no. 1, 1947, p. 45; no. 7, 1953, p. 5 (text by F. Sides, p. 3, R. Massat, p. 5); no. 8, 1954, p. 6 refers to presentation of "Le jubilé Frank Kupka" (1953).

535. Lonngren, Lillian. "Kupka: innovator of the abstract international style." *Art News*, 14 ill. (port.), Nov. 1957.

536. Siblik, Emmanuel. *François Kupka*. Prague, Aventium, 1928–[1929?].
No. 8, Musaion series; 650 copies in Czech, 100 in French; bilingual captions.

Lardera, Berto

537. Gindertael, R. V. "Les thèmes visuels de Lardera." *XXᵉ Siècle*, no. 21, May 1963.

538. Krefeld, Kaiser Wilhelm Museum. *Lardera*. Krefeld, Sept. 1956.
Catalogue and text by Paul Wember. Bibliography.

539. Kultermann, Udo. "Berto Lardera." *Das Kunstwerk*, Oct. 1961.

540. Seuphor, Michel. *Berto Lardera*. Neuchâtel, Griffon, 1960.
Texts and captions in French, English, German. Chronology and bibliography.

Larionov & Goncharova

541. Arts Council. *Larionov and Goncharova: Retrospective Exhibition*. London, Nov. 1961.
Essays by Mary Chamot and Camilla Gray.

542. Galerie de l'Institut. *Michel Larionov*. Paris, May 25–June 13, 1956.
About 40 canvases (1903–1925). Preface by W. George.

543. Gray, Camilla. *The Great Experiment: Russian Art 1863–1922*. London, Thames and Hudson, 1962.
Comprehensive study with numerous illustrations and references. Bibliography.

Le Corbusier

544. Choay, Françoise. *Le Corbusier*. New York, Braziller, 1960.
"Masters of world architecture" series. Bibliography.

545. Le Corbusier (Charles Edouard Jeanneret-Gris). *Creation is a Patient Search*. New York, Praeger, 1960.
Translated from the French. Chronology (1900–1960); bibliography. Complemented by his *New World of Space*, New York, Reynal & Hitchcock; Boston, Institute of Contemporary Art, 1948.

546. Papadaki, Stamo, ed. *Le Corbusier: Architect,*

Painter, Writer. Essays by J. Hudnut, S. Giedion, F. Leger, J. L. Sert, J. T. Soby. New York, Macmillan, 1948.

547. Paris, Union Centrale des Arts Décoratifs. *Le Corbusier.* Paris, March 3–May 16, 1966.
Photos by Lucien Hervé. Bibliography, 1918–1965.

Liberman, Alexander

548. Alloway, Lawrence. "Alexander Liberman's recent work." *Art International*, April 1964.

549. New York, Jewish Museum. *Alexander Liberman: Recent Sculpture.* New York, June 29–Sept. 15, 1966.
Text by Sam Hunter; chronology.

Linck, Walter

550. Bern, Kunsthalle. *Walter Linck: Skulpturen, Mobiles, Zeichnungen.* Sept. 11–Oct. 17, 1965.
Preface: A. Schulze Vellinghausen. Biography, bibliography.

551. Joray, Marcel. *La Sculpture Moderne en Suisse.* Neuchâtel, Griffon, 1955–1959.
Two vols. Biography.

552. Kunstlerlexikon der Schweiz: XX. *Jahrhundert.* Vol. 8, pp. 583–584. Frauenfeld, 1958.

Lippold, Richard

553. Bernier, Rosamund. "Richard Lippold." *L'Oeil,* no. 64, April 1960.

554. Kochnitzky, Léon. "Richard Lippold." *Quadrum,* no. 14, 1963.
French and English résumé.

555. Lippold, Richard. "Variation number 7: Full Moon." *Arts & Architecture*, May 1950.
Additional comment Aug. 1947 (pp. 22–23). For further articles and statements see: "Sculpture?" *Magazine of Art*, Dec. 1951; Statement in *15 Americans*; Museum of Modern Art, New York, 1952; Extracts from addresses (1953, 1957, 1958, 1961) in Willard Gallery, *Richard Lippold, 1952–1962*, New York, 1962.

556. Trier, Eduard. "Lippolds plastische Sonne." *Form* (Cologne), no. 2, 1958.
French and English summary.

Lissitzky, El

557. Eindhoven, Stedelijk van Abbemuseum. *El Lissitzky.* Eindhoven & Hannover, 1965.
Exhibited at Basel and Hannover. Comprehensive catalogue. Major bibliography by H. Richter includes "Literatur über Lissitsky und den Konstruktivismus."

558. Gray, Camilla. *The Great Experiment: Russian Art 1863–1922.* London, Thames & Hudson, 1962.
A major study with comprehensive commentary. Bibliography.

559. Kallai, Ernst. "El Lissitzky." *Cicerone*, v. 16, pp. 1058–1063, 1924.
Similarly in *Jahrbuch der Jungen Kunst*, 192♦, pp. 304–309.

560. Lissitzky, El. *Proun.* [Folge von 6 Blatt farbigen Lithographien und Titel]. Hannover, Verlag Ludwig Ey, 1923.
"Die Arbeiten entstanden in den für den Suprematismus entscheidenden Jahren 1919–1923 in Moskau und Berlin." Fifty numbered and signed folios.

561. ——— & Ehrenburg, Elie, eds. *Vesch, Gegenstand, Objet,* No. 1–2, March–April 1922.
Essay by Van Doesburg and others, published in Berlin by Verlag Skythen. Main trilingual article refers to "la naissance d'une grande époque constructive."

562. Lozowick, Louis. "El Lissitzky." *Transition*, no. 18, 1929.
Also text in his *Modern Russian Art*, New York, Société Anonyme, 1925.

563. Richter, Horst. *El Lissitzky: Sieg über die Sonne—Zur Kunst des Konstruktivismus.* Cologne, Czwiklitzer, 1958.
Illustration for edition of abstract lithographs; poem by A. Krutschenjich [Krutschenjich], Moscow 1913; Hannover 1923. Extensive bibliography.

Lohse, Richard

564. ———. [Beispiele für die heutigen Probleme der konkreten Kunst]. *Forum* (Amsterdam), no. 6–7, June–July, 1952.
Eight prints. Also accompanying observation by Aldo van Eyck.

565. ———. "A revised thematics for progressive art." *Trans/formation* (New York), no. 3, 1952.

566. Neuberg, Hans. *Der Bildraum und seine*

Gesetze: Zur Malerei von Richard P. Lohse. [15] pp., ill., n.d.

"Legenden von Richard P. Lohse—Erweiterte wiedergabe eines artikels aus der Zeitschrift *Werk.*" Notes by the artist in German, English, and French.

567. ———— & Lohse, Ida A., eds., *Richard P. Lohse.* Teufen, Niggli [1962].

Testimonials on his 60th birthday. For bibliography see Galerie Charles Lienhard catalogue (Zürich, Dec. 1960).

Louis, Morris

568. Boston, Museum of Fine Arts. *Morris Louis 1912–1962.* Boston, 1967.

Also exhibited Los Angeles County Museum, St. Louis Museum. Introduction by Michael Fried, chronology and bibliography. Clement Greenberg essay.

569. Greenberg, Clement. "Louis and Noland." *Art International*, no. 5, May 1960.

570. O'Doherty, Brian. "Art: Morris Louis plays on the eye." *New York Times*, Oct. 20, 1962.
Review of the Emmerich Gallery show.

571. Solomon R. Guggenheim Museum. *Morris Louis, 1912–1962.* Memorial Exhibition: Paintings from 1954–1960. New York, Sept.–Oct. 1963.

Note by T. Messer. Essay by Lawrence Alloway. Comprehensive bibliography by M. Tuchman.

Lye, Len

572. "Arts in architecture: the visionary art of Len Lye." *Craft Horizons*, May 1961.

Also: L'art visionnaire de Len Lye. *Art d'Aujourd'hui*, Feb. 1962.

573. Howard Wise Gallery. *Len Lye's Bounding Steel Sculptures.* New York, March 6–April 3, 1965.

Biographical note; description of five works.

574. Lye, Len. "Is film art?" *Film Culture*, no. 29, Summer 1963.

Dated New York, 1959. Includes "Filmography of Len Lye" (incomplete), 1928–1958.

575. ————. "Tangible motion sculpture." *Art Journal*, no. 4, Summer 1961.

Includes "Description of Roundhead I" (p. 228).

576. Weinberg, Gretchen. "Interview with Len Lye." *Film Culture*, no. 29, Summer, 1963.
Refers to kinetics, vibration, and sculpture.

Macdonald-Wright, Stanton

577. Coquiot, Gustave. *Cubistes, Futuristes et Passeistes.* Paris, Ollendorf, 1914.
References, pp. 177–187.

578. Los Angeles County Museum. *Stanton Macdonald-Wright.* Los Angeles, Jan. 19–Feb. 19, 1956.

Retrospective. Quotes artist's preface for Bernheim show (Paris, 1913), comment on recent work, bibliography.

579. Millier, Arthur. "Thirty five years of creative painting." *Art Digest*, Nov. 1, 1948.

Works shown at the Art Center school galleries.

580. Rose Fried Gallery. [Macdonald-Wright Exhibitions]. New York, 1950–1955.

Retrospectives, reviewed *Art Digest*, Dec. 1, 1950 (p. 14); *Art News*, Dec. 1950 (p. 47); *Art News*, March 1955 (p. 49); *Art Digest*, Feb. 15, 1955 (p. 24).

Mack, Heinz

581. Krefeld, Museum Haus Lange. *Ausstellung Mack, Piene, Uecker.* Jan. 1963.
Catalogue and bibliography by Paul Wember.

582. Mack, Heinz. "Dynamo Mack." *Zero*, no. 3 [1961].
Also in French and English.

583. ————. [Statement from Zero, v. 2, 1959]. In *Konkrete Kunst*, p. 51, Zurich, 1960.

584. Simmat, William E. "Heinz Mack." In *Europäische Avantgarde.* Frankfurt-am-Main, Galerie d, July 9–Aug. 11, 1963.

Extensive chronology, quotations, bibliography.

Magnelli, Alberto

585. Habasque, Guy. "L'architecture plastique d'Alberto Magnelli." *XXᵉ Siècle*, no. 19, June 1962.
Also essay in *L'Oeil*, no. 70, Oct. 1960.

586. Lassaigne, Jacques. *Magnelli.* Paris, Aimery-Somogny, 1948.

587. Liége, Musée de l'Art Wallon. *Magnelli—Arp—Hartung—Jacobsen.* Liége, July–Sept. 1958.

Magnelli, pp. 151–173, biography and comprehensive bibliography.

588. Mendes, Murilo, ed. *Alberto Magnelli.* Rome, Ateneo, 1964.
Editor's text in Italian, French, English. Biography; bibliography.

589. Ringström, Karl K. "Alberto Magnelli." *Metro,* no. 8, 1962.

Mahlmann, Max

590. Hamburg, Kunsthaus. *Josef Albers—J. Albert, M. Herrmann, M. Mahlmann, G. Piper, H. Stromberger, W. Michaelis.* Hamburg, Aug. 23–Sept. 25, 1963.

Malevich, Kasimir

591. Alvard, Julien. "Les idées de Malevich." *Art d'Aujourd'hui,* no. 5, July 1953.
Additional commentary on the artist, Jan. 1951, June 1952.

592. Braunschweig, Kunstverein. *Kasimir Malewitsch.* Feb. 16–March 16, 1958.
Essay by Peter Lufft. Fifty-five exhibits. Bibliography.

593. Malevich, Kasimir. *The Non-Objective World.* Chicago, Theobold, 1959.
Introduction by L. Hilberseimer. Translation by H. Dearstyne of *Die gegenstandlose Welt,* Munich, Langen, 1927 (Bauhausbücher 11). (See illus. on p. 256.)

594. ———. *Suprematismus—Die gegendstandlose Welt.* Cologne, Dumont Schauberg [1963].

595. ———. "Suprematism." In Camilla Gray, *The Great Experiment: Russian Art,* pp. 282-284, London, Thames & Hudson, 1962.
Excerpts from essay in: The Tenth State Exhibition, "Abstract Creation and Suprematism," Moscow, 1919. Also a 1915 manifesto, p. 193. Index pp. 324–325.

596. [Malevich Number]. *Plastique,* no. 1, Spring 1937.

597. Rome, Galleria Nazionale d'Arte Moderna. *Casimir Malevic.* Rome, May 5–June 2, 1959.
Introduction by P. Bucarelli; catalogue by G. Caradente. Bibliography. For recent English show see *Kasimir Malevich, 1875–1935,* London, Whitechapel Art Gallery, Oct. 1959.

Malina, Frank

598. Galleria Schwarz. *Frank J. Malina.* Milan, April 15–30, 1961.
Essay by J. Cassou: "Verso un'arte cinetica." Also in English and French.

Manzoni, Piero

599. Castellani, Enrico & Manzoni, Piero, eds. *Azimuth, rivista d'avanguardia.* Milan, Galleria Azimut, 1959 ff.
Includes catalogues, texts, etc.

600. Petersen, Jes. *Piero Manzoni: the Life and the Works.* Glücksburg, Hamburg, Paris, 1962.
Edition: 100 numbered copies (ca. 100 pp.) [Data from advertisement].

Mari, Enzo

601. Bill, Max & Munari, Bruno. *Enzo Mari.* Milan, Muggiani, 1959.

602. Ragghianti, Carlo L. *Richerche visive, strutture, design di Enzo Mari.* Milan, Tipografia La Cromotipo, 1962.

603. Studio B 24. *Enzo Mari. Esperimenta: colore—volume.* Milan, The Gallery, 1957.
Opening, May 10, 1957; introduction by Guido Ballo.

Martin, Kenneth

604. Forge, Andrew. "Notes on the mobiles of Kenneth Martin." *Quadrum,* no. 3, 1957.

605. Hodin, J. P. "Une fontaine en acier inoxydable." *Quadrum,* no. 12, 1962.

606. Lords Gallery. *Kenneth Martin: a retrospective exhibition.* London, Oct.–Nov. 1962.
Preface by Alan Bownes. Bibliography.

607. Martin, Kenneth. [Articles and statements]. 1956–1963.
Includes: *Architectural Design,* July 1956 ("Architecture and mobile"); *Arts and Architecture,* Feb. 1956 ("Architecture, machine, mobile"); *Broadsheet,* no. 1, 1951, no. 2, 1952; *Motif,* no. 9, 1962 ("Visual grammar of form"); *Structure,* no. 2, 1960 ("The mobile"), no. 1, 1963 ("Construction from within").

Martin, Mary

608. Alloway, Lawrence. *Nine Abstract Artists.* London, Tiranti, 1954.
With statement by Mary Martin.

609. London, Institute of Contemporary Arts. *Essays on Movement: Reliefs by Mary Martin. Mobiles by Kenneth Martin.* London, June 9–July 2, 1960.
     Illustrated catalogue, chronology, documentation.

610. Martin, Mary. [Articles in the magazine "Structure"]. 1961–1963.
     Ser. IV, no. 1 (1961): "Art, architecture and technology"; no. 2 (1962): "Art and philosophy"; Ser. V, no. 1 (1962): "Pro-art and anti-art"; Ser V, no. 2 (1963): "On construction." Biographical notes.

611. Zürich, Kunstgewerbemuseum. *Experiment in Fläche und Raum.* Zurich, Aug. 25–Sept. 30, 1962.
     Mary Martin, p. 24; biographical notes. Same as: *Experiment in Constructie* (Amsterdam, Stedelijk Museum, May 18–June 16, 1962) but omits bibliography.

Mavignier, Almir

612. Galerie Stuttgart. *Ausstellung Almir da Silva Mavignier.* Stuttgart, Nov. 20–Dec. 19, 1957.
     Essay by Max Bense in German and French.

613. Ulm, Museum. *Ausstellung Mavignier.* Ulm, Feb. 3–March 10, 1963.
     Illustrations, biographical note, preface by H. Pée.

McLaughlin, John

614. Felix Landau Gallery. *John McLaughlin: Recent Paintings.* Los Angeles, Jan. 29–Feb. 17, 1962.
     Introduction by Jules Langsner, statement by the artist, chronology.

615. Pasadena Art Museum. *Retrospective Exhibition: John McLaughlin.* Nov. 12–Dec. 12, 1963.
     Text by McLaughlin, biography.

Megert, Christian

616. Galerie d. *Christian Megert zeigt: unendliche Dimensionen.* Frankfort, Jan. 25–March 1, 1963.
     "Festival d'avant-garde 63." Catalogue, text.

617. Megert, Christian. *Texte von und über C. Megert, 1960–1965.* [1966?]
     Mimeographed (32 pp.). Includes English text: "A new space."

618. ——— & Laszlo. "Manifest für Luxus." [Basel, Panderma Verlag?], 1961.

619. Simmat, William E. "Christian Megert." In *Europäische Avantgarde,* Frankfurt-am-Main, Galerie d, July 9–Aug. 11, 1963.
     Text by the artist: "Ein neuer Raum." Chronology, bibliography.

Mies van der Rohe, Ludwig

620. Hilberseimer, Ludwig. *Mies van der Rohe.* Chicago, Theobald, 1956.

621. Johnson, Philip C. *Mies van der Rohe.* New York, Museum of Modern Art, 1947.
     Writings by the architect, chronology, bibliography. Extended edition: Stuttgart, Verlag Gerd Hatje, 1953.

Moholy-Nagy, László

622. Giedion, Siegfried. "Notes on the life and work of L. Moholy-Nagy, painter universalist." In *Architects' Year Book,* no. 3, London, 1949.
     Complemented by his and other multilingual texts in special Moholy-Nagy issue of *Telehor* (Brno), no. 1, (1936). Reprinted in first English exhibition catalogue: "L. Moholy-Nagy," London, London Gallery, Dec. 3, 1936–Jan. 27, 1937. List of films, bibliography.

623. Moholy-Nagy, László. *Kestnermappe 6: 6 Konstruktionen.* Hannover, Verlag Ludwig Ey, 1923.
     Six lithographs (2 col.); edition of 50, signed. Same series as Lissitzky's "Proun."

624. ———. *The New Vision, 1928, and Abstract of an Artist.* New York, Wittenborn, Schultz, 1949.
     Fourth rev. ed. First ed.: *Vom Material zur Architektur,* Bauhausbücher 14, 1929. Second ed. *The New Vision: From Material to Architecture,* New York, Brewer, Warren and Putnam, 1930 (also Norton, 1938). These contain the original plates with captions. Third rev. ed.: *The New Vision,* New York, Wittenborn, 1946.

625. ———. "Space-time problems in art." In *American Abstract Artists. Yearbook 1946,* pp. 5–6, 9–13, 16 ill., New York, 1946.

626. Moholy-Nagy, Sibyl. "Moholy-Nagy und die Idee des Konstruktivismus." *Die Kunst und das*

Schöne Heim, no. 9, June 1959.
Complemented by her authoritative biography *Moholy-Nagy: Experiment in Totality*, New York, Harper, 1950.

627. New London Gallery. *Moholy-Nagy.* London, May–June 1961.
Important introduction by E. Maxwell Fry.

Mondrian, Piet

628. Arts Yearbook 4. New York, Art Digest, 1961.
"Piet Mondrian: twenty years later" (pp. 55–86, ill.). Commentators on his New York period. Complemented by R. Welsh: "Landscape into music: Mondrian's New York period," *Arts Magazine*, Feb. 1966.

629. Mondrian, Piet. *Le Néo-Plasticisme.* Paris, L'Effort Moderne (Léonce Rosenberg) 1920.

630. ———. *Neue Gestaltung, Neoplastizimus, Nieuwe Beelding.* Munich, Langen, 1925.
Bauhausbucher 5, a translation of "Le Néoplasticisme," plus 4 essays, of which three appeared in *De Stijl* (1921–1923).

631. ———. "A new realism." In *American Abstract Artists*, New York, The Association, 1946.
Essay (7 pp.) dated April 1943. "Mondrian's last literary work . . . written especially for the AAA." Contemporaneous interview by J. J. Sweeney in *Museum of Modern Art Bulletin*, v. 13, no. 4–5, pp. 35–36, 1946. (Additional *Bulletin* data, v. 12, no. 4). Excerpts from Mondrian's unpublished writings, introduced by Harry Holtzman, appeared in *IT IS* (New York), no. 2, pp. 32–35, Autumn 1958: "Neoplasticism in the art of painting (1917)"; "Pure abstract art (1926)"; "The new art—the new life (1931)."

632. ———. *Plastic Art and Pure Plastic Art (1937) and Other Essays (1941–1943)*, New York, Wittenborn, 1945.
Introduction by Harry Holtzman.

633. Ragghianti, Carlo L. *Mondrian e l'arte del XX Secolo.* Milan, Edizioni di Communità, 1962.
A major work: 442 pp., 831 ill. (col.).

634. Seuphor, Michel. *Piet Mondrian: Life and Work.* New York, Abrams, 1956.
Monumental monograph with illustrated oeuvre-catalogue. Bibliography (pp. 435–440). Includes the artist's "Natural reality and abstract reality" (pp. 301–335). Also foreign editions.

635. Sweeney, James J. "Mondrian, the Dutch and De Stijl." *Art News*, no. 4, June–Aug. 1951.
Reproduces Mondrian letter.

Morellet, François

636. ———. [33 leaves. Paris, 1966?]
Brochure. On cover: 83, rue porte-baron-49-cholet. Includes photo: Visiteurs de la Biennale de Paris 1965 . . .

637. See Also: Groupe de Recherche d'Art visuel (Bibl. 475–481).

Mortensen, Richard

638. Galerie Denise René. *Mortensen.* Paris, June 1962.
Comprehensive chronology, bibliography. Similarly: *Richard Mortensen: Res et Signa*, Feb.–March 1961.

639. Johansson, Ejnar. "Mortensen." *Art International*, no. 6, June 1960.

640. Mortensen, Richard. *Richard Mortensen.* Munksgaard, Copenhagen, International Booksellers, [in process, 1964].

641. René, Denise, comp. *Catalogue des Ouvrages édités, 1949–1961.* Paris, Editions Denise René, 1961.
Detailed descriptions, with illustrations, of Mortensen albums and limited editions.

Munari, Bruno

642. Babila, Libreria. *Munari: ricostruzioni teoriche di oggetti immaginari.* Milan. Oct. 20–Nov. 6, 1956.
Introduction by the artist. Also reported in *Domus*, no. 326, Jan. 1957. To this should be added a series of "Libri illegibile," wordless books consisting of constructivist layouts, collages, perforations.

643. Munari, Bruno. "Concavo e convesso." *Domus*, no. 223–225, Oct.–Dec. 1947.
Complemented by articles and plates in many issues: no. 273, Sept. 1952; no. 274, Oct. 1952; no. 317, April 1956; no. 291, Feb. 1954; no. 359, Oct. 1959; no. 368, July 1960; no. 388, March 1962. Also note Bibl. 51–54.

644. ———. *Mostra d'Arte Programmata. Organizzata da Bruno Munari.* Milan, Società Olivetti, May 1962.
For details, see Bibl. 253.

645. Vigano, Vittoriano. "Munari et le mouvement." *Art d'Aujourd'hui*, no. 4, ill., Sept. 1955.

Nevelson, Louise

646. Hanover Gallery. *Louise Nevelson. First London Exhibition*. London, Nov. 6–Dec. 6, 1963.
Plates and chronology.

647. New York, Museum of Modern Art. *Sixteen Americans*. Edited by Dorothy Miller. Dec. 14, 1959–Feb. 14, 1960.
Statement, illustration, documentation.

648. Pace Gallery. *Nevelson*. New York, Nov. 17–Dec. 12, 1964.
Plates and chronology.

Nicholson, Ben

649. Galerie Charles Lienhard. *Ben Nicholson*. Zurich, Jan. 3–Feb. 7, 1959.
Text by the artist. Bibliography and chronology. Also 1960 catalogue with essay.

650. Hodin, J. P. *Ben Nicholson: the Meaning of His Art*. London, Tiranti, 1957.
Also essays and reviews by Hodin in: *Art News and Review*, no. 13, July 24, 1954; *Domus*, no. 305, April 1955; *Kroniek van Kunst en Kultuur*, no. 7, 1954; *Prisme des Arts*, no. 12, 1957; *The Dilemma of Being Modern* (London, 1956, pp. 106–119).

651. Read, Herbert. *Ben Nicholson: Paintings, Reliefs, Drawings*. London, Lund Humphries, 1948–1956.
Vol. 1: Text by the artist on abstract art. *Vol. 2:* Work since 1947. Bibliography.

652. Valsecchi, Mario. "Visita a Ben Nicholson." *Metro*, no. 1, 1960.
Texts also in French and English.

Noland, Kenneth

653. Galerie Charles Lienhard. *Kenneth Noland*. Zurich, March 1962.
Biographical and bibliographical notes. Ill. (port.); color cover.

654. Goossen, E. C. "Kenneth Noland." In *Noland*, Bennington College (Vt.), New Gallery, April 18–May 15, 1961.

655. Greenberg, Clement. "Louis and Noland." *Art International*, no. 5, May 1961.

Extract also in: *Kenneth Noland*, London, Kasmin Gallery Ltd., April 1963 (with chronology).

656. Lippard, Lucy R. "New York letter." *Art International*, no. 1, Feb. 1965.

657. Solomon R. Guggenheim Museum. *American Abstract Expressionists and Imagists*. New York, Oct.–Dec. 1961.
Text by H. H. Arnason, biography and bibliography.

658. Washington Gallery of Modern Art. *The Washington Color Painters*. Washington, D.C. June 25–Sept. 5, 1965.
Chapters on Morris Louis, Kenneth Noland, and others. Bibliographies.

NUL (Group)

659. Amsterdam, Stedelijk Museum. *Nul: Negentienhonderd vijf en zestig*. Deel 1: Teksten. Deel 2: Afbeeldingen. April 15–June 8, 1965.
Thirty-two participants, including Zero, Nul, T. Gutai groups. (See illus. on p. 271.)

660. Amsterdam, Stedelijk Museum. *Tentoonstelling Nul*. March 9–25, 1962.
Folded insert of pictures and texts titled: "O—Nul—Zero—Dynamo—Manifesto Blanco," etc.

661. Hague, Gemeentmuseum. *Nul: Armando, Henk Peeters, Schoonhoven*. March 20–May 18, 1964.
Biographies, bibliography.

662. Vries, Herman de. "Bibliographie—Nieuwe Konseptie—Zero—O—Nieuwe Tendenzen. *Museumjournal* 1963.
Bibliography published in ser. 9, no. 5–6 of *Museumjournal*. Also issued as 18 pp. separate, reporting periodicals, catalogues, exhibitions, artists, articles, etc., 1958–1963.

Pasmore, Victor

663. Alloway, Lawrence. "Pasmore constructs a relief." *Art News*, no. 4, June 1956.
Also *Art News and Review*, no. 3, March 1955, and *Art International*, no. 8, Nov. 1958.

664. Bowness, Alan. "The paintings and constructions of Victor Pasmore." *Burlington Magazine*, no. 686, May 1960.

665. Pasmore, Victor. [Articles, statements, etc.]. 1949.

Includes: *Abstract art.* Commentary by some artists and critics (Privately printed, 1949); "The artist speaks" (*Art News and Review*, no. 1, Feb. 10, 1951); "Abstract, concrete and subjective art" *(Penwith Society Broadsheet,* St. Ives, no. 3, 1952); "Connections between painting, sculpture and architecture" *(Zodiac,* no. 1, 1957); "Construction" *(New Departure,* no. 1, Summer 1959); "What is abstract art?" *(London Times,* Feb. 5, 1961).

666. Reichardt, Jasia. *Victor Pasmore.* London, Methuen, 1962.
      With artist's statement, chronology, bibliography.

Pevsner, Antoine

667. Massat, René. *Antoine Pevsner et le Constructivisme.* Paris, Caractères, 1956.
      Preface by J. Cassou. For corrective data, see bibl. 442.

668. Olson, Ruth & Chanin, Abraham. *Naum Gabo —Antoine Pevsner.* Introduction by Herbert Read. New York, Museum of Modern Art, 1948.
      Catalogue for exhibition. Bibliography.

669. Peissi, Pierre. *Antoine Pevsner: Tribute by a Friend. Antoine Pevsner's Spatial Imagination* by Carola Giedion-Welcker. Neuchâtel, Griffon, 1961.
      Biography, catalogue and bibliography.

670. Pevsner, Antoine. [Statements, texts, etc.] 1920–1959.
      Selected texts would include: "Thesen aus dem Realisten Manifest, Moskau 1920," *G* (Berlin), no. 1, July 1923; "Le réalisme constructeur," *XXᵉ Siècle,* no. 1, 1939; also n.s. no. 13, 1959; "Propos d'Antoine Pevsner; propos de Gabo et Pevsner," in Galerie René Drouin, *Pevsner,* Paris, June 1947; "Extraits d'une lettre de Gabo et Pevsner," *Réalités Nouvelles,* no. 1, 1947; "Espaces," *Réalités Nouvelles,* no. 4, 1950; "Message de la sculpture," *XXᵉ Siècle,* no. 1, 1951; [Sur l'espace], *Réalités Nouvelles,* no. 6, 1952; [Témoignage: l'espace], *XXᵉ Siècle,* no. 2, 1952; "Propos d'un sculpteur" (interview), *L'Oeil,* no. 23, Nov. 1956; "Antoine Pevsner über sich selbst," *Form* (Cologne), no. 1, 1958; "La science tue la poésie," *XXᵉ Siècle,* no. 12, 1959 (with English summary).

Picasso, Pablo

671. Argan, Giulio Carlo. *Scultura di Picasso.* Venice, Alfieri, 1953.
      Also English text.

672. Barr, Alfred H., Jr. *Picasso: Fifty Years of His Art.* New York, Museum of Modern Art, 1946.
      Includes illustrations, chronology, quotations, bibliography.

673. Gonzalez, Julio. "Picasso sculpteur." *Cahiers d'Art,* no. 6–7, 1936.

674. Kahnweiler, Daniel-Henry. *The Sculptures of Picasso.* London, Phillips, 1949.
      Photos by Brassai. Translated from Editions du Chêne, Paris, 1948.

Piene, Otto

675. Dorfles, Gillo. "Piene: luce e fumo." *Metro,* no. 7, 1962.

676. Galerie Schmela. *Piene: Ölbilder und Gouachen.* Dusseldorf, Sept.–Oct. 1963.
      Includes "Jetzt" (4 pp.) signed by the artist. Extensive documentation in: *Europäische Avantgarde,* Frankfort, Galerie d, July 9–Aug. 11, 1963.

677. Howard Wise Gallery. *Piene: Light Ballet.* Nov. 4–20, 1965.
      Essay by the artist, catalogue, chronology.

678. McRoberts & Tunnard Gallery. *Piene: light and smoke* [London, Oct. 1962?].
      Statement by the artist.

679. Piene, Otto. *Piene Texte.* Munich, Frankfort, [The Artist?], 1961.
      "Zahlreiche Textveröffentlichungen, erstmalig zusammengefasst."

Poons, Larry

680. Coplans, John. "Larry Poons." *Artforum,* no. 9, June 1965.

681. Johnson, Ellen H. "Three new, cool, bright imagists." *Art News,* no. 4, Summer 1965.
      Larry Poons, Charles Hinman, Neil Williams.

682. Smithsonian Institution, National Collection of Fine Arts. *The United States of America,* an exhibition organized by the Pasadena Art Museum for the Eighth Sao Paulo Biennial. Sao Paulo, Sept. 4–Nov. 28; Washington, D. C., Jan. 27–March 6, 1966.

Exhibitors: Newman, Bell, Bengston, Irwin, Judd, Poons, Stella. Chronology, bibliography.

683. Tillim, Sidney. "Larry Poons: the dotted line." *Arts Magazine*, Feb. 1965.

Reinhardt, Ad

684. Betty Parsons Gallery. *Ad Reinhardt, 1960. Twenty-five Years of Abstract Painting.* New York, Oct. 17–Nov. 5, 1960.
      Artist's texts from *Art News*. Chronology, Illustrations.

685. Leverkusen, Städtisches Museum. *Ad Reinhardt, New York—Francisco Lo Savio, Rome—Jef Verheyen, Antwerpen.* Leverkusen, Jan. 27–March 19, 1961.
      Prefaces by U. Kulturmann. Extracts from Reinhardt's essay on Chinese paintings (*Art News*, 1957, 1960). Biographical notes.

686. Miller, Dorothy C., ed. *Americana 1963.* With Statements by the Artists and Others. New York, Museum of Modern Art, 1963.

687. New York, Jewish Museum. *Ad Reinhardt.* New York, Nov.–Dec. 1966.
      Chronology, bibliography.

688. Reinhardt, Ad. "Art-as-art." *Art International*, no. 10, Dec. 20, 1962.

Richter, Hans

689. Bayl, Friedrich. "Gespräch mit Hans Richter." *Art International*, no. 1–2, 1959.
      Also English article, no. 10, Dec. 1960.

690. Berlin, Akademie der Künste. *Hans Richter: Ein Leben für Bild und Film.* Berlin, Oct. 17–Nov. 16, 1958.
      Variant catalogs for Kunstgewerbemuseum Zürich (1959), Museum Folkwang, Essen (1961). Modified format and documentation in: *40 ans de Peintures—Rouleaux* (Paris, Galerie Denise René, March 1960).

691. Richter, Hans. "Il film astratto e il futurismo." *Cinema Italiano* (Rome), no. 12, 1953.
      Complemented by no. 3 (1953): A. G. Bragaglia, "Richter e i Futuristi."

692. Turin, Galleria Civica d'Arte Moderna. *Hans Richter.* Turin, May 19–June 12, 1962.
      Text by F. Russoli. Bibliography.

Rickey, George

693. Corcoran Gallery of Art. *George Rickey: Six Years of Kinetic Sculpture.* Washington, D. C. Sept. 30–Nov. 20, 1966.
      Preface: Peter Selz. Quotes; chronology.

Riley, Bridget

694. Baro, Gene. "Bridget Riley: drawing for painting." *Studio*, v. 172, pp. 12–13, July 1966.

695. Ehrenzweig, Anton. "The pictorial space of Bridget Riley." *Art International*, no. 1, Feb. 1965.

696. Gallery One. *Bridget Riley.* London, Sept. 9–28, 1963.
      Texts by D. Sylvester, A. Ehrensweig. Also April–May 1962 catalogue, text by M. de Lausmarez.

697. Riley, Bridget. [Letter to George Rickey]. London, Sept. 3, 1963.
      Statement on artistic procedures and beliefs. Copy on deposit in Museum of Modern Art Library.

698. Tooth, Arthur & Sons. *1962—One Year of British Art.* London, 1963.
      A selection of 14 artists, including Riley. Reviewed by N. Lynton, *Art International*, no. 3, March 1963 (pp. 58–59).

699. Walker Art Center. *London: The New Scene.* Minneapolis, Feb. 6–March 14, 1965.
      Articles by M. Friedman, A. Bowness. Biographies and bibliographies by J. Reichardt. Riley, pp. 62, 71–72.

Rivera, José Ruiz de

700. Ashton, Dore. "The Sculpture of José de Rivera." *Arts* (New York), April 1956.
      Quoted in Gordon below. Additional commentary: *Art Digest* April 15, 1952, p. 14, *Arts & Architecture*, Nov. 1952, pp. 22–23, 34 (5 ill.).

701. Catalano, E. F. "Estructuras curvas de José de Rivera." *Revista de Arquitectura*, May 1947.

702. Gordon, John. *José de Rivera.* New York, American Federation of Arts, 1961.
      Monographic booklet for circulating exhibition. Statement by the artist, chronology, bibliography (pp. 27–29).

703. Miller, Dorothy C., ed. *12 Americans.* New York, Museum of Modern Art, 1956.
      Biographical note, statement by the artist (pp. 78–83, 96, 12 ill.).

Rodchenko, Alexander

704. Gray, Camilla. *The Great Experiment: Russian Art, 1863–1922*. London, Thames and Hudson, 1962.
      Rodchenko references: p. 195–196, 219–220, 224, 226–227, 244–245, 250, 252–254; 8 ill. Biography, pp. 292–294. English and Russian bibliography.

705. Klub V.S.P. *5 × 5 = 25. Vistavka Jivopisi. Khud: Varst, Vesnin, Popova, Rodchenko, Exter.* Moscow, Sept. 1921.
      "Mimeographed, with mss. illus."

706. Lozowick, Louis. *Modern Russian Art*. New York, Museum of Modern Art—Société Anonyme, 1925.
      On the Suprematists (pp. 18–27) and the Constructionists (pp. 29–45), including Rodchenko text and illustration.

707. Umanski, Konstantin. "Die neue Monumental-skulptur in Russland." *Der Ararat*, no. 5–6, March 1920.
      Supplemented by: *Neue Kunst in Russland, 1914–1919*, Potsdam & Munich, 1920.

Russell, Morgan

708. Dallas Museum. *American Genius in Review: No. 1.* May 4–June 1960.
      Five American painters. Biographical essay on Morgan Russell. Introduction by Douglas MacAgy.

709. Knoedler & Company. *Synchromism and Color Principles in American Painting, 1910–1930.* New York, Oct. 12–Nov. 6, 1965.
      Catalogue and text by William C. Agee. Includes American and European artists.

710. Russell, Morgan. [Statement from Bernheim Jeune catalogue, 1913] In Rose Fried Gallery, "Morgan Russell, 1884–1953," New York, Oct. 26–Nov. 1953.
      Text by H. Cahill.

Schöffer, Nicolas

711. Galerie Denise René. *Nicolas Schöffer: Micro-temps.* Paris, April–May 1966.
      Essay by the artist. Comprehensive biography and bibliography.

712. Joray, Marcel, ed. *Nicolas Schöffer*. Introduction by Jean Cassou. Texts by Guy Habasque and Jacques Ménétrier. Neuchâtel, Griffon, 1963.
      Translated from the French. Also French, English, and German editions with 150 serial reliefs in plexiglas and 150 serigraphs numbered and signed. Text by the artist; bibliography.

713. London, Institute of Contemporary Arts. *Schöffer.* London, July 7–30, 1960.
      "In collaboration with the Galerie Denise René." Translations of texts by J. Cassou and G. Habasque. Bibliography.

714. New York, Jewish Museum. *2 Kinetic Sculptors: Nicolas Schöffer and Jean Tinguely.* New York, October House, 1966.
      Essays by J. Cassou, K. G. Hultén, S. Hunter. Statement by Schöffer. Bibliography.

715. Schöffer, Nicolas. *Le Spatiodynamisme.* [Paris, Editions AA (*Art d'Aujourd'hui*), 1954].
      Lecture at the Sorbonne. Lists "études consacrées au spatiodynamisme."

716. ———. "Spatiodynamisme et synthèse des arts." *Réalités Nouvelles*, no. 8, 1954.

Servranckx, Victor

717. Brussels, Palais des Beaux Arts. *Ser Vranckx.* Préface du Léonce Rosenberg. Brussels, Editions du Centaure, Jan. 1947.
      Preface partially translated in *Collection of the Société Anonyme*, New Haven, Yale University Art Gallery, 1950 (p. 58, with bibliography).

718. Galerie Les Contemporains. *Hommage à Servranckx.* Brussels, May 11–29, 1957.
      Prefaces by M. Bilcke, L.-L. Sosset. Biography, critiques.

719. Lacomblez, J. "Victor Servranckx et Paul Joostens." *Art d'Aujourd'hui*, June 1960.

720. Servranckx, Victor. "Directives nouvelles dans les arts plastiques." *Guide de l'Amateur Art*, no. 3, March 5, 1929.
      More recent statements in *Réalités Nouvelles*, no. 6, 1952, no. 9, 1955.

Smith, David

721. *Arts* (New York). [Special Number] *David Smith.* Feb. 1960.
      Vol. 34, no. 5 (pp. 22–49 incl. ill.), consists of: Hilton Kramer, "The scupture of David Smith"; David Smith, "Notes on my work."

722. Fogg Art Museum. *David Smith, 1906–1965, a retrospective exhibition.* Cambridge, Harvard College, 1966.
     Chronology, bibliography. Texts by Smith, interview by K. Kuh.

723. Greenberg, Clement. "David Smith's new sculpture." *Art International*, no. 4, May 1964.
     Introduction from University of Pennsylvania exhibition.

724. Motherwell, Robert. "David Smith: A major American sculptor." *Studio International*, no. 880, Aug. 1966.
     Followed by Gene Baro: "David Smith, the art of wholeness."

725. New York, Museum of Modern Art. *David Smith*, by Sam Hunter. New York, 1957.
     Booklet for museum exhibition; chronology and bibliography. Also issued as *Bulletin*, no. [2] 1957. Complemented by current circulating exhibition with introduction by Frank O'Hara: Arts Council of Great Britain, "David Smith, 1906–1965," at the Tate Gallery, London, Aug. 18–Sept. 25, 1966. Bibliography.

Smith, Leon Polk

726. Alloway, Lawrence. New work and its origin. *Art International*, April 1963.
     Also v. 2, pp. 51–52, 1961: "London letter: six from New York," which reviews Tooth Gallery show.

727. Galerie Chalette. *Leon Polk Smith: Torn Drawings.* New York, Chalette, 1965.
     Prefatory note (unsigned). Portfolio of 10 facsimiles issued on occasion of exhibition. Edition: 500 copies.

728. Oeri, Georgine. "Leon Polk Smith." *Quadrum*, no. 12, 1962.

729. Smith, Leon Polk. [Statement]. *It Is* (New York), Spring 1960.

730. Solomon R. Guggenheim Museum. *American Abstract Expressionists and Imagists.* New York, Oct.–Dec. 1961.
     Essay by H. H. Arnason, references.

Soto, Jésus-Raphaël

731. Bremer, Claus. "Jésus-Raphaël Soto." In *Kinetische Kunst*, Zurich, Kunstgewerbemuseum, May–June 1960.

732. Krefeld, Museum Haus Lange. *Soto: Kinetische Bilder, Tableaux Cinétiques.* Krefeld, Nov.–Dec. 1963.
     Preface by Paul Wember.

733. Seuphor, Michel. "Soto." In his *Dictionary of Abstract Painting*, New York, Paris Book Center, 1958.

734. Simmat, Walter E. "Jésus-Raphaël Soto." In *Europäische Avantgarde*, Frankfurt-am-Main, Galerie d, July 9–Aug. 11, 1963.
     Chronology, quotation, bibliography.

735. "Soto." *Signals* (London), no. 10, Dec. 1965.
     Special issue; comprehensive documentation, p. 22.

Stazewski & Strzeminski

736. Galerie Chalette. *Six Contemporary Polish Artists.* New York, April 1961.
     Artists also represented in comprehensive show of 1960: "Construction and Geometry in Painting" (Bibl. 256).

737. Galerie Denise René. *Précurseurs de l'Art abstrait en Pologne.* Paris, Nov.–Dec. 1957.
     Texts by J. Cassou, J. Przybos. Extracts from Berlewi: *Mechanofaktura*. Reviewed: *Aujourd'hui, Art et Architecture* Dec. 1957 (p. 20).

738. Rostkowska, Maria. "Malewitch et l'art abstrait en Pologne." *XXe Siècle*, no. 10, 1958.
     On the occasion of the René show below. Illustrated; Berlewi, Malevich, Strzeminski.

739. Selz, Peter. *15 Polish Painters.* New York, Museum of Modern Art, 1961.
     Exhibition catalogue. Mentions Strzeminski (p. 6) and includes Stazewski (pp. 7, 54, 60, 63–64).

740. Stazewski, Henryk. [Statement: L'Art plastique . . .]. *Abstraction-Création, Art Non-Figuratif*, no. 1, 1932.
     Text (pp. 34–35) complemented by no. 2, pp. 39, 42 (ill.), 1933: [*Réponses*].

741. Strzeminski, Wladyslaw. [Statement: La ligne . . .]. *Abstraction-Création, Art Non-Figuratif*, no. 1, 1932.
     Text (p. 35) complemented by no. 2, p. 40 1933: [*Réponses*]. Articles both illustrated, also plates in no. 4, p. 29, 1935; no. 5, p. 26, 1936.

742. Warsaw, National Museum. [Sonderausstellung Henryk Stazewski]. Warsaw, 1959.
Mentioned in *Konkrete Kunst* (Zurich, 1960, p. 70). Recent exhibits have included: Grabowski Gallery (London, Sept. 1963), San Marino Biennale, 1963.

Stella, Frank

743. Fogg Art Museum. *Three American Painters: Kenneth Noland, Jules Olitski, Frank Stella.* Cambridge, Mass., Harvard University, April 21–May 30, 1965.
Exhibit and essay by Michael Fried. References. Chronologies. Also shown at Pasadena.

744. Leider, Philip. "Frank Stella." *Artforum*, no. 9, June 1965.

745. Lucie-Smith, Edward. "Studies in severity." *Art and Artists*, v. 1, no. 8, Nov. 1966.
On the occasion of show at Kasmin Gallery.

746. New York, Museum of Modern Art. *Sixteen Americans*. Edited by Dorothy Miller. Dec. 14, 1959–Feb. 14, 1960.
Statement, documentation. Additional bibliography in *Toward a New Abstraction* (New York, Jewish Museum, 1963, p. 39).

Stroud, Peter

747. Coplans, John. "Interview with Peter Stroud." *Artforum*, March 1966.

748. Leverkusen, Städtisches Museum. *Neue Malerei in England*. Sept. 18–Nov. 5, 1961.
Preface: Udo Kulturmann. Ten artists, including Peter Stroud.

749. Marlborough-Gerson Gallery. *Peter Stroud.* New York, Sept. 21–Oct. 18, 1966.
Preface: D. Ashton. Chronology, bibliography.

750. Stroud, Peter. "Personal statement." *Architectural Design*, Feb. 1961.
Similarly in *Gazette* (London), no. 2, 1961.

Taeuber-Arp, Sophie

751. Bill, Max. "Sophie Täeuber-Arp." *Werk*, no. 6, 1943.

752. Degand, Léon. *Sophie Taeuber-Arp.* Paris, Galerie Denise René; Basel, Galerie d'Art Moderne, 1957.
Introduction with 10 color plates in folio.

Additional Degand essays: *Art d'Aujourd'hui*, no. 1, Dec. 1951; *Sophie Taeuber-Arp*, Berne, March 6–April 19, 1954, (chronology, bibliography).

753. Galerie Chalette. *Jean Arp and Sophie Taeuber-Arp.* New York, Oct.–Nov. 1960.
Largely commentary by Seuphor: *The spiritual mission of art*, translated from the French of 1953, an essay supplemented by his *L'Art Abstrait* (1950).

754. Schmidt, Georg, ed. *Sophie Taeuber-Arp.* Basel, Holbein, 1948.
Contributors include Arp, Kandinsky. Oeuvre catalogue, exhibitions, bibliography.

Takis

755. Calas, Nicolas. "Takis." *XXe Siècle*, no. 26, Dec. 1964.

756. Hoctin, Luce. "Takis: conversation dans l'atelier." *Oeil*, no. 119, Nov. 1964.

757. Alexandre Iolas Gallery. *Takis: Dix Ans de Sculpture, 1954–1964.* New York, Paris, Geneva, 1964.
French texts. Insert: Takis, Oct. 8–Nov. 7, 1964. Chronology. See also artist's statement ("about the magnets"), dated 19.6.61 in earlier Iolas show, New York, 1961.

758. Schwarz, Arturo, Gallery. *Takis.* Milan, April 14–May 4, 1962.
Italian, French, English text.

759. Takis. *Estafilades.* [Paris], Ed. Juilliard, 1961.
Illustrated testament.

Tatlin, Vladimir

760. Annekov, G. "Tatlin och konstruktivismen" (Paris, January 1961). In *Rörelse i Konsten*, Stockholm, Moderna Museet, 1961.
Text (pp. 5–6), supplemented by biographical note (p. 31). Also comment and additional illustrations in appended essay by K. G. Hultén.

761. Punin, N. *Tatlin-Protiv Kubizma.* St. Petersburg, Gosudartsvennoe Izdatelisto, 1921.
"Against cubism." Pamphlet (25 pp.) includes plates and portrait.

762. Seuphor, Michel. *L'Art Abstrait.* Paris, Maeght, 1950.
Tatlin: pp. 52–56, 315. Ill.: pp. 226–229.

763. Vallier, Dora. "L'Art abstrait en Russe: ses origines, ses premières manifestations." *Cahiers d'Art*, v. 33–35, 1960.

Teana, Marino di

764. Galerie Denise René. *Di Teana: Sculptures en Acier*. Paris, Nov. 1960.
     Text by M. Seuphor. Chronology, bibliography. Reviewed in *Apollo*, Dec. 1960; *Aujourd'hui*, Dec. 1960.

765. Habasque, Guy. "Marino di Teana." *Quadrum*, no. 10, 1961.
     Additional comment in *L'Oeil* no. 87, 1962.

766. Ragon, Michel. "Marino di Teana." *Cimaise*, no. 55, Sept.–Oct. 1961.
     Quadrilingual text includes English.

767. Teana, Marino di. "Marino di Teana raconte comment il a trouvé sa voie." *Connaissance des Arts*, no. 136, June 1963.

Thépot, Roger-François

768. Galerie Hautefeville. *Roger-François Thépot*. Paris, March 14–April 15, 1961.
     Preface by M. Seuphor (from *Art de France*, Jan. 1959). Biographical and bibliographical notes.

769. Pan, Imre. *Roger-François Thépot*. Paris, Morphèmes, 1963.
     "Les artistes contemporains, 4." Sixty copies (10 with original gouache).

770. Thépot, Roger-François. *Texte inédit: projet pour introduction à une catalogue*. Paris, Dec. 1960.
     One page document (copy in Museum of Modern Art Library).

Tinguely, Jean

771. Descargues, Pierre. "Les nouvelles machines de Jean Tinguely." *XXe Siècle*, no. 27, June 1965.

772. Houston, Museum of Fine Arts. *Jean Tinguely Sculptures*. April 3–May 16, 1965.
     Text by J. J. Sweeney. Chronology, bibliography, films.

773. Hultén, K. G. "Une sculpture-machine de Tinguely pour les lecteurs de Metro." *Metro*, no. 6, June 1962.
     Text on reverse of diagrammatic drawing reproduced on folio sheet (insert).

774. New York, Jewish Museum. *2 Kinetic Sculptors: Nicholas Schöffer and Jean Tinguely*. New York, Nov. 23–Jan. 2, 1966.
     Essays by J. Cassou, K. G. Hultén, S. Hunter. Statement by the artist. Bibliography.

Tomasello, Luis R.

775. Belloli, Carlo. *Atmosphères mobiles: chromoplastiques de Tomasello*. Oct. 1962.
     Translated from Italian, "scheduled as preface for a forthcoming show at the Galerie Denise René, Paris."

776. Galerie Denise René. *Luis R. Tomasello*. Paris, Nov. 1962.
     Chronology and catalogue (one ill.). French and Spanish text by A. Pelligrini.

777. ———. *Tomasello*. Nov. 18, 1965–Jan. 15, 1966.
     Preface: Carlo Belloli. Biography.

Torrès Garcia, Joaquin

778. Amsterdam, Stedelijk Museum. *Joaquín Torrès Garcia*. Amsterdam, Dec. 1961–Jan. 1962.
     Thirty-five works (1927–1943) with illustrations, biography, list of exhibitions, and writings. Reproduces his "Raison et Nature" (Paris, Iman, 1932). Similar catalogue issued by Staatliche Kunsthalle, Baden-Baden, March 2–April 1, 1962.

779. Kirstein, Lincoln. *The Latin-American Collection of the Museum of Modern Art*. New York, Museum of Modern Art, 1943.
     Includes catalogue of exhibition. Biographical note. While bibliography refers to his *Circulo y Cuadro* (no. 1–7, Montevideo 1936–1938), related to *Cercle et Carré* (no. 1–3, Paris, 1930), edited jointly with Seuphor, it omits other references noted in *Collection of the Société Anonyme*, Yale University Art Gallery, New Haven, 1950 (p. 56).

780. Rose Fried Gallery. *J. Torrès Garcia: Paintings from 1930–1949*. New York, March 1960.
     Essay by Jean Cassou from *XXe Siècle*, Dec. 1959. Comments on the artist's *Universalismo Constructivo* (Buenos Aires, Poseidon, 1944).

781. Torrès Garcia, Joaquin. *Historia di Mi Vida*. Montevideo, La Associacion de Arte Constructivo, 1939.

Bibl. 773. Jean Tinguely. "Une sculpture-machine . . ." *Metro*, no. 6, 1962.

With author's illustrations. Text dated Oct. 1934. Complemented by his *La Tradicion del Hombre Abstracto* (Montevideo, 1938); *Constructivo: Contribution al Arte de las Tres Americas* (Montevideo, 1946).

Uecker, Günther

782. Howard Wise Gallery. *Uecker*. New York, Nov. 1–19, 1966.
    Essay by W. Sharp: "Uecker, Zero and the kinetic spirit." Biography.

783. Krefeld, Museum Haus Lange. *Ausstellung Mack, Piene, Uecker*. Jan. 1963.
    Extensive documentation by Paul Wember.

784. Sharp, Willoughby. *Günther Uecker—Ten Years of a Kineticist's Work*. New York, Kineticism Press, 1966.
    Boxed edition with original object (nail on white board). Bibliography.

785. Simmat, Walter E. "Günther Uecker." In *Europäische Avantgarde*, Frankfurt-am-Main, Galerie d, July 9–Aug. 11, 1963.
    Chronology, artist's statement, bibliography.

786. Uecker, Günther. *Weissstrukturen*. Dusseldorf, Hofhauspresse, 1962.
    An abstract white-on-white book (48 pp. incl. ill. and covers). List of exhibitions, artist's texts 1956–1962. Preface by J. A. Thwaites.

Uhlmann, Hans

787. Bremen, Kunsthalle. *Hans Uhlmann*. Berlin, 1960.
    Introduction by Seiler. Illustrations, chronology.

788. Giedion-Welcker, Carola. *Contemporary Sculpture*. Rev. & enl. ed. New York, Wittenborn, 1960.
    Biographical note, p. 354; text, p. 219; port., p. 348; bibliography, p. 394.

789. Hentzen, Alfred. "Sculpture." In *German Art of the Twentieth Century*, New York, Museum of Modern Art, 1957.
    Comment, pp. 176–178 (ill.); bibliography.

790. Ohff, H. "Hans Uhlmann." *Kunstwerk*, May 1964.

791. Schiff, Gert. "Hans Uhlmann." *Art d'Aujourd'hui*, no. 6, Aug. 1953.

Vantongerloo, Georges

792. Bill, Max, ed. *Georges Vantongerloo*. London, Marlborough Fine Art Limited, 1962.
    Documentation by Margit Staber. Texts by the artist.

793. Staber, Margit. "Georges Vantongerloo." *Art International*, no. 2, Feb. 1966.

794. Vantongerloo, Georges. *L'Art et Son Avenir*. Antwerp, "De Sikkel," 1924.
    Texts from 1919 to 1921. Part I, dated 1919, on the evolution of sculptural art. Additional writings: *De Stijl*, no. 9, 1918; no. 3, 1919; no. 5, 1919; no. 2, 1919; no. 4, 1920. *Abstraction-Création, Art Non-Figuratif*, no. 2, no. 4, no. 5. *Plastique*, no. 5, 1939. *Structure*, no. 2, 1960.

795. Vantongerloo, Georges. *Georges Vantongerloo: Paintings, Sculptures, Reflections*. New York, Wittenborn, Schultz, 1948.
    Preface by Max Bill. Biography and bibliography.

Vasarely, Victor

796. Belloli, Carlo. "Vasarely and the integration of the arts." *Metro*, no. 4–5, 1961.
    Also Italian text.

797. Brussels, Palais des Beaux Arts. *Vasarely*. Brussels, Jan. 30–Feb. 14, 1960.
    Extensive documentation and bibliography. Essay by F.-C. Legrand.

798. Habasque, Guy. "Vasarely et la plastique cinetique." *Quadrum*, no. 3, 1957.

799. Hague, Gemeentemuseum. *Victor Vasarely*. Sept. 4–Oct. 11, 1964.
    Comprehensive documentation, 1947–1964, by and on the artist.

800. Paris, Musée des Arts Décoratifs. *Vasarely*. Paris, March–April 1963.
    Article by the artist. Comprehensive bibliography. Preface by M. Faré.

801. Vasarely, Victor. "Fragments d'un journal." *Art International*, no. 3, April 1964.

802. ————. *Vasarely*. Introduction by Marcel Joray. Neuchâtel, Griffon, 1965.
    Comprehensive documentation and bibliography. Monograph includes plastic section with overlapping optical effects.

Vieira, Mary

803. Giedion-Welcker, Carola. *Contemporary Sculpture*. Rev. & enl. ed. New York, Wittenborn, 1960.
   Text and biography, pp. 221, 354; ill. p. 220, port. 348.

804. Leverkusen, Museum Morsbroich. *Brasilien Baut*. Leverkusen, 1956.
   Included Vieira section (catalogue, p. 13).

805. Vollmer, Hans. *Allgemeines Lexikon der Bildenden Künstler des XX. Jahrhunderts*, v. 5, p. 33, Leipzig, Seemann, 1961.
   Includes references. Omits review of Galerie d'Art Moderne show (Basel), *Werk*, Jan. 1959 (v. 46, suppl. p. 16, ill.).

Vordemberge-Gildewart, Friedrich

806. Galleria del Levante. *Friedrich Vordemberge-Gildewart*. Rome, Sept.–Oct. 1965.
   Chronology, bibliography, expositions. Includes photo of *Cercle et Carré* exhibitors, Paris 1930.

807. Lohse, Richard P., ed. *Vordemberge-Gildewart: eine Bild-Biographie*. Teufen (Switzerland), Niggli, 1959.
   "Dokumente, Fotografien, Zeichnungen und Bilder." Multilingual texts.

808. Sartoris, Alberto. "Vordemberge-Gildewart." *Gaceta de Arte* (Tenerife), no. 34, Nov. 1934.
   Accompanied by: Eduardo Westerdahl, "Conducta de la obra de Vordemberge-Gildewart."

809. Vordemberge-Gildewart, Friedrich. *Vordemberge-Gildewart: Époque Néerlandaise*. Amsterdam, Duwaer, 1949.
   Preface by Jean Arp.

810. ———. *Vordemberge-Gildewart*. Amsterdam, Duwaer, 1946.
   Limited edition (250 copies); 14 p. text, 33 plates (12 col.). Biography, bibliography.

Wiegand, Charmion von

811. John Heller Gallery. *Charmion von Wiegand*. New York, Jan. 4–21, 1956.
   New paintings and collages (25 works). Introduction by Koo Hsien Liang.

812. Wiegand, Charmion von. *The oriental tradition and abstract art*. In *The World of Abstract Art*, New York, Wittenborn, 1957.

813. ———. [Statement on art]. *Réalités Nouvelles*, no. 5, 1951.

814. ———. *The White Plane*. New York, Pinacotheca, 1947.
   Mimeographed introduction (3 pp.) to exhibit organized for that gallery, March 19–April 12.

Wilding, Ludwig

815. Galerie Wilbrand. *Ludwig Wilding: Arbeiten der Jahre 1960 bis 1965*. Münster (Westf.), [1965?].
   Chronology. Illustrations, 1951 ff.

Wilfred, Thomas

816. Wilfred, Thomas. "Composing in the art of lumia." *Journal of Aesthetics and Art Criticism*, Sept. 1948.

Zero (Group)

817. Atelier de Fontana. *Zero Avantgarde 1965*. March 27, 1965 ff.
   Also at Cavelino (Venice), May 4 ff. 31 artists.

818. Block, G. "Zero-Nul." In *De Nieuwe Stijl*. Deel 1. Amsterdam [1966?].
   English text (pp. 173–174) followed by: J. J. Schoonhoven, "Zero" (p. 175).

819. "Die Gruppe 'Zero.'" *Quadrum*, no. 14, 1963.
   An insertion with illustrations, including color.

820. Hannover, Kestner-Gesellschaft. *Heinz Mack, Otto Piene, Günther Uecker*. Hannover, 1965.
   Introduction by W. Schmied. Comprehensive texts, bibliography.

821. Howard Wise Gallery. *Zero: Mack, Piene, Uecker*. New York, Nov. 12–Dec. 5, 1961.
   Notes on the Group, texts by the artists, biographies.

822. Kestner-Gesellschaft. *O: Mack, Piene, Uecker*. Hannover, May 7–June 7, 1965.
   Comprehensive texts (185 pp.) including full documentation.

823. Pennsylvania University, Institute of Contemporary Art. *Group Zero*. Philadelphia, Oct. 30–Dec. 11, 1964.

824. Thwaites, John A. "The story of Zero." *Studio International*, no. 867, July 1965.
   Quotes Piene: "Zero and the attitude."

ADDENDA: *Numbers indicate proper position in preceding bibliography.*

10a. Battcock, Gregory, ed. *Minimal Art: A Critical Anthology.* New York, Dutton, 1968.

15a. Brett, Guy. *Kinetic Art: The Language of Movement.* New York, Reinhold, 1968.

15b. Burnham, Jack. *Beyond Modern Sculpture.* New York, Braziller, 1968.
"Effects of science and technology."

34a. Hill, Anthony, ed. *DATA: Directions in Art Theory and Aesthetics.* London, Faber & Faber, 1968.

34b. Hultén, K. G. Pontus. *The Machine as Seen at the End of the Mechanical Age.* New York, Museum of Modern Art, 1968.

61a. Popper, Frank. *Origins and Development of Kinetic Art.* London, Studio Vista, 1968; New York, New York Graphic Society, 1969.
Translation: *Naissance de l'art cinétique* (Paris, Gauthier-Villars, 1967) with new chapter.

62a. Reichardt, Jasia, ed. *Cybernetic Serendipity: The Computer and the Arts.* London, New York, Studio-International, 1968.
Special issue of *Studio International* to coincide with similar show at the Institute of Contemporary Arts, Aug. 2–Oct. 10.

111a. *Leonardo.* Editors: Frank J. Malina, *et al.* Paris, London, New York, Jan. 1968–current.
On the abstract, kinetic and experimental.

119a. Výtvarné Umění. ("Fine Arts," Czechoslovak Association of Artists). No. 8–9. Prague, 1967.
Special issue on Suprematism, Constructivism, Kineticism. Résumés in English, Russian, and German deal with Malevich, Tatlin, etc. Rare illus.

212a. Staber, Margit. "Konkrete Kunst." *Serielle Manifeste 66 (St. Gallen).* No. XI, Nov. 1966.

226a. Amsterdam. Stedelijk Museum. *Vormen van de kleur.* [New Shapes of Color]. Nov. 19, 1966–Jan. 15, 1967.

233a. Buffalo. Albright-Knox Art Gallery. *Plus by Minus: Today's Half-Century.* Mar. 3–Apr. 14, 1968.
Exhibit and text by Douglas MacAgy.

235a. Frankfurt. Frankfurter Kunstverein. *Konstruktive Malerei, 1915–1930.* Nov. 19, 1966–Jan. 8, 1967.

251a. Los Angeles County Museum of Art. *American Sculpture of the Sixties.* Editor: Maurice Tuchman. Apr. 28–June 25, 1967.
Essays, statements, bibliography.

251b. Milan. Galleria del Levante. *Il contributo russo alle avanguardie plastiche.* [Oct.–Nov.?] 1964.
Catalogue by Carlo Belloli.

254a. Minneapolis. Walker Art Center. *Light, Motion, Space.* Apr. 8–May 21, 1967.
Chart on "luminism" (W. Sharp).

258a. New York. Museum of Modern Art. *The Art of the Real: U S A, 1948–1968.* Editor: E. C. Goossen. New York, 1968.

262a. New York. Solomon R. Guggenheim Foundation. *Art of Tomorrow.* (opening) June 1939.

263a. New York. Solomon R. Guggenheim Museum. *Systemic Painting.* Sept.–Nov. 1966.
Text by Lawrence Alloway.

263b. New York. Whitney Museum of American Art. *Light: Object and Image.* July 23–Sept. 23, 1968.
Text by Robert Doty. Bibliography.

263c. Newcastle-upon-Tyne. King's College, Dept. of Fine Art. *Man, Machine & Motion.* University of Durham, 1955.
Catalogue notes by R. Banham.

273a. San Marino. Sesta Bieññale d'Arte. *Nuove Techniche d'Immagine.* July 15–Sept. 30, 1967.
Includes English and French texts.

276a. Washington, D.C. Washington Gallery of Modern Art. *New Aesthetic.* May 6–June 25, 1967.
Text by Barbara Rose.

407a. Eindhoven. Stedelijk van Abbe Museum. *Theó van Doesburg, 1883–1931.* Dec. 13, 1968–Jan. 26, 1969.

532a. Fédit, D. *L'Oeuvre de Kupka.* Paris, Éditions des Musées Nationaux, 1966.

561a. Lissitzky-Küppers, Sophie, ed. *El Lissitzky: Life, Letters, Texts.* Introduction by Herbert Read. Greenwich, Conn., New York Graphic Society, 1968.

595a. Malevich, Kasimir. *Essays on Art, 1915–1928.* Copenhagen, Borgen, 1968. Two Vols.
Edited by Troels Andersen. Translated from the Russian. Bibliography.

635a. Wijsenbeek, L. J. F. *Piet Mondrian.* Recklinghausen, Verlag Aurel Bongers, 1968.

Index

The numbers in boldface refer to discussions of illustrations in the text.